Books are to be returned on or before
the last date below.

**7 – DAY
LOAN**

LIBREX–

READING MUSIC

This outstanding collection of Susan McClary's work exemplifies her contribution to a bridging of the gap between historical context, culture and musical practice. The selection includes essays which have had a major impact on the field and others which are less known and reproduced here from hard-to-find sources. The volume is divided into four parts: Interpretation and Polemics, Gender and Sexuality, Popular Music, and Early Music. Each of the essays treats music as cultural text and has a strong interdisciplinary appeal. Together with the autobiographical introduction they will prove essential reading for anyone interested in the life and times of a renegade musicologist.

ASHGATE CONTEMPORARY THINKERS ON CRITICAL MUSICOLOGY SERIES

The titles in this series bring together a selection of previously published and some unpublished essays by leading authorities in the field of critical musicology. The essays are chosen from a wide range of publications and so make key works available in a more accessible form. The authors have all made a selection of their own work in one volume with an introduction which discusses the essays chosen and puts them into context. A full bibliography points the reader to other publications which might not be included in the volume for reasons of space. The previously published essays are published using the facsimile method of reproduction to retain their original pagination, so that students and scholars can easily reference the essays in their original form.

Titles published in the series
Critical Musicology and the Responsibility of Response
Lawrence Kramer
Music and Historical Critique
Gary Tomlinson
Taking Popular Music Seriously
Simon Frith
Music, Performance, Meaning
Nicholas Cook

Titles to follow
Sound Judgment
Richard Leppert

Reading Music

Selected Essays

SUSAN MCCLARY

Professor of Musicology, University of California at Los Angeles, USA

ASHGATE CONTEMPORARY THINKERS ON
CRITICAL MUSICOLOGY SERIES

ASHGATE

Published by
Ashgate Publishing Limited
Gower House
Croft Road
Aldershot
Hampshire GU11 3HR
England

Ashgate Publishing Company
Suite 420
101 Cherry Street
Burlington, VT 05401-4405
USA

Ashgate website: http://www.ashgate.com

ISBN 978-0-7546-2672-5

British Library Cataloguing in Publication Data
McClary, Susan
    Reading music : selected essays
    1. Music - History and criticism
    I. Title
    781

US Library of Congress Cataloging-in-Publication Data
McClary, Susan
Reading music : selected essays / by Susan McClary.
    p. cm. – (Ashgate Contemporary thinkers on critical musicology series)
  Includes bibliographical references and index.
  ISBN 978-0-7546-2672-5
  1. Music–History and criticism. I. Title.

  M60.M4955 2007
  780–dc22

                                                                2007016517

Printed and bound in Great Britain by TJ International Ltd, Padstow, Cornwall

Contents

PART FOUR   EARLY MUSIC

Acknowledgements

The author wishes to acknowledge the following publishers of the original work reproduced in this volume. Every effort has been made to contact copyright holders.

Cambridge University Press for 'Blasphemy of Talking Politics during Bach Year' in *Music and Society: The Politics of Composition, Performance and Reception,* Richard Leppert and Susan McClary (eds), 1987, 13–62.

University of California Press for 'Narrative Agendas in 'Absolute' Music: Identity and Difference in Brahms's Third Symphony' in *Musicology and Difference: Gender and Sexuality in Music Scholarship*, Ruth Solie (ed), 1993, 326–44; 'Thinking Blues' in Susan McClary *Conventional Wisdom: The Content of Musical Form*, 2000, Chapter 2; 'The Cultural Work of the Madrigal' in Susan McClary *Modal Subjectivities: Self-Fashioning in the Italian Madrigal*, 2004, Chapter 1.

Columbia University Press for 'Structures of Identity and Difference in Bizet's Carmen' in *The Work of Opera: Genre, Nationhood, and Sexual Difference*, Richard Dellamora and Daniel Fischlin (eds), 1997, 115–30.

University of Minnesota Press for 'A Material Girl in Bluebeard's Castle' in *Feminist Endings: Music, Gender, and Sexuality*, 1991, 3–34; 'Terminal Prestige: The Case of Avant-Garde Music Composition' in *Cultural Critique*, **12**, Spring 1989, 57–81.

Taylor and Francis/Routledge for 'Constructions of Subjectivity in Schubert's Music' in *Queering the Pitch: The New Gay and Lesbian Musicology*, Philip Brett, Elizabeth Wood and Gary Thomas (eds), 1994, 205–33; ''Same as it Ever Was': Youth Culture and Music' in *Microphone Fiends: Youth Music and Youth Culture*, Andrew Ross and Tricia Rose (eds), 1994, 29–40.

University of Texas Press for 'Living to Tell: Madonna's Resurrection of the Fleshly' in *Genders*, **7**, 1990, 1–21. The version reproduced here is from *Feminine Endings: Music, Gender, and Sexualities*, University of Minnesota Press, 1991.

University of Toronto Press for 'Cycles of Repetition: Chacona, Ciaccona, Chaconne, and *the* Chaconne' in *Ritual, Routine, and Regime: Institutions of Repetition*, Lorna Clymer (ed.), 2007, 21–45.

Introduction

The Life and Times of a Renegade Musicologist

I did not start off my career with the intention of shifting any paradigms. My goals have always been far more modest: I have simply wanted to deal with pieces of music as cultural texts, just as literary, art, and film critics engage with novels, paintings, and movies as a matter of course. But what has always seemed to me a self-evident endeavor – the cultural interpretation of pieces of music – was virtually eliminated in post-war musicology.

At the time I entered the discipline in 1968, musicologists acknowledged only three modes of professional activity: archival research, the production of scholarly editions, and quasi-mathematical formal analysis. History and the music itself appeared to occupy entirely separate intellectual compartments. Consequently, the possibility that the tensions of certain moments in social history might have influence musical processes or, conversely, that musical processes might have affected the historical events never arose. In essence, those of us called "new musicologists" have sought to bridge that gap between historical contexts and musical practices.

Before I began my graduate work, I had already spent many years as a coach. In that capacity, I helped other performers (singers, chamber musicians, conductors) bring notated scores to life by pointing out crucial formal details to them, helping them make sense of such details, and assisting them as they converted their readings into dramatic sound. This enterprise continues to be my principal point of departure, and much of my writing addresses would-be performers as well as listeners and other music historians.

In recent years, musicologists have increasingly turned their attention to performers and listeners. Influenced by the anthropological methods adopted by performance studies and ethnomusicology, they focus on the musicians whose bodies bring sounds into being and also on the listeners who ultimately decide for themselves how to understand what they hear. Those involved in such endeavors often denigrate score study as fetishistic and dehumanizing. Yet listeners can only hear what musicians make audible, and I have experienced far too many dull concerts to put my faith unconditionally in the testimonies of either performers or listeners, even though I care deeply about both. In fact, it was my dissatisfaction with uninflected performances and my concern for listeners who have learned to perceive all classical music as merely soothing that led me into musicology in the first place.

My coaching activities had concentrated on the standard canon – the European art-music repertories from Bach through the early twentieth century. By means of my intensive exposure to this music since childhood as well as my own piano training, I had internalized the grammar and codes necessary for understanding it before I studied formal music theory; in other words, I had absorbed classical music as my vernacular and had learned how to make sense of it the same way I had learned English. But when I first encountered repertories from before Bach in my undergraduate survey, I was both dazzled and challenged. I set off to graduate school with the misguided impression that musicologists knew how to deal with earlier musics in ways that paralleled my own approaches to Mozart or Brahms.

Strangely enough, given the prestige of Renaissance and Baroque repertories within the discipline, very little useful work existed along the lines I wished to pursue. A more pragmatic student would have put aside her preconceptions and adapted herself to the agendas condoned by the discipline. But although I went through the paces demanded of me in graduate school, I still headed down to the practice rooms in the basement when no one was looking to puzzle through the scores that so intrigued me. I devoted my dissertation, *The Transition from Modal to Tonal Organization in the Works of Monteverdi* (Harvard, 1976), to reconstructing the grammars and codes necessary for the analysis of sixteenth- and seventeenth-century repertories. With musical scores constantly in the foreground, I cobbled together my own theories by studying Renaissance treatises on the one hand and, on the other, concepts borrowed from contemporary linguistics concerning the structures of language change. At last I arrived (to my satisfaction, in any case) at frameworks that allowed me to interpret these remote repertories with the same degree of detail I brought to readings of compositions by Bach or Beethoven.

I did not anticipate, however, how very alien my projects would seem to the discipline. I joined the faculty at the University of Minnesota in 1977, but I had a great deal of difficulty getting any of my work accepted. Over and over again, I submitted manuscripts for publication, only to have them return with a note advising me that early music cannot be analyzed because its composers had not yet grasped how music is supposed to work. As the tenure clock kept ticking, I tried repackaging my ideas in ways that would make them intelligible – but to no avail.

In desperation I turned to other strategies. First, I initiated a series of what I thought of as "running for tenure" talks: lecture/demonstrations in which I showed how music produces cultural meanings. My examples ranged from seventeenth-century monodies to Bach concertos and Schubert impromptus. These presentations managed to convince my dean and colleagues from other departments of my work's value. Moreover, the objections raised by musicologists who attended (music has no cultural meanings, it is just sound) made it clear to the larger community why my manuscripts had not been accepted for publication within the discipline. Thus despite that fact that I had not a single item in print at the time, I received tenure, owing to the support of scholars from other fields. I learned later that many of my drafts had circulated samizdat-style, in paler and paler photocopies, among younger musicologists in North America and elsewhere.

Second, I began to write specifically for interdisciplinary readers, who proved eager to pay attention to someone who could bring music to discussions concerning cultural criticism. With its Theory and History of Literature series and the founding of *Cultural Critique*, the University of Minnesota had positioned itself at the forefront of cultural theory, and I discovered that many of the tools I needed for my work were being developed in humanities centers. Thanks to my dear friend Rose Rosengard Subotnik, I had already started to study

Theodor W. Adorno and Michel Foucault, both of whom have influenced me deeply. Now I also found myself involved with feminist theory (by far the most consequential area of cultural criticism of the 1980s), narratology, postcolonial studies, and the newly emerging field of postmodernist aesthetics. In addition, my immersion in cultural criticism convinced me that I had to cast off my life-long prejudice against popular music.

My first several publications appeared in journals such as *Cultural Critique* and as commissioned essays for Jacques Attali's *Noise* (1985) and Catherine Clément's *Opera, or the Undoing of Women* (1988). An international conference organized by my colleague Richard Leppert and myself yielded the volume *Music and Society: the Politics of Composition, Performance and Reception* (1987); I owe to Richard my determination to keep working within musicology. Finally, a compilation of talks I presented at interdisciplinary feminist conferences, *Feminine Endings: Music, Gender, and Sexuality* (1991), and a commissioned Cambridge Opera Handbook on *Carmen* (1992) appeared. Taken together, these publications helped to inaugurate critical musicology or (as its detractors called it) New Musicology. I braided together many of these apparently disparate interests in my Bloch Lectures in 1993 at the University of California – Berkeley, and these lectures were published in 2000 under the title *Conventional Wisdom: The Content of Musical Form*. In 1995, I received a MacArthur Foundation Fellowship.

After having proceeded through the classical canon, reinterpreting its central figures and genres in accordance with my theoretical approaches, I have finally found it possible to return to my still-favorite repertories: those of the sixteenth and seventeenth centuries. In 2004 I published *Modal Subjectivities: Self-Fashioning in the Italian Madrigal*, which offers both a theory of sixteenth-century modal practice and a cultural interpretation of the madrigal. A genre that sought explicitly to produce simulations in sound of complex interiorities, the madrigal introduced into music representations of emotions, desire, gender, reason, madness, and tensions between mind and body. It thereby recorded assumptions of the time concerning selfhood, making it an invaluable resource for understanding the history of Western subjectivity. A sequel, *Power and Desire in Seventeenth-Century Music*, is now close to completion.

Together, these two books finally present the work I developed within my 1976 dissertation; *Modal Subjectivities* won the Otto Kinkeldey Prize in 2005. A quick comparison will reveal that I still hold to the theoretical frameworks I originally formulated as a graduate student. Thanks to my exposure to interdisciplinary conversations, however, I now know much better how to understand both the conventional and idiosyncratic dimensions of pieces in terms of their cultural contexts, which is why I entered musicology in the first place. I also have substituted for the "objective" prose I was trained to emulate a more vivid, often comic style that strives to simulate the action of the music itself.

* * *

I have divided the items I have chosen to include in this volume into four clusters, which follow roughly the career trajectory sketched above. I have made my selection on the basis of several criteria. Some essays appear here because of their impact on the field; others because they were published in hard-to-find sources. Taken together, I believe that they offer a good representation of the various kinds of projects I have undertaken over the course of the last thirty years.

A.   Interpretation and Polemics

When I realized in the 1980s that my work on early music was not going to be accepted for publication any time soon, I decided to return to the bedrock of my musical and intellectual development: the interpretation of the classical canon. I thought that if I demonstrated how to understand the moves within well-known tonal pieces in cultural terms, I would soon be allowed to show how the same kinds of operations obtained within the modal repertory. In my naïveté, I actually imagined that musicologists would see how obvious this enterprise was; I had no idea how very solid the firewall was that "protected" music from cultural criticism.

I conceived of "Pitches, Expression, Ideology: An Exercise in Mediation" when a student complained to me that his piano teacher had dismissed a Schubert impromptu as incompetent because of its formal redundancies. After recovering from my shock, I walked the student through the piece and then presented it as a lecture/demonstration; I took the fact that many in the audience were weeping at the end of the performance as evidence not only of Schubert's competence (!) but also of the viability of my methods. When I converted the talk into a paper, I chose to focus on the strategic move to the flat sixth degree that figures so prominently in the music of composers from Beethoven and Schubert through Mahler, and I included a discussion of a movement from a Beethoven quartet along with the Schubert to demonstrate the expressive range made available by this strategy. By selecting a grammatical element this fundamental, I hoped to concentrate my efforts in this article on sketching out the process whereby one could connect formal idiosyncrasy with cultural beliefs.

The article appeared in *Enclitic*, an in-house literary journal at the University of Minnesota. It was my good fortune that Tom Conley, a distinguished scholar of French literature and film theory, was serving on the tenure committee when my case came through, and he volunteered to publish my work if no one else would. This essay was my first publication. I include it here not only for sentimental reasons but also because it presents in a systematic way the agenda and methods underlying nearly all my subsequent work.

"The Blasphemy of Talking Politics during Bach Year" arose from my amazement at hearing prominent scholars in 1985 claiming that Bach's music was divinely inspired and thus exempt from discussion. My contribution to the conference *Music and Society*, "Bach Year" first attracted widespread attention to my work. Like "Pitches, Expression, Ideology," this essay also developed from a lecture/demonstration – in this case, a performance of the opening movement of the Brandenburg Concerto No. 5 in which the harpsichord cadenza actually brought audience members to their feet in sheer suspense and excitement. Incidentally, I do not suggest in my text (as has been often stated) that this piece – from the 1720s – is contemporaneous with the French Revolution. I merely argue that the class-based resentments that finally toppled the French monarchy in 1789 had been brewing for several decades. "Bach Year" also contains my first account of differing temporalities in French and Italian musics and also my first attempt at feminist criticism.

The essay on Brahms's Third Symphony resulted from an invitation by literary critics who specialize in narratology; it was published in Ruth Solie's landmark collection,

Musicology and Difference. Although it employs narrative theory, as do many of my readings of instrumental music, it does not trace stories to substitute for structural listening but rather engages with the role of narrative-oriented musical procedures in the performance of basic cultural work. The essay also seeks to discredit the sacred cow of "absolute" music, which has done so much to convert sites of cultural meaning into pristine abstractions.

"Terminal Prestige" began as my contribution to the conference *The Economy of Prestige*, and it appeared in a special volume of *Cultural Critique.* At the time I wrote it, the serial mafia still dictated the kinds of musics deemed acceptable within the academy. While teaching at the University of Minnesota, I worked closely with a number of young composers who felt stifled by this ideology, and some of them eventually moved in directions just then emerging as critical postmodernism. If my other writing principally influences other scholars, this essay has succeeded as an intervention on the creative front.

B.   Gender and Sexuality

I first became involved with feminist theories because of the extraordinary intellectual ferment associated with such issues in the 1980s. Over the course of that decade, feminism transformed and reinvigorated most disciplines within the humanities and social sciences – as well as creative enterprises in literature, cinema, and the plastic arts. It seemed to me obvious not only that musicology too might benefit from engagement with questions related to gender and sexuality but also that interdisciplinary conversations would gain from the presence of music in their discussions.

I had other reasons to turn to feminism at this time. First, no matter how hard I had tried earlier in my career to declare my gender irrelevant to my work, the fact remained that I am a small female. Instead of continuing to battle against that truth, hoping somehow that no one would notice, I came to realize that I had access to a great many very interesting insights if I approached my work explicitly *as a woman.* I also believed that my larger project of understanding musical procedures in terms of cultural means would be more easily grasped if I concentrated on what I took to be self-evident representations. If qualities such as temporality or social class prove difficult to explain, I thought that surely we could all recognize the gendered dimensions of, say, opera characters. Moreover, the essays that eventually appeared in *Feminine Endings* had all been warmly received in interdisciplinary conferences; if anything, I seemed a bit conservative in those contexts.

I expected that *Feminine Endings* would principally add music to the myriad books on feminist theory then crowding the shelves in bookstores, though I must have had some trepidation as well. When I now reread the opening chapter, "A Material Girl in Bluebeard's Castle," I am struck with my casting of myself as Judith awaiting decapitation. Still, I did not quite anticipate the furor that ensued with the publication of this thin, drab-looking volume. I am including "A Material Girl" in this collection because it sets out most explicitly my reasons for turning my own work in this direction.

The essay on *Carmen* chosen for this collection seems to me the most succinct of my several treatments of Bizet's opera. After my book on *Carmen* appeared, I received many invitations to speak on this topic, and I needed to write something that drew together the themes of the book without duplicating it. "Structures of Identity and Difference" appeared as program notes for several productions of the opera, as a book chapter, and as a journal article.

I also include here my notorious essay on Schubert and sexuality – a topic I took up only with the strong encouragement of the late Philip Brett, without whose influence and support I could scarcely have produced any of what I wrote in the 1990s. Like most of my work, the reading of the "Unfinished" Symphony that appears here emerged from class discussions; I rarely offer such readings in my lectures, but as soon as I give students permission to take gender or sexuality into account, they readily produce such interpretations themselves.

C.   Popular Music

As I mentioned above, I came to popular music very late in my career. I had managed to make it through the birth of rock 'n' roll in the 1950s, the British Invasion, and the psychedelia of the 1960s with my ears tuned exclusively to earlier eras. Only when I faced the prospect of teaching a survey of twentieth-century music did I find that I could not in good conscience deal only with the continuation of the European canon. With the help of Robert Walser, I set about learning at least enough about jazz and rock to include them in my syllabus. I do not pretend to be an authority in this area. Yet at a time when musicologists still focused exclusively on classical music, I decided that I could at least produce methods for engaging with both ends of the cultural hierarchy.

"Same As It Ever Was" offers a very long view of popular music, stretching as it does from Plato and Saint Augustine to rock. I presented it at an interdisciplinary conference on youth culture held at Princeton in 1993, and it appeared in the book that resulted from that event. Pop-music specialists often dismiss any engagement of scholars with "the music itself." In my essay, I attempt to demonstrate what pop-music critics might learn from musicologists and, conversely, what musicologists – even those who specialize in earlier music – might learn from the study of popular culture. In addition to the diverse quotations I brought to bear on the topic, I also discussed two examples: Wilson Pickett's "Midnight Hour" and the seventeenth-century dance craze, the *ciaccona*. I end with one of my favorite lines: "The study of popular music should also include the study of popular music." Go ahead and carve it on my tombstone.

My essay on Madonna – by far the most frequently reprinted item I have written – emerged from my course titled *Women and the Arts*. Madonna happened to be passing through town on her *Who's That Girl?* tour, and I suggested to the members of my class that we see what all the ruckus was about. Although I had expected to be appalled by this woman so roundly despised by progressive critics, I found myself overwhelmed by her artistry, imagination, and sheer force of will; I have never altered that opinion. My essay is very dated now, for the Material Girl has reinvented herself at least a dozen times since I offered my account of her (now) early period. Few others, however, have bothered to deal with her music, so distracted are they by the spectacularity of her self-presentation. Surely the most successful woman in the history of music deserves more! For now, here is my contribution.

"Thinking Blues" appeared as one of my Bloch Lectures at Berkeley, later published as *Conventional Wisdom*. For that series of lectures, I wanted to show how to move between popular and classical musics: even though these repertories come from profoundly different worlds with radically divergent cultural priorities, they still operate dialectically between procedures freighted with social meanings and individual artistic decisions that make scores or recordings unique. I turned to this genre in order to demonstrate the extraordinary range of cultural projects – including those of Bessie Smith, Robert Johnson, and Eric Clapton – available even within so stringent a convention as the twelve-bar blues. I followed this talk/chapter with a similar account of eighteenth-century tonality: the convention (nearly as formulaic as the blues) that underlies the works of Bach and Mozart.

D.   Early Music

As the Dixie Chicks put it, I've taken the long way around. This admittedly circuitous route – through unlikely assistance from sources as diverse as feminist theorist Hélène Cixous and hip-hop artist Chuck D – has brought me back to where I started. The penultimate item in this collection, a remnant of my earliest work, counts among my most recent publications.

I first submitted versions of "The Cultural Work of the Madrigal" to journals in 1980, but, as I explained earlier, it was rejected. It appeared finally in 2004 as the opening chapter of *Modal Subjectivities.* I should warn the reader that this piece has quite a strong dose of music theory: musicologists have neglected to take seriously the syntax of music from before Bach, which hampers not only our ability to deal cogently with early music but also to explain why and how our standard point of reference – harmonic tonality – came into being when and as it did. My deconstructive essays from the 1980s and 1990s were concerned with showing that tonal repertories too should be understood as cultural products; I was motivated not by some nihilistic postmodernist agenda but by a desire to make sense of all musics. The project presented in this chapter lurks behind everything I have ever written.

Yet whereas my dissertation focused almost exclusively on structuralist issues in seventeenth-century music, the latterday manifestations of that work benefit from everything else I have encountered in the course of the last thirty years: cultural theory, feminism, and popular music. I can no longer even imagine an explanation of a musical procedure that does not relate to experiences of the body, social potentials and constraints, and much else, including structures of time. The last item in *Reading Music* is "Cycles of Repetition: Chacona, Ciaccona, Chaconne, and THE Chaconne," which traces the cultural history of a particular rhythmic groove as it travels from the New World, through rowdy European dance fests and a privileged place in the court of Louis XIV, to serve finally as a metaphor of entrapment in the works of J.S. Bach.

When the Chinese say "May you live in interesting times," they intend it as a curse. My career has been rather more like a rollercoaster ride than I had anticipated when I chose to specialize in Renaissance repertories. As I glance over my present bibliography, I can scarcely imagine how I would have reacted to such an eclectic list of items when I first started out in 1968; certainly nothing of its ilk existed at the time. In this narrative, I have tried to impose a kind of sense – historical, biographical, ideological – on what at times seemed a bewildering, through undeniably interesting journey. Enjoy the ride!

Bibliography

The Transition from Modal to Tonal Organization in the Works of Monteverdi. Harvard University Dissertation, 1976; Ann Arbor, UMI., 1977.

"Pitches, Expression, Ideology: An Exercise in Mediation." *Enclitic* 7/1 (Spring 1983): 76–86.

"The Politics of Silence and Sound." Afterword to Jacques Attali, *Noise*, trans. Brian Massumi. Minneapolis: University of Minnesota Press, 1985, 149–58.

"A Musical Dialectic from the Enlightenment: Mozart's *Piano Concerto in G Major, K. 453*, Movement II." *Cultural Critique* 4 (Fall, 1986): 129–69.

"Mozart's Women." *Hurricane Alice* 3 (1986): 1–4.

Music and Society: The Politics of Composition, Performance and Reception. Co-edited with Richard Leppert. Cambridge: Cambridge University Press, 1987.

"The Blasphemy of Talking Politics during Bach Year," in *Music and Society*, 13–62.

"The Rise and Fall of the Teleological Model in Western Music," in *The Paradigm Exchange* 2 (Center for Humanistic Studies, University of Minnesota, 1987): 26–31.

"Getting Down Off the Beanstalk: The Presence of a Woman's Voice in Janika Vandervelde's *Genesis II*." *Minnesota Composers Forum Newsletter* (January, 1987).

Susanna Does the Elders: Confessions of a Tanna Leaf Smoker (full-length music-theatre piece). Commissioned and premiered through OVERTONES, Southern Theater, Minneapolis, 1987.

"Feminism, or the Undoing of Opera." Foreword to Catherine Clément, *Opera, or the Undoing of Women*, trans. Betsy Wing. Minneapolis: University of Minnesota Press, 1988, ix–xviii.

"Terminal Prestige: The Case of Avant-Garde Music Composition." *Cultural Critique* 12 (Spring 1989): 57–81.

"Constructions of Gender in Monteverdi's Dramatic Music." *Cambridge Opera Journal* 1/3 (Fall 1989): 203–23.

Hildegard (collaborative music-theatre piece on Hildegard von Bingen; with Janika Vandervelde, composer, and Melisande Charles, video animator). Southern Theatre, Minneapolis, 1990.

"Start Making Sense: Musicology Wrestles with Rock." Co-authored with Robert Walser, in *On Record: Rock, Pop, and the Written Word*, ed. Simon Frith and Andrew Goodwin. New York: Pantheon Press, 1990, 277–92.

"Living to Tell: Madonna's Resurrection of the Fleshly." *Genders* 7 (March 1990): 1–21.

"This Is Not a Story My People Tell: Time and Space According to Laurie Anderson." *Discourse* 12/1 (Fall–Winter 1989–90): 104–28.

"Towards a Feminist Criticism of Music." *Canadian University Music Review* 10 (1990): 9–18.

"Getting Down Off the Beanstalk: The Presence of a Woman's Voice in Janika Vandervelde's *Genesis II*." *Music/Dance/Theatre Journal* (Summer 1990).

Feminine Endings: Music, Gender, and Sexuality. Minneapolis: University of Minnesota Press, 1991.

Review of Ellen Rosand, *The Rise of a Genre: Seventeenth-Century Opera in Venice*. *Historical Performance* 4/2 (Fall 1991): 109–17.

Review of Richard Middleton, *Studying Popular Music. Popular Music* 10/2 (May 1991): 237–42.

"Schubert's Sexuality and His Music." *Gay & Lesbian Study Group Newsletter* 2 (March 1992).

"Identity and Difference: The 'Funny People' in Bizet's *Carmen*." Essay for Los Angeles Opera production of *Carmen* (January, 1992).

Georges Bizet: Carmen. (Cambridge Opera Handbook). Cambridge: Cambridge University Press, 1992.

Review of Leo Treitler, *Music and the Historical Imagination. Notes* 48/3 (March 1992): 838–40.

"Structures of Identity and Difference in *Carmen*." *Women: A Cultural Review* 3 (Spring

1992): 1–15.

"A Response to Elaine Barkin." *Perspectives of New Music* 30/2 (Summer 1992): 234–38.

Review of Charles Ford, *Così? Sexual Politics in Mozart's Operas. Music & Letters* 73/4 (November 1992): 591–93.

"La costruzione dell'identità sessuale nelle opere drammatiche di Monteverdi." *Musica/ Realtà* 41 (August 1993): 121–44.

"Sexuality and Music: On the Rita Steblin/Maynard Solomon Debate." *19th-Century Music* 17/1 (Summer 1993): 83–88.

"Reshaping a Discipline: Musicology and Feminism in the 1990s." *Feminist Studies* 19 (Summer 1993): 399–423.

"Agonie und erotischer Taumel: Ausformungen der Geschlechtsspezifik in Monteverdis *L'Orfeo*," in program book to Monteverdi's *L'Orfeo*, Salzburg Festival, 1993, 61–85.

Review of Iain Fenlon and Peter Miller, *The Song of the Soul: Understanding "Poppea." Music & Letters* 74/2 (May 1993): 278–81.

"Narrative Agendas in 'Absolute' Music: Identity and Difference in Brahms's Third Symphony," in *Musicology and Difference: Gender and Sexuality in Music Scholarship*, ed. Ruth Solie. Berkeley: University of California Press, 1993, 326–44.

"Living to Tell: Madonna's Resurrection of the Fleshly," in *Culture/Power/History: A Reader in Contemporary Social Theory*, ed. Nicholas B. Dirks, Sherry B. Ortner, and Geoff Eley. Princeton: Princeton University Press, 1993, 459–82.

"Living to Tell: Madonna's Resurrection of the Fleshly," in *Desperately Seeking Madonna*, ed. Adam Sexton. New York: Delta, 1993, 103–29.

"Narratives of Bourgeois Subjectivity in Mozart's 'Prague' Symphony," in *Understanding Narrative*, ed. Peter Rabinowitz and James Phelan. Columbus: Ohio State University Press, 1994, 65–98.

"'Same as It Ever Was': Youth Culture and Music," in *Microphone Fiends: Youth Music and Youth Culture*, ed. Andrew Ross and Tricia Rose. New York and London: Routledge, 1994, 29–40.

"Constructions of Subjectivity in Schubert's Music," in *Queering the Pitch: The New Gay and Lesbian Musicology*, ed. Philip Brett, Elizabeth Wood, and Gary Thomas. New York and London: Routledge Press, 1994, 205–33.

"Ode to Cecilia: A Foreword," in *Cecilia Reclaimed: Feminist Perspectives on Gender and Music*, ed. Susan C. Cook and Judy S. Tsou. Urbana: University of Illinois Press, 1994, ix–xii.

"Blood Rites": Review of Laurie Anderson, *Bright Red. The Village Voice* (Dec. 1994).

"'Exoticism' in *Carmen*." Essay for Covent Garden production of *Carmen* (January 1994), 37–42.

Review of Eric Chafe, *Monteverdi's Tonal Language. Music Theory Spectrum* 16, No. 2 (1994): 261–66.

"A Response to Linda Dusman." *Perspectives of New Music* 32/2 (Summer 1994): 148–53.

"Of Patriarchs . . . and Matriarchs, too: The Contributions and Challenges of Feminist Musicology." *The Musical Times* 135 (June 1994: special 150-anniversary issue): 364–9.

"Theorizing the Body in African-American Music." Co-authored with Robert Walser. *Black Music Research Journal* 14 (Spring 1994): 75–84.

"Paradigm Dissonances: Music Theory, Cultural Studies, Feminist Criticism." *Perspectives of New Music* 32 (Winter 1994): 68–85.

"Wuthering Depths": Review of PJ Harvey, *To Bring You My Love. Village Voice* (March 1995).

"Music, the Pythagoreans, and the Body," in *Choreographing History*, ed. Susan Leigh Foster. Bloomington: Indiana University Press, 1995, 82–104.

Review essay of Marcia J. Citron, *Gender and the Musical Canon*; *Gender, Culture, and the Arts*, ed. Ronald Dotterer and Susan Bowers; and *Erotic Politics: Desire on the Renaissance Stage*, ed. Susan Zimmerman. *Signs* 21/1 (Autumn 1995): 168–72.

"'Same as It Ever Was': Youth Culture and Music," in *Rock She Wrote: Women Write about Rock, Pop and Rap*, ed. Evelyn McDonnell and Ann Powers. New York: Delta, 1995, 440–54.

Review of Richard Kramer, *Distant Cycles: Schubert and the Conceiving of Song. Notes* (March 1996): 777–80.

Review of Charles Rosen, *The Romantic Generation. Notes* (June 1996): 1139–42.

"Second-Hand Emotions: Toward a History of Western Interiority." *Contemporary Sound Arts: Essays in Sound* 3 (December 1996): 92–104.

"The Impromptu that Trod on a Loaf: How Music Tells Stories." *Narrative* 5/1 (January 1997): 20–34.

"Terminal Prestige: The Case of Avant-Garde Music Composition," reprinted in *Keeping Score: Music, Disciplinarity, Culture*, ed. David Schwarz, Anahid Kassabian, and Lawrence Siegel. Charlottesville: University Press of Virginia, 1997, 54–74.

"Dödlig Prestige: Fallet Avantgardekomposition." *Nutida Music* 1 (1997): 23–36.

Review of Linda Hutcheon and Michael Hutcheon, *Opera: Desire, Disease, Death. Journal of the American Musicological Society* 50/1 (Spring 1997): 175–81.

"*Feminine Endings* in Retrospect." Preface for Japanese edition of *Feminine Endings* (1997).

"Structures of Identity and Difference in Bizet's *Carmen*," in *The Work of Opera: Genre, Nationhood, and Sexual Difference*, ed. Richard Dellamora and Daniel Fischlin. New York: Columbia University Press, 1997, 115–30.

"Unruly Passions and Courtly Dances: Technologies of the Body in Baroque Music," in *From the Royal to the Republican Body: Incorporating the Political in Seventeenth and Eighteenth Century France*, ed. Sara Melzer and Kathryn Norberg. Berkeley: University of California Press, 1998, 85–112.

"Música y Cultura de Jóvenes: La Misma Historia de Siempre." *A Contratiempo* 9 (1997): 12–21.

"Rap, Minimalism, and Structures of Time in Late Twentieth-Century Culture." The Norman and Jane Geske Lecture, 1998. Lincoln: University of Nebraska Press, 1999.

"Different Drummers: Analyzing the Music of Women Composers," in *Musics and Feminisms*, ed. Sally MacArthur and Cate Poynton. Sydney: University of Western Sydney, Napean, 1999.

Review of Alice Echols, *Scars of Sweet Paradise: The Life and Times of Janis Joplin. Women's Review of Books* 16 (September 1999), 1–4.

Conventional Wisdom: The Content of Musical Form. Berkeley and Los Angeles: University of California Press, 2000.

"Gender Ambiguities and Erotic Excess in Seventeenth-Century Venetian Opera," in *Acting on the Past: Historical Performance Across the Disciplines*, ed. Mark Franko and Anne Richards. Hanover, N.H.: Wesleyan University Press, 2000, 177–200.

"Different Drummers: Interpreting Music by Women Composers," in *Frauen- und Männerbilder in der Musik: Festschrift für Eva Rieger*, ed. Freia Hoffmann, Jane Bowers, and Ruth Heckmann.Oldenburg: Bibliotheks- und Informationsystem der Universität Oldenburg, 2000, 113–26.

"Women and Music on the Verge of the New Millennium." *Signs* 25/4 (Summer 2000): 1283–86.

"Seksualna Politika u Klasicnoj Muzici." *ProFemina* 21–22 (Spring/Summer 2000): 172–96.

"Women and Music on the Verge of the New Millennium," in *Feminisms at a Millennium*, ed. Judith A. Howard and Carolyn Allen. Chicago: University of Chicago Press, 2000, 272–75. "Temporality and Ideology: Qualities of Motion in Seventeenth-Century French Music." *ECHO* 3 (November 2000). www.humnet.ucla.edu/ECHO

"Temp Work: Music and the Cultural Shaping of Time." *Musicology Australia* 23 (2000): 80–95.

Entries on Madonna, Laurie Anderson, and Feminist Musicology. *The New Grove Dictionary of Music and Musicians*. New York: Macmillan, 2000.

Entry on Feminist Musicology for *Routledge Encyclopedia of Feminist Theories*. New York and London: Routledge, 2001: 326–38.

Review of Raymond Monelle, *The Sense of Music: Semiotic Essays*. *Notes* 58/2 (December 2001): 326–28.

"This Is Not a Story My People Tell: Musical Time and Space According to Laurie Anderson," in *Women Making Art: Women in the Visual, Literary, and Performing Arts since 1960*, ed. Deborah Johnson and Wendy Oliver. Peter Lang Publishing Inc., 2001, 161–88.

Review of Naomi Cumming, *The Sonic Self: Musical Subjectivity and Signification*. *Social Semiotics* 12/1 (2002): 135–7.

"A Salute to Women Composers." *Sounding Board: American Composers Forum Newsletter* (March 2002).

"The 'Funny People' in Bizet's *Carmen*." Essay for San Francisco Opera production of *Carmen*, 2002.

"Schubert's 'Late' Quartets." Program essay for Aldeburgh Festival, 2002.

"Fetisch Stimme: Professionelle Sänger im Italien der frühen Neuzeit," in *Zwischen Rauschen und Offenbarung: Zur Kultur- und Mediengeschichte der Stimme*. ed. Friedrich Kittler, Thomas Macho, and Sigrid Weigel. Berlin: Akademie Verlag, 2002, 199–214.

"Feminine Endings in Retrospect." Preface to second edition of *Feminine Endings*. Minneapolis: University of Minnesota Press, 2002.

Feminine Endings: Music, Gender, and Sexuality, 2nd ed. Minneapolis: University of Minnesota Press, 2002.

Review of Sally Macarthur, *Feminist Aesthetics in Music. International Alliance for Women in Music Journal* 8/3 (2002): 48–49.

"On Ethics and Musicology." *Tijdschrift voor muziektheorie* 7/3 (November 2002): 182–85.

Reply to Joke Dame's "When Music(ology) signifies ..." *Tijdschrift voor muziektheorie* 7/3 (November 2002): 188.

"Bessie Smith: Thinking Blues," in *The Auditory Culture Reader*, ed. Michael Bull and Les Back. Oxford and New York: Berg, 2003, 427–34. (excerpted from *Conventional Wisdom*).

Foreword to the *New Historical Anthology of Music by Women*, ed. James Briscoe. Bloomington: Indiana University Press, 2004, ix–x.

Modal Subjectivities: Self-Fashioning in the Italian Madrigal. Berkeley and Los Angeles: University of California Press, 2004.

"Rap, Minimalism, and Structures of Time in Late Twentieth-Century Culture," in *Audio Culture: Readings in Modern Music*, ed. Christoph Cox and Daniel Warner. New York: Continuum/The Wire, 2004, 289–98.

"Egy anyagias lány Kékszukállú várában" and "Klasszikus zene és a szexualitás stratégiái."Hungarian translations of parts of *Feminine Endings*.Dániel Kodaj, *Replika* (2005). http://www.replika.hu

Review of Bernard Gendron, *From Montmartre to the Mudd Club: Popular Music and the Avant-Garde. Twentieth-Century Music* 1/1, 2005.

"The Symbiosis of Teaching and Research." *Current Musicology* (2005).

"*Carmen* as Perennial Fusion: From Habañera to Hip-Hop," in *Carmen: From Silent Film to MTV*, ed. Chris Perriam and Ann Davies. Amsterdam and New York: Rodopi Press, 2006, 205–16.

Review of Richard Taruskin, *The Oxford History of Western Music. Music & Letters* 87/3 (August 2006): 408–15.

"Remembering Philip Brett." Introduction to *Music and Sexuality in Britten: Selected Essays by Philip Brett*, ed. George Haggerty. Berkeley: University of California Press, 2006.

"Mounting Butterflies," in *A Vision of the Orient: Texts, Intertexts, and Contexts of Madame Butterfly*, ed. Jonathan Wisenthal et al. Toronto: University of Toronto Press, 2006, 21–35.

"Cycles of Repetition: Chacona, Ciaccona, Chaconne, and THE Chaconne," in *Ritual, Routine, and Regime: Institutions of Repetition*, ed. Lorna Clymer. Toronto: University of Toronto Press, 2007, 21–45.

"Mediterranean Trade Routes and Music of the Early Seventeenth Century," *Inter-American Music Review* 17, no. 1–2 (Winter 2007).

"Toward a History of Harmonic Tonality," in *Historical Theory, Performance, and Meaning in Baroque Music*. Ghent, Belgium: Orpheus Academy for Music Theory, 2007.

Italian edition of my *Georges Bizet: Carmen*, with new foreword by the author. Trans. Annamaria Cecconi. Milan: Rugginenti Editore, 2007.

"Minima Romantica," in *Beyond the Soundtrack: Representing Music in Cinema*, ed. Richard Leppert, Lawrence Kramer, and Daniel Goldmark. Berkeley and Los Angeles: University of California Press, 2007.

Part One

Interpretation and Polemics

CHAPTER 1

PITCHES, EXPRESSION, IDEOLOGY: AN EXERCISE IN MEDIATION

A prominent strategy in many musical compositions of the early 19th century involves the sudden interruption of a reasonably stable diatonic procedure by a self-contained passage on the minor sixth degree (i.e., A♭ major in C minor or C major). The interruption is usually abrupt, dramatic—clearly marked off from the surrounding context as significant; and the embedded passage is held apart not only by means of harmonic disruption but also through strongly contrasting thematic materials. In many instances, it seems the central issue of the composition: an exposed confrontation that defines the tonal/thematic axis on which the piece revolves. Whenever it occurs, the discontinuity and sharp justaposition provoke almost inevitably the question: what is THIS doing here? What does it signify?

＊

Most discussions that attempt to account for the strategies of musical compositions fall into one of two categories.[1] Those of the first sort deal with the intricacies of the notated score, but by means of a technical vocabulary that resists references to anything outside its own closed system.[2] The second group interprets pieces in terms of emotional expression or even cultural values, but usually without explicit grounding in the details of the musical surface.[3]

And there is, in fact, no *objective* way of making connections between the two. Pitches are, after all, simply sounds: they have no absolutely verifiable correlation with anything in the outside world of feelings or ideas.[4] Yet to listeners not bound by formalist skepticism, music seems regularly to suggest gestures, psychological states, narrative sequences, and ways of understanding life. Moreover, in most cases there is sufficient consensus among listeners to indicate that these reactions cannot be wholly subjective.[5] The impressions are, at least to some extent, produced by the relationships among pitches. But how does one bridge the gap between notes and meaning?[6]

＊

This essay is an attempt at demonstrating how particular configurations of pitches may be interpreted so as to be relevant to human experience. It concentrates on the single phenomenon described above: minor-sixth interruptions in early 19th-century music.

While any number of other configurations might have been selected, this device offers two major advantages. First, it is so strongly marked as significant that it virtually demands interpretation. Second, the strategy turns out to be one of the principal musical means of articulating certain key 19th-century cultural issues. By dealing with instances of this single device, it is possible to begin substantiating some of the perceptive (usually non-technical) interpretations of the repertory by such cultural historians and critics as Peckham, Adorno, and Subotnik.[7]

The first part of the essay examines the abstracted mechanism itself: its syntax, metaphorical implications, semiological connotations, and so on. The second part focuses on the interaction between the basic mechanism and the particularities of context in the production of meaning. For each of the two compositions that serve as models (Schubert's *Impromptu in C Minor, Op. 90 #1* and the slow movement of Beethoven's op. 127 quartet), the central minor-sixth interruption is explained in terms of its formal, expressive, and ideological significance.[8]

***

We shall begin with an inventory of the chord on the sixth degree in its natural diatonic habitat, the minor mode. The triad is made up of the sixth degree (as root), the tonic pitch, and the mediant of the home key (ex. 1a). It is major in quality, and as an isolated entity, it is consonant, stable, inert.

When placed within the framework of tonality, however, it acquired certain dynamic tendencies. The chord shares two pitches ($\hat{1}$ and $\hat{3}$) with the most stable function of the key, the tonic triad. These tend to retain their sense of stability, particularly when they are held as constants in the harmonic movement from i to VI (ex. 1b). The active ingredient is the sixth degree itself, which within tonality has such a strong tendency to descend the half-step to $\hat{5}$ that it often acts as a satellite to the dominant (ex. 1c).[9] The need for $\hat{6}$ to descend to $\hat{5}$ exerts such contrapuntal tension that the chord takes on some of the characteristics of a dissonance—even though it is, technically speaking, a perfectly consonant, major triad.

In other words, while acoustically more stable than most of the primary minor-key sonorities surrounding it, it is functionally unstable and demanding of resolution. This fundamental contradiction (accoustical stability/functional instability) is responsible for both its formal and expressive values.

When employed within simple chordal progressions, the function flickers by as a colorful (because major in a minor context) yet otherwise unremarkable diatonic element. We are not here investigating every conceivable use of the function, but only one special case: the interruption of a stable procedure by a sustained envelope on the sixth degree.

Such interruptions may emerge by means of very different harmonic pivots and in a wide variety of situations. The necessary factors are that there be continuity leading up to the event and that the appearance of the function suddenly divert the flow from its previously implied goal.

The most conventional sort of minor-sixth interruption occurs in a simple deceptive cadence. In such a situation, the materials leading up to the occurrence very strongly imply impending resolution. But just as the melody achieves closure on $\hat{1}$, the bass moves not to the expected tonic but rather up a half step, from the dominant to the sixth degree (ex. 2a). The continuous striving toward resolution is thus interrupted, and formal expectations are frustrated. But even though there is an element of frustration present and although the sixth-degree triad is functionally unstable and tentative (with its bass perched that half-step above $\hat{5}$), it is also a radiant major sonority that asserts itself as an attractive alternative to the expected minor-tonic sonority.

In most instances, the subsequent material remains within the original key (of which VI is a diatonic funtion), prepares once again for closure, and finally achieves it (ex. 2b). But in the strategy we are investigating, the unexpected sixth-degree triad establishes itself, at least temporarily, as its own stable key area. It hijacks the tonality (ex. 2c).

The beginning of an embedded passage may be compared to the open-parenthesis of a qualifying phrase, which signals that the whole entity is a self-contained interruption interjected into a larger context. Following the close-parenthesis, the progression of the principal line of thought continues, colored by the information provided by the qualifier but otherwise as though the interruption had not occurred.

The parenthetically enclosed passage ordinarily prolongs (by means of stable

78

diatonic harmony) the original surface function, thereby projecting it and its implications on a higher structural level. Thus, the diatonic prolongation of the triad on the sixth degree is a major-key area, and its inherent stability suggests that it might last indefinitely. But its contrapuntally unstable root $\hat{6}$, still requires the descent to $\hat{5}$.

This creates something of a paradox. The initial intrusion of the area on the sixth degree is jolting, yet the stability of the major-key material almost immediately seduces us into accepting it as the only point of reference. This stable region, however, because of its tentative mode of generation, carries with it the nagging realization that regardless of how long it is maintained, it is a structural dissonance and must be cancelled out. Its promise of major-key stability and the expectation of necessary closure in the original key are incompatible.

Thus far, we have dealt with the formal implications (harmonic, contrapuntal, structural) of the mechanism. It will have been noticed, however, that these implications already suggest analogies with emotional patterns. In particular, the formal paradox just described has much in common with various psychological experiences. For the process of moderation that closes the gap between notes and expression begins as soon as the phenomenon is plugged into its tonal framework. While notated pitches mean very little in themselves, the norms of the tonal idiom (defining degrees of tension/release, stability/instability, directionality/closure) cause them to cluster into recognizable gestures: purposeful growth, striving for stability, frustrated expectations, and so forth. Most listeners respond directly to these patterns, and because they have no technical expertise with which to justify their reactions, they regard them as subjective. But it is possible to account for these responses through a strongly dynamic interpretation of the pitch relationships themselves.

An additional mediating factor permits us to go even farther in the general explication of this device: the conventional association in the 19th century of major and minor respectively with positive and negative emotional qualities.[10] When this pair of oppositions and their connotations are applied to the mechanism of minor-sixth interruptions, an extremely potent set of expressive implications comes into play.

If the minor-mode context represents some negative emotional state (greater specificity than positive/negative being possible only within individual instances), then the sudden emergence of a stable major-quality area on the sixth degree represents an unexpected infusion of some positive state. But because of the contrapuntal implication that the function is in need of resolution, this prolongation brings with it from its inception the seeds of its own demise. If, for instance, the envelope in isolation suggests hope, it must be perceived in context as *false* hope.

The combination of syntax and semiological code permits us, even prior to individual instances, to understand this strategy as possessing a sense of disillusion and pessimism: stable, positive emotional states are rendered unfeasible and formally dissonant while the more unstable negative states are defined as the only reliable points of reference. This particular mechanism of attempted ascape from minor is doomed to failure even as it begins: $\hat{6}$ must resolve back to $\hat{5}$ and the original key.

Minor-sixth interruptions also occur in major-mode compositions. In several respects, this phenomenon is similar to the one in minor: the mechanism of interruption, parenthetical prolongation, and continuation is the same. Here too the triad and its region are both consonant and major—locally stable—while in contrapuntal context, the root still strongly implies that it must ultimately descend the half-step to $\hat{5}$.

Two factors, however, make it somewhat more complicated. First, the function can only appear through chromatic alteration: it hovers precariously between the normal sixth degree and $\hat{5}$ (ex. 3). The fact that it is deviant from the diatonic processes of the key intensifies its functional instability—its unnatural generation demands resolution all the more. The strategy in the minor context seems sufficiently disruptive, even though the embedded prolongation involves a triadic element that is part of its natural universe; in the major, only the slender thread of one common tone—the tonic—serves to link two essentially disjunct worlds. They are related to one another irrationally, since continuous diatonic procedure cannot connect them.

The second complication is that the major/minor opposition that facilitates interpretation of the strategy in minor-mode compositions is not applicable here. Both areas (tonic and minor sixth) are major, and in terms of the standard code, both reside on the positive side. Yet the confrontation between two presumably positive but incompatible affects is in itself disquieting. Generalizations beyond these few observations are difficult, for the expressive purpose of the device in major varies even more from piece to piece than in minor.

In both minor and major, the interruption strategy is articulated not only through harmonic disruption, but through other parameters as well. The impression that a foreign state invades the normal flow is projected by substantial alterations in melodic contour, rhythmic character, texture, and so on. These other parameters are responsible for rendering more specific the kinds of positive or negative emotional states involved in any given situation. In addition, the placement of the interruption in the course of the piece's narrative plan[11] influences heavily the way in which it is to be understood. And so, we must now turn to individual compositions.

***

The opening section (mm. 1-33) of Schubert's *Impromptu in C Minor, Op. 90 #1* presents an extremely concentrated image of confinement. All its parameters conspire in this. The melodic line tries continually to ascend, only to get stuck on repeated notes and then to fall back listlessly to the center of gravity. The level of rhythmic motion is restricted to the quarter-note, producing a tedious sense of plodding. The phrases are all four bars long, and each comes to a half or full stop—no momentum or purposeful activity beyond these is accomplished. The structure of the section is almost intolerably redundant, made up as it is of four pairs of antecedent-consequent presentations of the same

materials. And the harmonic plan tiresomely reiterates confirmations of the dominant and tonic. Attempts at moving to the relative major (occasional rays of hope) are invariably quashed by the inexorable returns to C minor and its most powerful component: *g*, the fifth degree and dramatic opening pitch.

All this adds up to a kind of stagnation, but not complacency, for there are also elements present that indicate growing dissatisfaction. First, the range of the piece (beginning in m. 2) grows from a single, pent-up melodic line in the middle of the keyboard, through ever wider circles of space until, at the end of the section, the materials fill out the entire canvas first set forth by the mysterious octave *g*'s at the beginning. Yet, while the range bumps up against those spatial boundaries, it seems unable to go beyond, to progress. Second, the dynamic level grows from *pianissimo* to the *fortissimo* also set as a limit by the opening octaves. Both of these dimensions—range and dynamics—attempt to break out by means of force, but they only succeed in intensifying the realization of confinement by their failure to bring about any change in pattern.[12]

This failure seems to be acknowledged in mm. 34-37 through the telescoping of the cycles of cadential confirmation. But almost as though inadvertently, the cadential pattern in m. 34 includes a hesitation on VI— inadvertently because the first time, it is overlooked and simply serves as a diatonic function in the march to C minor. It seems, however, that after the conclusion of the cadence, the potential of the sixth degree as a means of escape is recognized. The pattern is repeated—softly, for what force could not accomplish may now be achieved by careful manipulation of this function—and a sleight-of-hand, a melodic *db*, leads suddenly to a cadence on A*b* major. The grimness of the C minor area is left behind, but not by means of purposeful growth. It is simply abandoned, replaced by the area on $\hat{6}$, which has already been revealed (mm. 34-37) as a function that most naturally participates in the confirmation of C minor.

However, the shaky justification for its emergence is soon forgotten as the radiant A*b* major section systematically opens up all the elements previously expressive of

80

confinement. The melodic line (a modifica-
tion of the original material, connoting transformed identity) now soars beyond the bounds
of the first section's limits. The accompaniment pattern of flowing triplets provides a
sense of ongoing motion and raises the level
of rhythmic activity to the half-measure. The
phrases are five measures in length, gracefully
though willfully avoiding each time the
tendency to cadence after four. The harmonic
plan permits free modulatory exploration
through tangentially related areas that turn
out to pivot (unexpectedly, irrationally but
gratifyingly) back to Ab. Each potential threat
of minor is converted miraculously into major.
Finally, in m. 78, the material seems to
become airborne, moving in units of entire
measures that do not even touch down on the
downbeats because of the suspensions that
keep them aloft. The melody moves down by
gracious sequences to cadences on Ab: Utopia
achieved.

With a single stroke, the descent of ab to g
in m. 84 announces unceremoniously what we
should have known all along—that this whole
Ab excursion was a fantasy. Yet even the
wisest of listeners (those who recognized the
falseness of the excursion from its inception)
are bound to feel betrayed, for Schubert has
permitted—even forced—us to taste the
concretized experience of Utopia.

The remainder of the impromptu is
devoted to exorcising the seductive vision in a
succession of stages. First, the piece simply
returns to the confinement of the opening
material. This is now rendered brutal, ironically by means of those very features that had
contributed to the sense of freedom in the Ab
section: the triplets and the db that initially
served as pivot to Ab. The level of activity is
drawn down to the subdivisions within the
beat, as each member of the triplet is articulated by a thick, often dissonant cluster; and
db, far from providing a means of escape, is
held up for contempt in the harsh light of C-
minor reality. It becomes an unbearable,
grating dissonance.

Nor is this the extent of the negation. The
. conclusion of this section leads suddenly into a
reprise of the Ab material, but in a transformation so grotesque that it is almost
unrecognizable. It is now in minor, and the

brutal rhythmic jabs of the preceding section
continue. But, possibly most significant, the
entire section is imprisoned in the area on the
fifth degree, G minor: a sardonic recollection
of the Ab section from the vantage point of
the most repressive element of the C-minor
area (as defined in this piece). The lovely
remnants of the earlier vision are kicked to
bits, as though it is now recognized as a cruel
hoax—a betrayal.

But most devastating is the sudden
evaporation of hostility and the emergence of
the airborne section (m. 152), untransformed
except in two respects. First, it is in G major, is
still thus imprisoned. And second, its context
prevents us from believing in it. It no longer
grows out of a process of increasingly liber-
ated animation. It simply happens: the
vulnerable, nostalgic memory of a dream that
could never be.

The return of the original material in m.
160 does not require the wrenching reorientation that brought back reality the first
time. We never left it. The final section,
following attempts at escape, self-lacerating
negations, and sentimental recall, achieves
what may be the only possible solution in the
transformation of the self from C minor to C
major. Even here, the transformation is equivocal—the conclusion is an uneasy,
bittersweet compromise between minor and
major—but at least the c and g boundaries (as
definers of reality) are stabilized and accepted.

The sixth-degree interruption, its negation,
and reconciliation thus form the basis for the
plot of this composition. The factors
identified in the general syntactical discussion
(localized stability versus functional
instability, the falseness of the major-key
affect in this context, etc.) are responsible for
articulating the strategy, but the particular
materials permit much more specific
interpretation: grim reality, escape to illusory
freedom, return to an even grimmer reality,
hostile and nostalgic recollection, and finally
coming to terms with reality by accepting it
and transforming the self.[13]

Other minor-mode compositions employ
sixth-degree interruptions in similar fashions,
but because of particular materials and narrative contexts, the end results always differ
somewhat.[14] The original key area may seem

brooding, violent, tragic, and the sixth-degree envelope may project (against that backdrop) triumph (in Beethoven's *Ninth Symphony*[15]), banal complacency (Beethoven's *A Minor Quartet, Op. 132*), or lyrical freedom (as here or in Schubert's *Unfinished Symphony*). The particular contrast sets up the central dichotomy for the composition, and the remainder of the process is concerned with settling the conflict. Often the implications of the embedded passage are simply dismissed, and the original negative state asserts itself the more strongly at the end. (This particularly occurs in the first movement of a cyclic composition: Beethoven's *Ninth*, op. 132, and Schubert's *Unfinished*.) Sometimes, however, it is as though the memory of the experience eventually brings about a transformation to major of the original key. In both the Beethoven examples cited, the minor-sixth area (after having been suppressed in the first movement) emerges with distinctly religious materials in an internal movement, is subsequently negated in a violent manner, but ultimately serves as the catalyst for transcendence in the final movement.[16]

In any case, these all have in common an essentially pessimistic point of departure, interpolation of a more positive state, and subsequent negation and/or synthesis. Seen against the Classical-period, Enlightenment norms of continous dynamic process and "organic" achievement of tonal goals,[17] these indicate a rather new view of life. Existence is found in a harsh deterministic world in which refuge turns out to be illusion.

Within this framework, Beethoven struggles for and often seems to attain transcendence, though a vital element in these apparent triumphs is the fact that they have been forged from an unstable pact between tonic and sixth degree: they are based on hope, faith, heroic assertion of the will in the face of doubt—not on the seemingly rational growth processes of, say the *Eroica*.[18] Schubert, by contrast, rarely attempts the breakthrough to transcendence. In his pieces, the embedded passages of lyricism more often turn out to be pure illusion; the attempts at transformation become, to use Adorno's image, facets of a crystal—Plus ça change....[19]

Whether these differences in denouement reflect differences in personality or age (Beethoven lived through the exuberance of the French Revolution, Schubert experienced only post-Enlightenment disillusion), the problems posed are the same. Neither believes in rational solution. The ideology of the time is thus concretized in musical strategies by means of minor-sixth interruption.

***

The second movement of Beethoven's *Quartet in Eb Major, Op. 127*, is a set of variations. The theme itself seems at once supplicative, consoling, and quietly confident (achieved in part by its melody that grows gradually in waves from the 7th of its dominant, to the tonic, sixth, octave, and beyond—but that also reaches down continually, as if to make sure the hesitant accompanying voices are following). The two variations that follow increase in animation until the movement seems to dance with joy. The implication is that this growth process of ever increasing liveliness will continue (though just what it could do to follow the hops, trills, and passagework of the second variation is hard to fathom).

In fact, at the cadence of this variation, a mysterious pivot occurs (mm. 58-59): in octaves, all instruments play *c -c#-e* (in an A*b* Major context), which ushers in Variation III in E major, the enharmonic equivalent of F*b*, the minor sixth degree. There had been flirtations with *fb* (in conjunction with *db*—now *c#*) at the close of the second strain of each of the preceding three versions, but it had always seemed a momentary color change or, when it actually flaired (mm. 49 and 55), it had been cleared away rapidly into the secure diatonic framework of the theme.

Several factors combine to make this pivot seem unprepared and inexplicable from the point of view of normal procedure. One is the lifting of *db-fb* (now *c#-e*) out of the contrapuntal/harmonic context that had made it seem only a slight, easily absorbed inflection. Another is the visual aspect—the change in signature from four flats to four sharps looks like the sudden appearance of an

82

entirely different world.[20] If the original theme seemed simple, it now appears in retrospect to have been almost fussy, for here it is presented in a distilled, hymnlike essence. The increasing animation halts and is confronted with what seems a timeless and (because of the religious associations of the material) mystical state. Moreover, in the second strain, the variation twice pivots dramatically to its own lowered-sixth degree, suggesting the possibility of infinite regress through chains of these irrational progressions (mm. 64 and 74).

At the conclusion of this variation, the *e* is simply returned (in octaves) to the *eb* dominant of A*b*: the miraculous vision disappears and we find ourselves again on diatonic earth. The variation that follows employs the decorative style of figuration characteristic of the pre-E major variations, and through the very slow but purposeful harmonic rhythm (accomplished by the arpeggio that binds together each entire measure) seems to be regaining confidence. But at the conclusion of this variation (m. 94), the piece seems to lose its bearing. It is as though the memory of that E-major vision cannot be assimilated or forgotten.

An abortive fifth variation (from m. 96) begins with imitation between violin and viola, interrupted by an attempt at re-entering the world of four sharps. This time, only the *c#* is accomplished—the *e* to which it moved the first time is not forthcoming, suggesting that the revelation cannot be summoned by sheer will. The lines grope about in the rarified C# minor region, rather like St. Peter attempting to walk on the waters without the requisite faith. We are saved from drowning by a sudden pivot in m. 107 and a final variation in A*b*.

At the conclusion of the movement, a simple deceptive cadence on the lowered sixth degree (*fb* in the bass in m. 122 rather than *ab*) suddenly provides the key for entry into the inexplicable region. As *ab* is sustained (respelled as *g#*) as a common tone, the two apparently remote tonalities, A*b* and E, present themselves in simple cadential formulas, and the movement closes following this at least partial reconciliation of the two states.

This movement concretizes in music an encounter with the Sublime[21]. The E-major section—simple, unornamented, spiritual essence—suddenly just appears, a vision of another world. After the encounter, the piece cannot continue in what had been a purposeful, confident process of linear development. It returns to try to relive that moment—unsuccessfully. It searches in vain for the proper pivot. Only at the end is the key to the transformation revealed (the interrelationship among the dominant triad, its auxiliary triad on the lowered sixth degree, and the common-tone pivot of the tonic pitch). While it remains mysterious, the foreign key is no longer completely alien to the larger context. It has confronted the confident human state, baffled it, caused it considerable anxiety and inability to function as before, but finally altered it to achieve a higher level of consciousness: one that has access to mystical, unearthly understanding.

Other pieces that revolve around this relationship include Beethoven's *Les Adieux* and Op. 110, Schubert's posthumous B*b* piano sonata and *Moments musicals, Op. 94 #6*.[22] As with the phenomenon in minor, its meaning in context depends on the remainder of the piece. But all of them articulate central 19th-century problems of discontinuity, loss of confidence in the individual's ability to determine his or her fate, and the turn from rational processes to the irrationality characteristic of Romanticism. A dual perception of external versus internal realities and an inability (or reluctance) to reconcile them adequately is at the root of these compositions—as it is in the 19th-century novel, poetry, visual art, and political unrest.[23]

***

Musical signification is indeed difficult to interpret. Ambiguities, circular reasoning (the necessity of dealing with the notation in performance in such a way as to confirm in sound the original interpretation), and leaps of faith abound in the process just sketched. But if art derives its affective and communicative powers from the resonances evoked by metaphors, associations, conventional symbols, and so forth, then these slippery issues (with their inherent pitfalls and circles) need to be addressed, directly and with precision.

And not just for scholars with simply interdisciplinary interests. Both musicology and music theory have recognized the phenomenon of minor-sixth interruptions and have dealt with it objectively (citing statistics indicating their greater incidence in the early 19th-century repertory) or formally (demonstrating through reductions the underlying normality of such seeming deviations). But as satisfying as objective or formal treatments may be, neither can explain the purpose of such an interruption in any given compostition nor why such remote syntactical relationships became prominent features of 19th-century style. This study determines that such strategies are reflections

of ideology; the formal mechanisms that emerge in repertories are to a large extent the means by which views of the world and values find themselves articulated. Thus, in order to explain adequately the history of musical repertories and their formal strategies, involvement with meaning both expressive and ideological—is essential.

With sufficient consideration given to the tensions implied by basic syntactical mechanisms, to the particularities of context, and to those aspects of the outside world that lend themselves to musical embodiment, musical strategies can be handled in ways parallel to those used in the criticism of literature or the visual arts. If we are to begin treating musical compositions as meaningful products of culture, then we must begin to translate our formalisms into human terms.

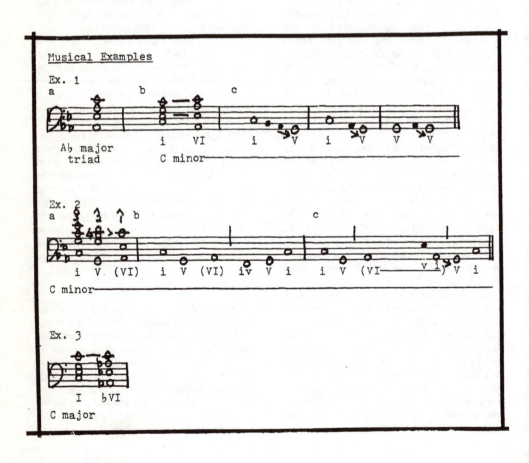

Musical Examples

Notes

1. A third option—the practice of a music criticism that deals seriously with the internal workings of compositions, but in ways that permit explanation in terms of human values—has been advocated in recent years, particulary in the following: Leonard B. Meyer, *Emotion and Meaning in Music* (Chicago, 1956) and *Explaining Music* (Berkeley, Los Angeles, London, 1973); Joseph Kerman, "How We Got into Analysis, and How to Get Out," *Critical Inquiry*, 7 (1980), 311-331; Leo Treitler, "History, Criticism, and Beethoven's Ninth Symphony" *19th Century Music*, 3 (1980), 193-210 and "'To Worship That Celestial Sound': Motives for Analysis," *Journal of Musicology*, 1 (1982), 153-70; Peter Kivy, *The Corded Shell: Reflections on Musical Expression* (Princeton, 1980); Edward T. Cone, "The Authority of Music Criticism," *Journal of the American Musicological Society*, 34 (1981), 1-18; and Robert P. Morgan, "Theory, Analysis, and Criticism," *Journal of Musicology*, 1 (1982), 15-18.

2. Ruth Solie's "The Living Work: Organicism and Musical Analysis," in *19th Century Music*, 4 (1980), 147-56 and Kerman's "How We Got into Analysis" offer expositions of the unspoken ideology that underlies this kind of insulated analysis. Most music theorists prefer to borrow models from the physical sciences (rather than from the humanties) and tend to take the regularities of the notated surface (rather than gesture, rhetorical devices, or semiological code, which are methodologically impure and "subjective") as the proper focus of study.

3. James Haar, in his "Music History and Cultural History" *Journal of Musicology*, 1, 1982, p. 10) writes: "A similar problem exists with many works on music in the context of cultural history: they are simply too far away from the notes, often to such an extent that one cannot tell from what is said about the music of a given period whether or not any of that music has survived. What readers are looking for is...intelligent description, comprehensive analysis, and critical judgment, in a historical framework supported by evidence from the other arts."

While Haar's point is well taken, the difficulty facing cultural historians of music is partly one of practicality. In a study dealing with broad issues, it is as impossible to build continually from the notes upward as for a literary critic to build always from letters, to words and sentences, and finally to some discussion of plot. The higher-level concerns, such as character, mood, or theme, are dependent on the words and their letters, but we usually do not expect to see the entire process set tediously before us—except in treatises on critical theory. But since connections between notes, local meaning and superstructure are not automatically assumed, such high-level interpretations of music often seem entirely arbitrary and subjective. If the mediating steps linking them can be reconstructed, however, these interpretations can perhaps be validated—at least to the extent that any critical account of literature or visual art can be.

4. A pre-occupation with "objectivity" has determined much of the course of academic music study in the past several decades. The search for verifiability has resulted in a flood of historical information and complex analytical technique, but it has also prevented us from dealing with the musical composition as a meaningful product of a society.

5. The same may be observed with any human sign system, all of which rely on convention, shared beliefs, semiological codes, and so on. Much of the recent work on metaphor has sought to undermine the stranglehold of the old objective/subjective distinction by demonstrating its inadequacy for explaining how we acquire concepts and understanding—even in the physical sciences. See, for instance, George Lakoff and Mark Johnson, *Metaphors We Live By* (Chicago, 1980), particularly Chapters 24-30.

Kivy's *The Corded Shell* is a serious philosophical attempt at accounting for our recognition of emotions in music. While the discussion is limited to the expression of static-state emotions (and not their changes or fluctuations through time), it is a necessary first step in the process of making respectable once again emotive descriptions of music.

6. It might be argued that there is no need to bridge this gap—that music is best experienced as direct sensuous presence, uncontaminated by verbal mediation. (See, for instance, Richard Taruskin's reviews of Kivy's *The Corded Shell*, the *Musical Quarterly*, 68 (1982), 293 or Roland Barthes' "The Grain of the Voice," in his *Image Music Text*, trans. Stephen Heath, N.Y., 1977, 179-89.) But for at least two groups, the process of reconstructing the connections between pitch

relationships and signification would seem indispensable.

The first of these are performers. Written music cannot speak for itself but is dependent on performers for reconstituting it in sound. Any gesture, image, or idea lying latent in the score will fail to materialize unless projected by the performer: the listener can experience only that which is thus presented. (See, for instance, Treitler's "History, Criticism," for a discussion of the problems involved in performing the beginning of Beethoven's *Ninth Symphony* and the importance of understanding syntactically, structurally, metaphorically, and ideologically its function.) Since interpretation, whether conscious or not, necessarily precedes the production of concretized sound in our tradition, the critical methods whereby the patterns in the score are realized deserve very serious attention.

The second group is made up of musicologists. The fact that we no longer agree about the ability of music to communicate emotions or ideas should not bar historians from performing what should be a central task of reconstructing what the musical strategies of a period meant to the composers and audiences of the day. If, for instance, music in the 19th century was believed to be capable of communicating those aspects of experience otherwise inexpressible (the infinite, the Sublime, etc.), what patterns were used to articulate them? When musicologists begin dealing with cultural encoding in music, they can begin to participate more fully with specialists in the other humanities in tracing society's projections of itself in its artifacts. (See Treitler, "History, Criticism," particulary p. 194.)

7. Morse Peckham, *Behond the Tragic Vision: The Quest for Identity in the Nineteenth Century* (N.Y., 1962); Theodore W. Adorno, "Spätstil Beethovens" and "Schubert," in *Moments musicaux* (Frankfurt, 1964), 13-36; Rose Rosengard Subotnik, "Adorno's Diagnosis of Beethoven's Late Style: Early Symptom of a Fatal Condition," *Journal of the American Musicological Society*, 29 (1976), 242-75 and "The Historical Structure: Adorno's 'French' Model for the Criticism of Nineteenth-Century Music," *19th Century Music*, 2 (1978), 36-60.

8. The word "ideology" here refers to cultural values or the shared assumptions (often non-explicit and unconscious) and ways of viewing the world characteristic of a society. The imprint of ideology on an artwork need not be deliberate; it is frequently a reflection of habits of thought so ingrained as to be transparent

initially, rendered visible only with changes in time or location.

9. Voice-leading is something of a problem in the resolution of this triad to the dominant, since its components would move down most naturally in illicit parallel motion. Indeed, this difficulty becomes an integral part of the interruption syndrome: very often , the resolution involves the abandonment of polyphony and the stark motion in unison or octaves of all voices from $\hat{6}$ to $\hat{5}$. See the discussions of the two compositions below.

10. The fact that these associations are not universal is here irrelevant. Music of this time utilizes the major/minor distinction quite consistently to project emotional qualities, and as a convention in a period that sought to communicate such matters, it is an essential tool for interpretation of this music.

11. Since music unfolds through time, it has more in common with narrative processes usually than with the architecture more frequently used as a model for explanation. But in the 19th century, the literary analogy becomes particularly germane, as both music and the novel manifest parallel involvements with long-term patterns of conflict/resolution, character (thematic) transformation, organicism, and so on. The pieces discussed below are extremely dependent on the particular sequence of their events, as in a plot, even though they follow the formal outlines of rondo and theme-and-variations respectively.

12. Hearing these images and patterns of tension/release in the ways described depends on the particular performance. If the score is played differently, the confinement/escape strategy may simply not be there. (There are those who find the impromptu tiresomely repetitious—a bad piece—and who patronizingly compensate for its faults by nuancing the surface throughout, hoping no one will notice the redundancy.) Interpretation (cognitive or intuitive) necessarily precedes performance. Thus, these comments indicate not only an explanation of the piece's logic, but also a way of playing the composition.

Note also that other interpretations of the same sequence of events are possible. I am less concerned with asserting this reading than with demonstrating a critical process.

13. In a letter to his brother Ferdinand on July 18, 1824, Schubert wrote: "True, it is no longer that happy time during which each object seems to us

86

to be surrounded by a youthful gloriole, but a period of fateful recognition of a miserable reality, which I endeavor to beautify as far as possible by my imagination (thank God). We fancy that happiness lies in places where once we were happier, whereas actually it is only in ourselves." in Otto Erich Deutsch, *Schubert: A Documentary Biography*, trans. Eric Blom (London, 1946), #484.

This says in words essentially what was conveyed in the *Impromptu*. But although the verbal statement is more explicit, the musical version is far more eloquent and precise: through the music (which does render beautiful this "fateful recognition"), we know exactly the feeling of that miserable reality, the particular qualities of happiness, and so on.

14. Instances of minor-sixth interruptions occur in Baroque and Classical music as well, but they tend to occur toward the ends of pieces, as a way of postponing closure through deception and surprise. The sudden explosions in Rossini overtures are usually based on this syntactical relationship as well. But in most of these cases, the interruption is a local event—not the central component in the plot. The pieces included in this discussion feature the strategy prominently in their structures and thus require special attention.

15. See Treitler's splendid interpretation of the *Ninth* in his "History, Criticism," 193-98 and "'To Worship'," 161-70.

16. This association of the area of unreality with religious materials represents not fantasy but faith: a state that likewise exists outside normal purposeful activity but that (unlike fantasy) holds out hope for transcendence.

17. See once again the sources cited in #7 for discussions of the breakdown of Enlightenment ideology. "A spirit of disillusionment, febrile and confused, succeeded the high certainties of the Age of Reason and the expectations voiced in the revolutionary creed. The philosophy of the Restoration was for many a thing of shreds and patches after the stark and glittering mirror-world the *philosophes* had held before the gaze of humanity, and the reversion to traditional pretensions, petty policies, checks and balances and compromises, though it might mark a return to sanity and repose, still left behind a despairing conviction that humanity had failed itself." Geoffrey Bruun, *Europe and the French Imperium, 1799-1814* (N.Y., 1963), 202.

18. In addition to sources cited in #7, see also Philip Downes, "Beethoven's 'New Way' and the *Eroica*, in *The Creative World of Beethoven*, ed. Paul Henry Lang (N.Y., 1970), 83-102 and Maynard Solomon, *Beethoven* (N.Y., 1977), 141-42.

19. "Schubert." This image forms the core of Adorno's essay.

20. The listener does not *see* the score and thus is not aware of the change in notation as such. It might be argued that the respelling is nothing more than a matter of convenience (F♭ major requires double-flats). But it might also be argued that the shift to four sharps is an essential part of Beethoven's strategy in that it contributes to the alienated quality of this variation. If the latter argument is accepted, the performer is responsible for projecting (through tone-color, articulation, etc.) some sense of this extraordinary dimension.

21. The "Sublime" in 18th and 19th-century aesthetic writing is a complex state (rather foreign to current categories) in which majesty, awe, and terror are intermixed. "The passion caused by the great and sublime in *nature*, when those causes operate most powerfully, is astonishment: and astonishment is that state of ths soul in which all its motions are suspended, with some degree of horror. In this case the mind is so entirely filled with its object, that it cannot entertain any other, nor by consequence reason on that object which employs it. Hence arises the great power of the sublime, that, far from being produced by them, it anticipates our reasonings, and hurries us on by an irresistible force. Astonishment, as I have said, is the effect of the sublime in its highest degree; and inferior effects are admiration, reverence, and respect." Edmund Burke, *A Philosophical Inquiry Into the Origin of our Ideas of the Sublime and Beautiful* (London, 1756), Part II, Section I.

22. See Edward T. Cone's superb discussion of this piece in "Schubert's Promissory Note," *19th Century Music*, 5 (1982), 233-41.

23. See again the sources cited in #7. Peckham in particular presents an extremely clear exposition of the reflections in literature, art, and music of the ideological upheavals in the 19th century.

CHAPTER 2

The blasphemy of talking politics during Bach Year

Introduction

The last great Bach Year, 1950 (the bicentennial of Bach's death), inspired the undertaking of many monuments of Bach scholarship we now find indispensible. The *Neue Bach Ausgabe* was initiated,[1] and it was during the course of preparing that new edition that the profound revision of Bach's compositional chronology began to emerge.[2] We now know, for instance, that his cantata composition was concentrated in a very few years, that his production of instrumental music occurred throughout his career, that he was far more ambivalent about his position as a church musician than had previously been recognized.[3] Moreover, our interest in the performance practices of early music intensified at that time, resulting in the proliferation of first-rate performers devoted to carefully reconstructed renderings of Bach's music.

But of all these extraordinary contributions to our understanding of Bach, my favorite souvenir of that last Bach Year remains Adorno's 'Bach defended against his devotees'.[4] In this classic essay, Adorno set forth a

---

[1] *Neue Bach Ausgabe*, ed. Johann-Sebastian-Bach-Institut, Göttingen, and Bach-Archiv, Leipzig (Kassel and Basel, 1954–).

[2] See Georg von Dadelsen, *Beiträge zur Chronologie der Werke Johann Sebastian Bachs* (Trossingen, 1958), and Alfred Dürr, 'Zur Chronologie der Leipziger Vokalmusik J.S. Bach', *Bach Jahrbuch*, 44 (1957), pp. 5–162.

[3] See, for instance, Robert Marshall, 'Bach the progressive: observations on his later works', *The Musical Quarterly*, 62 (1976), pp. 313–57, and Friedrich Blume, 'Outlines for a new picture of Bach', *Music and Letters*, 44 (1963), pp. 214–27.

[4] Theodor Adorno, *Prisms*, trans. Samuel Weber and Shierry Weber (1967; reprint ed. Cambridge, Mass., 1981), pp. 133–46.

14   SUSAN McCLARY

model of how Bach's music might be understood in social contexts: both
Bach's own and those of subsequent (especially post-war) generations.
Unlike the other new directions for Bach scholarship suggested in the
1950s, however, Adorno's insights have had negligible impact on musicology or on the common reception of Bach.[5] Indeed, as 1985 (the ter-
centenary of Bach's birth) arrived, it became clear that the matters that
concerned Adorno had changed very little in the intervening thirty-five
years – except, perhaps, to move even farther in directions Adorno would
recognize with the ironic satisfaction a paranoid derives from seeing worst-
possible scenarios fully realized.

As a scholar classified as a Baroque music specialist, I participated during
1985 in several Bach Year celebrations: panel discussions in which my contributions were modest attempts at resituating Bach in his social, political,
ideological context. To my overwhelming joy (again as paranoid confronted with worst-possible scenario), I was told outright by prominent
scholars that Bach (unlike 'second-rate' composers such as Telemann) had
nothing to do with his time or place, that he was 'divinely inspired', that his
music works in accordance with perfect, universal order and truth. One is
permitted, in other words, to deal with music in its social context, but only
if one agrees to leave figures such as Bach alone. Thus the time seems ripe
to take up Adorno's enterprise, to re-examine the ways in which Bach's
music can be said to bear the imprint of its social origins, to reconsider the
place of Bach's music in present-day culture.

I shall begin by inquiring how and why music is treated differently than
the other arts in our culture and also by examining our preconceptions and
ideological uses of eighteenth-century music, Bach's in particular. By way
of contrast, the second section will present a sketch of Bach's social context
and discuss two of his compositions in order to demonstrate the kinds of
insights that can be gleaned from socially grounded interpretation. In the
final section, I shall consider what is to be gained by dealing with Bach in
political terms.

The Pythagorean dilemma

Why should the act of talking about music – especially Bach's – in a political context be regarded as blasphemous? To some extent, music's history of

[5] See, however, Laurence Dreyfus, 'Early music defended against its devotees: a theory of
historical performance in the twentieth century', *The Musical Quarterly*, 69 (1983),
pp. 297–322.

reception parallels that of literature and the visual arts in that it was displaced during the course of the nineteenth century to a 'separate sphere', replete with pseudo-religious rituals and attitudes.[6] At the very moment that music was beginning to be produced for a mass bourgeois audience, that audience sought to legitimize its artifacts by grounding them in the 'certainty' of another, presumably more absolute, realm – rather than in terms of its own social tastes and values.

I wish to argue, however, that music has a much longer history of claiming autonomy from social practice – indeed a history that can be traced at least as far back as Pythagoras and the discovery of a correspondence between harmonious tones and numerical proportions.[7] (Later theorists found similar correspondences between triads – the building blocks of the tonality of the bourgeois era – and properties of physical acoustics[8] or attempted to validate compositions on the basis of their apparently mechanical generation from pitch class sets.)[9] In other words, from very early times up to and including the present, there has been a strain of Western culture that accounts for music in non-social, implicitly metaphysical terms. But parallel with that strain (and also from earliest times) is another which regards music as essentially a human, socially grounded, socially alterable construct.[10] Most polemical battles in the history of music theory and criticism involve the irreconcilable confrontation of these two positions.

[6] See, for instance, Jacques Barzun, *The use and abuse of art* (Princeton, 1974); Janet Wolff, *Aesthetics and the sociology of art* (London, 1983); Terry Eagleton, *Literary theory* (Minneapolis, 1983), and *The function of criticism* (London, 1984); and Susan McClary's series, 'Historical deconstructions and reconstructions' in the *Minnesota Composers Forum Newsletter*, especially 'The roots of alienation' (June, 1982), 'Autonomy and selling out' (June, 1983), and 'The living composition in social context' (February and March, 1984).

[7] What we know of Pythagoras' philosophy was transmitted principally through Philolaus, Plato, and Aristotle. See the discussion in Richard Norton, *Tonality in Western culture* (University Park, Penn. and London, 1984), pp. 80–104.

[8] As much as they may differ in specific argument, the two most influential theories of tonality, those by Rameau and Schenker, agree at least in their desire to account for tonality on a non-social basis. See Jean-Philippe Rameau, *Traité de l'harmonie* (Paris, 1722), trans. Philip Gossett (New York, 1971), and Heinrich Schenker, *Der freie Satz* (Vienna, 1935), trans. Ernst Oster (New York and London, 1979). For discussions linking these to the Pythagorean position see Norton, *Tonality*, pp. 22–55, and Susan McClary, 'The politics of silence and sound', the afterword to Jacques Attali, *Noise: the political economy of music*, trans. Brian Massumi (Minneapolis, 1985), pp. 150–2.

[9] See Allen Forte, *The structure of atonal music* (New Haven, 1973), and David Epstein, *Beyond Orpheus* (Cambridge, Mass., 1979).

[10] Plato deals seriously in the *Republic* with the ethical dimensions of various kinds of musical practice and considers some to be socially beneficial, others to be pernicious. Major stylistic changes in the history of Western music have frequently been accompanied by justifications indicating that new styles are products of changes in social values. For instance, the polemics of the early seventeenth-century 'seconda prattica' assert that abstract rules of

16   SUSAN McCLARY

Clearly, my sympathies are with the latter position. But since I consider the problem to lie in that fundamental difference, I would like to explore briefly why the Pythagorean model, with all its subsequent manifestations, is so seductive.

Music enters through the ear – the most vulnerable sense organ. It cannot be closed or used selectively: one can avert one's eyes from the decor of an elevator but not one's ears from its Muzak. And especially in Western culture, in which the visual and the verbal are privileged as sources of knowledge, sound and music tend to slip around and surprise us.[11] The impact of the phenomenon seems immediate: one appears to experience concretely and intimately whatever the music dictates.

Moreover, music appears to be non-representational, at least as representation is usually construed. Unlike literature or the visual arts (which at least make use of characters, plots, color, and shapes that resemble phenomena in the everyday world and that can be referred to by means of ordinary language), music seems to be generated from its own self-contained, abstract principles. It is obviously much easier to demonstrate the content (both literal and ideological) of stories and pictures than of patterns of tones, for which most people have no verbal vocabulary and therefore no conscious cognition.

In music one enters a strange rarified world in which, for instance, the phenomenon of a d♭ can move one to tears, can appear either to affirm (as though inevitably, absolutely) one's expectations or to shatter one's most fundamental beliefs.[12] Now a d♭ all by itself in the real, extra-musical world signifies nothing. It can only do so by appearing in a highly structured, ordered context – a context dependent on norms, rules, and those apparently self-contained, abstract principles known explicitly only by initiated practitioners.

Thus, on the one hand, we have a priesthood of professionals who learn principles of musical order, who come to be able to call musical events by name and even to manipulate them; and, on the other hand, we have a

harmony no longer govern the new music, but rather considerations of text and passionate expression influence its composition. See Monteverdi's foreword to his *Fifth book of madrigals* (1605) as it was glossed by his brother, Giulio Cesare, in *Scherzi musicali* (1607) in *Source readings in music history*, ed. Oliver Strunk (New York, 1950), pp. 405–12. Schoenberg's move into 'atonality' was understood by him at times as a new abstract order, but at other times as a self-conscious rejection of bourgeois values. See Carl Schorske's account in *Fin-de-siècle Vienna* (New York, 1981), pp. 344–64.

[11] See, for instance, Don Ihde, *Listening and voice: a phenomenology of sound* (Athens, Ohio, 1976).

[12] See, for instance, the discussion of the function of the d♭ in Schubert's Impromptu, Op. 90, No. 1 in Susan McClary, 'Pitches, expression, ideology: an exercise in mediation', *Enclitic*, 7 (1983), pp. 76–86.

Talking politics during Bach Year   17

laity of listeners who respond strongly to music but have little conscious critical control over it. Because non-professional listeners usually do not know how to account intellectually for how music does what it does, they respond either by mystifying it (ascribing its power to extra-human sources – natural or implicitly supernatural) or by domesticating it (trivializing or marginalizing it, asserting that it does not really bear meaning).

Neither priest nor consumer truly wants to break the spell: to reveal the social grounding of that magic. Thus the priesthood prattles in its jargon that adds a metaphysical component to the essence of music and abdicates responsibility for its power; and listeners react as though mystically – not wanting to attribute to mere mortals the power to move them so. For if one recognizes the power of music to manipulate through unknown means, one at least wants to believe that human hands are not working the controls. Or, conversely, if one is working the controls, one most understandably wants to deny responsibility, to displace it elsewhere. Both musician and layperson collude in this mystification, both resist establishing connections between the outside, social world and the mysterious inner world of music.

If one feels comfortable and identifies with what is being articulated in a particular kind of music, one is likely to be happy ascribing to it universality and extra-human truth. It is only when one is dissatisfied with that music and its implicit social agenda – when, for instance, one's own voice is being silenced by its prestige and its claim to universal autonomy – that the music's ideological constructedness will become an issue: a *political* issue. In other words, advocates of dominant culture tend to take refuge in a neo-Pythagorean position (that is, 'we didn't make this up: this is simply the order of things'). Opponents to reigning order, however, rightly seek to deconstruct its social ideology.

Jacques Attali, in his book *Noise*,[13] develops a means of deciphering socio-political agendas in apparently self-contained music by focusing on the dialectic between order on the one hand and violence on the other. Music must have some degree of order: otherwise it reduces to undifferentiated noise. But it must also have some elements that deviate at least occasionally from that order, or else there is no semblance of motion, no interest, no art. Different repertories arrange themselves variously on a continuum between pure order and pure noise, depending both on the values of the society within which they are produced and also on those of the musicians who compose or even perform the music. By understanding as ideological constructs both the norms of a repertory and also the devia-

[13] Originally published as *Bruits: essai sur l'économie politique de la musique* (Paris, 1977).

18   SUSAN McCLARY

tions against those norms in particular compositions, one can begin to discern the most fundamental principles of social order of a period as well as individual strategies of affirmation and opposition.

One can also begin to distinguish between two very different groups of people who participate in music: (1) those who seek to immerse themselves in what they wish to regard as the pure order of music in order to escape what they perceive as the chaos of real life and (2) those who turn to music in order to enact or experience vicariously the simulacrum of opposition to the restrictiveness of real life (with 'real life' represented by those abstract though socially grounded norms). The ways in which one composes, performs, listens, or interprets are heavily influenced by the need either to establish order or to resist it.

We find ourselves today embedded in a society that is very anxious to secure for itself order in the face of potential or actual violence, in the face of pluralistic claims of the right to cultural production. Our theories of music (the means by which institutions train musicians) try to account for all events in a piece of music as manifestations of self-contained order, rather than as a more complex dialectical relationship between conventional norms and codes on the one hand and significant particularities and strategies on the other. And, consciously or not, our performance practices for the most part are designed to produce literal, note-perfect, reassuring but inert renditions of virtually all musics, whether originally affirmative or oppositional.

The music that dominates the concert repertory today is that of the eighteenth-century Enlightenment: the music that was first shaped in accordance with the social values of the stabilizing middle class.[14] This music appears (at least on some levels) to present itself as harmonious, perfect, organic, unified, formally balanced, capable of absorbing and resolving all tensions.[15] In this way, it is very much unlike either the music produced in the seventeenth century (which celebrates in its fragmented structures, its illegitimate dissonances, and in its ornate, defiant arabesques the disruptive, violent struggles of the emerging bourgeoisie against the norms of the church and the aristocracy)[16] or in the nineteenth century (which dramatizes the conflicts between the subjective self and the con-

---

[14] See Susan McClary, 'The rise and fall of the teleological model in Western music', to be published in *The paradigm exchange* (Minneapolis, 1987), and Norton, *Tonality*, pp. 169–230. Compare Terry Eagleton's account of the rise of the novel as a similar means of securing cultural hegemony for the English middle class in *The rape of Clarissa* (Minneapolis, 1982).

[15] See Susan McClary, 'A musical dialectic from the Enlightenment: Mozart's Piano Concerto in G Major, K. 453, movement II', *Cultural critique* 4 (Fall, 1986), pp. 129–69.

[16] See McClary, 'Politics', pp. 154–6.

Talking politics during Bach Year   19

straints of bourgeois society).[17] In the music of both the seventeenth and nineteenth centuries the ideological dimensions are far more evident, because their symbolic enactments of social antagonisms are to a large extent the message.

But, in fact, no less ideological are the 'classics', which pretend (at least on some levels) to be manifestations of perfect, absolute, universal form and truth. Surely the overt defiance of eighteenth-century convention that begins in Beethoven means to be unmasking precisely this claim. And even within what we frequently like to perceive as the pure order of eighteenth-century music itself, the tension between order (indeed, competing claims to legitimate order) and deviation – if not outright violence – is readily apparent if we permit ourselves to hear it.[18]

Bach's music as social discourse

This is the case even with the great, universal Bach, whose music is so widely thought to transcend the conditions of his time, place, career, and personality. However, once we understand each of the styles Bach appropriated as an articulation of a set of social values, then we can begin to detect details in his celebrated stylistic synthesis that connect his particular eclectic mode of composition with his thorny social and professional relationships and even with his situation with respect to the broader political context.

To begin with the larger picture, Bach's collected works could only have been produced by someone occupying a de-centered position with respect to acknowledged, mainstream musical cultures. As a German, he belonged to a society that had long been culturally colonized – by the music of the church and later, in the secular realm, by Italian opera and the musical manifestations of French Absolutism.[19] Others of his contemporaries

---

[17] See Theodor Adorno, 'Spätstil Beethovens', and 'Schubert' in *Moments musicaux* (Frankfurt, 1964), pp. 13–36; Morse Peckham, *Beyond the tragic vision: the quest for identity in the nineteenth century* (New York, 1962); Rose Rosengard Subotnik, 'Adorno's diagnosis of Beethoven's late style: early symptom of a fatal condition', *Journal of the American Musicological Society*, 29 (1976), pp. 242–75, and 'The historical structure: Adorno's "French" model for the criticism of nineteenth-century music', *19th Century Music*, 2 (1978), pp. 36–60; and McClary, 'Pitches'.

[18] See McClary, 'Musical dialectic' and also the discussion of Bach's Brandenburg Concerto No. 5, below.

[19] See Christoph Wolff's article on Bach, *The new Grove dictionary of music and musicians*, ed. Stanley Sadie, 20 vols. (London, 1980), I, pp. 785–840, for a presentation of Bach's career that is sensitive to social contexts. See also Barbara Schwendowius and Wolfgang Dömling, eds., *Johann Sebastian Bach: life – times – influence* (Kassel, 1976), trans. John Coombs, Lionel Salter and Gaynor Nitz (Hamburg, 1977).

20   SUSAN McCLARY

aligned themselves with one or another of the dominant options and wrote more or less systematically within its genres and for its market.[20] But Bach chose to retain his marginalized position, to appropriate all available musical discourses while clinging fiercely to his own German heritage, and to forge perhaps not so much a unified totality as a set of eclectic hybrids.

To have thus flown in the face of each of his spheres of influence required a certain kind of personality. Bach's career was mapped on the same forcefield of attractions and ambivalences as his style collection: never willing to commit himself entirely to any single context and its attendant ideology, he continued to shuttle among them, creating antagonisms with superiors while acting out possible means of reconciliation among these various contradictions only within his music.[21]

Seen against this social backdrop, the music itself ceases to appear as the pure mathematical order often suggested by theorists. For the styles Bach assembles are not simply different with respect to surface mannerisms: each has its own peculiar quality of moving through time. To combine in a single composition the on-rushing goal orientation of the Italian opera or concerto with the more sober, static, contrapuntal ideal of the German Lutheran repertory and the motion-arresting graces of French dance is to produce at times a highly conflicted procedure.[22] Yet Bach's genius lies in his ability to take these components that are highly charged – both ideologically and with respect to dynamic musical impulse – and to give the impression of having reconciled them.

Examples

I would like now to demonstrate how this synthetic procedure is manifested in two of Bach's compositions: the first movement of the Brandenburg Concerto No. 5 and Cantata 140, *Wachet auf*. My approach differs fundamentally from those of mainstream music theory which, because it is in search of deep-structural universals, disregards the idiosyncrasies of pieces – or regards them as surface difficulties to be explained away, to be reduced back to the norm.

This is not to say that I am uninterested in norms. Since signification in

---

[20] Handel, for instance, adopted far more fully the genre of Italian opera and later altered his style to fit the changing tastes of English audiences.

[21] A very high proportion (indeed most) of the surviving documents written by Bach are connected with disputes with authorities. These are collected in *The Bach reader*, ed. and trans. Hans T. David and Arthur Mendel (New York, 1945).

[22] See the discussion below of Bach's cantata *Wachet auf*.

music is in part a product of the socially invested meanings of the individual elements themselves, both of these presentations will require that their components be discussed to some extent in the abstract: it is only up against the norms and semiotic conventions of a style that the strategies of an individual piece can be perceived as significant. Thus the reconstruction of both the norms and the semiotic codes upon which a piece relies is essential.[23] But inasmuch as every piece of music assembles and problematizes very different elements of the shared semiotic code, the interpretive process is by definition both ad hoc (it derives its strategies from the specific demands and features of the individual composition) and dialectical (it strives to account for particularities in terms of the norms they affirm or oppose).

1. *Brandenburg Concerto No. 5, first movement*[24]

a. *Tonality*

On the most basic level, this concerto is a tonal composition (as are most of Bach's pieces). Tonality is, in short, a set of structural and syntactical procedures that emerged in Western music during the course of the seventeenth century and that underlies the concert music of the eighteenth and nineteenth centuries.[25] It is so familiar to us that we often accept it as 'the way music is supposed to go', though its career of rise and decline happens to articulate through musical terms the course of the European bourgeoisie.[26]

Tonality as a procedure relies on the interaction between at least two mutually dependent levels: a background progression and surface strategies. Each informs the other and makes the other meaningful. The background progression is responsible for giving the impression of long-term

[23] We are fortunate in that there existed in the eighteenth century an area of inquiry that strongly resembles semiotics, known today as the *Affektenlehre* or doctrine of the affections. Theorists such as Bach's contemporary, Johann Mattheson, in *Der vollkommene Capellmeister* (Hamburg, 1739), trans. Ernest Harriss (Ann Arbor, 1981), systematically codified both the various signs available for constructing representations of the affections and also the ways in which they could be combined in composition.

[24] The *Concerts avec plusieurs instruments* (French name, Italian forms, German dedication) were presented in autograph to the Margrave of Brandenburg in 1721. Bach had written them, however, between 1718 and 1721 for performance by his own ensemble at Cöthen, where he was employed. The fifth of them is thought to have been the last of the set to be composed.

[25] See Christopher Small, *Music – society – education* (2nd ed. rev., London, 1980), especially chapters 1, 3 and 4.

[26] See Norton, *Tonality*, and McClary, 'Rise and fall'.

coherence. Normally it begins in a home-key called the tonic, proceeds through a series of other keys (each of which is articulated heavily by a cadence), and returns at the end to re-affirm the tonic. The surface activities in a piece of tonal music are concerned with sustaining dynamic tension between the points of arrival that punctuate the background progression. This is largely accomplished by means of a complex harmonic syntax that continually implies what the next cadence in the background ought to be – while deferring the actual arrival until the composer sees fit to produce it.

This process is intensively teleological in that it draws its power from its ability to make the listener desire and finally experience the achievement – usually after much postponed gratification – of predetermined goals. It also seems rational, in that the harmonic procedures are always regulated and controlled by the constraints of tonal harmonic convention. The social values it articulates are those held most dear by the middle class: beliefs in progress, in expansion, in the ability to attain ultimate goals through rational striving, in the ingenuity of the individual strategist operating both within and in defiance of the norm.

In Bach's early eighteenth century, there were several different dialects of tonal procedure. The music of the German Lutheran sphere made use of tonal procedures in some respects (especially the harmonic strategies of implying and postponing goals),[27] but this repertory had other priorities (for instance, long-term structures based on traditional chorale melodies rather than on strictly 'logical', abstract background progressions) that resisted total conversion to tonal procedures. The French musical establishment under Louis XIV recognized all too well the destabilizing, exuberant, subversive character of tonality and tried to prevent its infiltration; the braking quality of French Baroque music (so peculiar to our tonally-trained ears) is the result of its attempt to appropriate the rational power of tonality while constantly draining off its energy.[28]

[27] There had been several moments of Italian influence in Germany before this time. In the early seventeenth century, Praetorius employed the polychoral Venetian style, Schein adapted the affective extremes of the madrigal to the sacred motet, and Schütz experimented with these as well as with monody and *stile recitativo* in the context of Lutheran church music. Influence of the later seventeenth-century Italian *bel canto* style is evident in the music of Buxtehude and others.

[28] While French musical style was not of particular concern in Italy, the flamboyant, noisy Italian style was a prominent political issue in France, where it was heatedly discussed and often even banned. See Robert Isherwood, *Music in the service of the king* (Rochester, 1973), for a discussion of the connections between musical institutions and politics in the French court. For contemporary French polemics comparing Italian and French musical styles in terms of a noise/order dichotomy, see François Raguenet, *Parallèle des Italiens et des Français* (Paris, 1702), and Le Cerf de la Viéville, Seigneur de Freneuse, *Comparaison de la musique*

Talking politics during Bach Year   23

The dynamic procedures just described are most characteristic of Italian music. Bach came into contact with the Italian musical language in the 1710s by way of the fashionable Vivaldi concertos being circulated throughout Europe,[29] and, to a great extent, he adopted it as his principal tongue. Yet (like many who write or speak primarily in a second language) his strategies continually treat tonal procedures as a construct, always under scrutiny, always being informed by the properties of the native tongue.

The opening movement of the Brandenburg Concerto No. 5 qualifies as a tonal composition. Its background progression opens in a key it unambiguously defines as its tonic (D Major), proceeds through a number of other keys (in order: A Major, B Minor, and F♯ Minor), then returns to re-establish the tonic key, thus achieving tonal closure. And throughout, its surface harmonic syntax is unrelentingly devoted to directing the ear to the next goal, instilling desire in the listener for attainment of that goal, and playing with (teasing and postponing, gratifying) the expectation of imminent closure. I will deal with Bach's more unusual strategies in fuller detail below.

b. *Concerto grosso procedure*

The movement's formal structure likewise is indebted heavily to the model Vivaldi developed and made popular. The concerto grosso involves two principal performing media: a large, collective force (the concerto grosso – literally, the 'big ensemble') and one or more soloists. These two forces enact metaphorically – and as a spectacle – the interactions between individual and society.

The fact that this genre developed in the early eighteenth century is not surprising, given that it so systematically addresses the tensions between the dynamic individual and stable society – surely one of the most important issues of the increasingly prominent middle class. By contrast, the medium favored by the sixteenth century was equal-voiced polyphony in which the harmony of the whole was very carefully regulated. The seventeenth century saw the emergence of solo genres (sonata, cantata, opera) that celebrate individuality, virtuosity, dissonance, and extravagant dynamic motion. In the eighteenth century, most musical genres testify to a widespread interest in integrating the best of both those worlds into one in

---

italienne et de la musique française (Paris, 1705), selections of both translated in *Source readings*, ed. Strunk, pp. 473–507.

[29] Bach studied Vivaldi's collection of concertos, *L'Estro armonico* (Amsterdam, 1712), shortly after they were published. He not only made arrangements of several of these pieces for organ and wrote many Vivaldi-style concertos himself, but he applied its formal principles to almost every other genre with which he was concerned.

which social harmony and individual expression are mutually compatible. The concerto, the new formalized opera aria, and the later sonata procedure all are motivated by this interest.

The standard Vivaldi-style concerto grosso movement begins with the presentation by the large group of a stable block of material, the ritornello. A ritornello represents a microcosm of the entire movement: it defines the tonic and principal thematic material, introduces at least a moment of instability in its middle, and then returns to the stable tonic and closing material to conclude. True to its name ('the little thing that returns'), it reappears throughout the piece to punctuate points of arrival in the background progression, thus throwing the unfolding structure into high relief. Such movements also end with a restatement of the ritornello, which articulates broadly the re-establishment of tonal and thematic order.

In a concerto grosso, the soloist enters between statements of the ritornello. This soloist is almost invariably a virtuosic exhibitionist, the individualism of which flaunts the collectivity of the larger ensemble. It is the active agent in the piece – it is primarily responsible for dynamic motion, for destabilization, the striving toward and achievement of each successive goal (which the large group greets and punctuates with a ritornello).

The convention itself, then, comes with an agenda attached. Given the high value placed on closure in eighteenth-century style, we already know prior to any particular piece (1) that the group will represent stability and the soloist, individual mobility; (2) that the two forces will operate dialectically – with the soloist providing movement, desire, and noise, the group acknowledging and appropriating the soloist's achievements; (3) that regardless of the oppositional tensions between the two in the course of the piece, the tonic key area and the group ritornello will have the last word – thus containing or absorbing the excesses of the soloist; and (4) that individual expression and social harmony will finally be demonstrated to be compatible.

The first movement of Brandenburg Concerto No. 5 shapes itself in accordance with these principles: it begins with a full-ensemble ritornello, alternates ritornello fragments with materials from the soloists in the body of the movement, and concludes with a complete statement of the opening ritornello (Ex. 1).

But the movement starts to present its own problems when the soloists enter. It begins as though it is going to be a concerto for solo flute and violin, but it soon becomes clear that there is a darkhorse competitor for the position of soloist: the harpsichord. Because today we are so accustomed to keyboard concertos, our senses are perhaps dulled to what

Talking politics during Bach Year   25

Ex. 1: Schematic overview of movement [* = missed cadence or failed closure]

mm. 1–9	mm. 9–19	mm. 19–20	mm. 20–9	mm. 29–31	mm. 31–9	mm. 39–42
Ritornello I	Soloists	*Rit. IIa*	Soloists	*Rit. IIb*	Soloists	*Rit. III*
D Major	DM to AM	*AM*	AM	*AM*	AM to Bm	*Bm*

mm. 42–58	mm. 58–61	mm. 61–101	mm. 101–2	mm. 102–21	mm. 121–5	mm. 125–36
Soloists	*Rit. IV*	Soloists	*Rit. V*	Soloists	*Rit. VIa*	Soloists
Bm to DM	*DM**	DM, F#m, AM	*AM*	AM to DM	*DM**	DM

mm. 136–9	mm. 139–54	mm. 154–219	mm. 219–27
Rit. VIb	Soloists	*Harpsichord cadenza*	*Rit. VII*
DM*	DM	[DM]	*DM*

this emergence of the harpsichord as a soloist signified in terms of the norms in Bach's day. And since this use of the harpsichord turns out to be one of the most unusual and most critical elements in the movement, a word on the conventional early eighteenth-century functions of the harpsichord is in order.

c. Harpsichord

Harpsichords are almost invariably present in Baroque ensembles, but they normally play a service role. They are part of the continuo section, along with a melodic bass instrument, that provides the normative harmonic and rhythmic foundation for the group. Baroque ensembles cannot do without the continuo, but it usually blends in with the background like a custodian that, in insuring continuity, permits the expressive liberties of the soloists. Yet it is frequently the composer or group leader – the brains of the operation – who occupies the position of harpsichordist. Thus as self-effacing as the role may seem, the harpsichordist is often a Svengali or puppet master who quietly works the strings from behind the keyboard.

Anyone who has served as an accompanist knows the almost complete lack of recognition that comes with that position. As an active keyboardist, Bach was very familiar with this role and – if the narrative of this piece can serve as an indication – with its attendant rewards and frustrations. For in this concerto (in which he would have played the harpsichord part

26   SUSAN McCLARY

himself),[30] he creates a 'Revenge of the continuo player': the harpsichord
begins in its rightful, traditional, supporting, norm-articulating role but
then gradually emerges to shove everyone else, large ensemble and conventional soloists alike, out of the way for one of the most outlandish displays
in music history. The harpsichord is the wild card in this deck that calls all
the other parameters of the piece – and their attendant ideologies – into
question.

d. Discussion

The premises of the styles within which Bach has chosen to operate (tonality and concerto grosso procedure) presuppose both the simulacrum of
dynamic motion and ultimate reconciliation, closure, collective order. The
specific characters in Bach's narrative are:

(1) the large ensemble and its ritornello, which is confident (note the self-
assured arpeggiation of the opening), unified, slightly smug (the repetition
of each note of the unison arpeggio yields a quality of complacency or self-
satisfaction), and self-contained (Ex. 2);

Ex. 2: Brandenburg Concerto No. 5, mm. 1–9

[30] The scoring for the concerto is unusual in that it requires only one violin part instead of the
normal two. Bach ordinarily played viola with his group, but if he were occupied with the
virtuosic harpsichord part, there would be one string player missing from his standard
ensemble. See Friedrich Smend, *Bach in Köthen* (Berlin, 1951), p. 24.

28   SUSAN McCLARY

Ex. 2: (cont.)

(2) the conventional soloists – the flute and violin, which are marked by eighteenth-century semiotics as somewhat sentimental (Ex. 3: note the elaborate ornamental filagree of mm. 13–16, the conventional sighs of mm. 20–1) and yet dynamic enough to accomplish modulations to other keys;

(3) the harpsichord, which first serves as continuo support (see Ex. 2) then begins to compete with the soloists for attention (Ex. 4a), and finally over-throws the other forces in a kind of hijacking of the piece (Ex. 4b).

I use the word 'overthrow' because the harpsichord's solo emergence is written so as *not* to appear as an orderly event in the planned narrative. The ritornello seems to know how to deal with the more well-behaved soloists, how to appropriate, absorb, and contain their energy. But in the passage just prior to the cadenza (the extensive harpsichord solo), Bach composes the parts of the ensemble, flute, and violin to make it appear that *their* piece has been violently derailed. They drop out inconclusively, one after another, exactly in the way an orchestra would if one of its members started making up a new piece in the middle of a performance. Their parts no

Talking politics during Bach Year   29

Ex. 3: mm. 9–22

30   SUSAN McCLARY

Ex. 3: *(cont.)*

Talking politics during Bach Year 31

32   SUSAN McCLARY

Ex. 3: (cont.)

longer make sense. They fall silent in the face of this affront from the
ensemble's lackey, and all expectations for orderly reconciliation and harmonic closure are suspended.

    The cadenza is extremely unusual in several respects. First, it is presented
by the wrong instrument: initially the piece appeared to be a concerto for
sentimental flute and violin, yet the cadenza is delivered by a frenzied continuo instrument. Second, it occupies a full quarter of the movement's
entire length. Most cadenzas at the time would have been a very few measures long – a slightly elaborate prolongation and preparation before capitulation to the ritornello and the final resolution. Third, sustaining a cadenza
of this length requires extraordinary ingenuity. Recall that if the soloist's
pace should slacken, the ensemble could leap in (theoretically in any case)
and impose closure. Thus in order to maintain necessary energy the harpsichord part must resort to increasingly deviant strategies – chromatic
inflections, faster and faster note values – resulting in what sounds like a
willful, flamboyant seventeenth-century toccata: in its opposition to the

Talking politics during Bach Year 33

Ex. 4a: mm. 47–8

34   SUSAN McCLARY

Ex. 4b: mm. 151–5

Talking politics during Bach Year 35

36   SUSAN McCLARY

ensemble's order, it unleashes elements of chaos, irrationality, and noise until finally it blurs almost entirely the sense of key, meter, and form upon which eighteenth-century style depends (Ex. 5a). Finally, it relents and politely (ironically?) *permits* the ensemble to re-enter with its closing ritornello (Ex. 5b).

Ex. 5a: mm. 196–214

Talking politics during Bach Year 37

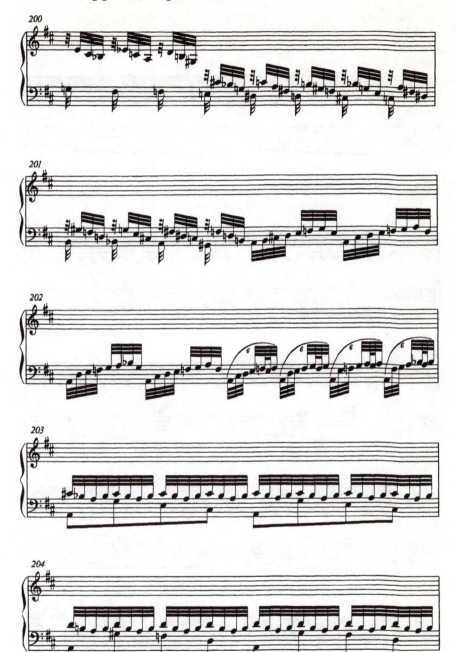

38   SUSAN McCLARY

Ex. 5a: (*cont.*)

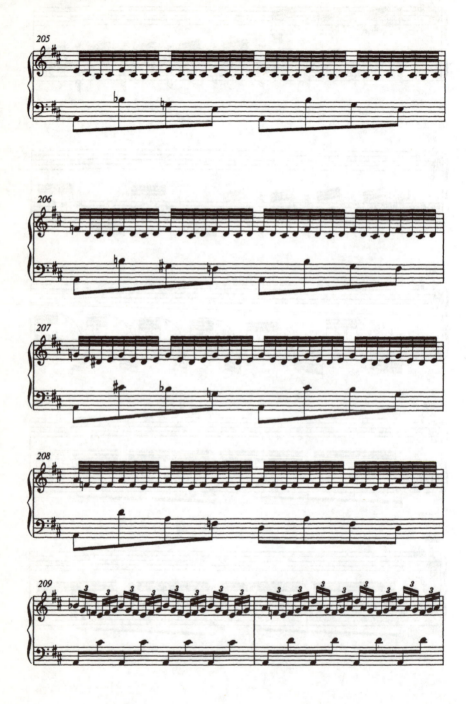

Talking politics during Bach Year 39

Ex. 5b: mm. 215–19

Cembalo

40   SUSAN McCLARY

Ex. 5b: (*cont.*)

On the surface, closure is attained; but the subversive elements of the piece seem far too powerful to be contained in so conventional a manner. We are relieved at this closure (the alternative seems to be madness) but surely also somewhat troubled by its implications. The usual nice, tight fit between the social norm, as represented by the convention of concerto procedure, and specific content is here highly problematized. Certainly social order and individual freedom are possible, but apparently only so long as the individuals in question – like the sweet-tempered flute and violin – abide by the rules and permit themselves to be appropriated. What happens when a genuine deviant (and one from the ensemble's service staff yet!) declares itself a genius, unconstrained by convention, and takes over? We readily identify with this self-appointed protagonist's adventure (its storming of the Bastille, if you will) and at the same time fear for what might happen as a result of the suspension of traditional authority.

Bach thus articulates very powerfully precisely the dilemma of an ideology that wants to encourage freedom of expression while preserving social harmony. The possibility of virtual social overthrow, and the violence implied by such overthrow, is suggested in the movement, and the reconciliation of individual and social hierarchy at the end – while welcome – may seem largely motivated by convention. To pull this dramatization back within the limits of self-contained structure and order may seem to avoid the dilemma, but it does so at the expense of silencing the piece. For Bach is here enacting the exhilaration as well as the risks of upward mobility, the simultaneous desire for and resistance of concession to social harmony.

2. *Wachet auf*[31]

The shaping principles of both tonality and concerto (and their attendant ideologies) are operative in Cantata 140 as well. But because the cantata is tied to a clear extra-musical, liturgical tradition, Bach also has available to him in the writing of the cantata an explicit semiotic code of conventional signs and associations. It is thus possible to become far more specific with regard to signification in the cantata than in the strictly instrumental concerto. Yet Bach's compositional process never is reducible to the assembling of ready-made meanings. As is the case with all of his pieces, meaning is produced by virtue of particular choices and contextual juxtapositions. I would like here to address a cluster of issues that are engaged by Bach in the cantata: national identity, orthodoxy/Pietism, and gender construction.

a. *National identity*

Bach had access to three distinguishable national styles, each with its own social priorities, codes, ways of understanding and organizing the world. The Italian style had been associated with virtuosity and theatricality since the early seventeenth century. Its practitioners had developed carefully during that period (1) a code by which various flamboyant emotion-types could be constructed and (2) the goal-oriented motion described above in the section on tonality. The French, by contrast, had produced most of

---

[31] The cantata is designated for the twenty-seventh Sunday after Trinity – an occasion that occurred but twice (1731 and 1742) during Bach's mature career. It is thus thought to have been written in 1731 and probably repeated in 1742. The chorale on which the cantata is based, 'Wachet auf', was written by Philipp Nicolai in the late sixteenth century. The librettist is unknown. See Alfred Dürr, *Die Kantaten von Johann Sebastian Bach* (Kassel, 1971), pp. 531–5, and also the *Norton critical scores* edition of the cantata, with commentary by Gerhard Herz (New York, 1972).

their officially recognized music in the context of Louis XIV's absolutist court. Much of it was self-consciously anti-Italian: in particular the emotional dimension of Italian music was regarded as excessive and the onrushing quality of motion as dangerously close to chaos.[32] In this rarified world in which Platonic order and regimented dance ruled, music was restrained both in its expressivity (for the sake of *bon goût*) and in its characteristic quality of motion. Whereas the aim of Italian music was to sustain tension as long as possible, continually deferring relaxation to moments of orgasmic release, the French constantly drained off excess tension, often once or twice per measure, leaving only enough energy to provide a modicum of movement.

German music in the eighteenth century was heavily influenced by both Italian and French modes of composition. Several waves of Italian style had washed over Germany since the early seventeenth century, and each left a kind of hybrid behind in its wake.[33] French music had likewise been imported, especially by the nobility who aspired to emulate the example of Versailles.[34] What remained constant and recognizable in German music was the traditional tie to the Lutheran liturgy. Regardless of the stylistic surface of this music, to the extent that it incorporated chorale melodies it was still identifiably German.

Moreover, the dedication to chorale-based composition resulted in other, more specifically musical characteristics. For instance, if one was committed to utilizing a sixteenth-century, pre-tonal chorale as the structural underpinning for a movement, the formal demands of the chorale's cadential patterns had to be adjusted to the demands of conventional tonal background progressions – or vice versa. One had to decide whether to abide by the ways of God (as represented by the chorale's archaic – or 'irrational' – characteristics),[35] to follow the ways of Man (as represented by Italianate

[32] See n. 28.

[33] See n. 27.

[34] According to his son, C.P.E., while Bach was a student in Lüneburg he had some access to the Francophile ducal court in Celle and became familiar with the French style there.

[35] See, for instance, Bach's Cantata No. 77, *Du sollt Gott, deinen Herren, lieben* (Leipzig, 1723). The underlying pre-existent material in the opening movement is the traditional chorale, 'Dies sind die heil'gen zehn Gebot" ('These are the Holy Ten Commandments'), a modal chorale that is organized irrationally with respect to tonal norms. To compound the difficulty, Bach sets the chorale as a complex canon (a pun on law). The law of God – the old, pre-Enlightenment law – thus circumscribes many times over the movement's procedure. And while it abides by this law, in musical terms it sounds almost arbitrary in its unfolding. For the old law, it seems, is not compatible with the new eighteenth-century bourgeois tonal procedures that we tend to hear as absolute, timeless, and universal. If the movement makes us uneasy, this is no accident. It is meant to demonstrate how far removed our sense of propriety is from God's and to call the believer back from the false security of secular reason to the unfathomable truth of God. The arias that follow in the

Talking politics during Bach Year   43

tonal convention), or to try to bring about a reconciliation. And the composers of the German church had retained their taste for complex polyphonic counterpoint, in part because the sixteenth-century motet repertory continued to be used in Lutheran services well into the eighteenth century, in part because of a greater commitment to community (as opposed to Italian unimpeded individual – soloistic – progress), and in part because of an implicit, multileveled metaphysics still fashionable among certain of the German intelligentsia.[36] This penchant for imitative layering gave German music a richer, more ponderous quality of motion that becomes obvious when one compares, say, a concerto of Vivaldi with a concerto by Bach written in the 'Italian style'.[37]

A German composer had the option of pursuing these various styles side by side or meshing them in relatively unproblematic ways.[38] Bach often calls attention to the separate implications of the various components of which he makes use and then seems to overcome the dichotomies in order to fashion a world (always centrally German) in which aspects of each style can co-exist. The first movement of *Wachet auf* is a case in point.

The movement is framed as an Italian concerto, with a self-contained orchestral ritornello that opens, punctuates, and concludes the structure (Ex. 6). Yet the tonal motion within the movement (between statements of the ritornello) is determined by the cadential demands of the pre-existent German chorale melody, 'Wachet auf'.[39] This means that the on-going progressive characteristics of the concerto must be made compatible with the repetitive, relatively static AABA structure of the tune. Bach's solution

cantata are humble pleas for God to teach us His ways. This cantata presents an unusual strategy for Bach in that he stresses incompatibility of his sources rather than enacting his more typical synthesis.

[36] The collection of sixteenth-century motets *Florilegium portense* (compiled 1603) remained in use in Leipzig, for instance, during Bach's tenure, and Bach became especially drawn to this archaic style in his last years. See Christoph Wolff, *Der stile antico in der Musik Johann Sebastian Bachs* (Wiesbaden, 1968) for a detailed study of Bach's complex relationship with archaic styles.

[37] The first movement of Brandenburg Concerto No. 2 is an excellent example of a composition that utilizes Vivaldi's formal model but that renders it far more complex by means of permutations and imitative overlapping among the four soloists. The concerto-like first movement of the Sonata in B Minor for flute and harpsichord, BWV 1030 becomes so convoluted in its contrapuntal overlap that the linear narrative of the Vivaldi model threatens to break down altogether.

[38] Handel, for instance, made use of all the national styles with which he had had contact, but he rarely proceeded by juxtaposing self-consciously his various semiotic systems for the sake of forging new meanings – with socio-political implications – from that juxtaposition.

[39] The chorale was first published in 1598 and was incorporated (unlike many hymns composed after the canon was established) into official hymnals. It is extremely regular with regard to melodic contour, formal patterning, and cadential articulation – thus there is no musical dilemma inherent in fusing it with eighteenth-century tonal procedures.

44 SUSAN McCLARY

satisfies both dimensions while managing to comment on each and even to make the apparent non-fit thematically meaningful.

Ex. 6: Schematic outline of *Wachet auf*, movement 1

mm. 1–17	17–53		53–69	69–105	105–17	117–24	124–7
Rit. I	Chorale, lines 1–3		*Rit. II*	Chorale, 4–6	*Rit. III*	Chorale, 7	*Rit. IV*
E♭M	E♭M		E♭M	E♭M	E♭M *to* B♭M	E♭M	E♭M

mm. 127–34	135–56		156–60	161–89		189–205
Chorale, 8	Extended alleluia		*Rit. V*	Chorale, 9–11		*Rit. VI*
E♭M	Gm to Cm		CM	A♭M, Cm, E♭M		E♭M

The movement also bears, especially at the beginning, essential references to French music – indeed to the original contextual functions of the stylistic borrowings. For the piece sounds initially as though it is going to be a French overture, a genre developed for the ceremonial entrances of the Sun King to his entertainments[40] (Ex. 7). Two details mark the beginning in ways that illustrate Bach's intentions: (1) while French overtures, like most processional genres, are normally in duple meters, this one is in a *triple* meter and (2) the piece is in E♭, the key of *three* flats. This, then, is music for the entrance of a king – but of the Trinitarian King, which is, in fact, the subject of the chorale and cantata text.

As befits French style, the opening four measures are grand but also rather deliberate and static. They move, in other words, like a French piece. Now Bach seems willing on occasion to simulate briefly the quality of motion characteristic of French music. But even in his French-style dance suites, he quickly becomes impatient: once the French reference has been made, he modulates rapidly into the more congenial Italian on-rushing quality of motion.[41] This affective modulation has extremely interesting

[40] For further reading on the impact of Louis' personal imagery on the politics of representation and the absolutist state, see Louis Marin, *Le portrait du roi* (Paris, 1981), to be published in translation by University of Minnesota Press. Louis XIV appropriated many of the signs formerly associated with theological authority and suited them to his own use. Here Bach reverses the process and appropriates Louis' images back to theology, but this reversal underscores how close the two semiotic systems were at the time.

[41] This modulation from French rigidity to Italianate exuberance occurs repeatedly in Bach's most French genre, the dance suite. For instance, in the Partita in D major for harpsichord (the most self-consciously French of the entire set) virtually every movement operates according to this principle. The opening 'Ouverture' couples a French overture beginning and an Italian concerto continuation; the 'Courante' commences with the regular braking action of Louis' favorite court dance but soon converts to impetuous Italian motion; and the 'Sarabande' takes an extravagant courtly gesture and teaches it to flow. I know of very few movements by Bach in which he maintains a French quality of motion after he has referred to it.

Ex. 7: mm. 1–4

1. Chorale

ideological implications, for Bach is, in effect, continually setting up a rigid aristocratic structure in order to transform it into the dynamic mobility with which he seems to identify.

The Italian ritornello of this German-chorale movement, then, begins as though it will be a French overture; but another motive enters in the fifth measure – syncopated, scattered, and halting at first (Ex. 8a), then increasingly capable of continuous motion until it leads to a quintessentially Italian spill-over (Ex. 8b), contained only at the very end by the return of the dotted French rhythms which brake the energy and conclude (Ex. 8c). And, of course, the French/Italian ritornello as a whole serves as the

46   SUSAN McCLARY

Ex. 8a: mm. 5–6

Ex. 8b: mm. 9–10

Talking politics during Bach Year 47

Ex. 8c: mm. 16–17

introduction that ushers in the true musical king of this cantata: the traditional German chorale melody.

The alternation of static, regal processional music with exuberant, onrushing mobility remains characteristic of the entire movement. A similar effect is drawn from the superimposition of the monolithic, cantus-firmus presentation of the chorale melody and the imitative commentary of the remainder of the choir, though the semiotic associations are different: the chorale stands for the timeless voice of orthodox tradition, while the chattering counterpoint represents human response (Ex. 9).

48   SUSAN McCLARY

In the terms of the text, the advent of the Trinitarian King is announced, and the sleepers awake and rush excitedly to join the procession. And Bach makes use of all these various elements from his various codes in order to produce a particular quality – that of moving repeatedly from the stasis of the regal or the timeless to the excited goal-oriented expectation of the human congregation and on to a tantalizing foretaste of synthesis or reconciliation.

On one level, the movement is a set of relatively autonomous microcosmic distillations, one nested inside the next, of the cantata's overall plot:

Ex. 9: mm. 17–25

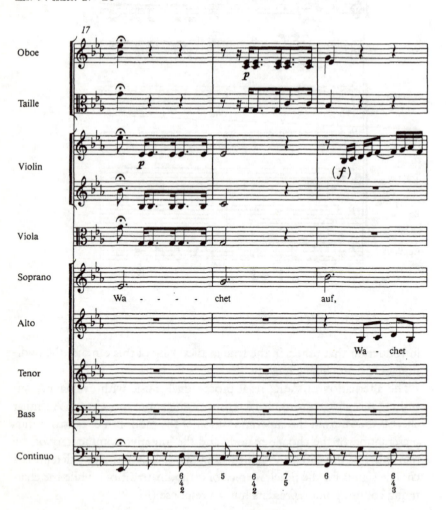

Talking politics during Bach Year   49

Ex. 9: (*cont.*)

the ritornello, the triple-phrased A-section of the chorale setting, and the movement as a completed structure all present on different levels the regal beginning, the rushing forward, and the reconciliation. On still a higher level (since final narrative closure – the longed-for union – is deferred until the end of the cantata), this movement converts into a huge opening gesture for the whole multi-movement complex. The architectural plan of the cantata follows the same phenomenological progression as the various layers of the first movement, with this part serving as a grand, French overture, the middle chorale-based movement concerned almost exclusively with the exploration of on-rushingness, and the closing chorale presenting final arrival, absorption into a timeless Lutheran orthodoxy that transcends and contains all the properties (French, Italian, German) that went into its accomplishment (Ex. 10). After hearing such a piece in which

Talking politics during Bach Year   51

so many interlocking levels all finally achieve closure, who could fail to believe in the overdetermination of salvation? In the specifically German plan of salvation?

Ex. 10: Overview of cantata
1. Chorale Fantasia _____ 4. Chorale-based movement
                                                    7. Chorale
[2. Recit.] 3. Duet I_____[5. Recit.] 6. Duet II

The cantata enacts a synthesis of all available national styles in such a way as to appropriate them all and put them in the service of an expressly Lutheran agenda. The monad that contains the whole world is located, significantly, on German soil.

b. Orthodoxy/Pietism

One of the principal ideological disputes with which Bach was continually entangled was that between the more orthodox strains of Lutheranism versus the pietistic.[42] While this split is no longer of pressing interest to us, it did affect Bach's career directly (and, quite frequently, uncomfortably), and it informed his compositional choices.

Very briefly, orthodox congregations were more concerned with collective worship, with doctrine, with the traditional liturgy and hymnody. Elaborate 'art music' (performed by special choirs and instrumentalists and incorporating complex, often secular, styles) was included in services for the 'greater glory'. By contrast, Pietism focused on the personalized relationship between the individual and God. The intervention of elaborate, professionally performed music in that relationship was considered distasteful. Instead, Pietists preferred either straight congregational singing or else, in the context of devotionals, songs in which the lyrics dealt in sentimental – sometimes even erotic – terms with the one-to-one empathy between the Soul and Jesus.[43]

Much of Bach's church music attempts a reconciliation between these two

---

[42] For more on orthodoxy and Pietism, see Friedrich Blume, *Protestant church music*, trans. in collaboration with Ludwig Finscher *et al.* (London, 1975), Section II, pp. 125–316. For a detailed study of Bach's particular theological situation, see Günther Stiller, *Johann Sebastian Bach and liturgical life in Leipzig* (Berlin, 1970), trans. Herbert Bouman, Daniel Poellot, and Hilton Oswald (St. Louis, 1984).

[43] The chorale 'Wachet auf' is one of the most famous of the personalized Jesus hymns. It is one of the few hymns of Pietist leanings to be canonized in the mainstream chorale tradition, and thus it already suggests the possibility of reconciliation between the orthodox and mystical within itself. See Blume, *Protestant*, p. 140.

positions. On the one hand, most of it clearly falls in the orthodox camp by virtue of its complexity and theatricality, a fact brought to his attention repeatedly by displeased employers of Pietist leanings. But, on the other, he had an insatiable taste, as did many of the writers of cantata libretti, for the vivid, personalized imagery of Pietism. Indeed, the cantata *as a genre* represents a strange fusion between the opera-inspired techniques welcome only in orthodox contexts and the obsessions with Mystical Union, pain, and sentiment that might have seemed repugnant to many of the orthodox. To a Baroque poet or composer, however, this fusion offered an irresistible combination: virtuosity *and* extravagant emotional expression.

The libretto for *Wachet auf* is concerned with integrating both orthodox and pietistic approaches to faith. The structure of the text pursues two parallel strands: the opening, central and concluding movements (which all utilize the traditional chorale melody) address the collective response to the announced advent, while the two Soul/Jesus duets that separate these chorale-based movements involve the individual Christian's response. As we have seen, the collective strand first contains the heralding of the Bridegroom's coming, then the rushing forth of the guests to meet Him, and finally a stable, collective chorale celebrating the arrival. The duets first articulate the Soul's passionate longing for that advent (in explicit bride/groom imagery) and then the mutual bliss of the Union, followed by the concluding chorale in which the congregation, the individual Soul, and Christ are all unified. Both orthodox and Pietist visions of salvation are satisfied. The two camps are thus demonstrated to be mutually compatible. If Bach could not effect such a solution in real life, he could at least enact it through his creative imagination.

c. Gender

Questions concerning the construction of gender rarely enter into discussions of music.[44] The absence of a feminist critique in music is not *necessarily* owing, however, to an anti-woman bias.[45] Until there exists some way

[44] By 'construction' I mean the modes developed in our musical traditions for representing men and women. I am thus assuming that while the sex of an individual is a biological given, the ways in which we understand gender are socially defined and transmitted by – among many other means – music. One of the profound musical achievements of the seventeenth century was the invention of a vocabulary by means of which women characters in operas could be portrayed. That vocabulary is an ideological construct, and it is informed by (male) attitudes of what women are, how they behave and feel, and so forth. Both the code itself and its uses in particular compositions can tell us a great deal about how gender was (and is) socially shaped.

[45] For accounts of how and why American musicology has resisted criticism see Joseph Kerman, *Contemplating music* (Cambridge, Mass., 1985), and Rose Rosengard Subotnik, 'The role of ideology in the study of Western music', *Journal of Musicology*, 2 (1983), pp. 1–12.

of dealing with music in general as a social discourse, gender will remain a non-issue. In this, it is treated no differently than any other matter one might wish to examine critically or ideologically.

The Soul/Jesus duets, however, raise some interesting questions in connection with gender that I would like to discuss. The convention of casting the individual believer as female, incomplete and longing for satisfaction and fulfillment from the divine male, is ancient and Bible-sanctioned. As was mentioned above, it was resurrected and exploited extensively in Pietist poetry concerned with the Mystical Union between the Soul as Bride and Christ as Bridegroom, and it provides one of the two narrative strands of *Wachet auf.*

I am not interested here in bringing charges of 'sexism' against Bach as an individual. He clearly was a product of his time, shaped by attitudes toward religion, politics, and gender then prevalent. It is, however, interesting to note the ways in which Bach brings the musical apparatus of his day to bear on the construction of gender, especially in the first duet.

The duet operates on the conceit that the Soul, unable to perceive Christ's presence or his responses, longs impatiently for him, continually asking when he will arrive. The Soul is presumably gender-free (male souls are also supposed to long in this manner for Christ's coming, after all), yet the musical images Bach uses mark it as specifically female, or as femininity is frequently construed in his – and our – culture, in any case. Put quite simply, the Soul here is a nagging, passive-aggressive wife, insecurely whining for repeated assurances of love and not hearing them when they are proferred (Ex. 11).

Ex. 11: Movement 2, mm. 8–18

54   SUSAN McCLARY

Ex. 11: (cont.)

One might counter that this is, in fact, the way we *all* are with respect to the Patriarch, that this is a universal condition. Yet underlying Bach's musical metaphors is an analogy: just as a husband patronizingly puts up with a complaining mate because he knows that her insecurity stems from her emotional dependence, so God tolerates (uni-sex) us and our frailties.

Interestingly, though not really surprisingly, men listening to this duet tend to situate themselves differently with respect to its dialectic than do women. In class discussions I have discovered that the men unselfconsciously identify with the male character (with Christ!) and sneer at the Bride's tiresomeness. And the women realize that they are supposed to identify with the Bride but resent the pleading insecurity with which she is portrayed.

That Bach was simply drawing on the stereotypes of female behavior familiar to him and deriving a kind of down-to-earth, homey realism from what was taken to be 'shared truth' – at least among the men in his day – is not in question. Indeed, that is precisely the point. Bach's music is indelibly marked with the concerns and conventional social constructs of his time and place. It is not universal, nor does it represent pure order. Like any product of human social discourse, it is subject to critique – even feminist critique.

Bach reception

Far from appearing universal, Bach's audacious synthesis of all available cultures – with Germany at its center – was not likely to have pleased many of his contemporaries, not even most Germans. Perhaps not surprisingly, he was canonized as representing pure order only after the codes on which his semiotic strategies had relied and their accompanying social contexts had become inactive.[46] Universality was achieved only at the expense of specific, concretely articulated meaning.

The strategy of defining one's own ideology as pure, non-social order clearly is empowering; but it is not entirely advantageous, not even to the artists who most obviously benefit from it. For, as we have seen, such absolutist redefinitions remove whatever was being articulated within the

---

[46] Bach's music was known to a few connoisseurs in subsequent generations. Van Swieten, for instance, introduced his music (primarily the fugues) to both Mozart and Beethoven, but it was the skilled craftsman and pedagogue in Bach that they admired. By the time Mendelssohn resurrected the *St Matthew Passion* in 1829, the contexts within which Bach had composed it had long vanished. For more on the reception of Bach's music before the Mendelssohn revival, see Gerhard Herz, *Essays on J.S. Bach* (Ann Arbor, 1985), pp. 1–124.

56   SUSAN McCLARY

music in terms of signification and convert the composition – or even the repertory as a whole – to the status of icon. If all is perfect order, pure and simple, then no compositional choice can *mean* anything, except by virtue of a kind of closet metaphysics: as evidence of something beyond, which is the source of all perfection.

As is the case with most composers, Bach both revealed his project – throughout his career juxtaposing these widely divergent, ideologically antagonistic styles – and concealed his political agenda in seeming just to be writing notes. His 'devotees', however, by taking very seriously the claim to autonomy and by having lost access to the codes through which Bach revealed his meanings, have flattened him out into pure order.

Many factors have had a hand in this recasting of Bach as icon: the German nationalists of the early nineteenth century who wanted covertly to colonize the world culturally by means of 'absolute music' (that is, German music with the ideology camouflaged);[47] those nostalgic for periods of strong religious authority;[48] music theorists who derive their rules and norms from the study of his music;[49] the objectivists and combinatorialists of abstract expressionism who claim Bach as their forerun-

---

[47] The first biographer and advocate of Bach, J.N. Forkel (1802), makes no secret of his nationalistic agenda: 'This undertaking [Bach's biography] is not only of the highest advantage, in every respect, to the art itself, but must contribute more than any other of the kind to the honor of the German name. The works which John [*sic*] Sebastian Bach has left us are an invaluable national patrimony, with which no other nation has anything to be compared.' Forkel continues at some length in this vein. See the translation by 'Mr. Stephenson' (1808) in David and Mendel, eds., *The Bach reader*, p. 296. There is, of course, nothing inappropriate in the promotion of one's national cultural treasures – it is frequently on that basis that canons are constructed. The problem enters only when this interest becomes suppressed.

[48] See Adorno, 'Devotees', especially pp. 135–6, for a treatment of this mode of reception.

[49] Much of Bach's music was originally designed at least in part for pedagogy: the *Orgel-Büchlein*, the *Well-tempered Clavier*, the *Clavier-Übung*, and the *Art of Fugue* all have obvious educational dimensions. And it was as a teacher, a lone transmitter of the old style of rigorous compositional technique, that Bach was noted in his day and in the generations that followed. (See n. 46.)

But gradually, as familiarity with the codes within which Bach's music operates has eroded, his compositions have been seen not as instances of reconciled tensions but as order, pure and simple. Thus the chorale settings, which to Bach presented the challenge of taking traditional modal melodies and 'rationalizing' them through tonal harmonic syntax, are taken as paradigms of tonal propriety. We take these pieces, in which modal patterns frequently force Bach to resort to outlandish strategies in order to make us believe in their tonal logic, and we teach students that this is how tonality works – without any recognition of the dialectical strain inherent in the genre. Similarly Bach's fugues have been reduced to formula, to structural analysis, and to chord labeling, thus obscuring once again the extraordinary tension between his determination to integrate the old-fashioned multi-leveled polyphonic style with the new on-rushing Italian procedures.

ner;[50] the recording industry that peddles 'authenticity' while sacrificing interpretation to the demands of efficient sound engineering;[51] and performers whose sensibilities have been formed by vastly different cultures and who have no familiarity with – and, indeed, no interest in – Bach's socio-historical context.[52] The result is a politically neutralized cultural figure whose whole opus signifies greatness while none of the events in particular pieces can be said to mean anything at all.

Why do we still need to locate perfection, universality, extra-human truth in this music at the expense of stifling it? What is our sense of the history of the bourgeoisie that we want to cling to its early documents as 'divinely inspired' (a bizarre aspiration, to be sure, for secular humanism), that we do not want them to have been constructed by *us*, that we want our regulations to have extra-human authority – yet to have no god per se onto whom to place the responsibility? In today's crisis of liberal humanism, we appear especially to be trying to hold onto the shreds of evidence for the universal truth-content of bourgeois ideology. And eighteenth-century music seems to offer the best source because it hides its social agenda inside what appear to be pure, self-contained patterns of tones.

Bach's music is especially marked in our culture as a repository of *truth*. Its particular authority is, to be sure, partly owing to its expressly religious

[50] See, for instance, Schoenberg's essay from 1950 on Bach, in *Style and idea*, ed. and trans. Leo Black (Berkeley and Los Angeles, 1975), pp. 393–7. The essay opens as follows: 'I used to say, "Bach is the first composer with twelve tones."' In the same collection, see also 'New music, outmoded music, style and idea', pp. 116–18 and 'National music (2)', p. 173. I by no means intend to criticize Schoenberg for this self-interested appropriation. Indeed, like Adorno ('Devotees', p. 146), I see this self-empowering reinterpretation as the path away from cultural stagnation. But a new 'misreading' is past due.

[51] The proponents of 'authentic' performance practice in Adorno's day were frequently inept performers located in university musicology programs – thus his sarcastic comments in 'Devotees', pp. 142–6. In the last fifteen years, however, technically proficient performers have begun to participate in early music, and a wide range of highly polished, elaborately produced recordings are now available. In certain respects, new versions of old music have become the current vanguard, satisfying the demand for novelty and thus replacing the need for new music. Many talented young musicians, who in another time would have been composers, devote their efforts to reconstructing this year's definitive, new and improved *Messiah*. 'Authenticity' has become a marketing catchword in this new mass culture industry, with virtually every recording of Baroque music announcing in big letters its particular claim: authentic instruments, authentic score, authentic acoustical setting, or whatever. What often (though not always – see below, n. 60) gets obscured by the obsession for technical and technological perfection is careful interpretation of the music itself. Adorno's statement, p. 144, concerning adequate interpretation remains a powerful guideline.

[52] Some of the leading proponents of 'authentic' early music performance are keenly aware of the necessity of understanding the music within its original social context. See especially Nicolas Harnoncourt's *Musik als Klangrede* (Salzburg and Vienna, 1982). See also Richard Taruskin, Daniel Leech-Wilkinson, Nicholas Temperley, and Robert Winter, 'The limits of authenticity: a discussion', *Early Music*, 12 (1984), pp. 3–25.

subject matter. Much, for instance, is made of Bach's habit of dedicating his music to the Glory of God (though the same people who find great significance in Bach's dedications respond quite differently to the same gesture when delivered by the rock star, Prince).[53] But there is plenty of sacred music available that is not regarded with the same reverence. Why Bach?

As Adorno pointed out in his essay, Bach's music participates fully in musical procedures that are primarily products *not* of a medieval, ritualistic society but of the eighteenth-century Enlightenment bourgeoisie.[54] To be sure, this music abounds with self-conscious archaisms and references to earlier traditions; but the parts that we treasure most – the ones that appear to grant us tastes of what we like to consider universal transcendent truth – are those constructed by means of virtuoso, individualistic defiant techniques of the Italian Baroque: the techniques Bach learned from Vivaldi concertos.

Yet at the same time that this music shapes itself in terms of bourgeois ideology (its goal orientation, obsessive control of greater and greater spans of time, its willful striving, delayed gratification and defiance of norms), it often cloaks that ideology by putting it at the service of an explicit theology. The tonal procedures developed by the emerging bourgeoisie to articulate their sense of the world here become presented as what we, in fact, want to believe they are: eternal, universal truths. It is no accident that the dynasty of Great (bourgeois) Composers begins with Bach, for he gives the impression that *our* way of representing the world musically is God-given. Thereafter, tonality can retain its aura of absolute perfection ('the way music goes') in its native secular habitat. This sleight of hand earned Bach the name 'the fifth evangelist',[55] and his gospel informs and legitimizes the

---

[53] Prince always includes a statement such as 'All thanks 2 God' on his record jackets along with the other acknowledgments. He seems to mean it, even though those unfamiliar with the fusion of physical and divine forms of ecstasy characteristic of Gospel traditions (and, one might add, of Lutheran Pietism) tend to regard these as blasphemous.

[54] 'Devotees', pp. 135–9.

[55] Blume includes this term among others in his attack on theologized notions of Bach in 'Outlines', p. 217. Blume's secularizing of Bach perhaps went a bit too far in denying Bach's commitment to the church, but it succeeded admirably in stimulating a new wave of scholarship that attempts to relocate Bach in his Lutheran setting without undue mystification. Herz 'Toward a new image of Bach', (originally from the 1970 issue of *Bach*, reprinted in his *Essays on Bach*, pp. 149–84) is a direct attempt at refuting Blume's 'Marxism', and Stiller's *Bach and liturgical life in Leipzig* likewise readdresses these issues in great detail. The old mystified Bach lives on, however, in Wilfrid Mellers, *Bach and the dance of God* (New York and Oxford, 1981).

The question is not whether Bach was a believer, but whether his faith caused his music to possess some extrahuman aura. It seems to me quite inescapable that Bach was (among many other things) a Christian; but regardless of how strong his belief, his music remains a human, social construct.

remainder of the German canonic tradition, especially the music of the pre-lapsarian Enlightenment (that is, the time when we had it all together rationally, before we began to destroy it with self-indulgent romanticism).

Bach in today's cultural politics

I would now like to invert my title: to address the blasphemy of talking about Bach in a context concentrating primarily on political issues in the current musical scene. Why bother with Bach if one is aware of issues concerning ideological reproduction, if one recognizes the suffocating effect the canon has on those whom it marginalizes? Is it not hypocritical or cowardly to pretend, on the one hand, that one's allegiances are to various forms of post-modern performance and to continue, on the other, to lavish time and energy on the canon?

The fact is that Bach does not go away simply because one refuses to talk about him. Culture is not produced in a vacuum but in a social context with a tradition that, for us, very prominently contains Bach. By turning away to alternative, contemporary forms and leaving him exclusively to his devotees, one may inadvertently contribute to the canon's stranglehold – to the implicit claim by the mainstream that '*we* have truth and universals while *you* only have noise and fads'. Only if those claims, those dominant modes of composition and of reception are scrutinized critically can Bach be perceived in a perspective that permits the music of today to exist on an equal methodological footing.[56]

Let me return for a moment to Adorno and his attack on Bach's devotees. While much of his analysis of ideological tensions in Bach's music and in the reception of that music is extremely insightful and useful, it is difficult fully to endorse his position on how we ought to regard Bach and how we ought, in light of Bach, to proceed. For Adorno is still operating within and on behalf of the autonomous German canon, which he continued to regard as a repository of truth.[57] Adorno's autopsy of Western

---

[56] By this I do not mean necessarily that Bach and (say) Prince are of equal value, but simply that both need to be critically evaluated in terms of their social contexts, functions, and agendas, that neither is exempt from scrutiny.

[57] Virtually all of Adorno's program is concerned either with discerning the truth articulated in German music from Bach (the fountainhead, as we have seen, of German national music) through Schoenberg or attacking other musics, whether jazz (see 'Perennial fashion – jazz', *Prisms*, pp. 121–32) or Stravinsky (see *Philosophy of modern music*, trans. Anne Mitchell and Wesley Blomster (New York, 1973)).

This concentrated obsession with German culture is understandable, given his own social context, but it presents obstacles to the generalization of his insights. In working with Adorno, one must attempt both to reconstruct the intellectual/political environment

culture and his strategic stance of resignation offer few options and little
room to maneuver for the post-World War II artist, especially those (such
as blacks and women – indeed, non-Germans) whom he consistently excluded from cultural production. His discussion of Bach seeks on the one
hand to relocate Bach's compositional enterprise in a social context but, on
the other, to wrest him from the degradation of social reception for the
sake of his music's autonomous truth-content.

My problem with current Bach reception is not simply that the devotees
have got it all wrong or even that we are spending too much of our finite
energies on a repertory 275 years old (though both of those considerations
do, in fact, motivate me to some extent), but that the way in which our
society regards Bach serves as an obstacle and blinder to new contributions
to culture. Thus we must *confront* Bach and the canon and resituate him in
such a way as to acknowledge his prominence in musical and non-musical
culture while not falling victim to it.

What I am suggesting here is deconstruction as a political act. It is not
coincidental that most deconstructive enterprises have centered on classic
texts of the eighteenth-century Enlightenment, for, as we have seen, these
are the texts (and the musical repertories) that most powerfully articulated
the social values of the emergent bourgeoisie under the guise of universal
rationality, objectivity, truth.[58] Indeed, so powerful and successful were
these articulations – with their hidden ideological underpinnings – that
they still shape the ways in which we understand the world and our place as
individuals within it.

My proposed project would involve at least three levels. The first is the
deconstruction of the canon. For until we can perceive the artifacts of the
eighteenth century as human constructs, created in particular social contexts and for particular ideological interests, we cannot, in a sense, be free
to produce our own articulations of our own times and interests. The claim
to transcendental truth that attaches to Bach and Mozart especially will
continue to undercut our efforts until we can begin to define all these various kinds of artistic production as social practice. This program is not
intended to reduce Bach's achievement. Indeed, the more one knows
about his social and working conditions and the musical codes within
which and against which he produced meaning, the more one ought to

within which he formulated his statements and to distill a general methodology that can be
applied to repertories excluded by Adorno.
[58] See, for instance, Eagleton, *The function of criticism* and *The rape of Clarissa*, deconstructing
respectively the institutions of criticism and the novel in eighteenth-century England, and
also Jacques Derrida, *Of grammatology*, trans. Gayatri Spivak (Baltimore and London, 1976),
pp. 95–316, deconstructing notions of writing in Rousseau.

Talking politics during Bach Year   61

admire his endeavor, for the compositional choices and inflections in his music will become significant in the sense of *producing socially grounded meaning*, rather than significant as antiquarian relics that have value simply by virtue of possessing 'aura'.

Second, these reinterpretations need to be put into practice. So long as the performances of Bach to which we are subjected are of the pure-order, brain-dead variety, what I have been talking about cannot, in fact, be perceived.[59] In order to make audible the daring syntheses of opposing ideological forces in his compositions, the performer has to be aware of the faultlines in the pieces (that is, how to identify the various components, to be able to render them so as to make their individual qualities of motion heard), and then to *appear* to transcend them by sheer force of will and ingenuity. To play pieces in manners that make accessible the kinds of interpretations suggested above is to contribute insight both into Bach as a human being with desires and frustrations and into the social tensions of his day; to be more responsive to the notation as indicative of highly inflected, significant choices; and to produce a more dramatic, musically compelling reading than is usual.[60] To be sure, those who seek in Bach's music their principal refuge of order become highly indignant with such readings which reintroduce the violent element into his compositions. The greatest blasphemy of all is to perform Bach's music such that it speaks its encoded story of order and noise. But I would contend that *not* to articulate audibly the violent dimensions of music so strongly marked with deviation and resistance – to reduce it to orderliness – is to practice a more pernicious form of violence: *forceable silencing*.

Finally, I would propose the age-old strategy of rewriting the tradition in such a way as to appropriate Bach to our own political ends. Just as Renaissance mannerists justified their subjective excesses by appealing to principles of ancient Greek theory,[61] so each group since the early nine-

---

[59] Adorno's descriptions of a selection of Bach's fugues in 'Devotees' are excellent recipes for exciting, dialectical performances, though I know of no recording that seems informed by them. One has to play the fugues oneself in accordance with Adorno's interpretations in order to hear them as he describes them.

[60] There are performers of Bach's music who are extremely dynamic and in whose performances one can hear enacted the strains to which Adorno points. These include (among others) Gustav Leonhardt, Franz Brüggen, Nicolas Harnoncourt, and the Kuijkens. For remarkable presentations of the extravagantly theatrical side of Bach's production, listen to Edward Parmentier, a young American harpsichordist.

[61] For instance, Nicolo Vicentino, in his *L'antica musica ridotta alla moderna prattica* (1555), tried to legitimize his use of prohibited chromaticism and dissonances by appealing to the chromatic and enharmonic genera of Greek theory, hitherto empty categories in Renaissance musical practice. Vincenzo Galilei, in his *Dialogo della musica antica e della moderna* (1581), sought to replace what he regarded as the decadence of contrapuntal polyphony with popular-song style by making use of Aristotle's descriptions of Greek music.

62   SUSAN McCLARY

teenth century has found it necessary to kidnap Bach from the immediately preceding generation and to demonstrate his affinity with the emerging sensibility.[62] My portrait of Bach presented earlier clearly exhibits characteristics of the post-modern eclectic, of the ideologically marginalized artist empowering himself to appropriate, reinterpret, and manipulate to his own ends the signs and forms of dominant culture. His ultimate success in this enterprise can be a model of sorts to us all. In actively reclaiming Bach and the canon in order to put them to our own uses, we can also reclaim ourselves.

[62] See the Schoenberg references in n. 50 and also the description of Bach by Wagner in David and Mendel, eds., *The Bach reader*, p. 374. This latter is clearly also a self-portrait of Wagner himself (in his own mind the never-sufficiently-appreciated nineteenth-century genius/artist); yet it is strikingly more consonant with my post-modern eclectic Bach than are the objectified, orderly versions of Bach favored by the editors of *The Bach reader*.

CHAPTER 3

Narrative Agendas in "Absolute" Music: Identity and Difference in Brahms's Third Symphony

The proper object of musical criticism may be music, but only if what we mean by "object" is a goal and not a possession. Music is all too easy to treat as an Abstract Entity, something in but not of culture and history. Perhaps the impulse to idealize music in these terms betrays a need to establish a preserve, a protected area where the compromises and brutalities of the world cannot encroach. Freud once compared our conscious fantasies—daydreams—to preserves like Yellowstone Park; perhaps the compositions we idealize are the national parks of high culture.[1]

Of all the sacrosanct preserves of art music today, the most prestigious, the most carefully protected is a domain known as "Absolute Music": music purported to operate on the basis of pure configurations, untainted by words, stories, or even affect.[2] This category first appeared in the nineteenth century for the purpose of distinguishing presumably autonomous instrumental music from opera, song, and programmatic music. Musicologists have tended to practice different modes of criticism for these various repertories, addressing texted or programmatic music according to the terms set by the verbal or referential components but restricting their observations of string quartets or symphonies to whatever can be discerned through formal analysis alone.

An earlier version of this essay was written for a colloquium on narrative theory at the Wesleyan University Center for the Humanities. I have benefited from the comments of Nancy Armstrong, Christine Bezat, Michael Cherlin, Michael Harris, Lawrence Kramer, Andrew Jones, Bruce Lincoln, Thomas Nelson, Nancy Newman, Richard Ohmann, Jann Pasler, Sanna Pederson, Peter Rabinowitz, Jane Stevens, David Sylvan, Leonard Tennenhouse, Gary Thomas, Robert Walser, and Winifred Woodhull.

1. Lawrence Kramer, "Dangerous Liaisons: The Literary Text in Musical Criticism," *19th-Century Music* 13 (1989): 165.

2. See the critical overview in Roger Scruton, "Absolute Music," *The New Grove Dictionary of Music and Musicians*, ed. Stanley Sadie (New York, 1980), vol. 1, pp. 26–27.

In *The Idea of Absolute Music* Carl Dahlhaus traces the history of this notion that some instrumental music is self-contained, innocent of social or other referential meanings.[3] The concept of Absolute Music arose with the beginnings of German romanticism, in the writings of E. T. A. Hoffmann, Ludwig Tieck, Wilhelm Heinrich Wackenroder, and others, although it was not called by this term until the midcentury debates of Richard Wagner and Eduard Hanslick over texted versus untexted music.[4] Dahlhaus reveals how and for what ideological purposes music was withdrawn from the public sphere of the eighteenth-century Enlightenment and reassigned to the domain of metaphysics. Along the way he observes that this new, nonreferential ideal of wordless music was closely related to the phenomenon of German pietism, that the cult of Absolute Music took on the trappings of religious spirituality.[5] In Hoffmann's words, instrumental music "leads us forth out of life into the realm of the infinite."[6] The early romantics sought in symphonies and quartets the subjective, transcendent experience of mystical union that formerly had been available principally through pietistic devotion. And they sought universal domination for German culture by means of this textless music that does not betray its place of origin.

A subsequent generation (around midcentury) took the autonomous concept of instrumental music from this crypto-sacred, nationalistic context and reclothed it in "objectivity." As Hanslick, the chief polemicist for the absolutists, wrote in 1854: "To the question: What is to be expressed with this musical material? the answer is: Musical ideas. A fully realized musical idea, however, is already something beautiful by itself, is its own purpose, and is in no way merely means or material for the representation of feelings and thoughts. . . . Tonally moving forms are the sole content and object of music."[7] This philosophy still regulates much of musicology, blocking all but the most formalistic approaches to criticism. Indeed, even though Dahlhaus painstakingly delineates this history whereby a social discourse was appropriated and redefined first by romantic mystics and then by objectivists, he continues to respect the prohibitions of that

---

3. Carl Dahlhaus, *The Idea of Absolute Music*, trans. Roger Lustig (Chicago, 1989).

4. See Carl Dahlhaus, "The History of the Term and Its Vicissitudes," in his *The Idea*, pp. 18–41.

5. Ibid., pp. 5, 86, and 90.

6. As quoted in ibid., p. 67.

7. *On the Beautiful in Music* (Leipzig, 1854); as translated in Dahlhaus, *The Idea*, p. 109. Compare this statement concerning "absolute" art with one by Charles Baudelaire: "Into this horrible book I have put all my *heart*, all my *tenderness*, all my (travestied) religion, all my *hatred*, all my *bad luck*. It is true I will write the contrary, I will swear up and down that it is a book of *pure art*, of mummery and acrobatics, and I will be lying like a con man." Letter to Narcisse Ancelle, 18 February 1866, as quoted in Jerrold Seigel, *Bohemian Paris: Culture, Politics, and the Boundaries of Bourgeois Life, 1830–1930* (New York, 1986), p. 122.

tradition of objectivity. In his *Nineteenth-Century Music* he practices only structural analysis on instrumental music, and he scorns those who would venture into hermeneutic studies of symphonies.[8]

Yet despite—and perhaps because of—Dahlhaus's warning, I find it necessary to rush in where he, among others, feared to tread, into what Lawrence Kramer calls this "protected area where the compromises and brutalities of the world cannot encroach." Nor am I am alone in this venture. One of the most important trends in recent musicology has been the demystification of Absolute Music, the demonstration that those compositions long exalted as autonomous rely—no less than operas or tone poems—on codes of social signification such as affective vocabularies and narrative schemata.[9] The treasured distinction between the musical and the so-called extramusical is starting to dissolve, allowing hermeneutic readings of compositions traditionally held to be exempt from interpretation.

My own interest in Absolute Music extends beyond hermeneutics, although I rely heavily on the kinds of insights offered by studies of narrative and semiotics. I wish to understand what this music apparently intends to convey through its use of publicly shared signs, but I also want to subject it to social critique.[10] For Absolute Music articulates the same dominant social beliefs and tensions as other cultural artifacts of the nineteenth century; indeed, its patterns represent habits of thought so fundamental that they can even be transmitted without verbal cues. Given

8. Carl Dahlhaus, *Nineteenth-Century Music*, trans. J. Bradford Robinson (Berkeley, 1989), pp. 11, 94. See also his *The Idea*, p. 37. It is illuminating to read Dahlhaus in tandem with Terry Eagleton, *The Ideology of the Aesthetic* (Oxford, 1990), and the nineteenth-century segments of Denis Hollier, ed., *The History of French Literature* (Cambridge, Mass., 1989). All three projects investigate the history of "autonomous" art, but only Dahlhaus attempts to preserve intact what he has himself helped to demystify.

9. See Anthony Newcomb, "Once More 'Between Absolute and Program Music': Schumann's Second Symphony," *19th-Century Music* 7 (1984): 233–50; "Schumann and Late Eighteenth-Century Narrative Strategies," *19th-Century Music* 11 (1987): 164–74; and "Sound and Feeling," *Critical Inquiry* 10 (1984): 614–43. See also Lawrence Kramer, *Music as Cultural Practice, 1800–1900* (Berkeley, 1990); Fred Maus, "Music as Drama," *Music Theory Spectrum* 10 (1988): 65–72; and Jann Pasler, "Narrative and Narrativity in Music," in J. T. Fraser, *Time and Mind: Interdisciplinary Issues* (Madison, Conn., 1989), pp. 233–57. Carolyn Abbate, in her *Unsung Voices: Opera and Musical Narrative in the Nineteenth Century* (Princeton, 1991), has raised some important questions concerning narrative readings of instrumental music. I hope to respond at length elsewhere to her arguments.

10. I have written elsewhere about music as social discourse. See, for example, "The Blasphemy of Talking Politics During Bach Year," in Richard Leppert and Susan McClary, eds., *Music and Society: The Politics of Composition, Performance and Reception* (Cambridge, 1987), pp. 13–62; "A Musical Dialectic from the Enlightenment: Mozart's Piano Concerto in G Major, K. 453, Movement 2," *Cultural Critique* 4 (1986): 129–69; and the methodological discussion in the first chapter of my *Feminine Endings: Music, Gender, and Sexuality* (Minneapolis, 1991).

that these covert patterns have managed to operate successfully for two centuries, they stand very much in need of interrogation.[11]

This project owes a great deal to the music criticism of Theodor W. Adorno, who traced the history of bourgeois subjectivity and its contradictions through the same instrumental music that seems so impervious to such analyses. Much of this essay stands as a particularized elucidation of a few extraordinarily provocative pages by Adorno concerning late nineteenth-century Absolute Music:[12] it attempts to make explicit the kinds of mediating steps that enabled Adorno to link musical procedures with society. But my analysis differs from his in that it also addresses issues such as gender and race—issues which were not among Adorno's priorities.

The viability of apparently autonomous instrumental music depends on the powerful affective codes that have developed within the referential domains of vocal music.[13] Familiarity with this network of cultural associations permits us to recognize even in textless music traditional signs for grief, joy, or the heroic. But signification extends far beyond the surface in instrumental music: its formal conventions—often held to be neutral with respect to meaning—are likewise socially encoded. Stuart Hall has written, with respect to narrative, that

> meanings are already concealed or held within the forms of the stories themselves. Form is much more important than the old distinction between form and content. We used to think form was like an empty box, and it's really what you put into it that matters. But we are aware now that the form is actually part of the content of what it is that you are saying. So then one

11. See Stuart Hall, "The Narrative Construction of Reality," *Southern Review* [Adelaide] 17 (1984): 3–17, for a theoretical discussion of the ways narrative conventions permeate virtually all cultural constructs. "In any society we all constantly make use of a whole set of frameworks of interpretation and understanding, often in a very practical unconscious way, and those things alone enable us to make sense of what is going on around us, what our position is, and what we are likely to do. . . . What is it that is secured, put in place, by those being the ways in which we talk to ourselves about life, experience, emotions, new situations? . . . Who is it that benefits? . . . Why do [these stories] take that shape? . . . What are the stories we don't tell ourselves?" (pp. 7–12).

12. See Theodor W. Adorno, "Class and Strata," *Introduction to the Sociology of Music*, trans. E. B. Ashton (New York, 1976), pp. 55–70. See also Rose Rosengard Subotnik, "The Historical Structure: Adorno's 'French' Model for the Criticism of Nineteenth-Century Music," *19th-Century Music* 2 (1978): 36–60.

13. These codes emerged self-consciously in seventeenth-century music and were theorized during the eighteenth century as the *Affektenlehre*, by writers such as Johann Mattheson and Johann David Heinichen. Even though these social codes of signification were no longer acknowledged by most nineteenth-century aestheticians, they are no less operative in the music. Traditional semiotics had been so thoroughly absorbed that they had become transparent or "natural." See the references in note 10.

has to ask why it is that certain events seem to be handled, predominantly in our culture, in certain forms.[14]

What, then, of the forms that guarantee and sustain Absolute Music?

Classical instrumental music depends on two interlocking narrative schemata, tonality and sonata. I am referring here to tonality, not in the broad sense of pitch-centeredness (which would include most of Western music), but in the more specific sense of the grammatical and structural syntax of eighteenth- and nineteenth-century European musics. I have written elsewhere about the early history and also the decline of tonal procedures.[15] For our present purposes it is sufficient to recognize that the history of tonality was shaped by its social contexts and that tonality operates according to a standard sequence of dynamic events, giving the music it organizes a distinctly narrative cast.

Tonality emerged as a way of arousing and channeling desire in early opera,[16] although instrumentalists quickly adopted its procedures for their own repertories. In fact, Tieck, one of the early theorists of Absolute Music, described instrumental music as "insatiate desire forever hieing forth and turning back into itself."[17] On both local and global levels, tonality is intensely teleological; it works through the simple mechanism of suggesting a particular pitch for purposes of release, but then withholding that pitch while continuing to imply (through a particular brand of harmonic syntax) that the goal is nearly within reach. The surface of the tonal piece thus alternates between carefully sustained tension or protracted longing and periodic moments of relief.

The tonal composition (with a few idiosyncratic exceptions) ends in the same key in which it began. Consequently, from the very outset of the composition listeners know its probable ultimate goal. Yet that goal can be truly meaningful only if it is called into question. It therefore becomes necessary for the piece to leave the tonic key area and to enact an adventure in which other key areas are encountered and tonal identity is at least temporarily suspended. Regardless of the twists and turns of the composition's particular chain of events, however, the outcome—the inevitable return to the tonic—is always known in advance. To the extent that "Other" keys stand in the way of unitary identity, they register as dissonances and must finally be subdued for the sake of narrative closure.

14. Hall, "The Narrative Construction," p. 7.

15. See, for instance, my "The Transition from Modal to Tonal Organization in the Works of Monteverdi," Ph.D. diss., Harvard University, 1976; and *Feminine Endings*.

16. See my "Constructions of Gender in Monteverdi's Dramatic Music," *Cambridge Opera Journal* 1 (1989): 202–23. I am at present writing a book titled *Power and Desire in Seventeenth-Century Music*, to be published by Princeton University Press.

17. As quoted in Dahlhaus, *The Idea*, p. 18.

Difference is thus not coincidental to this schema. Without dissonance, without excursions into other keys, there would be no plot, no long-term dynamic tension. Yet those dissonances and other keys must eventually be purged—sometimes violently—if the composition is to end satisfactorily. The schema thus outlines a kind of narrative based on identity and certainty on the one hand, and difference and excitement (with at least the illusion of risk) on the other. Each individual piece of tonal music fleshes out the paradigm in its own way, principally through its choice of key relationships, its affective vocabulary, and its strategies for manipulating desire. But all of these choices are socially based and socially intelligible insofar as they draw on the powerful social conventions of normative tonality.

My account of tonality differs from most in that it regards as ideologically significant these oppositions between self and Other and the predetermined terms of resolution. But a few other music theorists have also noticed the political implications of the tonal schema, most explicitly Arnold Schoenberg, who writes in his *Theory of Harmony*:

> For [our forebears] the comedy concluded with marriage, the tragedy with expiation or retribution, and the musical work "in the same key." Hence, for them the choice of scale brought the obligation to treat the first tone of that scale as the fundamental, and to present it as Alpha and Omega of all that took place in the work, as the patriarchal ruler over the domain defined by its might and its will: its coat of arms was displayed at the most conspicuous points, especially at the beginning and ending. And thus they had a possibility for closing that in effect resembled a necessity.[18]

In other words, Absolute Music enacts a kind of absolutist political narrative merely by virtue of assuming tonality as a natural imperative.[19]

An additional stratum of narrative convention makes possible the nineteenth-century symphony: namely, sonata procedure—a particular schematic arrangement within tonality. The sonata exposition typically articulates the two initial key areas (tonic and its primary Other) with distinctive themes. In the eighteenth century, composers often replicated the opening theme at the level of the secondary key, thereby maintaining the identity of the implied protagonist throughout the tonal adventure; but in the nineteenth, thematic contrast became central to the paradigm. Thus the tension between identity and difference with respect to keys, which is already fundamental in tonality, is thrown into high dramatic relief by the additional tension between the two thematic types.

18. Arnold Schoenberg, *Theory of Harmony*, trans. Roy E. Carter (Berkeley, 1978), p. 129.
19. In fact, when Wagner coined the term *Absolute Music*, he intended it as a taunt. It is ironic that the term was quickly adopted by those he meant to parody.

S U S A N   M c C L A R Y

James Webster's article in *The New Grove Dictionary of Music* offers the following, presumably neutral, description of this tension and its narrative consequences:

> The second group in the exposition presents important material and closes with a sense of finality, but it is not in the tonic. This dichotomy creates a "large-scale dissonance" that must be resolved. The "sonata principle" requires that the most important ideas and the strongest cadential passages from the second group reappear in the recapitulation, but now transposed to the tonic. The subtle tension of stating important material in another key is thus "grounded," and the movement can end.[20]

Later in this article Webster mentions that mid-nineteenth-century theorists began referring to these themes respectively as "masculine" (the opening material identified with what Schoenberg calls the "patriarchal" tonic) and "feminine" (the theme predestined to be "grounded" in the key of the first). For instance, in 1845 theorist A. B. Marx wrote: "The second theme, on the other hand, serves as contrast to the first, energetic statement, though dependent on and determined by it. It is of a more tender nature, flexibly rather than emphatically constructed—in a way, the feminine as opposed to the preceding masculine."[21]

This convention of designating themes as "masculine" and "feminine" was still common in pedagogy and criticism of the 1960s,[22] although musicology has since repudiated it and has attempted to expunge the memory that such gender-typing ever occurred or, in any event, that it ever truly meant anything. However, eliminating this terminology does not erase the issue of gender from the musical structures of this period: because many of the themes in question draw on the semiotics of "masculinity" and "femininity" as they were constructed in opera or tone poems, they are easily recognized in their respective positions within these musical narratives. We do not need to express verbal confirmation, such as A. B. Marx offers, in order to proceed.

Nor is this a trivial matter of labeling. We have already seen that these "masculine" and "feminine" themes are located in particular slots in the conventional schemata of tonality and sonata, that their respective fates are already cast before the composition begins. The "masculine" tonic is predestined to triumph, the "feminine" Other to be (in Webster's words) "grounded" or "resolved." In this respect, sonata replicates with uncanny

---

20. James Webster, "Sonata Form," *The New Grove Dictionary*, vol. 17, p. 498.

21. As cited and translated in a communication from Peter Bloom to *Journal of the American Musicological Society* 27 (1974): 162.

22. Not only are themes gendered in this way, but also cadences and, occasionally, triads. The underlying rationale always involves relative strength and "naturalness." See my discussion in chapter 1 of *Feminine Endings*.

accuracy the narrative paradigms of myth delineated by narratologists such as Vladimir Propp and Jurij Lotman.[23] As Teresa de Lauretis observes with respect to Lotman's schema:

> The hero must be male, regardless of the gender of the text-image, because the obstacle, whatever its personification, is morphologically female. . . . If the work of the mythical structuration is to establish distinctions, the primary distinction on which all others depend is . . . sexual difference. . . . The hero, the mythical subject, is constructed as human being and as male; he is the active principle of culture, the establisher of distinction, the creator of differences. Female is what is not susceptible to transformation, to life or death; she (it) is an element of plot-space, a topos, a resistance, matrix and matter.[24]

The reason, then, that Absolute Music appears to make itself up without reference to the outside social world is that it adheres so thoroughly to the most common plot outline and the most fundamental ideological tensions available within Western culture: the story of a hero who ventures forth, encounters an Other, fights it out, and finally reestablishes secure identity. So long as composers agreed to stick to the standard narrative, they and their audiences could pretend to be listening in on the utterances of Hegel's *Geist* or Schopenhauer's *Will*: an illusion always heavily circumscribed by convention, always ideologically saturated.

Instrumental composers who wanted to tell other stories risked unintelligibility. One popular solution was to provide listeners with alternative metaphorical grids, conveyed in titles or programs, through which to understand unorthodox formulations—a solution that also offered composers a potentially infinite range of idiosyncratic formal designs.[25]

23. Vladimir Propp, *Morphology of the Folktale*, ed. Louis A. Wagner (Austin, 1968); and Jurij M. Lotman, "The Origin of Plot in the Light of Typology," trans. Julian Graffy, *Poetics Today* 1 (1979): 161–84.

24. Teresa de Lauretis, "Desire in Narrative," in *Alice Doesn't: Feminism, Semiotics, Cinema* (Bloomington, 1984), pp. 118–19.

25. Richard Strauss states this explicitly in a letter to Hans von Bülow in 1888: "I have found myself in a gradually ever increasing contradiction between the musical-poetic content that I want to convey a[nd] the ternary sonata form that has come down to us from the classical composers. . . . Now, what was for Beethoven a 'form' absolutely in congruity with the highest, most glorious content, is now, after 60 years, used as a formula inseparable from our instrumental music. . . . If one wants to create a work of art which is unified in its mood and consistent in its structure . . . this is made possible only by inspiration through a poetic idea, whether it is introduced as a programme or not. I consider it a legitimate artistic method to create an appropriate new form for each subject." As translated in James Hepokoski, "Fiery-Pulsed Libertine or Domestic Hero? Strauss's Don Juan Reinvestigated" (unpublished typescript, 1990). I wish to thank Professor Hepokoski for permitting me to see a copy of this paper.

Critics such as Hanslick condemned the verbal cues of programs for sullying music's purity. But there was even more at stake: programs threatened to blow the lid off the metaphysical claims of the absolutists, for tone poems employed the same codes, the same gestural vocabulary, the same structural impulses—although always acknowledging (at least in part) what they signified.[26]

The schemata of tonality and sonata persisted in organizing European music for about two centuries, but they were anything but static.[27] Some of the transformations resulted from the prevalent anti-authoritarianism of romanticism, for no sooner had tonal or sonata conventions crystallized than composers began rebelling against their constraints; if these paradigms continued to underwrite composition and interpretation, they also provided the terms for resistance. But other shifts were the products of changing social attitudes toward questions of identity and difference, especially as they related to gender.[28] Consequently, no composition can be reduced simply to the narrative conventions that informed it: its historical moment and its particular strategies must also be taken into account. But the specific details of any given piece are intelligible only insofar as they engage dialectically with those conventions.

Thus I would now like to examine a work by a composer who represents the Old Faithful within the Yellowstone Park of Absolute Music, Johannes Brahms's Third Symphony (1883). When Brahms was a mere twenty years old, Robert Schumann hailed him as the hope for German music, the defense against the corruption of programmatic excess, the

26. Some programs, of course, do not fully divulge their agendas. For instance, the last movement of Debussy's *La Mer* ("Dialogue Between the Wind and the Sea") articulates in sound an extremely violent encounter between what are semiotically marked as a "masculine" force (the wind) and a "feminine" one (*la mer/la mère*), even though it does not acknowledge verbally that this is the case. See also Hepokoski, "Fiery-Pulsed Libertine." This rereading of Strauss's *Don Juan* observes much more about this tone poem's sexual narrative than the program admits explicitly.

27. Jay Clayton has recently criticized literary narratologists for the ahistoricity of their structures and analyses. See his "Narrative and Theories of Desire," *Critical Inquiry* 16 (1989): 33–53.

28. Eighteenth-century cultural artifacts typically reach closure in ways that seem unforced, as though the preordained hierarchies of class and gender are simply natural. During the nineteenth century, however, as such hierarchies were destabilized (in part by women who refused to assume subordinate positions), conflicts and attempts at closure became far more violent. This trajectory in literature has been traced by Nancy Armstrong, *Desire and Domestic Fiction: A Political History of the Novel* (Oxford, 1987); Peter Gay, *The Bourgeois Experience, Victoria to Freud.* Vol. 1: *The Education of the Senses* (Oxford, 1984); and Sander L. Gilman, *Difference and Pathology: Stereotypes of Sexuality, Race, and Madness* (Ithaca, 1985). It would be possible to do the same for the history of Absolute Music. This essay attempts to examine one moment; *Feminine Endings* addresses other repertories.

rightful heir to Beethoven, who represented the cornerstone of Absolute Music.[29] Through his rhetoric Schumann deliberately positioned himself as John the Baptist heralding the advent of Christ. Predictably, the young Brahms was almost paralyzed by Schumann's excess and the inflated expectations it raised; he was not to premiere a symphony until twenty-three years later.

When he did finally begin releasing symphonies, they were cast self-consciously in Beethovenian molds and were received in that spirit as well. The first of them was compared to Beethoven's Ninth, the second to the "Pastoral" Symphony.[30] And both stood as evidence that the metaphysical spirit of Absolute Music still smiled on Germany. Brahms's Third Symphony was, like Beethoven's Third, referred to as the "Eroica" or heroic—even by upholders of the absolutist faith, such as Hanslick.[31] The presumed "heroic" quality of the symphony might be denied by today's latterday objectivists, although most listeners can easily recognize the opening gesture of the symphony as belonging to a family that would also include Richard Strauss's Don Juan, Franz Liszt's triumphant Faust, or John Williams's Indiana Jones (mm. 1–3). The opening motto is loud, forcefully played by a band of brasses and winds, and it shoves up by means of apparently herculean effort to a point of release that hurls us into the first movement's narrative. Its sonority, volume, aggression, and rocketlike gesture mark it semiotically as "masculine."[32] Thus the symphony earns its heroic label right off the bat. But the symphony's claim to heroicism extends far beyond mere thematic character: like Beethoven's "Eroica," Brahms's narrative unfolding illustrates how heroic behavior is constituted, but it also revisits and critiques the formal terms of Beethovenian heroicism.

29. Robert Schumann, "New Paths," *Schumann on Music: A Selection from the Writings*, ed. and trans. Henry Pleasants (New York, 1988), pp. 199–200.

30. Eduard Hanslick, *Music Criticisms 1846–99*, ed. and trans. Henry Pleasants (Baltimore, 1950), p. 211.

31. Ibid., pp. 210–13.

32. Tradition has it that this motto—F-A♭-F—was a private sign between Brahms and his friend Joseph Joachim that meant "frei aber froh" (free but glad). This was supposed to have been Brahms's response to Joachim's motto, F-A-E, or "frei aber einsam" (free but lonely), by which he expressed his dissatisfaction with bachelor life. By contrast, the version ascribed to Brahms celebrates bachelorhood, the absence of entanglements with women. See the original anecdote in Max Kalbeck, *Johannes Brahms*, 2d ed. (Berlin, 1908–1914), vol. 1, p. 98.

Michael Musgrave has called this tradition into question because its authenticity cannot be substantiated. See "Frei aber Froh: A Reconsideration," *19th-Century Music* 3 (1980): 251–58. Yet this symphony (the principal composition that utilizes this motto) resonates powerfully with the gist of that "free but glad" slogan, struggling as it always is to throw off "feminine" influence. It is easy to see how this tradition may have arisen from the narrative tensions of the Third Symphony itself.

SUSAN McCLARY

For although Brahms follows carefully in Beethoven's footsteps, some of the tensions that were audible even in Beethoven's own music had become almost unworkable by the time Brahms received them.[33] In the eighteenth century Haydn found it relatively unproblematic to enact the dynamic processes of tonality and sonata and to make the reconciliation between themes and forms sound natural, rational, unforced. But Beethoven began to question what it would mean for his protagonist—regardless of its individuating idiosyncrasies—to go through the same tonal and formal paces as every other composition. Beginning with his "Eroica," he began trying to make it seem that the protagonist was inventing itself and determining from its own quirks its own tailor-made succession of narrative events, while still holding on to the norms of tonality and sonata that guaranteed intelligibility.[34] Therein lies the revolutionary heroism of that symphony. But this tension between individual expression and social convention became exacerbated over the course of the nineteenth century, so that Brahms inherited both a desire to emulate the classical narrative model and, at the same time, a profound distrust of its strictures—including even what it means to be in a key or to achieve closure.

I introduced the initial gesture of Brahms's symphony as though it were a straightforward sign of heroic swagger. But that opening motto is, in fact, extremely complex. The symphony is ostensibly in F Major, characterized by a bright, sunny A♮. But the motto presents as its second sonority A♭, in direct opposition to the key's fundamental triad. Although the third sonority in the motto sets the mode "right" again with the return of A♮ in the harmony, this confusion over the proper mediant poses the terms of the entire symphony.

For the motto's identity is not reconcilable with the demands of tonality itself, and the symphony vacillates throughout between adhering to the thorny idiosyncrasy that spells this particular self and surrendering to the security, the false consciousness, the law of convention. The placid terrain of plain old F Major, with its consistent A♮, and keys that themselves highlight A♮ stand for enticements to abandon the struggle, while A♭ (which typically veers away from the affirmative into rage or melancholy) represents the attempt to hold on to the anomaly that gives this piece its identity. Yet despite all this individuation, we know that, according to the premises of musical narrative, tonal pieces cannot end in a key other than the one that opened the piece—especially not if the trajectory moves from

33. See Adorno, "Class and Strata," pp. 63–65; and Subotnik, "The Historical Structure."

34. For a narratological reading of the "Eroica," see Philip G. Downes, "Beethoven's 'New Way' and the Eroica," in Paul Henry Lang, ed., *The Creative World of Beethoven* (New York, 1970), pp. 83–102.

triumphant major into dismal minor.[35] If Beethoven first called the narrative model into question, Brahms plunged headlong into the fissures that had opened up in the aftermath of Beethoven's critique.

In the first section of his exposition Brahms's idiosyncratic motto, rather than selling out to the banality of tonal syntax, attempts to blaze its own harmonic path. Underneath the theme, the motto replicates itself end to end like Tinker Toys or a strand of DNA. The result is a sequence of chords that swing among distantly related keys as though arbitrarily, cut loose from the garden-variety tonal syntax that gives the music of this period its illusion of rationality. By avoiding convention the motto may succeed in devising its own solipsistic process, but it is a process that verges on the socially unintelligible.

Moreover, after a mere fourteen bars the motto seems to have run its course: the contradiction apparently cannot be sustained indefinitely. What follows is a serene little tune from which all evidence of A♭ has been expunged (mm. 15–19). In the wake of the heroic flailing that precedes it, however, this theme sounds almost lobotomized. The motto comes back (m. 19), first disguised in a diatonic transformation and then in earnest. When the little tune returns (m. 23), it has been flipped around to D♭ Major, in accordance with the dictates of the motto and in defiance of convention.

We now begin to approach the second key area. Ordinarily, the second key would be on the fifth scale-step. But given the specific tensions of this piece, such a choice could only mean blind adherence to convention. Thus Brahms makes the second key relevant to this particular narrative. It is A Major; the A♮ that has been so problematized as the option spelling loss of identity here asserts itself as a rival key center. We arrive at A Major, moreover, through a sleight-of-hand (mm. 29–35) in which the treasured A♭ is gradually reinterpreted as G♯ resolving dutifully into A. David Brodbeck has argued that these measures refer explicitly to the moment from the Venusburg scene in Wagner's *Tannhäuser* in which sirens seductively beckon "Naht euch dem Strande."[36] And as our sign of heroic resistance loses its vitality, we are delivered over to the second theme.

Let's pretend we have no idea that second themes were sometimes called "feminine." The score marks this one as *grazioso* (in contrast to the opening theme's *passionato*). A dancelike meter emerges, with an ara-

---

35. Among the few tonal pieces that progress from major to minor is the last of Schubert's Impromptus, Op. 90. This piece is so odd that theorist Edward T. Cone was compelled to write a narrative account of it. See his "Schubert's Promissory Note," *19th-Century Music* 5 (1982): 233–41.

36. David Brodbeck, "Brahms, the Third Symphony, and the New German School," in Walter Frisch, ed., *Brahms and His World* (Princeton, 1990), pp. 67–68. Brodbeck interprets the principal tension in the movement in terms of Brahms's ambivalence toward Wagner.

besque tune in the clarinet that weaves around teasingly over a static, nonprogressing bass. This bass drone contributes what Brodbeck describes as a "pastoral atmosphere," especially after the intellectual torments of the opening (mm. 36–49).[37] Its alignment with "nature," stasis, seduction, and the physicality of the dance indicates that this theme already occupies a position on the "feminine" side of nineteenth-century cultural semiotics.

But it is possible to go further. Hermann Kretzschmar, a critic from the turn of the century who broke rank by writing in hermeneutic terms about the Absolute Music of his day, refers to this theme as Delilah, pointing to the Oriental exoticism, the dizzying rhythms, and the seductive sensuality of this section.[38] Indeed, this theme serves to rob the movement's implied trajectory of its energy, "to lull the powerful elements of the composition to sleep with gentle feelings."[39] It shears off the crucial $A\flat$ that is the secret of the hero's strength and domesticates that pitch for its own purposes—as the $G\sharp$ that leads back inevitably to $A\natural$.

However, like Samson after his first encounters with Delilah or like Tannhäuser after Venus, the motto gradually awakens (beginning in m. 49) and throws off the influence of this second theme. It reestablishes its original meter and aggressiveness; and although it is temporarily stuck with A as tonic, its heroic move is to cancel out the affirmative, alluring quality of that key by ending the exposition forcefully in a stoic A Minor. This leads to a return to the explosive beginning of the exposition for a second presentation of self, seduction, and resistance—a dramatic sequence that now threatens to become cyclic rather than resolvable.

I should mention at this point that the story of Samson and Delilah was especially popular in the late nineteenth century, when this symphony was written. Saint-Saëns's opera of that name had appeared six years earlier, in 1877; other operas with vampirish, treacherous women (often marked as racially Other) and victimized heroes were becoming prevalent, *Carmen* being the best known of them.[40] As Peter Gay and Sander Gilman have demonstrated, the story of a white male protagonist ren-

37. Ibid., p. 69.

38. Hermann Kretzschmar, *Führer durch den Konzertsaal: Sinfonie und Suite*, vol. 2, ed. Hugo Botstiber, 7th ed. (Leipzig, 1932), pp. 95–100. The subordinate theme in this symphony may not sound Oriental to our ears, for we are far better acquainted with actual Asian music than was Brahms. Kretzschmar's testimony is helpful because it points up for us what would have been conceived and perceived as "Oriental" within the codes of that time. Tchaikovsky's Symphony No. 4 has a similarly Orientalist "feminine" second theme. See my discussion in "Sexual Politics."

39. Kretzschmar, "The Brahms Symphonies," trans. Susan Gillespie, in Frisch, ed., *Brahms and His World*, p. 136.

40. See my discussion of *Carmen* in "Sexual Politics," and also my *Georges Bizet's Carmen* (Cambridge, 1992).

dered impotent by an exotic temptress appealed enormously to Europeans in the last third of the nineteenth century.[41] And Brahms the absolutist was not oblivious to these trends: when *Carmen* was first produced in Vienna in 1876, he went twenty times to see it.[42]

The development section of the symphony (from m. 71) presents a knock-down-drag-out confrontation between the two forces. It opens with the heroic materials in both low and high instruments, both rightside up and upside down. The protagonist has consolidated its forces and militance, yet its accents are all rhythmically displaced, rendering it unstable. And as soon as it reaches temporary closure, the second theme enters in a savage transformation (m. 77). No longer enticing, it now matches the aggression of the first theme. Our contemporary witness Kretzschmar hears this as wrathful, hysterical, distorted with rage, and he describes the scene with a virtuosity of alliteration that would give Wagner pause.[43]

Gradually, however, its energy dissipates, and we are led into the development's other surprise: the heroic motto transformed into a serene, lyrical melody (m. 101). It is tender, yearning, rather than striving; and although it still twists around harmonically to irrationally related keys in a kind of infinite regress of its idiosyncrasy, it does so without force. We get a glimpse here of the hero's privatized subjectivity. Kretzschmar, in keeping with his Samson trope, refers to it as a dreamer or sleeper and says that it sounds like a nocturne, a genre strongly associated with women and femininity.[44] This passage occupies flat keys: the hero's identification with flats remains intact, but without the antagonism of the other side of the dialectic it lacks vitality. We also seem very far away from the determining tonic.

The heroic theme then enters haltingly in m. 112, divorced from the motto that had always animated it. It sinks down without resistance in

41. Gay, "Offensive Women and Defensive Men," in *Education of the Senses*, pp. 169–225; and Gilman, *Difference and Pathology*. See also Mieke Bal, "Delilah Decomposed: Samson's Talking Cure and the Rhetoric of Subjectivity," in her *Lethal Love: Feminist Literary Readings of Biblical Love Stories* (Bloomington, 1987), pp. 37–67.

42. Mina Curtiss, *Bizet and His World* (New York, 1958), p. 426. Brahms presented the *Carmen* score to Clara Schumann. Tchaikovsky likewise was enamoured of *Carmen*, as were Wagner and Nietzsche. For more on Brahms's ambivalence toward women, see Peter F. Ostwald, "Johannes Brahms, Solitary Altruist," in Frisch, ed., *Brahms and His World*, esp. pp. 28–31.

43. Kretzschmar, *Führer*, p. 97: "Ganz unversehens tritt da das zweite Thema herein, aber es ist hier ganz anders gemeint als in der Themengruppe: . . . es kommt in Moll grollend, grimmig abweisend, hoch erregt, mit Zusätzen, die es verzerren und verhöhnen, es wird mit einem schliesslich komischen Eifer abgelehnt under zurückgewiesen."

44. Ibid., p. 97. See Jeffrey Kallberg, "The Harmony of the Tea Table: Gender and Ideology in the Piano Nocturne," *Representations* 39 (1992): 102–33.

what seems like free-fall, its major mediant converting to minor but otherwise without any semblance of its original gritty identity. But at what seems like the last moment before irreversible catatonia, the bass catches on F, the tonic pitch (m. 118). With a gigantic effort requiring that it redouble itself, the motto launches back into the original key, the opening theme complex, and the formal recapitulation (m. 120).

The development thus presents an inversion in power between the first and the second theme, as the "feminine" theme betrays its latent ferocity and the heroic theme lies impotent, effeminized, and helpless, summoning up the strength to escape only at the last moment. The purpose of the recapitulation is to reestablish the rightful relationship and begin the push toward closure. Yet, oddly enough, it is at this moment of apparent narrative triumph that the constraints of sonata itself begin to chafe. Sonata had its beginnings in the Enlightenment and so was originally concerned with formal balance. In Haydn, when the recapitulation repeated the events of the exposition, it served to celebrate the reconciliation of social order with individual will. But in the nineteenth century, when the quality of "becoming" was the ideal, the recapitulation constituted an awkward holdover from that earlier time: a section of the piece where narrative progression suddenly gives way to formal reiteration.

As is typical, Brahms's recapitulation goes through the paces of the exposition once again, restating the themes in their original guises. The second theme, which had threatened to usurp agency in the development, now reappears as it was at the outset, but transposed—not to the tonic, but to D Major, a key that balances symmetrically with its original key (m. 149). By thus presenting the second theme symmetrically and in its initial version, it may be that Brahms reduces it to a mere vestige of the Enlightenment's demand for structural balance. But in withholding the second theme from the control of the "patriarchal" tonic, Brahms also suggests that it remains ungrounded and unresolved, especially since the recapitulation ends with its final (D Minor) rather than with the movement's tonic.

However, it might best be argued that the "feminine" theme is less a threat in and of itself than it is a projection of the hero's own ambivalence. In a sense, the "feminine" Other here is gratuitous, a mere narrative pretext. For the principal dilemma in the symphony is finally oedipal: the archetypal struggle of the rebellious son against the conventional Law of the Father, the struggle that underlies so many Western narratives.[45] As Jessica Benjamin has written of this paradigm, "The struggle for power takes place between father and son; woman plays no part in it, except as prize or temptation to regression, or as the third point of a triangle. There

45. See Ostwald, "Johannes Brahms," pp. 25–28.

is no struggle between man and woman in this story; indeed, woman's subordination to man is taken for granted."[46]

In this movement the principal tension is not between first and second theme (a tension resolved with little difficulty), but, rather, between a first theme that is dissonant with respect to the conventions that sustain its narrative procedures and those conventions themselves. To the extent that the heroic theme bears marks of Otherness with respect to "patriarchal" tonal custom, it itself stands in danger of being purged for the sake of tonal propriety. The remainder of the movement focuses on the resolution of the composition's real dilemma: how to define closure in a piece in F Major that insists on maintaining a defiant A$\flat$ for purposes of identity.

The movement's coda (from m. 183) proceeds with saber-rattling triumph for a while; yet although this enacts a return to the original heroic affect and key, it does little toward solving the A$\flat$/A$\natural$ dilemma. Commentators from Kretzschmar to objectivists such as Hanslick have remarked on the strangeness of the ending. The energy of the movement simply subsides: the motto gives one last appearance (mm. 216–20), and then the heroic theme drifts downward without resistance to resigned acceptance of closure in standard F Major. At the conclusion of what is otherwise an austere formal analysis, Dahlhaus himself grasps at a quasi-programmatic explanation, writing of this ending, "The subject immures itself to the world and turns ultimately to silence."[47]

The remaining movements of the symphony extend these narrative tensions further, first by moving to a serene choralelike movement (recalling the connections of Absolute Music with Lutheran pietism), but then making increasing forays onto the dark side until the final movement returns us, not to the expected F Major, but to F Minor, with its four flats. The struggles for identity that characterized the first movement become even more militant in this finale, which presses relentlessly against any surrender to convention. Yet its conclusion parallels that of the first movement: the minor evaporates, yielding to a replay of the earlier movement's last-minute capitulation, now enhanced with prayerlike chorales.

This conclusion may be read in a number of ways. The unsettling compromise at the end of each of the two critical movements may indicate defeat: the inability either to maintain indefinitely or to solve the contradictions that had initially hurled the symphony into motion. Or the chorale references at the end (also characteristic of transfiguring

---

46. Jessica Benjamin, *The Bonds of Love: Psychoanalysis, Feminism, and the Problem of Domination* (New York, 1988), pp. 6–7. See also Eve Kosofsky Sedgwick, *Between Men: English Literature and Male Homosocial Desire* (New York, 1985).

47. Dahlhaus, *Nineteenth-Century Music*, p. 269.

encounters with the sublime in Beethoven)[48] may imply apotheosis rather than defeat, a transcendence of the struggle. Yet the fact that tonal banality is the only form of closure available at the end of this and every other composition in the tonal repertory means that the normative term of the dilemma, the conventional A♮, is allowed to prevail after all—that, in some important sense, the struggle was always just an illusion.[49]

Thus if Brahms's symphony is intelligible by virtue of his adherence to his inherited narrative paradigms, its principal conflict involves not so much its own internal thematic elements as the restrictiveness of tonal procedures and of nineteenth-century formal conventions themselves: conventions concerning what it means to be in a key, to undergo recapitulation, to acquiesce to closure in keeping with classical models. Adorno writes: "The ideological side of Brahms also turns musically wrong when the standpoint of the subject's pure being-for-itself keeps compromising with the traditional collective formal language of music, which is not that subject's language any more."[50] Schoenberg's radical solution was, of course, to scrap intelligibility along with the social contracts upon which it had depended.[51]

I have not invaded the Yellowstone Park of Absolute Music to vandalize it. Part of my motivation is to examine the paranoid agendas relating to gender and even to race (in the guise of the treacherous, Oriental temptress) that show up regularly in this music that wants to resist any and all critiques. I hasten to add that Brahms was no guiltier of such narratives and constructions than were most of his contemporaries: the point is not to single him out for castigation, but, rather, to indicate that these mod-

48. For a discussion of musical representations of the sublime in Beethoven and Schubert, see my "Pitches, Expression, Ideology: An Exercise in Mediation," *Enclitic* 7 (1983): 76–86.

49. For a similar reading of another composition by Brahms, see Christine Bezat, Andrew Jones, Thomas Nelson, and Nancy Newman, "Brahms' Intermezzo, Op. 116, no. 4" (unpublished paper, 1990). I wish to thank the four of them for stimulating discussions of these issues. See also Thomas Nelson, "A Sublime Object of Ideology: Case Study #116/4" (unpublished paper, 1990). I am also grateful to Sanna Pederson for permitting me to read her "The German Symphony After Beethoven" (unpublished paper, 1990).

50. Adorno, "Class and Strata," p. 65.

51. See Schoenberg, *Style and Idea*, trans. Leo Black (Berkeley, 1975), and his *Theory of Harmony*. See also Adorno, "Arnold Schoenberg, 1874–1951," in *Prisms*, trans. Samuel and Shierry Weber (Cambridge, Mass., 1981), pp. 147–72. Again Jessica Benjamin's analysis proves insightful, as we consider the serial aftermath of Schoenberg's revolution: "The sons who overthrow the father's authority become afraid of their own aggression and lawlessness and regret the loss of his wonderful power; and so they reinstate law and authority in the father's image" (*The Bonds of Love*, p. 6).

els were so pervasive that they informed even Brahms's presumably abstract compositions. Moreover, such narratives still prevail in Western society, reproduced and transmitted in part by prestigious public texts such as symphonies. Thus we cannot afford to let Absolute Music pass unexamined: even those of us who would like to get beyond issues of gender difference can do so only if we perceive the extent to which culture—even High Culture—traffics in such images and stories.

Far from dismissing this symphony, however, I want to take it seriously as a cultural artifact, an object that tells us something about the values of the historical moment from which it emerged and of subsequent generations who have found meaning in such works—a document that speaks of heroism, adventure, conflict, conquest, the constitution of the self, the threat of the Other, and late-nineteenth-century pessimism. If the Enlightenment wished to maintain that individual will and social contract were mutually compatible, by the late nineteenth century this belief was seen by many as an untenable fairytale.[52] But the formal processes of classical music, which were developed during the Enlightenment, continued, regardless of the composer's intentions, to transmit something of that story. Brahms's Third Symphony presents tonality and sonata in a state of narrative crisis. It takes on and attempts to derail those Enlightenment assumptions, thus giving voice to the increasing self-alienation of the late-nineteenth-century individual (usually assumed to be male) and his feelings of impotence in a totalizing world that always defeats in advance his challenges to its absolute authority.

To be sure, the blame for these feelings of impotence was all too often displaced onto feminine and ethnic Others, as it is in the second-theme subplot of this symphony. But we do not have to agree with Brahms's particular narrative arrangements in order to admire the integrity with which he articulated and grappled with the problems. We need to be able to understand him not as a universal oracle but, rather, as a witness to and participant in a cluster of tensions specific to late-nineteenth-century Austro-Germany.[53] And if we do not want to accept his solutions, we must find other ones—without, however, losing sight of the complex moment in our cultural history about which he testifies so eloquently.

Ironically, perhaps, in this process of excavating the suppressed narrative strategies of composers such as Brahms, we can learn a great deal about the music itself—not just its formal intricacies, but its human and

52. For instance, see again the quotation in the text, from Schoenberg, and in note 25, from Richard Strauss.

53. See Leon Botstein, "Time and Memory: Concert Life, Science, and Music in Brahms's Vienna," in Frisch, ed., *Brahms and His World*, pp. 3–22.

historical dimensions as well. For we have long stifled the violence, the anxieties, the pain, the ideological contradictions of this music so as to exalt it as manifesting pure order. If removing Brahms's Third Symphony from the Yellowstone Park of Absolute Music opens it to critique, this same critique permits it to live and speak again.

CHAPTER 4

Terminal Prestige: The Case of Avant-Garde Music Composition

> Good evening. Welcome to Difficult Listening Hour.
> The spot on your dial for that relentless and
> impenetrable sound of Difficult Music
> [Music . . . Music . . . Music . . .]
> So sit bolt upright in that straight-backed chair,
> button that top button,
> and get set for some difficult music:
> Ooola.
> —Laurie Anderson, "Difficult Listening Hour"[1]

When composer/performance artist Laurie Anderson performs "Difficult Listening Hour" as part of her extended work, *United States*, she satirizes several aspects of the present-day music scene. Perhaps the first thing that strikes one is the sound of her voice. As she

---

1. Laurie Anderson, "Difficult Music," *United States*, part II. Recorded live at the Brooklyn Academy of Music, February 7-10, 1983. Available from Warner Bros Records Inc., 1984. The texts are also published in book form (New York: Harper and Row, Publishers, 1984).

speaks into a vocoder, the pitch of her voice is thrown down into a much lower range so that she no longer sounds like a woman at all. Rather, she evokes the insinuating delivery typical of announcers on classical music stations—the low, velvety, patriarchal voice that soothes and seduces while congratulating the listener on his or her status as a connoisseur of elite music. Ordinarily such "cultured" voices serve to render affirmative and nonthreatening their presentations of high art: kick off your shoes, sit back, and relax to (say) *Death and Transfiguration*. By contrast, Anderson instructs us (with that familiar congenial/sinister voice) to deny ourselves all the usual trappings of physical comfort as she braces us for that most alienating of musical experiences: the encounter with the avant-garde, with Difficult Music.

Lest we miss the lethal accuracy of Anderson's satire of the avant-garde, I would like to turn first to a strikingly parallel formulation from Roger Sessions's essay, "How a 'Difficult' Composer Gets That Way" (1950): "I have sometimes been told that my music is 'difficult' for the listener. There are those who consider this as praise, those who consider it a reproach. For my part I cannot regard it as, in itself, either the one or the other. But so far as it is so, it is the way the music comes, the way it has to come."[2] Sessions (presumably the agent who composes these pieces) is strangely absent from this explanation: it is *the music itself* that can't help it, that demands the kind of complexity that listeners by and large find incomprehensible. While Sessions professes not to care whether the assessment of "difficult" is intended as praise or reproach, the title and tone of the essay make it quite clear that he wears "difficult" as a badge of honor.

Better still, this is Arnold Schoenberg's "How One Becomes Lonely" (1937):

> But as soon as the war was over, there came another wave which procured for me a popularity unsurpassed since. My works were played everywhere and acclaimed in such a manner that I started to doubt the value of my music. This may seem like a joke, but, of course, there is some truth in it. If previously my music had been difficult to understand on account of the peculiarities of my ideas

2. Roger Sessions, "How a 'Difficult' Composer Gets That Way," in *Roger Sessions on Music: Collected Essays*, ed. Edward T. Cone (Princeton: Princeton University Press, 1979), 169.

and the way in which I expressed them, how could it happen that now, all of a sudden, everybody could follow my ideas and like them? Either the music or the audience was worthless.[3]

One of the accusations directed at me maintained that I composed only for my private satisfaction. And this was to become true, but in a different manner from that which was meant. While composing for me had been a pleasure, now it became a duty. I knew I had to fulfil a task: I had to express what was necessary to be expressed and I knew I had the duty of developing my ideas for the sake of progress in music, whether I liked it or not; but I also had to realize that the great majority of the public did not like it.[4]

Here again we find that a piece is worthless if it is not so "difficult" as to be incomprehensible, and that acceptance on the part of the audience indicates failure. Note, too, that what is described in the first of these paragraphs as Schoenberg's own oppositional idiosyncracies ("the peculiarities of my ideas") becomes in the second "the duty of developing my ideas for the sake of progress in music, whether I liked it or not": once again, it is the music itself that demands such sacrifices by community and artist alike.

Finally, here is Milton Babbitt in his "The Composer as Specialist," infamously—though probably appropriately— retitled by the editors of *High Fidelity Magazine* as "Who Cares if You Listen?" (1958):

> I dare suggest that the composer would do himself and his music an immediate and eventual service by total, resolute, and voluntary withdrawal from this public world to one of private performance and electronic media, with its very real possibility of complete elimination of the public and social aspects of musical composition. By so doing, the separation between the domains would be defined beyond any possibility of confusion of categories, and the composer would be free to pursue a private life of professional achievement, as opposed to a public life of unprofessional compromise and exhibitionism.[5]

3. Arnold Schoenberg, "How One Becomes Lonely," in *Style and Idea*, ed. Leonard Stein, trans. Leo Black (Berkeley: University of California Press, 1975), 51.

4. Ibid., 53.

5. Milton Babbitt, "Who Cares if You Listen?," *High Fidelity Magazine* 8, no. 2 (February 1958): 126.

I

Music functions and is valued variously in different human societies: it may participate in ritual, facilitate the physical motions of dance or labor, serve as entertainment, provide pleasure, stand as a manifestation of ideal beauty or order, and so on. Within many societies, there exists a hierarchy among musical discourses that attributes greater prestige to some of these functions than to others.

Perhaps only with the twentieth-century avant-garde, however, has there been a music that has sought to secure prestige precisely by claiming to renounce all possible social functions and values, just as Wagner's Alberich renounced human love in exchange for the Rheingold. Schoenberg was relieved and gratified when audiences again turned against him:[6] it had not been his fault that they had thought temporarily that they liked him—they really had not understood him in the first place. The prestige value of this music, in other words, is inversely correlated with public response and comprehension.

This strange posture was not invented in the twentieth century, of course. It is but the *reductio ad absurdum* of the nineteenth-century notion that music ought to be an autonomous activity, insulated from the contamination of the outside social world.[7] The motivation for this position can be traced in part to the breakdown of the aristocratic patronage system and to the problems the composer faced as a free-lance artist, reluctantly dependent on the bourgeois audience. Within the context of industrial capitalism, two mutually exclusive economies of music developed: that which is measured by popular or commercial success and that which aims for the prestige conferred by official arbiters of taste. Pierre Boulez, for instance, in defending the integrity of avant-garde music against the option of pluralism, states: "The economy is there to remind us, in case we get lost in this bland utopia: there are musics which bring in money and exist for commercial profit; there are musics that cost something whose very concept has nothing to do

---

6. Schoenberg, "How One Becomes Lonely," 51-53.

7. See Janet Wolff, "The Ideology of Autonomous Art," foreword to *Music and Society: The Politics of Composition, Performance and Reception*, ed. Richard Leppert and Susan McClary (Cambridge: Cambridge University Press, 1987), 1-12. See also the introduction by Leppert and McClary in the same volume, xi-xix.

with profit. No liberalism will erase this distinction."[8]

The terms for this double economy are already recognizable in Robert Schumann's criticism in the *Neue Zeitschrift für Musik*, with his castigations of what he perceived as the vulgar virtuosity of Philistine Goliaths such as Liszt and his championing (through his imaginary group of aesthetic underdogs, the "League of David") of the cerebral, organic constructs of composers such as Brahms.[9] If Schumann helped set the groundwork for the Great German Canon that is still the mainstay of the bourgeois concert audience, he also articulated a position that would ultimately lead to the self-alienation of the composer from that same audience.

Schumann's writing is to some extent motivated by the social idealism that marks much of European culture in the first half of the nineteenth century—by a desire to wean the indiscriminate middle-class audience from empty, manipulative display and to instill in it what he regarded as the liberatory, dialectical habits of thought articulated in the complex music of serious composers. Adorno's interpretation of Schoenberg argues compellingly that his private-language games likewise are motivated by the impulse of social critique, even if Schoenberg's solutions end up reinscribing the very contradictions he sought to transcend.[10]

But idealism thwarted easily turns into contempt. In this century (especially following World War II), the "serious" composer has felt beleaguered both by the reified, infinitely repeated classical music repertory and also by the mass media that have provided the previously disenfranchised with modes of "writing" and distribution—namely recording, radio, and television. Thus even though Schoenberg, Boulez, and Babbitt differ enormously from each other in terms of socio-historical context and music style, they at least share the siege mentality that has given rise to the extreme position we have been tracing: they all regard the audience as an irrelevant annoyance whose approval signals artistic failure.

---

8. Michel Foucault and Pierre Boulez, "Contemporary Music and the Public," trans. John Rahn, *Perspectives of New Music* 23 (Fall and Winter 1985): 8.

9. Robert Schumann, *Gesammelte Schriften über Musik und Musiker*, 2 vols. (Leipzig: Breitkopf and Härtel, 1883). Several collections of these essays exist in English translation.

10. Theodor W. Adorno, "Schoenberg," in *Prisms*, trans. Samuel Weber and Shierry Weber (Cambridge: MIT Press, 1981), 147-72.

But no musical repertory can truly be autonomous from social values and networks. If it can be demonstrated that these composers disdain commercial and popular success or even political effect (for instance, contributing to the utopian enlightenment of the masses), this does not mean that they are entirely indifferent to socially conferred reward nor that they can truly exist as artists independent of any social framework.

Quite the contrary—the avant-garde composer requires a discursive community for support every bit as much as does any musician, but the constitution of this community and its values are those of the ivory tower. Babbitt, for instance, writes:

> But how, it may be asked, will [the withdrawal from the audience] secure the means of survival for the composer and his music? One answer is that after all such a private life is what the university provides the scholar and the scientist. It is only proper that the university, which—significantly—has provided so many contemporary composers with their professional training and general education, should provide a home for the "complex," "difficult," and "problematical" in music.[11]
>
> Granting to music the position accorded other arts and sciences promises the sole substantial means of survival for the music I have been describing. Admittedly, if this music is not supported, the whistling repertory of the man in the street will be little affected, the concert-going activity of the conspicuous consumer of musical culture will be little disturbed. But music will cease to evolve, and, in that important sense, will cease to live.[12]

By aligning his music with the intellectual elite—with what he identifies as the autonomous "private life" of scholarship and science (this at the height of the Cold War!)—Babbitt appeals to a separate economy that confers prestige, but that also (it must be added) confers financial support in the form of foundation grants and university professorships.[13]

The rhetoric of survival—the survival not merely of serial or electronic music, but of music *tout court*—runs through virtually all of these

---

11. Babbitt, "Who Cares," 126.
12. Ibid., 127.
13. See Serge Guilbaut, *How New York Stole the Idea of Modern Art: Abstract Expressionism, Freedom, and the Cold War*, trans. Arthur Goldhammer (Chicago: University of Chicago Press, 1983).

documents. We are back to the Fall of Rome with the barbarians at the gates; we are encouraged to perceive the serious composer as an endangered species and to provide public subsidies underwriting music that most proudly announces itself as incomprehensible. Babbitt's rhetoric has achieved its goal: most university music departments support resident composers (though many, including the composers in my own department, find the "Who Cares if You Listen" attitude objectionable); and the small amount of money earmarked by foundations for music commissions is reserved for the kind of "serious" music that Babbitt and his colleagues advocate.

In many ways, however, the academic prestige market is even less stable than the commercial market. Within the commercial market, it is at least clear that (for whatever reasons) a certain number of concert tickets or recordings have been sold. A popular artist may go from adulation to obscurity overnight, but some measure of that short-term fame will have been evident. By contrast, the claim that one's music is valuable precisely because of its autonomy from social function is itself precariously dependent on particular social definitions of prestige.

Those definitions have been shifting for about the last twenty years. Perhaps Philip Glass signalled best the beginning of the end of that era when he described his contact with the Boulez scene in Paris as "a wasteland, dominated by these maniacs, these creeps, who were trying to make everyone write this crazy creepy music."[14] For a while, avant-garde music's glory lay in the illusion that it had transcended social context altogether—that it was too difficult for the uninitiated to comprehend. But proud declarations of uselessness can be—and are now beginning to be—seen as *admissions* of uselessness. The obvious question becomes: "Who cares if you compose?"

Babbitt's claim that music will cease to exist if academic music is not publicly subsidized rests on an extraordinary assumption: that there really is no other music. Boulez's argument acknowledges the existence of other artifacts parading as music, though he summarily dismisses them as commercial. But just who are the barbarians in this picture? What is the whistling repertory of Babbitt's man in the street?

It would undoubtedly come as a surprise to that whistling barbarian

---

14. Quoted in John Rockwell, "Philip Glass," in *All American Music: Composition in the Late Twentieth Century* (New York: Alfred A. Knopf, 1983), 111.

that music is an endangered species, the last remnants of which are being carefully protected in university laboratories. Because to anyone
who has not been trained in terms of the modernist partyline, it is
quite obvious that the twentieth century has witnessed an unparalleled
explosion in musical creativity. But whereas the music of the canon is
the repository of aristocratic and, later, hegemonic middle-class values,
this unruly explosion in the twentieth century is the coming to voice of
American blacks and latinos, of the rural and working classes, of wom-
en, and (in the case of those we might call postmodern) of those whose
training in those creepy institutions did not quite take.

For all the rhetoric of survival and attempts at eliminating other
forms of musical productivity by simply refusing to acknowledge them,
these arguments have had very little influence on the musical world or
ultimately, I would predict, on music history. The music produced under those hothouse conditions has been heard by few and has had next
to no social impact. It is the last hurrah of a historical bloc that lost its
hegemonic grip on culture at the turn of the century.

As the end has become increasingly evident, supporters have occasionally called upon the avant-garde to recast its rhetoric of difficulty-
for-the-sake-of-difficulty. In a sympathetic open letter in *The Village
Voice* in 1984, Gregory Sandow invited Babbitt to explain what his music is about *in human terms*.[15] A couple of years before, Sandow had criticized Paul Griffiths's *Modern Music* for continuing the tradition of writing about Babbitt's music exclusively in terms of the quasi-mathematical models Babbitt himself had formulated.[16] Sandow even sketched
out why he liked Babbitt's music *as music*: as works of art that resonate
with the human condition in the mid-twentieth century, that could (if
explained and presented differently) even come to influence the listener's perception of the world and the self.

But in his recent article "The Unlikely Survival of Serious Music,"
Babbitt argues quite adamantly that he still prefers to hold the hard
line.[17] He continues to exalt difficulty, to denigrate the alternatives as

---

15. Gregory Sandow, "An Open Letter to Milton Babbitt," *The Village Voice*, 5 June
1984, 81-82.

16. Gregory Sandow, "A Fine Madness," *The Village Voice,* 16 March 1982, 73.

17. Milton Babbitt, "The Unlikely Survival of Serious Music," in *Milton Babbitt:
Words about Music*, ed. Stephen Dembski and Joseph N. Straus (Madison: University of
Wisconsin Press, 1987), 163-83.

Terminal Prestige   65

"public circuses of music, the citadels of show biz," to characterize his own position at Princeton as "our little humble house," and to define thus the kind of understanding he expects the listener to have of his music:

> not that kind of understanding which reduces the rich manifestations, the rich ramifications, of musical relationships to some mundane banalities, not some sort of many-one mapping of all those wonderfully rich ramifications of musical relations to some sort of representation of the world out there . . . but understanding of music and understanding of a great many other things by a fairly obvious process.
>
> I'm not going to try to summarize, and I've certainly not offered you anything more than what is a description of one aspect of this crisis in music, with no solution being offered because I know of no solutions. I think therefore you can understand why those of us who dare to presume to attempt to make music as much as it can be rather than as little as one can get away with—music's being under the current egalitarian dispensation—and who've entered the university as our last hope, our only hope, and ergo our best hope, hope only that we're not about to be abandoned.[18]

It seems necessary at this point to confront the inevitable charge of "anti-intellectualism," for the avant-garde has consistently protected its endeavors by hurling this invective at its would-be critics. To deal with the human (i.e., expressive, social, political, etc.) dimension of this music need not qualify as retreating into anti-intellectualism, as Babbitt repeatedly suggests. On the contrary, the orthodox, self-contained analyses that appear in *Perspectives of New Music* (the official Princeton-based journal of the musical avant-garde) require little more than a specialist's grasp of combinatorial techniques; by contrast, explication of this music as historical human artifact would involve not only knowledge of serial principles, but also grounding in critical theory and extensive knowledge of twentieth-century political and cultural history.

We would gain from such discussions of avant-garde music a greater sense of human connectedness—the repertory can be heard as articulating poignantly some of the contradictions human subjects are experiencing at this moment in social and musical history. But at the same time, we would lose the mystique of difficulty, which might well be replaced by the acknowledgement of human vulnerability. What if underneath

---

18. Ibid., 182-83.

all that thorny puzzle-playing and those displays of total control there lurked the fear and confusion (clearly recognizable in all the defensive quotations already cited) that mark most other forms of contemporary culture? In other words, one could, as Sandow does, explain on many levels how this music is meaningful in other than quasi-mathematical terms. But the point is that such an agenda would violate the criteria of prestige the avant-garde has defined for itself. Better to go down with the ship than to admit to meaning. We have here, in other words, a case of terminal prestige.

By retreating from the public ear, avant-garde music has in some important sense silenced itself. Only to the tiny, dwindling community that shares modernist definitions of the economy of prestige does the phenomenon make the slightest bit of sense: thus the urgency with which Babbitt throws himself on the mercy of "the mightiest of fortresses against the overwhelming, outnumbering forces, both within and without the university, of anti-intellectualism, cultural populism, and passing fashion."[19] For if the patronage of the university fails,

> to consign us to the great world out there, however seriously or however viciously, is to consign us to oblivion. Out there in that world outside the university, our music and our words are bound to fall on unheeding or, at least, uncomprehending ears. Don't forget, out there we're an academic, and there's no more sturdy vestige of anti-intellectualism than the fact that the very term academic is conceived to be an immediate, automatic, and ultimate term of derogation.[20]

In the face of this pathetic scenario, only a Simon Legree would press for eviction. Why not extend refuge? What does it matter, after all, if a few people in universities continue to write music intended only for themselves and a few colleagues?

II

The presence of this group of artists in universities has had several perhaps unexpected but nevertheless serious consequences besides the

19. Ibid., 163.
20. Ibid., 180.

presumably benign survival of the avant-garde. First, because the prestige of these composers (and, not coincidentally, their livelihood) is dependent on the transmission of their antisocial assumptions to subsequent generations of musicians, academic music study has gradually and subtly become restricted to the reproduction of this ideology. Most studies of twentieth-century music manage to ignore completely the existence of jazz or rock.[21] In the last decade, the popular success of certain postmodern musicians (Philip Glass, Laurie Anderson, Steve Reich, Meredith Monk) has precipitated a vigorous response on the part of academic composers who are attempting to reassert their greater prestige. Ironically, the "avant-garde" no longer identifies with the new: institutionalized as it is in the universities, it has become the conservative stronghold of the current music scene, for it holds stringently to difficulty and inaccessibility as the principal signs of its integrity and moral superiority.

The power of the avant-garde lobby within higher education is such that both popular and postmodern musics are marked as the enemy, and there is still considerable effort exerted to keep them out of the regular curriculum. American popular music, when taught at all in music departments, is usually presented as part of "ethnomusicology"—the culture of the "primitive," the ethnic "Other": a clear indication of the economy of prestige at work. More often such popular music is left for American Studies or sociology departments to deal with on the grounds that it really isn't music at all.

The treatment of newer forms of experimental music by the academy is perhaps even more puzzling at first glance. Neo-tonal composers such as David Del Tredici or George Rochberg have had to be extremely defensive about moving into terrain that most people in cultural circles would readily recognize as postmodern: the composition of music that draws upon images and gestures of past repertories.[22]

---

21. Very few studies have tried to present pictures of twentieth-century music that do not honor the high art division between "serious" and "popular" musics and that deal with many kinds of musics on an equal footing. See, for instance, Rockwell, *All American Music*, and Billy Bergman and Richard Horn, *Recombinant Do. Re. Mi: Frontiers of the Rock Era* (New York: Quill, 1985).

22. See Rockwell, "David Del Tredici: The Return of Tonality, the Orchestra Audience and the Danger of Success," in *All American Music*, 71-83, and George Rochberg, *The Aesthetics of Survival* (Ann Arbor: University of Michigan Press, 1984). For fuller treatments of the phenomenon of postmodernism in music, see Georgina Born, "Modern

When I gave a talk about Glass at the Walker Art Center in Minneapolis after a local performance of his *The Photographer* a few years ago, I was chastised by colleagues for having broken rank. The fact that Glass has attracted a considerable following is regarded by some as prima facie evidence of his lack of seriousness: in Boulez's terms, one can attain money or prestige, but not both. (One wonders a bit here about Boulez's professional fees and his base of institutional support in contrast to those of a black, working-class musician dreaming of producing a Top 40 hit.) As is the case with popular music, postmodern composers are discussed (if at all) in programs devoted to cultural studies or in sociology.

Self-proclaimed "serious" musicians often make a great deal of the artificial demand for popular music created by means of advertisement and image manipulation. But an interesting irony here is that much of the university curriculum is devoted to a usually futile attempt at instilling a very artificial demand for academic music in young musicians. We shame students for their incorrigible tastes in popular music and browbeat them with abstract analytical devices in hopes that they will be influenced by, say, stochasticism and will maintain the illusion that this kind of abstract experimentation informs the future of music. For everything rests on *some* community continuing to think that this audienceless music is prestigious: otherwise, prestige simply evaporates. It begins to feel a bit like the make-believe worlds of *The Glass Menagerie* or *The Wizard of Oz*, in which enormous amounts of energy are poured into keeping a fantasy of denial alive.

Since students (despite all our efforts) have access to the outside world, most of them are aware of these other musics on some level—even if they have bought into the academic prestige racket. But the influence of the avant-garde on universities has been more extensive than simply its attempted blackout of the competition. Because avant-garde music's prestige relies on its having transcended social use or signification, its advocates have naturalized this position and have projected it back onto the whole of the European canon. It has become heretical to address the signifying practices of, say, Bach or Beethoven for at least two interrelated reasons: first, their present-day prestige in the modernist academy hinges on the abstract patterns of order in their music rather than on signification;[23] second, the argument that their music likewise is nothing but abstract constructs in turn helps legitimize the avant-garde. The more obviously socially grounded sources of meaning in the music are bracketed and declared irrelevant, if not causes for embarrassment.

In the introduction to *Beyond Orpheus* (which boasts a foreword by Milton Babbitt), David Epstein writes:

> The fact that Schoenberg's approach to music had at its roots concepts from studies of tonal music from Bach through Brahms is of more than purely historical interest. It suggests that serial concepts themselves—as explicit viewpoints and procedures—may yield insights into similar viewpoints and concepts of earlier, tonal music.[24]

He goes on to set the limits of his project, first to the classic-romantic tradition from Haydn through Brahms and then to the German-Viennese tradition ("the most seminal [sic] body of music that emerged during this broad period"[25]). Finally, he says that his studies "are confined to absolute music":

> Our understanding of structure is still sufficiently unclear that it seems advisable to avoid the further complications of words and/ or dramatic action—implicit or explicit—and their relations to structure, or their effects upon it.
>
> A . . . final limitation: the matter of "expression" in music is beyond the confines of these studies. . . .The limitation here is a practical one alone; the question of what music "says" is vast and complex and demands separate study. . . .[Music's] materials are the means as well as the medium of its communication. Indeed, in attacking this problem it is first of all essential clearly to perceive, to recognize, and to comprehend what it is we hear, free of external or misconstrued meanings.[26]

---

23. For an account of traditional classical music as socially grounded discourse, see Susan McClary, "The Blasphemy of Talking Politics during Bach Year," in Leppert and McClary, eds., *Music and Society*, 13-62. For a response to this position that argues in favor of autonomy, see Nicolas Temperley, "Tonality and the Bourgeoisie," *Musical Times*, December 1987, 685-87.

24. David Epstein, *Beyond Orpheus: Studies in Musical Structure* (Cambridge: MIT Press, 1979), 5.

25. Ibid., 11.

26. Ibid.

He then proceeds to explicate Beethoven's *Eroica* as the efficient genetic unfolding of two pitch cells: a triad and a chromatic cluster. Epstein claims to leave open the possibility of dealing with "expression" for other studies. However, if one has really accepted his structuralist account as, in fact, what we are able "to perceive, to recognize and to comprehend, free of external or misconstrued meanings," then one would be rather hard pressed to come up with anything in the realm of meaning other than the implicit one that meaning inheres in such efficient genetic unfolding of two pitch cells.

Now this tends to be the way many music theorists—the individuals responsible for teaching students how music operates—are currently being trained, especially in the most prestigious departments on the east coast which also house the most prestigious composers. Any music that is worth bothering with (i.e., that is sufficiently prestigious to warrant attention) *was always already difficult music*. Only the ignorant—Babbitt's whistling man on the street—could have responded to music as though it had anything to do with desire, with experience of the body, with social meaning. I recently spoke with a prominent music theorist who thought I was very bizarre to suggest that Debussy's *Prélude à l'après-midi d'un faune* might be erotic.

These strange priorities also infect anyone who tries to play the prestige game with other musics. Recently jazz has been introduced into elite musicological and music theory circles, but it is permitted a place in the limelight only if its social context is scraped off and its artifacts are demonstrated to be every bit as complex and difficult to hear as serial music.[27]

---

27. See, for instance, Wynton Marsalis, "What Jazz Is—And Isn't," *New York Times*, 31 July 1988. Marsalis advocates rule-bound, difficult-music accounts of jazz in an attempt at elevating it to the status of high art. To be sure, the old mystified stories Marsalis argues against, in which jazz artists spring full-blown as the unmediated products of their miserable social conditions, are detestable; and, indeed, jazz must be acknowledged as the most significant musical genre to emerge in the first half of this century. But such revisions in jazz reception cannot afford to erase the oppressive social conditions that shaped the discursive practices of jazz, within and in spite of which its extraordinary practitioners worked to develop their complex art. One of the better attempts at dealing structurally with jazz is Lewis Porter, "John Coltrane's *A Love Supreme*: Jazz Improvisation as Composition," *Journal of the American Musicological Society* 38 (Fall 1985): 593-621. While Porter concentrates on formal matters in this article, he also states in his introduction: "Furthermore, Coltrane required more than abstract interest from his music. He used it to express profound spiritual moods. While retaining the goal of intellectual involvement, he sought to communicate nobility, dignity, peace, or even violent outrage" (593).

In his bid to be granted prestige by serious music circles, Anthony Braxton, for instance, has written program notes every bit as abstruse as those of any electronic composer, and, as Ronald Radano has demonstrated recently, Braxton has paid the price of being held as somewhat suspect by both avant-garde and jazz communities.[28] As long as Philip Glass was straddling the fence between the academy and the audience, he wrote program notes that explained in excruciating, abstract detail how his compositional constructs operated.[29] However, now that he has attracted an audience and has become comfortable about composing for people, his writing is extremely accessible and deals precisely with those matters Epstein fastidiously bracketed: the relationships among music, words, movement, and drama.[30]

III

Thus far I have presented my argument as though the only "enemies" against which the avant-garde has pitted itself were popular culture, postmodernism, and—in general—socially grounded signification. But a position has begun to emerge recently among cultural critics and historians that recognizes High Modernism as having been also strongly motivated as a repudiation of femininity. In "Mass Culture as Woman: Modernism's Other," Andreas Huyssen traces the retreat of "serious artists" from the contaminating qualities regarded as "feminine" (e.g., expression, pleasure, community) to that refuge of masculine prestige which is modernism.[31]

This repudiation can, of course, be understood as targeting not actual women, but rather what is feared to be the "feminine" dimension of the male artist—or even the practice of art itself, which is often classified as an "effeminate" activity: it is perhaps more obviously a product of homophobia and anxiety over masculine identity than of misogyny

---

28. See Ronald Radano, "Braxton's Reputation," *Musical Quarterly* 72, no. 4 (1986): 503-22.

29. See Glass's formal "Notes on *Einstein on the Beach*," included with the recording (CBS Records, 1976).

30. Philip Glass, *Music by Philip Glass* (New York: Harper and Row, Publishers, 1987).

31. Andreas Huyssen, "Mass Culture as Woman: Modernism's Other," in *Studies in Entertainment: Critical Approaches to Mass Culture*, ed. Tania Modleski (Bloomington: Indiana University Press, 1986), 189-207.

per se. However, Eve Kosofsky Sedgwick's *Between Men: English Literature and Male Homosocial Desire* reveals the ways in which masculine anxiety, homophobia, and misogyny form a tight system of pathological
interdependencies in Western culture.[32]

Thus, not surprisingly, the retreat to the boy's club of modernism
was not simply a matter of sloughing off soft, sentimental, "feminine"
qualities for the sake of more difficult, "hard-core" criteria. Littering
the path of this retreat are countless mutilated representations of wom-
en—the self-conscious defacements of what had previously been up-
held in art and society as "the beautiful"—which have been protected
from critical scrutiny by modernist appeals to autonomy, objectivity,
abstraction, artistic liberation from bourgeois constraints, stylistic innovation, and progress. The debate raging at the moment over Picasso—the visual artist of modernism's early avant-garde—is finally forcing the issue of the misogyny that marks the content of much of his
art:[33] the content which has often made me flinch from his paintings as
though they were images of criminal atrocities, but which I (as a "cultured" individual) could protest only at the risk of exposing my Philistine ignorance or "feminine self-interest." Susan Gubar and Sandra
Gilbert are presently analyzing these issues with respect to modernist
literature,[34] and Klaus Theweleit's *Male Fantasies* documents (perhaps
far more thoroughly and enthusiastically than one would wish) the links
between German modernist culture and its backlash against the
masses, Jews, and female contamination—all of which turn out to blur

---

32. Eve Kosofsky Sedgwick, *Between Men: English Literature and Male Homosocial Desire*
(New York: Columbia University Press, 1985).

33. This controversy has become very public with the publication of Arianna
Stassinopoulos Huffington's sensationalist *Picasso: Creator and Destroyer* (New York: Simon and Schuster, 1988). Huffington concentrates too heavily on Picasso's personality
in accounting for his imagery, thus making this dimension of his art seem exclusively a
product of his own psychopathology. However, similar readings of modernist art—
which emphasize discursive conventions rather than individual idiosyncracy—had already been available. See, for instance, Carol Duncan, "Virility and Domination in
Early Twentieth-Century Vanguard Painting," in *Feminism and Art History: Questioning the
Litany*, ed. Norma Broude and Mary D. Garrard (New York: Harper and Row, Publishers, 1982), 293-314. See also Leo Steinberg, "The Philosophical Brothel" (1972), reprinted in *October* 44 (Spring 1988): 7-74, for a pioneering discussion of the sexual politics articulated in Picasso's paintings, especially *Les Demoiselles d'Avignon*, and of how
formalist criticism serves to mask such issues.

34. Sandra M. Gilbert and Susan Gubar, "Tradition and the Female Talent," in *The Poetics of Gender*, ed. Nancy K. Miller (New York: Columbia University Press, 1986), 183-207.

into a single threatening "red tide."[35]

Feminism has been very late in making an appearance in music criticism, and this is largely owing to the success composers, musicologists, and theorists have had in maintaining the illusion that music is an entirely autonomous realm. But the gender politics which assign prestige to "masculinity" mark the emergence of modernism in music as much as in the other arts. Witness, for instance, Charles Ives's pathetic insistence on his own exaggerated masculinity and his homophobic renunciations of predecessors and contemporaries (including friends and colleagues);[36] Adorno's hysteria over the "castrating" effect of mass culture;[37] the on-going resistance to admitting women into the field of composition; formalist attitudes of revulsion in the face of expression (i.e., effeminate romantic excess); and, of course, the celebration of the unyielding, "hard-core" procedures of academic music apparent in virtually all the quotations above.

---

35. Klaus Theweleit, *Male Fantasies* (Minneapolis: University of Minnesota Press, 1987), vol. 1, *Women, Floods, Bodies, History*, trans. Stephen Conway.

36. This obsession is manifest in almost every document Ives wrote. For instance: "Well, I'll say two things here: 1) That nice professor of music is a musical lily-pad [one of Ives's several derogatory terms for insufficiently masculine men]. He never took a chance at himself, or took one coming or going. 2) His opinion is based on something he'd probably never heard, seen, or experienced. He knows little of how these things sounded when they came 'blam' off a real man's chest. It was the *way* this music was sung that made them big or little—and I had the chance of hearing them big. . . . a man's experience of men!" (*Charles Ives' Memos*, ed. John Kirkpatrick [New York: W.W. Norton and Co., Inc., 1972], 131). For a psychoanalytic discussion of this and other aspects of Ives's character, see Maynard Solomon, "Charles Ives: Some Questions of Veracity," *Journal of the American Musicological Society* 40 (Fall 1987): 466-69. Solomon writes: "he [Ives] is both drawn to music and repelled by it. 'As a boy [I was] partially ashamed of music,' he recalled—'an entirely wrong attitude but it was strong—most boys in American country towns, I think felt the same. . . . And there may be something in it. Hasn't music always been too much an emasculated art?' To ward off such feelings, Ives would eradicate the traces of the 'soft-bodied' and the 'decadent' in his own work, perhaps employing the techniques of modernism to conceal the atmospheric, lyrical, yielding strata which often underlie his first ideas" (467).

37. "The aim of jazz is the mechanical reproduction of a regressive moment, a castration symbolism. 'Give up your masculinity, let yourself be castrated,' the eunuchlike sound of the jazz band both mocks and proclaims, 'and you will be rewarded, accepted into a fraternity which shares the mystery of impotence with you, a mystery revealed at the moment of the initiation rite' " (Adorno, "Perennial Fashion-Jazz," *Prisms*, 129). Robert Walser has written extensively about Adorno's castration tropes in his writings on jazz in "Retooling with Adorno: Bach's Ontology and the Critique of Jazz" (unpublished paper, 1988).

It is symptomatic of the modernist attitude that the most widely used undergraduate textbook on twentieth-century music, Joseph Machlis's *Introduction to Contemporary Music*, is heavily illustrated with famous modernist paintings of female nudes (giving the book a deceptively interdisciplinary and "liberal" appearance) with captions that exclusively address formal considerations. The reader is offered these images for delectation, yet at the same time is bullied into regarding them not as the bodies of women, but rather as innovative ways of construing line, color, and form.[38]

Much of the avant-garde musical repertory similarly both flaunts and conceals its misogynist content. On the one hand, modern music claims autonomy—demands that one focus on the combinatoriality that gave rise to the technical choices in the compositional process. But, on the other hand, the violations of musical continuity and of traditional bourgeois expectations that characterize modern music are coupled (far more often than can be purely coincidental) with texts that feature the slashing of women. In other words, the most prestigious games in town (both the battle for artistic license—which regards the violation of social taboos as evidence of the artist's liberation—and also the battle for stylistic innovation) tend to be played out over female bodies. In piece after piece, some of the most extraordinarily vicious subject matter is trotted out unproblematically in the interest of artistic freedom and progressive experimentation with sound: see, for instance, Hindemith's *Murderer, Hope of Women*, Berg's *Lulu*, or Morton Subotnick's "The Last Dream of the Beast" from *The Double Life of Amphibians* (in which a beast dies during his "final love moment" with a blind, armless woman). The masculine prestige of modernism both protects and encourages such content.

To be sure, one wants to avoid reducing the accomplishments and complexity of modernist culture to simple expressions of misogyny. There are ways of interpreting the literary and musical content of

---

38. For instance, the caption for a reproduction of Modigliani's *Nude, 1917* (painting of a sleeping woman in full frontal nudity) appears as follows: "The economy and purity of style which characterizes Webern's music may also be found in the elegant simplicity of Modigliani's work. A supreme draftsman, his elongated figures are linear yet sculptural in the impression of roundness and volume which they convey" (Joseph Machlis, *Introduction to Contemporary Music*, 2nd ed. [New York: W.W. Norton and Co., Inc., 1979], 272). See also the captions for Manet's *Le Déjeuner sur l'herbe*, 84, and Gauguin's *The Spirit of the Dead Watching*, 17.

many modernist pieces that would argue for the artists's sensitivity with respect to the female victims represented. To take what may be an especially sympathetic instance, Babbitt's *Philomel* (its Ovid-inspired text by poet John Hollander was commissioned by the composer) can be read quite straightforwardly as an *anti-rape* statement, in which the victim is transformed into the nightingale to sing about both her suffering and her transcendence.[39] The violent distortions and ruptures of the singer's voice in the piece bear witness to Philomel's rape and to the fact that her tongue has been ripped out. The shattered fragmentation of her human voice (which is reassembled serially into "a million Philomels"), her change from material being into music ("I am becoming my own song," "As if a new self/Could be founded on sound"), and her forging of triumph from violence ("Suffering is redeemed in song") all serve to acknowledge the horror of the crime and yet the possibility of survival. They also resonate strongly with many of the modernist problematics (the anxiety over decentered identity; the reconstitution of subjectivity through complex recombinant procedures; the retreat from the material world into pure, autonomous sound) discussed throughout this paper. Anyone who has seen Bethany Beardslee perform this piece live—who has watched her as her own shredded, electronically transformed voice is thrown back at her from loud speakers—can attest to the great theatrical and emotional power of *Philomel*.

Yet Babbitt's writings discourage one from attempting to unpack his composition along these lines. Indeed, he warns us not to get hung up trying to map the events of pieces onto the "mundane banalities" of real life, for it is in this objective, unsentimental attitude that prestige resides. But if content is really not at issue, why such horrendous subject matter? Many of my female students have trouble listening passively to *Philomel* as yet another instance of serial and electronic manipulation: they have difficulty achieving the kind of objective intellectual attitude that would permit them to focus on considerations of sterile compositional technique. For to most women, rape and mutilation are not mundane banalities that can conveniently be bracketed for the sake of art: especially an art that attaches prestige to the celebration of such violations.

---

39. Babbitt, *Philomel* (1964), recorded by Bethany Beardslee on AR, in collaboration with Deutsche Grammophon.

IV

I am not arguing that composers should cease to be housed in the university. But I am no longer willing to be party to the transmission of the "prestige" ideology—especially when that means abdicating responsibility for problematic content or silencing the kind of music criticism that aims to understand music in its social context. I am especially concerned that we cease blocking the teaching of popular and postmodern music, for these are the musics (for better or for worse) most influential in shaping lives, subjectivities, values, and behaviors at the present moment. The avant-garde must be studied as well, to be sure, though not exclusively in accordance with the autonomous terms it has tried to enforce. All music—even that of the most austere avant-garde composer—is inevitably tied to the social conditions within which it is produced, transmitted, preserved, or forgotten. Among the conditions that need to be explored by the historian striving to make sense of the mid-century avant-garde are the formation of the university-as-discursive-community and also the economy of prestige upon which this music has depended for survival.

As we have seen, "survival" is a key word that appears over and over again in these documents—and even in compositions such as *Philomel*. Recent titles of essays concerning new music continue to announce this doomsday orientation: see, for instance, Rochberg's *The Aesthetics of Survival* or John Struble's article in a recent *Minnesota Composers Forum Newsletter*, "Survival Strategies for the End of the Millenium," a critique that resonates with Sandow's and my own.[40] As Babbitt (once again) puts it:

> But I am not prepared to admit that anything less than, anything other than, sheer *survival* is at stake, and that such *survival* seems unlikely when the conditions necessary for that *survival* are so seriously threatened. These conditions are the corporal *survival* of the composer in his [sic] role as a composer, then the *survival* of his [sic] creations in some kind of a communicable, permanent, and readable form, and finally, perhaps above all, the *survival* of the university in a role which universities seem less and less able or willing to assume [my emphasis].[41]

---

40. Rochberg, *Aesthetics of Survival*, and John Warthen Struble, "Survival Strategies for the End of the Millenium," *Minnesota Composers Forum Newsletter* (April 1988): 5-7.
41. Babbitt, "The Unlikely Survival," 163.

Threatened with extinction, the serious composers who have confined their interests to their own careers and to the perpetuation of a music they themselves refuse to justify continue to hurl invectives at the "rubbish" of popular culture.

But the avant-garde holds no monopoly on survival rhetoric. In that popular rubbish, one can also find survival as a central theme—though not the survival of the avant-garde for the avant-garde's sake. As I was writing this paper, I found that whenever I typed the word "survival," I began humming a tune that was very popular in 1987: "System of Survival" by Earth, Wind and Fire.[42] Moreover, this strange, oblique intrusion from the dreaded popular realm was far from annoying: the fortuitous presence of this song in my own cultural memory had the effect of undercutting the gravity of all those doomsday arguments, since each appearance of the "S-word" triggered not the intended gloom but rather the infectious rhythms of Earth, Wind and Fire. Finally, it proved impossible to remain too morose over predictions that "music will cease to evolve . . . will cease to live" in the face of such an irrepressible counterexample. Thus, while the connection between Babbitt's appeals and this *particular* popular song is admittedly rather tenuous, I wish to close by examining "System of Survival" and the ways in which it presents quite a different raison-d'être for music—a different economy of prestige—than that articulated by the avant-garde.

To begin, let us address forthrightly the issue of money: yes, the recording is commercial. I bought it at a store, as did some hundred-thousands of others. Yes, it aimed to be, and succeeded in being, a popular hit: for those traditionally excluded from the marketplace, the achievement of a commercial hit accrues extraordinary prestige (though valuing commercial success is not the same, as Boulez suggests, as producing music solely for profit—only someone in very comfortable conditions could thus disparage economic gain). Without question, the song is multiply-mediated through musical discursive practices, electronic technology, marketing decisions, and the recording industry's distribution patterns: no more than any other piece of music is it the pure representation of authentic experience. However, its message—namely, that music can provide sustenance to those who somehow

---

42. Skylark, "System of Survival," on Earth, Wind and Fire: *Touch the World*, produced by Maurice White for Kalimba Productions (CBS, Inc., 1987).

continue living in the face of institutional contempt and neglect, that the joyful engagement of one's body in dance can be the oppositional moment in lives almost overwhelmed by poverty and racism, that the survival of a people and its values can occur through the medium of music—is extremely eloquent up against the *"musique, c'est moi"* harangues of our last descendents of musical absolutism.

To be sure, its many levels of complex mediation are rendered as transparent as possible to facilitate communication—if one is familiar with the discursive norms of fusion, one can respond strongly to it on first hearing without a special seminar in advanced analytical methods. But this is not to say that "System of Survival" is simplistic or conventional in its construction, for musical excellence and imagination are demanded as much within this economy of prestige as within the modernist academy.

"System" begins with a montage of snippets from recent political news broadcasts, which provides the political backdrop up against which the song articulates its exuberant opposition. The song itself is marked by the intricate communality of performer participation characteristic of Afro-based music, a communality that stands in stark contrast to the alienated composerly control of Schoenberg or Babbitt. The virtuosity of the singers—especially the highly controlled, apparently effortless falsetto of Phillip Bailey—might qualify as "extended vocal technique" if presented in the context of experimental music. Survival itself is enacted musically in this song through the pungent dissonances that refuse to resolve, the continual resistance to harmonic closure (which would spell rhythmic death), and the effusive sax solo which dramatizes the noise of defiance. Moreover, the bassline enters only after a considerable length of time—the group sings of survival, even in the absence of the secure harmonic foundation that ordinarily grounds such music, yet the rhythm track is constantly present to inform the dance and to guarantee continuity.

As is the case with most Afro-American music, the rhythm itself constitutes the most compelling yet most complex component of the song. I would argue that the skill required to achieve and maintain a groove with the degree of vitality characteristic of "System of Survival" is far greater than that which goes into the production of the self-denying, "difficult" rhythms derived by externally generated means. One need only observe professional classical performers attempting to capture anything approaching "swing" (forget about funk!) to appreciate how *truly* difficult this apparently immediate music is.

Of course, "System of Survival" also requires tremendous technological sophistication for its execution. A recent volume of *Roland Users Group* (a trade magazine for musicians who use electronic gear in music production) presents a daunting "difficult music" description of the electronic devices and computer hook-ups necessary for duplicating Earth, Wind and Fire's studio compositions in live performance. The following is actually one of the simpler passages in the article, but it is included here as an example because it pertains to the song under discussion:

> For the song "System of Survival," McKnight [the keyboard technician and programmer] had to take the opening dialogue ("The biggest unanswered question is, Where is the money?"), a cash register sound, the vocoder encoded "System of Survival" and the words "Everybody Get Up" and sample them into the S-550 so that Phillip Bailey could play the various parts from different pads on his Roland Octapad (PAD-8). For their older material, McKnight had to recreate the analog sounds that were in vogue when the original albums came out. "The JX-10 is perfect for those types of analog sounds," Mike says. "One of the things I do is take the ROM presets from the JX-10, copy them to one of the blank slots and just go nuts."[43]

The exhaustive discussions of the mechanical details of execution in this article strongly resemble many program notes for "serious music." For anyone who continues to demand complex, jargon-laden analyses for the appreciation of music, such an article might serve to confer [modernist] prestige on the group: if you want difficulty, you've got it. At the very least, one can no longer pretend that their music is "natural" or "primitive," given their sophisticated control of state-of-the-art electronics, which shames much of the homemade sounding electronic music produced through university laboratories. However, no one in Earth, Wind and Fire or in popular music criticism would mistake such technical descriptions for the content of the pieces. The electronic nuts-and-bolts dimension of the music is highlighted in this

---

43. Tony Thomas, "The Sound of Earth Wind & Fire," *Roland Users Group* 6, no. 2 (1988): 49.

trade journal partly for the sake of other professionals (who indeed are interested in how certain effects were achieved) and partly for the sake of advertising Roland equipment. But this mechanical display is not the intended reception of the song—this is not what it means, and this is not the principal way it strives to acquire prestige.

The kind of intelligence that shines through this song is of quite a different order: it is an intelligence that accepts the experiences of the body—dance, sexuality, feelings of depression and elation—as integral parts of human knowledge that accrue value precisely as they are shared and confirmed publicly. "System of Survival" is, in other words, a song that gives no credence whatsoever to the mind/body split or to the defensive autonomy that infects so much of Western music, especially that of the avant-garde which fetishizes intellectual work for its own sake. At the same time, it is an extremely *smart* piece: musically, socially, politically. It draws upon and celebrates forms of sedimented cultural memory that have miraculously survived a history of extraordinary oppression and that threaten to persist indefinitely—even if not acknowledged within the academy.[44]

Adorno and others (including the composers cited above) have regarded modernism and mass culture as inseparable opponents in the same cultural world and have consequently bestowed prestige upon the avant-garde as a defense against the degradation of mass culture. But at this moment in the history of the dichotomy, the terms of the debate have shifted so much as to make earlier definitions and moral positions no longer credible. This is in part owing to the avant-garde's deliberate self-reification from the inside—most explicitly displayed by the "who cares if you listen" attitude. But it is probably the case that the avant-garde was always fighting a losing battle. If one reflects on the demographic shifts of this century, the emergence of energetic, previously disenfranchised voices to displace a moribund, elite status quo is not at all surprising. Nor, I think, is it cause for lamentation. Debates over culture now tend to concentrate on the various models articulated and distributed through the popular media. Some of these models are worthy of celebration, others seem highly problematic with

---

44. The concept of sedimented cultural memory in popular music is being most eloquently developed by George Lipsitz. See, for instance, his "Cruising around the Historical Bloc—Postmodernism and Popular Music in East Los Angeles," *Cultural Critique* 5 (Winter 1986-1987): 157-78.

respect to images of violence and misogyny—though none more so than much of what the avant-garde has consistently dished up. In any case, the avant-garde is scarcely even a factor in cultural discussions now, except in a few sealed rooms in the academy.

This is not to suggest that there are no longer standards or that anything goes. Rather, there are now many alternate sites of prestige-formation—all with their own stringent criteria—that correspond to communities hitherto excluded from the musical elite's crumbling economy of prestige.[45] In describing "System of Survival" above, I discussed some of the qualities that have made Earth, Wind and Fire an extremely influential group during the last fifteen years. The fact that this song reaches a wide audience, that it speaks in a comprehensible language of exuberant hope in the face of hardship is regarded not as evidence of selling out, but as a mark of success in an economy of prestige that rewards communication and political effectiveness. Earth, Wind and Fire cares if you listen.

> Everybody get up
> Do your dance
> Stay alive. . . .
>
> —Earth, Wind & Fire, "System of Survival"

---

45. For an excellent discussion of "popular culture" as a site of class struggle, see Stuart Hall, "Notes on Deconstructing 'The Popular,'" *People's History and Socialist Theory*, ed. Raphael Samuel (London: Routledge and Kegan Paul, 1981), 227-39.

Part Two

Gender and Sexuality

CHAPTER 5

A Material Girl in Bluebeard's Castle

In the grisly fairy tale of Bluebeard, the new bride, Judith, is given keys to all the chambers in her husband's castle with strict instructions that she is never to unlock the seventh door. Upon opening the first six doors, Judith discovers those aspects of Bluebeard that he wishes to claim—his wealth, strength, political dominion, love of beauty, and so on. Bluebeard offers a form of symbolic self-representation in these chambers: he reveals himself as the man he wants Judith to adore. But throughout her explorations— behind every door—she finds traces of something else, something hidden that sustains all she is actually shown, something that resonates with the old tales of horror she has heard. And in opening the final door she comes face to face with that unspoken, forbidden factor.

In some versions of the Bluebeard story, what Judith discovers behind the forbidden door are the mangled bodies of previous wives who likewise went too far in their quests for knowledge. Bruno Bettelheim assumes that she and Bluebeard's other hapless victims must have committed carnal transgressions of the magnitude of adultery in order to be deserving of such dreadful ends.[1] But it is also possible to interpret the story rather more literally: Judith and her sisters were simply not satisfied with the contradictory versions of reality given to them by a self-serving patriarch, and they aspired to discover the truth behind the façade.

The version of the story set by Bartók in his opera *Bluebeard's Castle* tends to support such a reading. Judith discovers not only Bluebeard's crimes but also his pain, his fears, his vulnerability. For this she is not executed but rather is exiled into darkness along with the other still-living wives, away from the light of his presence. The last speech is uttered by Bluebeard, whose tragedy this opera finally is. He is forever being betrayed by women who do not take him at his word, who insist on knowing the truth: the truth of his human rather than transcendental status. And he cannot live with someone who thus understands his mortality and materiality. Thus he is fated always to live alone, yet safe with his delusions of control and magnanimity—at least so long as no one tampers with that seventh door.

As a woman in musicology, I find myself thinking about Judith quite often—especially now, as I begin asking new kinds of questions about music with the aid of feminist critical theory. Like Judith, I have been granted access by my mentors to an astonishing cultural legacy: musical repertories from all of history and the entire globe, repertories of extraordinary beauty, power, and formal sophistication. It might be argued that I ought to be grateful, since there has really only been one stipulation in the bargain—namely, that I never ask what any of it means, that I content myself with structural analysis and empirical research.

Unfortunately that is a stipulation I have never been able to accept. For, to put it simply, I began my career with the desire to understand music. I suppose this must also be true of most other music professionals. Yet what I desired to understand about music has always been quite different from what I have been able to find out in the authorized accounts transmitted in classrooms, textbooks, or musicological research. I was drawn to music because it is the most compelling cultural form I know. I wanted evidence that the overwhelming responses I experience with music are not just in my own head, but rather are shared.

I entered musicology because I believed that it would be dedicated (at least in part) to explaining how music manages to create such effects. I soon discovered, however, that musicology fastidiously declares issues of musical signification to be off-limits to those engaged in legitimate scholarship. It has seized disciplinary control over the study of music and has prohibited the asking of even the most fundamental questions concerning meaning. Something terribly important is being hidden away by the profession, and I have always wanted to know why.

Just as Bartók's Judith discovers telltale traces of blood on the treasures in the first six chambers (even though Bluebeard adamantly refuses to corroborate her observations), so I have always detected in music much more than I was given license to mention. To be sure, music's beauty is often overwhelming, its formal order magisterial. But the structures graphed by theorists and the beauty celebrated by aestheticians are often stained with such things as violence, misogyny, and racism. And perhaps more disturbing still to those who would present music as autonomous and invulnerable, it also frequently betrays fear—fear of women, fear of the body.

It is finally feminism that has allowed me to understand both why the discipline wishes these to be nonissues, and also why they need to be moved to the very center of inquiries about music. Thus I see feminist criticism as the key to the forbidden door: the door that has prevented me from really being able to understand even that to which I was granted free access. To the extent that I live in a world that is shaped profoundly by musical discourses, I find it necessary to begin exploring whatever lies behind the last door, despite—but also because of—disciplinary prohibitions.

1

When feminist criticism emerged in literary studies and art history in the early 1970s, many women musicologists such as myself looked on from the sidelines with interest and considerable envy. But at the time, there were formidable obstacles preventing us from bringing those same questions to bear on music. Some of these obstacles were, of course, institutional: the discipline within which we were located was still male-dominated, and most of us were loath to jeopardize the tentative toeholds we had been granted.

Nevertheless, a few of the more courageous women began to excavate the history of women composers and musicians. And even though these projects were initially regarded with scorn, they have uncovered an enormous amount of rich material: the long-forgotten music of such extraordinary figures as Hildegard von Bingen, Barbara Strozzi, Clara Schumann, Ethel Smyth, Ruth Crawford Seeger, and many others is being made widely available for the first time.[2] Likewise the history of women performers, teachers, patrons, and civic promoters of music has been brought to light, as well as the history of the conditions that consistently have served to exclude or marginalize female participation in music.[3] As a result of this research, our understanding of music institutions and of specific people engaged in musical activities has been substantially altered.

Yet until very recently, there was virtually no public evidence (that is, in official conferences or refereed journals) of feminist music criticism. I am painfully aware that this volume—one of the first books of feminist criticism in the discipline of musicology—is being assembled at a time when cynical voices in many other fields are beginning to declare feminism to be passé. It almost seems that musicology managed miraculously to pass directly from pre- to postfeminism without ever having to change—or even examine—its ways.

Indeed, one of the few signs that the discipline has even noticed the challenges feminism has presented elsewhere is that musicology appears to be in the vanguard of antifeminist backlash. Norton's specially reprinted collections from *The New Grove Dictionary of Music* (the principal disciplinary reference tool since its publication in 1980) are entitled "Masters of Italian Opera," "Masters of the Second Viennese School," and so forth, perhaps taking their cue from the successful "Masters of the Universe" series on Saturday morning television.[4] There is also a prestigious new series of books and videos on the various periods of music history from Prentice-Hall called *Man and Music*, and still another new set of videos from Brown called *The Music of Man*.[5] It is impossible to believe that anyone who has lived through the last fifteen years can have failed to observe that terms such as "master" or "man" have been so thoroughly problematized that they are no longer in general circulation in most academic communities. If musicology has lagged behind in admitting feminist criticism to its list of legitimate areas of inquiry, it is way ahead of the game in its efforts to expunge all evidence that feminism ever existed.

Yet all is not hopeless in the field. Two conferences occurred in spring 1988—one at Carleton University in Ottawa and the other at Dartmouth—in which feminist criticism was highlighted.[6] Moreover, the program committee for the 1988 meeting of the American Musicological Society actively solicited and accepted several papers in feminist criticism, and the 1989 meeting offered the first discipline-sponsored workshop in feminist theory and music.[7] The most important consequence of these conferences is that they have enabled those of us who have been trying to develop and perform feminist criticism in isolation to become aware of others who have been grappling with similar issues and methods. Feminist critics of music, encouraged by the knowledge that a community does in fact exist, are currently organizing at least two anthologies of feminist music criticism.[8] Furthermore, several professional journals have begun to request feminist articles.

Most of the essays in this collection predate this recent surge of interest in feminist criticism, and they are virtually all marked by a sense of disciplinary solitude. They are often as concerned with questioning why there has been no feminist criticism in musicology as in exploring what one might do with such methods if one were allowed to pursue them. To that extent, these pieces bear the traces of a moment in the history of the discipline, and I have decided not to erase them. It is heartening, however, to know that it may no longer be necessary to concentrate quite so heavily on the issue of whether or not there ought to be a feminist criticism of music. That battle seems perhaps to have been won, at least in sympathetic quarters. Whether or not the mainstream of the discipline approves, feminist music criticism does exist. However, the more interesting questions remain: What would a feminist criticism of music look like? What issues would it raise, and how would it ground its arguments theoretically?

2

The roads taken by other feminist music critics have been similar to mine in some respects, very different in others. All of us are heavily indebted to the feminist theory and criticism that has taken shape in disciplines such as literary or film studies over the last twenty years. This work makes it possible for us to proceed without having to define *ex nihilo* such basic concepts as gender, sexuality, and femininity. We are able to benefit from the debates that have enlivened feminist scholarship and to arrive at our tasks with a sophisticated theoretical apparatus already at hand.

Nevertheless, it is not possible to transfer the key questions of other branches of feminist study directly to music, for music has its own constraints and capabilities that have to be identified and queried. As pioneering feminist critics of music, we have developed rather different agendas and procedures reflecting our intellectual training, our musical tastes, and the particular versions of feminist theory to which we have been exposed. At this moment, I cannot begin to give any kind of overview of the rich variety of approaches that appear to be emerging within the discipline. Therefore, I will only address my own work—the issues I have found most compelling and the circuitous methodological route that has permitted me at last to feel I can responsibly address some of the concerns of feminist criticism in music.

The questions I have pursued in my feminist work cluster into five groups. They are not always entirely separable; in fact, most of the essays in this collection engage with all five sets of questions in some way or other. Nevertheless, it seems useful to outline them at this point for the sake of setting out a provisional methodology.

1. *Musical constructions of gender and sexuality*. This is probably the most obvious aspect of feminist music criticism. In most dramatic music, there are both female and male characters, and usually (though not always) the musical utterances of characters are inflected on the basis of gender. Beginning with the rise of opera in the seventeenth century, composers worked painstakingly to develop a musical semiotics of gender: a set of conventions for constructing "masculinity" or "femininity" in music. The codes marking gender difference in music are informed by the prevalent attitudes of their time. But they also themselves participate in social formation, inasmuch as individuals learn how to be gendered beings through their interactions with

cultural discourses such as music. Moreover, music does not just passively reflect society; it also serves as a public forum within which various models of gender organization (along with many other aspects of social life) are asserted, adopted, contested, and negotiated.[9]

These codes change over time—the "meaning" of femininity was not the same in the eighteenth century as in the late nineteenth, and musical characterizations differ accordingly. To be sure, many aspects of the codes are strikingly resilient and have been transmitted in ways that are quite recognizable up to the present: for instance, musical representations of masculine bravura or feminine seductiveness in Indiana Jones movies resemble in many respects those in Cavalli's seventeenth-century operas. But if some aspects of the codes prove stable, it is not because music is a "universal language," but rather because certain social attitudes concerning gender have remained relatively constant throughout that stretch of history. Thus the musical semiotics of gender can tell us much about the actual music (why *these* particular pitches and rhythms as opposed to others). And studying music from this vantage point can also provide insights into social history itself, insofar as repertories testify eloquently to the various models of gender organization (whether hegemonic or resistant) available at any given moment.

Music is also very often concerned with the arousing and channeling of desire, with mapping patterns through the medium of sound that resemble those of sexuality. While the topic of sexuality is rarely broached in musicology, it has received considerable attention in recent literary and film theory. As a result of this investigation, much of what had been assumed as biological and immutable in human sexual experience has been radically reinterpreted as socially constructed. Stephen Heath sums up the revisionist position well when he writes:

> There is no such thing as sexuality; what we have experienced
> and are experiencing is the fabrication of a "sexuality," the
> construction of something called "sexuality" through a set of
> representations—images, discourses, ways of picturing and
> describing—that propose to confirm, that make up this sexuality
> to which we are then referred and held in our lives, a whole
> sexual fix precisely.[10]

As reasonably clear instances of "fabrications of sexuality" in music, we might consider the prelude to Wagner's *Tristan und Isolde*, Debussy's *Prélude à l'après-midi d'un faune*, or Madonna and Prince's recent duet, "This Is Not a Love Song." Even though such pieces may seem extraordinarily erotic—as though they have managed to bypass cultural mediation to resonate di-

rectly with one's own most private experiences—they are in fact constructions. Indeed, the three tunes just mentioned present very different notions
of what qualifies as "the erotic" (most listeners would tend to identify one
or two of them as representations of desire and to reject the others as incomprehensible or as rubbish). Because such pieces influence and even constitute
the ways listeners experience and define some of their own most intimate
feelings, they participate actively in the social organization of sexuality.
Thus, one of the principal tasks of feminist music criticism would be to examine the semiotics of desire, arousal, and sexual pleasure that circulate in
the public sphere through music.

2. *Gendered aspects of traditional music theory*. The images of gender or sexuality addressed above are usually rhetorically generated; that is, they are produced by more or less deliberate choices by composers, along with other
dramatic and affective strategies of particular pieces. This is not to say that
every element of every construction of, say, "femininity" must be entirely
intentional, for these codes often are taken to be "natural"—when composing music for a female character, a composer may automatically choose
traits such as softness or passivity, without really examining the premises
for such choices. But still, the fact that gender or arousal is at stake is reasonably clear.

My next two groups of issues are less obvious but are far more crucial to
the enterprise of feminist criticism, especially given that musical institutions
like to claim that music for the most part is not concerned with mundane
issues such as gender or sexuality. Most of the essays in this collection seek
to identify and analyze the ways in which music is shaped by constructions
of gender and sexuality—not only in the context of opera or programmatic
music, but also in some of the most fundamental of musical concepts and
procedures.

For instance, music theorists and analysts quite frequently betray an explicit reliance on metaphors of gender ("masculinity" vs. "femininity") and
sexuality in their formulations. The most venerable of these—because it has
its roots in traditional poetics—involves the classification of cadence-types
or endings according to gender. The 1970 edition of the *Harvard Dictionary
of Music*, for instance, includes the following entry:

> **Masculine, feminine cadence**. A cadence or ending is called
> "masculine" if the final chord of a phrase or section occurs on
> the strong beat and "feminine" if it is postponed to fall on a
> weak beat. The masculine ending must be considered the normal
> one, while the feminine is preferred in more romantic styles.[11]

This standard definition makes it clear that the designations "masculine" and "feminine" are far from arbitrary. The two are differentiated on the basis of relative strength, with the binary opposition masculine/feminine mapped onto strong/weak. Moreover, this particular definition betrays other important mappings: if the masculine version is ("must be considered") normal, then the implication is that the feminine is abnormal. This is so self-evident that the author, Willi Apel, does not think it worthy of explicit mention. Instead, he engages yet another binary: if the feminine is preferred in "more romantic styles," then the masculine must be (and, of course, *is*) identified with the more objective, more rational of musical discourses. In two brief sentences focused ostensibly upon a technical feature of musical rhythm, Apel has managed to engage some of the most prominent of Western beliefs concerning sexual difference. The "feminine" is weak, abnormal, and subjective; the "masculine" strong, normal, and objective. And this whole metaphysical apparatus is brought to bear and reinscribed in the conventional terminology used to distinguish mere cadence-types.

It might be argued that no one takes the gender implications of that music-theoretical distinction literally anymore, that these are but the reified traces of dead metaphors. But how, then, is one to explain theorist Edward T. Cone's strangely moralistic discussion of the performance "problem" of feminine cadences in Chopin?

> Even in the case of movements that seem to remain *incorrigibly feminine*, some differentiation can still be made. In the case of Chopin's Polonaise in A major, for example, a clever emphasis on one of the concealed cross-rhythms at the cadence can make the last chord sound, *if not precisely masculine*, at least like a strong tonic postponed by a suspension of the entire dominant.[12] (my emphasis)

Cone is concerned here with "butching up" a polonaise, a genre that is distinguished from other dances by what Apel labels as "feminine" endings. Now, Chopin's polonaise is a remarkably vigorous, even aggressive composition, and I would argue that it is precisely the emphatic stress on the second ("weak") beat that gives the polonaise its arrogant swagger, its quality of always being poised to plunge into the next phrase. But given that this technicality is conventionally classified as "feminine," Cone feels the need to rescue the piece from its "incorrigibly feminine" endings. He can do so only by violating Chopin's score and in effect weakening the rhythmic integrity of the composition. But at least then the cadences won't sound "feminine" (even if the resulting performance concludes with what sounds like a failure of nerve, a normalization that "corrects" the groove's idiosyncrasy).

Cone's nervousness over the "feminine" cast of this ending suggests that more must be at stake than mere "weakness." Apel defines "feminine endings" as those in which the final sonority is postponed beyond the downbeat. But we could also describe such events in terms of *excess*—a feminine ending then becomes one that refuses the hegemonic control of the barline. Such a description alters the assumed power relationship between the two types, but it begins to account for the anxiety that marks Cone's discussion of these "incorrigible" moments. For his proposed solution attempts to manipulate the music so that it *sounds* as though its "feminine" components are complying with the law of the downbeat. If gendered terminology can lead astray Edward Cone, who is unquestionably one of the finest theorists and analysts in the field, then it certainly needs to be interrogated seriously.

Nor are masculine/feminine distinctions limited to cadences. The eighteenth-century theorist Georg Andreas Sorge explained the hierarchical distinction between major and minor triads in terms he regarded as both natural and God-given—the respective powers of male and female:

> Just as in the universe there has always been created a creature more splendid and perfect than the others of God, we observe exactly this also in musical harmony. Thus we find after the major triad another, the minor triad, which is indeed not as complete as the first, but also lovely and pleasant to hear. The first can be likened to the male, the second to the female sex. And just as it was not good that the man (Adam) was alone, thus it was not good that we had no other harmony than the major triad; for how far would we come in a progression from one chord to the other? . . . And just as the womanly sex without the man would be quite bad, thus with music it would be in a bad way if we had no other harmony than that which the minor triad gives. We could not once make an authentic cadence.[13]

Because it might be objected that Sorge is a figure too far in the past to be relevant to anything today, I offer here a later mapping of major/minor onto masculine/feminine in Arnold Schoenberg's *Theory of Harmony*: "The dualism presented by major and minor has the power of a symbol suggesting high forms of order: it reminds us of male and female and delimits the spheres of expression according to attraction and repulsion. . . . The will of nature is supposedly fulfilled in them."[14] This passage occurs in a context in which Schoenberg has just defined the major mode as "natural," minor as "unnatural," and his mapping of masculine/feminine onto modes follows the same logic as Apel's, Cone's, or Sorge's. Yet even though he bears witness to this received wisdom, it is important to note that Schoenberg (unlike most others) also calls it into question and strives to resist it. For *Theory of Harmony* is in large measure an attempt at imagining a musical language that could eschew binarisms, whether they be major/minor, consonance/dissonance, or masculine/feminine. After the passage just quoted, he goes on to express his longing for a musical discourse that is, like the angels, "asexual"—a discourse no longer driven by the attraction and repulsion between major and minor. His success at locating the metaphysical categories (such as gender) that structure musical thought and his struggle to transcend them make his an exceptionally brave, if tortured, intellectual agenda.[15]

Sometimes sexual metaphors are used to structure musical concepts without reference to gender distinctions. For instance, the theoretical writings of Heinrich Schenker often draw explicitly on analogies to sexuality. Throughout *Harmony*, he describes musical logic—whether motivic or harmonic—as the product of "procreative urges":

> Obviously, every tone is possessed of the same inherent urge to procreate infinite generations of overtones. Also this urge has its analogy in animal life; in fact, it appears to be in no way inferior to the procreative urge of a living being. This fact again reveals to us the biological aspect of music, as we have emphasized it already in our consideration of the procreative urge of the motif.[16]

One explanation for such a passage is that Schenker simply found this particular verbal trope of sexuality handy for describing the dynamic quality of pure, abstract tonal music. Yet the nineteenth-century repertory he is accounting for was itself generated in accordance with a crucial set of biological, "organic" metaphors.[17] Schenker's tropes spring from and participate in the same cultural milieu that gave rise to the music he analyzes. They merely testify in words to the processes that likewise underwrite the musical imagery.[18]

3. *Gender and sexuality in musical narrative.* Not only do gender and sexuality inform our "abstract" theories, but music itself often relies heavily upon the metaphorical simulation of sexual activity for its effects. I will argue throughout this volume that tonality itself—with its process of instilling expectations and subsequently withholding promised fulfillment until climax—is the principal musical means during the period from 1600 to 1900 for arousing and channeling desire. Even without texts or programs, tonal compositions ranging from Bach organ fugues to Brahms symphonies whip

up torrents of libidinal energy that are variously thwarted or permitted to gush. The principal theorist to acknowledge and examine this aspect of tonality systematically is Schenker: the purpose of his quasi-mathematical diagrams (in addition to his explicitly sexualized tropes) is to chart simultaneously the principal background mechanisms through which tonal compositions arouse desire and the surface strategies that postpone gratification. Through rigorous theoretical language and graphing techniques, he plots out the mechanisms whereby certain simulations of sexual desire and release are constituted within the musical medium.

His mystical statements of intention to the contrary, Schenker's graphs can be read as demonstrating in fully material terms that the excitement achieved in these pieces is *constructed* (is not, in other words, the tracing of the German *Geist* or Schopenhauer's Will). And any medium—whether music or fiction—that regularly achieves such powerful effects needs to be studied carefully, not only technically (as in Schenker), but also ideologically. What are the assumptions that fuel these mechanisms so often called by the neutral name of "tension and release" (or by Schoenberg's explicitly sexualized "attraction and repulsion")? Whose models of subjectivity are they, given that they are not universal? To what ends are they employed in compositions? What is it, in other words, that the listener is being invited to desire and why?

Similarly, the various narrative paradigms that crystallized during the history of tonality contain many features that are in effect gendered. This is especially clear in the case of sonata-allegro procedure, for which there even used to be the custom of calling the opening theme "masculine" and the subsidiary theme "feminine." To be sure, this custom extends back only as far as the mid-nineteenth century. Theorist A. B. Marx seems to have been the first to use this terminology, in his *Die Lehre von der musikalischen Komposition* (1845):

> The second theme, on the other hand, serves as contrast to the first, energetic statement, though dependent on and determined by it. It is of a more tender nature, flexibly rather than emphatically constructed—in a way, the feminine as opposed to the preceding masculine. In this sense each of the two themes is different, and only together do they form something of a higher, more perfect order.[19]

The convention of designating themes as masculine and feminine was still common in pedagogy and criticism of the 1960s, although musicology by and large has since repudiated it—especially its application to sonata movements that antedate Marx's formulation.

14   Introduction

However, the fact that themes were not referred to in this fashion until
the mid-nineteenth century does not mean that earlier pieces are free of gendered marking: the themes of many an eighteenth-century sonata movement draw upon the semiotics of "masculinity" and "femininity" as they
were constructed on the operatic stage, and thus they are readily recognizable in their respective positions within the musical narratives. To identify
them as such is not to commit an anachronism: the gender connotations of
the opening "Mannheim rockets" or "hammerstrokes" and the sighing second themes in Stamitz symphonies are so obvious as to border on the car-
toonish, even if neither he nor his contemporaries actually called the respective themes "masculine" and "feminine."

Nor is it merely a matter of deciding whether or not to label themes as
"masculine" and "feminine" in what are otherwise neutral narrative processes. Drawing on the structuralist work of the Soviet narratologists
Vladimir Propp and Jurij Lotman, Teresa de Lauretis has demonstrated with
respect to traditional Western narrative that:

> The hero must be male, regardless of the gender of the text-
> image, because the obstacle, whatever its personification, is
> morphologically female. . . . The hero, the mythical subject, is
> constructed as human being and as male; he is the active
> principle of culture, the establisher of distinction, the creator of
> differences. Female is what is not susceptible to transformation,
> to life or death; she (it) is an element of plot-space, a topos, a
> resistance, matrix and matter.[20]

Furthermore, as de Lauretis and other narratologists have demonstrated, regardless of the manifest content of particular stories, these two functions interact in accordance with a schema already established in advance—the masculine protagonist makes contact with but must eventually subjugate
(domesticate or purge) the designated [feminine] Other in order for identity
to be consolidated, for the sake of satisfactory narrative closure.[21]

This narrative schema is played out quite explicitly in opera.[22] But it is
no less crucial to the formal conventions of "absolute" music: indeed,
large-scale instrumental music was not feasible before the development of
tonality, which draws on the model of these powerful narrative paradigms.
In its early manifestations in the late seventeenth and early eighteenth centuries, the course of a movement traces the trajectory from a home base
(tonic), to the conquest of two or three other keys, and a return to tonic for
closure. Schoenberg, for one, was explicitly aware of the narrative demands
of tonality:

> For [our forebears] the comedy concluded with marriage, the
> tragedy with expiation or retribution, and the musical work "in
> the same key." Hence, for them the choice of scale brought the
> obligation to treat the first tone of that scale as the fundamental,
> and to present it as Alpha and Omega of all that took place in
> the work, as the patriarchal ruler over the domain defined by its
> might and its will: its coat of arms was displayed at the most
> conspicuous points, especially at the beginning and ending. And
> thus they had a possibility for closing that in effect resembled a
> necessity.[23]

Thus, the Other may be merely an alien terrain through which the monologic subject of the piece passes (and secures cadentially) on its narrative adventure away from and back to tonic. However, the sonata procedure that
comes to characterize instrumental music of the eighteenth and nineteenth
centuries features a more polarized version of that basic narrative paradigm.
In sonata, the principal key/theme clearly occupies the narrative position of
masculine protagonist; and while the less dynamic second key/theme is *necessary* to the sonata or tonal plot (without this foil or obstacle, there is no
story), it serves the narrative function of the feminine Other. Moreover, satisfactory resolution—the ending always generically guaranteed in advance
by tonality and sonata procedure—demands the containment of whatever is
semiotically or structurally marked as "feminine," whether a second theme
or simply a non-tonic key area.

In his entry on sonata form in *The New Grove Dictionary*, James Webster
is careful to mention the terminology of "masculine" and "feminine"
themes only when he gets to the repertories and theories contemporary with
A. B. Marx. Yet in his opening structuralist account of the sonata paradigm,
he writes the following:

> The second group in the exposition presents important material
> and closes with a sense of finality, but it is not in the tonic. This
> dichotomy creates a "large-scale dissonance" that must be
> resolved. The "sonata principle" requires that the most
> important ideas and the strongest cadential passages from the
> second group reappear in the recapitulation, but now transposed
> to the tonic. The subtle tension of stating important material in
> another key is thus "grounded," and the movement can end.[24]

As abstractly worded as this statement may be, it reveals that the sonata and
likewise tonality are manifestations of the same cultural paradigms as the
mythic narratives schematically laid bare by Propp, Lotman, and de Lauretis. They depend upon the logic that assumes as natural the tonic protago-

nist's necessary subjugation ("resolution," "grounding") of whatever "large-scale dissonance" occupies the second narrative position.

Of course, the Other need not always be interpreted strictly as female—it can be anything that stands as an obstacle or threat to identity and that must, consequently, be purged or brought under submission for the sake of narrative closure. Robert Walser has suggested that the terms of tonality and sonata might be dealt with productively through methods expounded by cultural theorist Fredric Jameson in his analysis of *Jaws*. Jameson argues that the reason the film had such a powerful impact on the public imagination is that its narrative tensions could be interpreted in terms of a wide range of social tensions. In other words, the shark is not necessarily just a shark, but is available as a stand-in for any force (untamable nature, commodity culture, or even—in keeping with classical narratology and the shark's grotesque resonance with traditional iconography—the vagina dentata) that threatens the individual spectator. The danger posed by that "Other" is raised to an excruciating level and then resolved, granting at least momentarily the experience of utopia.[25]

Likewise, the paradigms of tonality and sonata have proved effective and resilient in part because their tensions may be read in a variety of ways. I do not want to reduce two centuries of music to an inflexible formula. Yet the heavily gendered legacy of these paradigms cannot be ignored either. In literature, even if the second narrative slot is not occupied by a woman character, whoever or whatever fills the fatal slot is understood on some fundamental cultural level as a "feminine" Other: to conquer an enemy is to "emasculate" him as he is purged or domesticated. Similarly, chromaticism, which enriches tonal music but which must finally be resolved to the triad for the sake of closure, takes on the cultural cast of "femininity."[26] The "feminine" never gets the last word within this context: in the world of traditional narrative, there are no feminine endings.

These are features of composition and reception that are taken for granted as aspects of autonomous musical practice, as simply "the way music goes." They are usually not considered actively by composers, are not "intended." They simply are the elements that structure his or her musical (and social) world. Yet they are perhaps the most powerful aspects of musical discourses, for they operate below the level of deliberate signification and are thus usually reproduced and transmitted without conscious intervention. They are the habits of cultural thought that guarantee the effectiveness of the music—that allow it to "make sense"—while they remain largely invisible and apparently immutable. Most of the essays that follow concentrate heavily on these conventions, for it is through these deeply engrained habits that gender and sexuality are most effectively — and most problematically — organized in music.

4. *Music as a gendered discourse.* Throughout its history in the West, music has been an activity fought over bitterly in terms of gender identity. The charge that musicians or devotees of music are "effeminate" goes back as far as recorded documentation about music, and music's association with the body (in dance or for sensuous pleasure) and with subjectivity has led to its being relegated in many historical periods to what was understood as a "feminine" realm. Male musicians have retaliated in a number of ways: by defining music as the most ideal (that is, the least physical) of the arts; by insisting emphatically on its "rational" dimension; by laying claim to such presumably masculine virtues as objectivity, universality, and transcendence; by prohibiting actual female participation altogether.[27]

If the whole enterprise of musical activity is always already fraught with gender-related anxieties, then feminist critique provides a most fruitful way of approaching some of the anomalies that characterize musical institutions. Some of this work is already available. For instance, Linda Austern and Richard Leppert have demonstrated that one reason the English have produced so little music is that they — more than their German or French neighbors — have long associated music strongly with effeminacy.[28] The English effectively prevented themselves as a society from participating in musical culture, except as connoisseurs and consumers, and Anglo-Americans have followed suit. As Maynard Solomon writes of Charles Ives:

> [Ives] is both drawn to music and repelled by it. "As a boy [I was] partially ashamed of music," he recalled — "an entirely wrong attitude but it was strong — most boys in American country towns, I think felt the same. . . . And there may be something in it. Hasn't music always been too much an emasculated art?" To ward off such feelings, Ives would eradicate the traces of the "soft-bodied" and the "decadent" in his own work, perhaps employing the techniques of modernism to conceal the atmospheric, lyrical, yielding strata which often underlie his first ideas.[29]

Likewise, the polemics that proliferate around moments of stylistic change are frequently expressed in terms of sexual identity. Early Romanticism, for instance, was in part an appropriation of what the Enlightenment had defined as subjective, "feminine" imagination, and the battles over the relative status of structure and ornamental excess, between rationality and irrationality in early nineteenth-century music were understood as battles over the proper constitution of the bourgeois male. Similarly, the turn from late Romantic hysteria and popular music to the refuge of rigorous Modernism is a gesture partly informed by the desire to remasculinize the discourse.[30]

Even the strange absence of criticism in the discipline may well be related to gender-related anxieties. A particularly poignant manifestation of such anxiety in action is Schumann's celebrated essay on Schubert's Symphony in C Major. The essay carefully establishes a dichotomy between the masculine example of Beethoven and the more sensitive, romantic Schubert; and throughout the essay, Schumann shields himself from Schubert's influence by calling upon Beethoven's "virile power" at moments when he is about to be overwhelmed by Schubert's charm. At the end, after he has succumbed to a rhapsodic account of what it is like to listen to the Schubert symphony, he seeks to recover his masculine authority by abruptly informing the reader: "I once found on Beethoven's grave a steel pen, which ever since I have reverently preserved. I never use it save on festive occasions like this one; may inspiration have flowed from it."[31]

Despite the deeply conflicted nature of Schumann's essay, he does risk revealing himself in print as a man given to strong emotional impulses, perhaps even as one who is as attracted to the seductive grace of Schubert as to the virility of Beethoven. Most music analysts today do not have the nerve to follow Schumann's example—and thus, for instance, the recent outcropping of daunting structuralist graphs used to distance and objectify the passionate music of nineteenth-century opera. For if to admit that music moves one affectively means that one may not be a proper masculine subject, then one's study of music will systematically avoid addressing such issues.[32]

The consequences of such anxieties are enormous—for individual musicians, for the history of music as it unfolds, and for the questions and methods admitted in the course of its academic study by theorists and musicologists. Even though these are extremely difficult and delicate issues, they have to be addressed seriously if music criticism of any sort is to proceed beyond surface details.

5. *Discursive strategies of women musicians.* There have been many obstacles preventing women from participating fully (or, at some moments in history, from participating *at all*) in musical production. Most of these have been institutional: women have been denied the necessary training and professional connections, and they have been assumed to be incapable of sustained creative activity. The music that has been composed by women (despite all odds) has often been received in terms of the essentialist stereotypes ascribed to women by masculine culture: it is repeatedly condemned as

pretty yet trivial or—in the event that it does not conform to standards of feminine propriety—as aggressive and unbefitting a woman.[33]

Within the last two generations, it has finally become possible for relatively large numbers of women to enter seriously into training as composers. Composers such as Joan Tower, Ellen Taaffe Zwilich, Thea Musgrave, Pauline Oliveros, Libby Larsen, and many others have successfully challenged the pernicious and absurd stereotypes that have plagued women for centuries. They prove that women can and do compose first-rate music, and they are fully capable of deploying the entire range of the semiotic code they have inherited—not merely the sweet and passive, but the forceful aspects as well. Many superb women composers insist on making their gender identities a nonissue, precisely because there still remain so many essentialist assumptions about what music by women "ought" to sound like.[34] That they are determined to demonstrate that they too can write MUSIC (as opposed to "women's music") is understandable. Moreover, it is an important political position and strategy, given the history of women's marginalization in this domain.

However, I am no longer sure what MUSIC is. Given that my first three sets of questions are concerned with laying bare the kinds of gender/power relationships already inscribed in many of the presumably value-free procedures of Western music, it becomes difficult to stash that information and simply analyze MUSIC, even if is produced by women. For even though women have managed to enter into composition as professionals, they still face the problem of how to participate without unwittingly reproducing the ideologies that inform various levels of those discourses.

Thus I am especially drawn to women artists who, like myself, are involved with examining the premises of inherited conventions, with calling them into question, with attempting to reassemble them in ways that make a difference inside the discourse itself, with envisioning narrative structures with feminine endings. The work of these women broadens the range of possible musics, as it comments both on the assumptions of more traditional procedures and on the problematic position of a woman artist attempting to create new meanings within old media.

3

How does one go about grounding arguments of the sort these questions would require? The intellectual obstacles that have impeded the development of feminist music criticism are rooted in the assumptions that have long informed and sustained academic musicology in general. It is important to remember that there really is very little resembling criticism *of any sort* in musicology.[35] For many complex reasons, music has been and continues to be almost entirely exempted from criticism as it is practiced within other humanities disciplines: even those scholars who produce work resembling that of the old-fashioned New Criticism of literary studies still count as radicals in musicology. In other words, feminist criticism has not necessarily been singled out for exclusion—to a very large extent, its absence is merely symptomatic of the way the discipline as a whole is organized. Consequently, it is not a matter of simply adding feminist issues to a well-established tradition of critical inquiry: before we can address the questions concerning gender and sexuality discussed above, it is necessary to construct an entire theory of musical signification.

It is an intimidating task to try to unlock a medium that has been so securely sequestered for so long. There does exist, of course, a sophisticated discipline of music theory, but this discipline by and large restricts the questions it acknowledges to matters of formal process as they appear in musical scores. To be sure, the contributions of music theory are indispensable to feminist or any other kind of criticism. Far from setting the score aside and concentrating on extramusical issues, my work is always concerned with explaining how it is that certain images or responses are invoked by particular musical details. But as long as we approach questions of signification *exclusively* from a formalist point of view, we will continue to conclude that it is impossible to get from chords, pitch-class sets, or structures to any other kind of human or social meaning. Indeed, the more deeply entrenched we become in strictly formal explanations, the further away we are from admitting even the *possibility* of other sorts of readings, gendered or otherwise.[36]

Yet music need not be—and has not always been—defined exclusively in terms of its atomic bits. In the seventeenth and eighteenth centuries, for instance, music was typically discussed in terms of affect and rhetoric. Monteverdi wrote letters in which he openly recounted his invention of various kinds of musical signs: ways of representing madness, military ferocity, and so forth. Bach's contemporaries Mattheson and Heinechen wrote lexicons cataloguing affective devices, and composition teachers of the time instructed students on how to produce passionate responses in listeners through rhetorical manipulation. And even though the musicians of the nineteenth century sought to give the illusion that they wrote by inspiration and with disdain for social codes, the documents produced by composers and critics testify to a belief in the emotional power of music, even if they wished that power to be regarded as unmediated and transcendent.

Likewise today most people who have not been trained as academic musicians (who have not had these responses shamed out of them) believe that music signifies—that it can sound happy, sad, sexy, funky, silly, "American," religious, or whatever. Oblivious to the skepticism of music theorists, they listen to music in order to dance, weep, relax, or get romantic. Composers of music for movies and advertisements consistently stake their commercial success on the public's pragmatic knowledge of musical signification—the skill with which John Williams, for instance, manipulates the semiotic codes of the late nineteenth-century symphony in *E. T.* or *Star Wars* is breathtaking. As Galileo is reported to have uttered after he was forced to recant his theories before the Inquisition, "And yet it moves." It doesn't really matter that academic disciplines have tried to insist that music is only music, that it cannot mean anything else. In the social world, music achieves these effects all the time.

Like any social discourse, music is meaningful precisely insofar as at least some people believe that it is and act in accordance with that belief. Meaning is not inherent in music, but neither is it in language: both are activities that are kept afloat only because communities of people invest in them, agree collectively that their signs serve as valid currency. Music is always dependent on the conferring of social meaning—as ethnomusicologists have long recognized, the study of signification in music cannot be undertaken in isolation from the human contexts that create, transmit, and respond to it.

However, this is not to suggest that music is nothing but an epiphenomenon that can be explained by way of social determinism. Music and other discourses do not simply reflect a social reality that exists immutably on the outside; rather, social reality itself is constituted within such discursive practices. It is in accordance with the terms provided by language, film, advertising, ritual, or music that individuals are socialized: take on gendered identities, learn ranges of proper behaviors, structure their perceptions and even their experiences. But it is also within the arena of these discourses that alternative models of organizing the social world are submitted and negotiated. This is where the ongoing work of social formation occurs.

Most members of a given social group succeed in internalizing the norms of their chosen music and are quite sophisticated in their abilities to respond appropriately. They know how to detect even minor stylistic infractions and to respond variously with delight or indignation, depending on how they identify themselves with respect to the style at hand. Yet very few people are able to explain verbally to themselves *how* music affects them.

I am interested first and foremost in accounting for the ways music creates such effects. On the informal level, my work has always been strongly influenced by my own perceptions: the perceptions of a member of this society who has been immersed in musical "high culture" for forty-four years and professionally engaged with it for over thirty. I always begin by trusting that my own reactions to music are legitimate. By "legitimate," I do not mean to suggest that my readings are identical with everyone else's or are always in line with some standard version of what a piece is taken to mean. Indeed, the essays that follow diverge quite consistently from received wisdom.

But neither would I accept the charge that my readings are "subjective" in the sense that they reflect only my own quirks. Rather, I take my reactions to be in large part socially constituted — the products of lifelong contact with music and other cultural media. Thus I regard them as invaluable firsthand evidence of how music can influence listeners affectively, how it can even participate in social formation.[37] If most other music professionals are reticent about confessing music's effects on them, I can at least draw upon my own experiences. Miraculously, thirty years in the profession have not succeeded in destroying my faith in that fundamental storehouse of knowledge.

But if I pay close attention to my own reactions (instead of shoving them to the side for the sake of an objectivity that will always prevent in advance the examination of music's impact), I am also very much concerned with the reactions of others. Since I want to be able to argue that music is socially grounded, I have conducted extensive field research (or, if you prefer, "reality testing") over the past twenty years. That is, I play pieces of music for and invite responses from many other kinds of people: inner-city high school students, professional string quartets, groups of senior citizens, musicology graduate students, literary critics, New Music America audiences. What I have learned is that nonprofessionals are extremely adept at comprehending and even explaining affect and rhetoric in music, while professionals tend to divide into two camps: those who think they are above such nonsense and who supply formal explanations for everything they hear, and those who have not surrendered their conviction that music signifies but who have kept this carefully hidden, rather as though they were adults who still believe in the Tooth Fairy.

But mere gut reactions (my own or those of others) are only the beginning — although without these, it would be impossible to discuss signification at all. My primary concerns are first with justifying those reactions through musical analysis, social history, critical theory, and much else. But once the validity of such reactions is established, I am further concerned with interrogating them: it is important to ascertain that Bizet does, in fact, make our pulses race at the end of *Carmen*, sweeping us ineluctably forward to Carmen's murder, and also to account for how he accomplishes this musically. But then it also becomes necessary to explain why — in Bizet's day and in ours — such a musico-narrative device has been regarded as so compelling and even pleasurable. And the question then arises of whose interest is being served by the public deployment of such devices.

My eclectic tool kit of methods has been assembled over the years out of whatever has seemed handy in unlocking particular musical problems, for music continually (and unpredictably) draws upon everything available in the social domain. In the various essays I have written—feminist or otherwise—I have made use of whatever helped me to make sense of the composition at hand. Thus I have no sense of loyalty to any particular orthodox position. To be sure, my various theoretical acquisitions invite me to make connections that would not be available to those who refuse categorically to look beyond the literal details of the musical notation. But my focus is invariably on the music itself—or, to be more precise, on the music as it operates within human contexts.

4

By far the most difficult aspect of music to explain is its uncanny ability to make us experience our bodies in accordance with its gestures and rhythms. Yet this aspect is also what makes music so compelling. If music were not able thus to move us, the human race would not have bothered creating any of it for formalists to dissect, for musicologists to catalogue, or for sociologists to classify. In a recent song, the Doobie Brothers sing, "Music is a doctor, makes you feel like you want to." And Raymond Williams too has stressed the impact of music on the body, albeit in rather more academic terms:

> We are only beginning to investigate this on any scientific basis, but it seems clear from what we already know that rhythm is a way of transmitting a description of experience, in such a way that the experience is re-created in the person receiving it, not merely as an "abstraction" or an emotion but as a physical effect on the organism—on the blood, on the breathing, on the physical patterns of the brain. . . . it is more than a metaphor; it is a physical experience as real as any other.[38]

Although Williams claims that what he is talking about is "more than a metaphor," the best way of grounding what he is addressing is philosopher Mark Johnson's recent epistemological work on metaphor. Johnson argues convincingly that metaphors are not mere figures of speech (which seems to be how Williams construes the word), but rather are the fundamental means through which we as embodied beings orient ourselves with respect to the world and thereby structure our discourses and our cognition. His work

constructs a theory of knowledge that avoids the splits between mind and
body, between objectivity and subjectivity that have plagued Western
thought since Plato:

> The body has been ignored by Objectivism because it has been
> thought to introduce subjective elements alleged to be irrelevant
> to the objective nature of meaning. The body has been ignored
> because reason has been thought to be abstract and transcendent,
> that is, not tied to any of the bodily aspects of human
> understanding. The body has been ignored because it seems to
> have no role in our reasoning about abstract subject matters.
>   Contrary to Objectivism, I focus on the indispensability of
> embodied human understanding for meaning and rationality.
> "Understanding" is here regarded as populated with just those
> kinds of imaginative structures that emerge from our experience
> as bodily organisms functioning in interaction with an
> environment. Our understanding involves many preconceptual
> and nonpropositional structures of experience that can be
> metaphorically projected and propositionally elaborated to
> constitute our network of meanings.
>   My purpose is not only to argue that the body is "in" the
> mind (i.e., *that* these imaginative structures of understanding are
> crucial to meaning and reason) but also to explore *how* the body
> is in the mind—how it is possible, and necessary, after all, for
> abstract meaning, and for reason and imagination, to have a
> bodily basis.
>   *Any adequate account of meaning and rationality must give a central*
> *place to embodied and imaginative structures of understanding by which*
> *we grasp our world.*[39]

I have quoted Johnson at length because I believe that it is only by adopt-
ing such an epistemological framework that we can begin accounting for
how music does what it does. Certainly the acoustician's sound waves in
and of themselves cannot be demonstrated to possess any of the powers
Williams describes. Yet when those sound waves are assembled in such a
way as to resemble physical gestures, we as listeners are able to read or make
sense of them, largely by means of our lifelong experiences as embodied
creatures.[40]

Thus to say that one hears sexual longing in the *Tristan* prelude is not to
introduce irrelevant "subjective" data into the discussion. Surely that is the
point of the opera, and we are missing the point if we fail to understand
that. The process by means of which Wagner's music accomplishes this is
not at all mystical. In part, his music draws on his own (excessively docu-
mented) experiences in the sexual realm, and we as listeners perceive long-

ing in his music likewise because we are human beings with bodies who have experienced similar feelings firsthand. But this is not to suggest that music works on the basis of essences or that this communication between bedroom and ear happens without extensive symbolic mediation. Wagner's music relies heavily on the traditional semiotics of desire available in the musical styles he inherited, and listeners understand his music in part because they too have learned the codes (the minor sixths demanding resolution, the agony of the tritone, the expectation that a dominant-seventh chord will proceed to its tonic, and so on) upon which his metaphors depend.

Moreover, the musical conventions for representing such human experiences are far from timeless or ahistorical. Desire, for instance, was configured differently in seventeenth-century music, in part because Baroque social codes of signification and even norms of harmonic syntax were very different: some of the techniques exploited by Schütz in "Anima mea liquefacta est" resemble distantly those in *Tristan* and can be grasped by the modern listener without special tutoring; but many more of them depend upon the listener's familiarity with the relevant set of grammatical expectations. Musical imagery, in other words, is heavily mediated through the available syntax, sound forces, genres, and much else.

Nor are the bodily experiences engaged by musical metaphors stable or immutable.[41] Indeed, music is a powerful social and political practice precisely because in drawing on metaphors of physicality, it can cause listeners to experience their bodies in new ways—again, seemingly without mediation. The explosion of rock 'n' roll in the mid-1950s brought a vocabulary of physical gestures to white middle-class kids that parents and authorities quite rightly perceived as subversive of hegemonic bourgeois values. Sheltered Northern adolescents picked up on the dance rhythms of the Southern honky-tonk and black R & B, and their notions of sexuality—their perceptions of their own most intimate dimensions of experience—split off irrevocably from those of their parents. Even if it is difficult to account definitively for how music precipitates such transformations, its political potency must be acknowledged. And any human discourse with this much influence not only warrants, but demands serious scrutiny.

As the Wagner and rock examples indicate, much is at stake in the sets of apparently "natural" metaphors that inform various musics. For music is not the universal language it has sometimes been cracked up to be: it changes over time, and it differs with respect to geographical locale. Even at any given moment and place, it is always constituted by several competing repertories, distributed along lines of gender, age, ethnic identity, educational background, or economic class. Because musical procedures are heavily inflected over history and across social groups, they function extensively within the public domain and are thus available for critical investigation.

Given its centrality in the manipulation of affect, social formation, and the constitution of identity, music is far too important a phenomenon *not* to talk about, even if the most important questions cannot be definitively settled by means of objective, positivistic methodologies. For music is always a political activity, and to inhibit criticism of its effects for any reason is likewise a political act.[42]

5

The project of critical musicology (of which feminism would be an important branch) would be to examine the ways in which different musics articulate the priorities and values of various communities. Fortunately, we are not required to reinvent the wheel, for this is, of course, one of the principal activities of ethnomusicology. Because the musical images produced by people foreign to us are usually somewhat opaque, discouraging us from thinking that we can hear straight through to universal meanings, we tend to be aware that there are many levels of social mediation involved in the production of other musics.[43] Accordingly, ethnographers regularly analyze the musical institutions and procedures of non-Western or folk communities in terms of social organization. But much less work is available that asks ethnographic questions of Western art music. For it is one thing to recognize the social basis of the activities of remote societies, and it is quite another to begin examining the relativity of our own cherished habits of thought.[44]

To do so demands two very different kinds of work: analytical and historical. On the one hand, the techniques and codes through which music produces meaning have to be reconstructed. Because the music theories available at present are designed to maintain the illusion that music is formally self-contained, very little exists in Anglo-American musicology to facilitate such a project. Having to trace over and over again the processes by which musical elements such as pitch or rhythm can be said to signify is extremely tedious, especially within a discipline that refuses even to acknowledge musical affect. Yet it is impossible to go on to finer points of interpretation so long as the question of whether music means anything at all arises to block any further inquiry.

The chapters in this book focus on substantive issues rather than on this basic methodological problem — although fundamental questions about musical signification are addressed continually throughout. But elsewhere I have published three essays devoted to demonstrating how formal musical details may be connected to expression and even to social ideology. Two of them present step-by-step readings of pieces by Mozart and Bach.[45] The third examines a very particular device in nineteenth-century music: narrative interruptions by the key of the flatted submediant.[46] Admittedly, this last project looks arcane on paper. But the reactions of listeners to flat-six interruptions are almost unfailingly immediate and dramatic, even if they do not know technically how to explain their perceptions of discontinuity. All three of these essays account for musical signification in part through details of the score: by means of historical semiotics, generic expectations, deviations from syntactical or structural norms, and rhetorical devices such as continuity, disruption, intensification, and so forth.

But these three essays also locate generic norms and strategies of deviation within historical and cultural contexts. Genres and conventions crystallize because they are embraced as natural by a certain community: they define the limits of what counts as proper musical behavior. Music theory has often been a more or less legislative branch of music that seeks to rationalize and prescribe the preferences of a particular dominant group. Yet crystallization or legislation also makes those norms available for violation, making music itself a terrain on which transgressions and opposition can be registered directly: as Jacques Attali has argued, music is a battleground on which divergent concepts of order and noise are fought out.[47]

For instance, Monteverdi's violations of Renaissance rules of dissonance treatment succeeded in polarizing authorities and advocates of the new practices, and the resulting polemics reveal quite clearly that much more was at stake than an occasional unprepared discord. When Bob Dylan first walked onto the stage with an electric guitar, he was thought to have betrayed the folk community with which he had been identified and threw into confusion the social categories of the 1960s. In our own day, Tipper Gore's PMRC has brought the censorship of rock both to Capitol Hill and to the recording industry because of the kinds of sexual images she claims the music transmits to her children.

In other words, music and its procedures operate as part of the political arena—not simply as one of its more trivial reflections. So long as music reaffirms what everyone expects, it can manage to seem apolitical, to serve as a mere frill. But as soon as it transgresses some deep-seated taboo, it can bring boiling to the surface certain antagonisms or alliances that otherwise might not have been so passionately articulated. The incidents involving the character Radio Raheem in Spike Lee's film *Do the Right Thing* illustrate this point with extraordinary clarity: Raheem is a loner whose identity is wrapped up in his boombox, on which he incessantly plays Public Enemy's "Fight the Power" at earsplitting volume. When he refuses to turn it off in

the pizza shop, the white owner (who displays only photos of Italian-
American celebrities on his walls, despite the objections of his all–black clientele) smashes the boombox, triggering the violence that escalates eventually to the looting of the shop, defacement of his cultural icons, Raheem's
murder, and a race riot. Struggles over musical propriety are themselves political struggles over whose music, whose images of pleasure or beauty,
whose rules of order shall prevail.

Consequently, it is difficult to understand why in certain repertories
some images and constructions dominate, why others are prohibited, unless
one has a strong sense of social history. The kind of history musicology has
typically adopted is that of chronology. There are no power struggles in
such histories, to say nothing of sensitive issues such as gender or sexuality.
It is in part because history is presented as orderly, settled, and unproblematic that it has appeared to be largely irrelevant to the ways music itself is
organized.

Therefore, the other principal task facing a music critic who wants to find
the traces of history in musical texts is to discover alternative modes of historiography. Fortunately, a considerable amount of work has already been
done toward this end, first through the Frankfurt School critics—
exemplified especially in the aesthetic theories and finely nuanced analyses
of Theodor Adorno—and more recently through Michel Foucault's "ar-
chaeologies of knowledge."

Adorno is the only major cultural theorist of the century whose primary
medium was music, as opposed to literature, film, or painting.[48] Thus
much of what he accomplished does not require the kind of disciplinary
translation that virtually all other critical theorists do. His work, while pa-
rochially grounded in the German canon of great composers from Bach to
Schoenberg, provides the means for understanding how compositions of
the tonal repertory are informed by the fundamental social tensions of their
time. His conceptual framework opens up that sacrosanct canon to questions of great social and political urgency.

Writing between the world wars, from the historical vantage point of the
horrific collapse of German high culture, Adorno dismisses with contempt
those who would regard this music as a set of icons and insists upon treating
it as a medium within which the bourgeois contradictions between individual free will and social pressures to conform were played out in increasingly
pessimistic ways. The illusion of total order and control cherished by traditional musicologists is stripped away by his readings, which focus unremit-
tingly on historical human dilemmas rather than on transcendent truth. In
his hands, the presumably nonrepresentational instrumental music of the
canon becomes the most sensitive social barometer in all of culture. It is

thereby made available to social criticism and analysis. Without my study of Adorno, I could not have undertaken any of the projects presented in this volume, for I would have had no way of getting beyond formalism. Yet there are many areas of human experience that Adorno overlooks or denigrates as regressive, such as pleasure or the body.

These are precisely the areas Foucault opens up to critical and historical investigation: in book after book, he has demonstrated that such apparent universals as knowledge, sexuality, the body, the self, and madness all have histories bound up with institutional power.[49] Moreover, he theorizes how these have been—and are—variously defined, organized, and constituted by means of cultural discourses such as literature or music. Social critics have typically been scornful of the pleasurable aspects of the arts, favoring those works that could be shown to have the proper political stance; to dwell on the actual details of the artifice was to be seduced by it into false consciousness, to be drawn away from the central issues of the class struggle. However, far from finding pleasure to be trivial, Foucault locates the efficacy of cultural discourses in their ability to arouse and manipulate. Pleasure thereby becomes political rather than private—it becomes one of the principal means by which hegemonic culture maintains its power.

While they offer extraordinary insight into the political machinations of culture, Foucault's formulations often are somewhat pessimistic, for they rarely admit of the possibility of agency, resistance, or alternative models of pleasure.[50] Here the models of political criticism developed by Antonio Gramsci or Mikhail Bakhtin can serve as empowering correctives, in that they recognize and focus on cultural contestation, counternarratives, and carnivalesque celebrations of the marginalized.[51] They conceive of culture as the terrain in which competing versions of social reality fight it out, and thus they permit the study of the ideological dimensions of art while avoiding the determinism that too often renders such analyses reductive.

Inspired in part by Foucault, Gramsci, and others, the practices of history and literary criticism have changed profoundly during the last decade. Historians are increasingly making use of anthropological questions as they interrogate who WE are: why we organize gender and sexuality as we do, how we came to assume certain notions of subjectivity, and how various discourses operate to structure, reproduce, or transform social reality. Consequently, the study of the arts has become a far more central, more urgent enterprise than it was in its Great Books phase. From various angles, writers such as Fernand Braudel, Stephen Greenblatt, Joan Kelly, and Nancy Armstrong have begun to set forth a very different picture of European/American history—a history no longer just of a privileged people, but of an extended community with beliefs and customs as peculiar as those of any so-called primitive society, a community that structures and reproduces it-self by means of cultural discourses.[52]

The essays that follow owe much in terms of method and information to these new directions in historiography. For if we reject the idea that European music is autonomous, then much about the changing world in which it was enmeshed must be reconstructed. Unfortunately for those who want their investigations to be methodologically tidy, the history of that "outside" world is not stable. We are at present in the midst of extensive revisions of the histories of Europe and the United States. Much of what one would like to know about (e.g., attitudes toward sexuality and gender throughout the centuries) is only now being pieced together.

It might be argued that it is foolhardy to jump in to try to account for music before the revised picture of the outside world has been solidified. But if music is one of the cultural terrains on which such issues get worked out, then our picture of the outside world will always be incomplete until music is figured in. Cultural critics have already discovered how absurd it is to write histories of the 1960s without paying close attention to the crucial roles played by music. I suspect that this is true of most other moments in Western history as well.

To the large extent that music can organize our perceptions of our own bodies and emotions, it can tell us things about history that are not accessible through any other medium. This is not to dismiss the importance of verbal documents: indeed, far more than flattened-out historical narratives, historical documents help us to locate music within the ideological struggles that leave their traces on its procedures. Consequently, my essays refer continually to a wide variety of documents and social histories. But for the study of music, music itself remains the best indicator, if we only permit ourselves to listen self-reflexively and to think.

The essays in this collection attempt to sketch out what several of these historical, analytical, and theoretical projects would look like. If the arguments sometimes seem circular—the analyses depend on particular constructions of the social world that are in part constituted by the music at hand—then this only points to the inseparability of music and the social world within which it operates. What usually motivates a project is that an odd musical detail catches my attention; but in order to explain that detail, I am required to undertake extensive historical excavation. And likewise, my historical studies make me aware of the significance of many musical details I might never have noticed otherwise.

My detour into critical and cultural theory has been interpreted by some as an abandonment of musicology. I have at times even been called a sociologist (though never by actual sociologists, who usually take me to be overconcerned with textual analysis). Yet, once again, it has always been music itself that has compelled me into these dark alleys, that has kept me searching for explanations beyond the scope of the autonomous analytical techniques musicology and music theory offered me. For if the principal obstacle to dealing with music critically has been its claim to nonrepresentationality, then critical and cultural theories make it possible to challenge not only the more superficial aspects of music (the setting of song texts, the delineation of characters in operas, the references to explicit literary sources in program music) but, more important, its very core: its syntactical procedures and structural conventions. Thus it is at this level that much of my critique is aimed—at the narrative impulses underlying sonata-allegro form and even tonality itself.

6

This is a collection of essays written between 1987 and 1989. Together they set out the beginnings of a feminist criticism of music. Although the essays address a wide range of periods and repertories (from the beginnings of opera in the seventeenth century to Madonna's most recent music videos), they are not packaged together here arbitrarily.

As I have considered the ways music might be opened to feminist critique, I have found it useful to develop a practice of scanning across many historical periods. For to focus exclusively on a single repertory is to risk taking its formulations as natural: its constraints and conventions become limits that cease to be noticeable. It is only, I believe, by continually comparing and contrasting radically different musical discourses that the most significant aspects of each begin to fall into relief. There are, consequently, extensive cross-references among repertories in the essays—Monteverdi's spectacles are intersected with those of heavy metal, Laurie Anderson's narratives with those of the nineteenth-century symphony. However, to thus violate period and genre boundaries does not mean losing sight of the specificity of sociohistorical contexts. On the contrary, such scanning facilitates the reading of repertories against the grain—it is the best way to lay bare the unquestioned assumptions that guarantee each repertory, to identify the most important historical questions.

The first three essays are concerned with examining compositions in the standard canon from a feminist point of view. The first of these, "Constructions of Gender in Monteverdi's Dramatic Music," concerns the emergence of a semiotics of gender in early seventeenth-century opera. Drawing on Foucault's *History of Sexuality* and his work on the rise of modern institutions of control in the seventeenth century, Gramscian models of cultural hegemony and resistance, and Bakhtin's concept of carnival, I explore how power relationships connected with gender and class are inscribed in these pieces. This essay examines the artificial codes Monteverdi devises for distinguishing between male and female characters, but it also traces the crisis in gender representation that occurred almost immediately as a result of unforeseen contradictions in the cultural terms of gender propriety.

"Sexual Politics in Classical Music" deals with how music (even classical music) is involved in creating particular models of libidinal desire and also how the standard schemata of narrative organization that inform both opera and instrumental music are loaded with respect to gender and power. The compositions it examines in particular are Bizet's *Carmen* (which also requires that treatments of race and class be addressed) and Tchaikovsky's Symphony No. 4, for which I introduce questions of gay criticism: does the fact that Tchaikovsky was homosexual have any bearing on his musical narratives?

"Excess and Frame: The Musical Representation of Madwomen" continues the study of gender representation and musical narrative conventions by exploring how madwomen from Monteverdi's lamenting nymph to Lucia and Salome are portrayed. It takes much of the work on the social history of madness by Foucault, Elaine Showalter, Klaus Doerner, and others and demonstrates how music participates in that history. However, the depiction of madness in music often is used to justify the flagrant transgression of musical convention (transgressions that become marks of status in the "antibourgeois" phase of bourgeois art). Thus this examination of musical dementia leads to a reexamination of the treatments of musical deviation by music theorists, especially Schoenberg. "Excess" concludes with a discussion of the work of Diamanda Galas, a contemporary performance artist/composer who takes onto herself the musical signs of the madwoman and uses them aggressively in political pieces designed to protest variously the treatment of AIDS patients and victims of the Greek junta. Galas's work makes it possible to compare the politics of representation versus self-representation. It also serves as a convenient bridge to the second set of essays.

The essays in the second group focus on recent music by women composers who deliberately problematize their sexual identities within their musical discourses: respectively so-called serious composition,[53] postmodern performance art, and popular music. I have concentrated here on new music for a couple of reasons. First, these essays were originally written in response to specific conference invitations, all of which happened to be concerned with examining contemporary issues. And second, the political climate of the 1980s has been more hospitable to participation and experimentation by women artists than any previous moment in music history. For the first time, there exists something like a critical mass of women composers and musicians. Moreover, the theoretical work of feminists in literary and art criticism has cleared a space where women can *choose* to write music that foregrounds their sexual identities without falling prey to essentialist traps and that departs self-consciously from the assumptions of standard musical procedures.

I believe it may be possible to demonstrate that various women composers in history (Hildegard von Bingen, Barbara Strozzi, Clara Schumann, Fanny Mendelssohn) likewise wrote in ways that made a difference within the music itself. Now that the music of these women is becoming available, we are able to begin examining their strategies for the first time. But the essays included in this volume concern only women artists who we can be relatively sure are engaged in the kinds of deconstructive enterprises I discuss.

The first of these, "Getting Down Off the Beanstalk: The Presence of a Woman's Voice in Janika Vandervelde's *Genesis II*," deals with the artistic development of Minnesota composer Janika Vandervelde who began to recognize certain masculinist traits in many of the techniques she had been taught or had absorbed from her lifelong exposure to classical music. Her response was to problematize these procedures in a piece that counterpointed them explicitly against new ways of organizing time. The result was the piece *Genesis II*, which is discussed at length in the essay.

"This Is Not a Story My People Tell: Musical Time and Space According to Laurie Anderson" takes up many of these same issues, but in the context of postmodern performance art. Drawing upon the feminist work on cinema and narrative of Teresa de Lauretis, Mary Ann Doane, and others, this essay focuses on the problem of the female body in performance, on electronic mediation, and on the compositional procedures of two songs: "O Superman" (*United States*) and "Langue d'amour" (*Mister Heartbreak*).

The final essay, "Living to Tell: Madonna's Resurrection of the Fleshly," moves into the realm of popular music. Yet it continues several of the threads already developed in the previous two pieces, including the deconstruction of inherited conventions and the possibility of new modes of organizing musical time. Like the piece on Laurie Anderson, it also deals with issues surrounding the female body, although—needless to say—this question is far more urgent in Madonna's case. Roland Barthes has written of the text as that "uninhibited person who shows his behind to the *Political Father*."[54] And Madonna's cheeky modes of self-representation habitually greet the anxieties so often ascribed to women's bodies by "mooning" them: she flaunts as critique her own unmistakably feminine ending. Thus, the essay also discusses Madonna's music videos, especially the ways in which their visual scenarios interact with her music.

Despite their obvious differences, these four contemporary women musicians—Galas, Vandervelde, Anderson, and Madonna—are similar in that they have inherited the sometimes oppressive conventions examined in the first group of essays. Each is concerned with carving out a niche for herself within the highly resistant medium of music; each is at least intuitively aware of the premises of the tradition; and each strives to rework those premises such that she can tell new and different stories.

In short, they accomplish within the music itself the kinds of deconstructions I present throughout this book in analytical prose. They too are Material Girls who find themselves in Bluebeard's castle, and they too refuse to abide by the house rules. They have entered resolutely into the forbidden chamber with its dark, hidden codes and have transformed it into a carnival—a playground of signifiers—for their own pleasure. And just as they dare to write compositions with feminine endings, so I conclude this collection with their voices.

Notes

Chapter 1. Introduction: A Material Girl in Bluebeard's Castle

1. Bruno Bettelheim, *The Uses of Enchantment: The Meaning and Importance of Fairy Tales* (New York: Vintage Books, 1977), 299–303.

2. See, for instance, Carol Neuls-Bates, ed., *Women in Music: An Anthology of Source Readings from the Middle Ages to the Present* (New York: Harper & Row, 1982); Jane Bowers and Judith Tick, eds., *Women Making Music: The Western Art Tradition, 1150-1950* (Urbana: University of Illinois Press, 1986); James R. Briscoe, ed., *Historical Anthology of Music by Women* (Bloomington: Indiana University Press, 1987); and Nancy B. Reich, *Clara Schumann: The Artist and the Woman* (Ithaca: Cornell University Press, 1985).

3. See, for instance, Bowers and Tick, *Women Making Music*; Eva Rieger, *Frau, Musik und Männerherrschaft* (Frankfurt: Ullstein, 1981); Ellen Koskoff, ed., *Women and Music in Cross-Cultural Perspective* (Westport, Conn.: Greenwood Press, 1987); and Judith Lang Zaimont, ed., *The Musical Woman: An International Perspective, 1983* (Westport, Conn.: Greenwood Press, 1984).

4. Stanley Sadie, ed., *The New Grove Dictionary of Music and Musicians* (New York: W. W. Norton, 1980).

5. The *Man and Music* videos were produced and shown by Granada Television International in 1986, and the books are now beginning to be released by Macmillan Press, with Prentice-Hall as the American publisher. Stanley Sadie serves as series editor and adviser for the videos, which are available through Films for the Humanities, Inc. (Princeton, N.J.). *The Music of Man* series is designed to accompany a textbook by K. Marie Stolba, *The Development of Western Music: A History* (Dubuque, Iowa: Wm. C. Brown, 1990). Ironically, Stolba is the first to incorporate some of what we now know about women composers and musicians into a general music history textbook.

6. The Ottawa conference "Alternative Musicologies" was organized by John Shepherd, and its proceedings are being published by the *Canadian University Music Review* and in a collection, *New Musicology*, edited by Shepherd for Routledge. The conference at Dartmouth, "Music and Literature," sparked many kinds of lively critical discussions. The principal feminist contribution was Ruth Solie's superb

169

"Whose Life? The Gendered Self in Schumann's *Frauenliebe* Songs." I wish to thank Prof. Solie for permitting me to read a copy of this paper.

7. There were two sessions devoted specifically to feminist issues at the meeting: "Feminist Scholarship and the Field of Musicology," organized by Jane Bowers, and panel, "The Implications of Feminist Scholarship for Teaching," organized by Susan Cook. In addition, there were several explicitly feminist talks scattered throughout many other sessions, including papers by Suzanne Cusick, Linda Austern, Jenny Kallick, and Marcia Citron. I list them here because the public surfacing of these women was such an extraordinary event.

8. The two anthologies are Ruth Solie, ed., *Music and Difference* (Berkeley: University of California Press, forthcoming); and Susan Cook and Judy Tsou, eds., *Cecilia: Feminist Perspectives on Women and Music.*

9. There are a few studies of musical semiotics available, though most of them prove not to be especially useful for my purposes. Jean-Jacques Nattiez, *Fondements d'une sémiologie de la musique* (Paris: Union Générale d'Éditions, 1975), is probably the most elaborate work to address these issues, though his theory operates entirely within a self-contained, formalistic context with scrupulous disregard for social signification. At the other extreme, Deryck Cooke, *The Language of Music* (London: Oxford University Press, 1974), presents a semantics of Western music, the usefulness of which is limited by his failure to ground his observations socially or historically. For astute analyses of the politics of "apolitical" semiotics, see Teresa de Lauretis, "Semiotics and Experience," *Alice Doesn't* (Bloomington: Indiana University Press, 1984), 158-86; and Edward W. Said, *The World, the Text, and the Critic* (Cambridge, Mass.: Harvard University Press, 1983).

10. Stephen Heath, *The Sexual Fix* (New York: Schocken Books, 1982), 3. I wish to thank Gary Thomas for bringing this formulation to my attention. See Chapters 2, 3, and 5 for more detailed expositions of gender and sexuality in music.

11. Willi Apel, *Harvard Dictionary of Music*, 2nd ed., rev. and enlarged (Cambridge, Mass.: Harvard University Press, 1970), 506. The entry "Feminine cadence," reads: "See Masculine, feminine cadence."

12. Edward T. Cone, *Musical Form and Musical Performance* (New York: W. W. Norton, 1968), 45. I should add that I find this to be the most insightful book available on the practical relationship between analysis and performance, and it is required reading for some of my courses.

13. Georg Andreas Sorge, *Vorgemach der musicalischen Composition* (1745–47), trans. Allyn Dixon Reilly (Ph.D. dissertation, Northwestern University, 1980), 179-80. I wish to thank Lawrence Zbikowski for bringing this passage to my attention.

14. Arnold Schoenberg, *Theory of Harmony* (1911), trans. Roy E. Carter (Berkeley: University of California Press, 1983), 96. My thanks to Andrew Jones for this citation.

15. See Chapter 4 for a more extensive discussion of the politics of Schoenberg's *Theory of Harmony* and of his musical compositions. Because it would have been problematic for Schoenberg to have put himself on the side of the "feminine" along with chromaticism and dissonance, he carefully remapped the conventional binarisms in terms of the struggle against class oppression. He then could valorize and even identify with what had traditionally been relegated to the "feminine" side of the equations. The passage cited above is one of the few that slip back into gendered terms.

16. Heinrich Schenker, *Harmony*, ed. Oswald Jonas, trans. Elisabeth Mann Borgese (Cambridge, Mass.: MIT Press, 1973), 28. See also xxv, 6, 28, 30. My thanks again to Larry Zbikowski. Schenker likewise subscribes to the nineteenth-

century concept of the "unconscious genius" who appropriates the passivity and breeding qualities from the female. See *Harmony*, 60 and 69, and *Der freie Satz*, trans. and ed. Ernst Oster (New York: Longman, 1979), xxv.

17. For an examination of "organicism" in musical thought, see Ruth Solie, "The Living Work: Organicism and Musical Analysis," *19th-Century Music* 4, no. 2 (Fall 1980): 147-56. For an analysis of the nineteenth-century identification of "genius" and organicism with male sexuality, see Christine Battersby, *Gender and Genius: Towards a Feminist Aesthetics* (London: Women's Press, 1989).

18. See Mark Johnson, *The Body in the Mind: The Bodily Basis of Meaning, Imagination, and Reason* (Chicago: University of Chicago Press, 1987), for a superb epistemological theory that posits metaphor as the principal means by which humans orient themselves to the world. Johnson analyzes verbal tropes not as decorative language but as evidence of the basic analogues that structure thought. Cultural discourses such as music are likewise meaningful because they draw upon the organizing metaphors shared by a particular social group. For a demonstration of how central cultural tropes organize ostensibly objective writing about music, see Janet M. Levy, "Covert and Casual Values in Recent Writings about Music," *Journal of Musicology* 5 (1987): 3-27.

19. As cited and translated in the communication from Peter Bloom in *Journal of the American Musicological Society* 27 (1974): 161-62. This communication presents a succinct account of the origins of the verbal convention of "masculine" and "feminine" themes.

See also the analysis of the description of sonata procedure from *Musik in Geschichte und Gegenwart* in Eva Rieger, " '*Dolce Semplice*'? On the Changing Role of Women in Music," *Feminist Aesthetics*, ed. Gisela Ecker, trans. Harriet Anderson (Boston: Beacon Press, 1985), 139-40.

20. Teresa de Lauretis, "Desire in Narrative," *Alice Doesn't*, 118-19.

21. De Lauretis, "Desire in Narrative," 103-57, and "The Violence of Rhetoric: Considerations on Representation and Gender," *Technologies of Gender* (Bloomington: Indiana University Press, 1987), 31-50. See also Vladimir Propp, *Morphology of the Folktale*, 2nd ed., rev. and ed. Louis A. Wagner (Austin: University of Texas Press, 1968); and especially Jurij Lotman, "The Origin of Plot in the Light of Typology," trans. Julian Graffy, *Poetics Today* 1, no. 1-2 (Autumn 1979): 161-84.

These narratological models have the drawback, however, of being relatively ahistorical. See the critique in Jay Clayton, "Narrative and Theories of Desire," *Critical Inquiry* 16 (Autumn 1989): 33-53. The essays in this volume are concerned with problematizing the historicity of narrative processes in music, even though they draw on the formulations of de Lauretis for purposes of explicating the musical repertories most devoted to the schemata she describes.

22. For an analysis of the ways the narrative structures of the principal operas of the standard repertory demand the subjugation of women, see Catherine Clément, *Opera, or the Undoing of Women*, trans. Betsy Wing (Minneapolis: University of Minnesota Press, 1988). If her litany is depressingly redundant, so are the schemata of dominant narratives. See also Chapters 3 and 4.

23. Schoenberg, *Theory of Harmony*, 129. For a more extensive discussion of Schoenberg's agenda, see Chapter 4.

24. James Webster, "Sonata Form," *New Grove* 17, 498.

25. Fredric Jameson, "Reification and Utopia in Mass Culture," *Social Text* 1 (1980): "Now none of these readings can be said to be wrong or aberrant, but their very multiplicity suggests that the vocation of the symbol—the killer shark—lies less in any single message or meaning than in its very capacity to absorb and orga-

nize all of these quite distinct anxieties together. As a symbolic vehicle, then, the shark must be understood in terms of its essentially polysemous function rather than any particular content attributable to it by this or that spectator. Yet it is precisely this polysemousness which is profoundly ideological, insofar as it allows essentially social and historical anxieties to be folded back into apparently 'natural' ones, to be both expressed and recontained in what looks like a conflict with other forms of biological existence" (142).

26. See Chapters 3 and 4 for more extensive discussions of chromaticism as gendered.

27. See Rieger, *Frau, Musik und Männerherrschaft*, and Battersby, *Gender and Genius*.

28. Linda Austern, " ' Alluring the Auditorie to Effeminacie': Music and the English Renaissance Idea of the Feminine," paper presented to the American Musicological Society, Baltimore (November 1988); Richard Leppert, *Music and Image: Domesticity, Ideology and Socio-cultural Formation in Eighteenth-Century England* (Cambridge: Cambridge University Press, 1989). Jeffrey Kallberg's "Genre and Gender: The Nocturne and Women's History" (CUNY Graduate Center, April 1989) also addresses the anxiety over the perceived effeminacy of certain genres. I wish to thank Prof. Kallberg for permitting me to read a copy of this paper.

Debussy reception has likewise been waged in terms of the "masculinity" or "effeminacy" of his musical style. See Daniel Gregory Mason, *Contemporary Composers* (London: Macmillan, 1929): "Sybaritism, too, has its own vulgarity; the question of aim is fundamental in art; and in judging the distinction of Debussy's aims we cannot evade the question whether physical pleasure, however refined, is the highest good an artist can seek. His charm, beyond doubt, is great enough to justify his popularity. Yet it would be regrettable if the student of modern French music, satisfied with this charm, were to neglect the less popular but more virile, more profound, and more spiritual music of Cesar Franck, Ernest Chausson, and Vincent d'Indy" (151). See also Robin Holloway, *Debussy and Wagner* (London: Eulenburg Books, 1979); and Robert Schmitz, *The Piano Works of Claude Debussy* (London: Duell, Sloan, and Pearce, 1950). I am indebted to Karen Schoenrock for these citations.

29. Solomon, "Charles Ives: Some Questions of Veracity," *Journal of the American Musicological Society* 40 (Fall 1987): 467.

30. For other discussions of the genderings of these style periods, see Jochen Schulte-Sasse, "Imagination and Modernity: Or the Taming of the Human Mind," *Cultural Critique* 5 (Winter 1986-87): 23-48; Alan Richardson, "Romanticism and the Colonization of the Feminine," in *Romanticism and Feminism*, ed. Anne Mellor (Bloomington: Indiana University Press, 1988), 13-25; Marlon B. Ross, "Troping Masculine Power in the Crisis of Poetic Identity," also in Mellor, *Romanticism*, 26-51; Andreas Huyssen, "Mass Culture as Woman: Modernism's Other," *Studies in Entertainment: Critical Approaches to Mass Culture*, ed. Tania Modleski (Bloomington: Indiana University Press, 1986), 188-207; Sandra M. Gilbert and Susan Gubar, *No Man's Land: The Place of the Woman Writer in the Twentieth Century* (New Haven, Conn.: Yale University Press, 1988); and Christine Buci-Glucksmann, *La raison baroque de Baudelaire à Benjamin* (Paris: Éditions Galilée, 1984). See also Chapter 4.

31. Robert Schumann, "Schubert's Symphony in C," *Neue Zeitschrift für Musik*, 10 March 1840. The translation of these concluding lines is by Sanna Pederson. A translation of the complete essay is available in *Schumann on Music*, trans., ed., and annotated Henry Pleasants (New York: Dover, 1988), 163-68. I wish to thank Ms. Pederson for bringing this essay to my attention.

32. For critiques of the crippling effect of this masculinist epistemology, see Carol Gilligan, *In a Different Voice: Psychological Theory and Women's Development* (Cambridge, Mass.: Harvard University Press, 1982); Mary Field Belenky et al., *Women's Ways of Knowing: The Development of Self, Voice, and Mind* (New York: Basic Books, 1986); Evelyn Fox Keller, *Reflections on Gender and Science* (New Haven, Conn.: Yale University Press, 1985); and Sandra Harding, *The Science Question in Feminism* (Ithaca: Cornell University Press, 1986).

33. See the documents included under the heading of "The 'Woman Composer Question'" and "The 'Woman Composer Question' Revisited" in Neuls-Bates, ed., *Women in Music*, 206–27 and 278–302. For classic accounts of the exclusion and denigration of women artists and writers, see Linda Nochlin, "Why Have There Been No Great Women Artists?" *Art and Sexual Politics*, ed. Thomas B. Hess and Elizabeth C. Baker (New York: Collier Books, 1973), 1–43; and Sandra M. Gilbert and Susan Gubar, *The Madwoman in the Attic: The Woman Writer and the Nineteenth-Century Literary Imagination* (New Haven, Conn.: Yale University Press, 1979), 3–104.

34. See the responses by women composers to Elaine Barkin's questionnaire published in *Perspectives in New Music* 19 (1980-81): 460–62; and 20 (1981-82): 288–330. See also Nicola LeFanu, "Master Musician: An Impregnable Taboo?" *Contact: A Journal of Contemporary Music* 31 (Autumn 1987): 4–8, for an argument similar to mine by a woman composer.

35. Joseph Kerman has explained the historical conditions that led to this state of affairs in American musicology. See his *Contemplating Music: Challenges to Musicology* (Cambridge, Mass.: Harvard University Press, 1985), 31–59.

There is, to be fair, a tiny cadre of American musicologists that has persistently advocated and practiced music criticism for the last thirty years. They include most prominently Edward T. Cone, Joseph Kerman, Leonard B. Meyer, Charles Rosen, Maynard Solomon, and Leo Treitler. Over the years, these critics have been a salutary presence in an otherwise arid discipline, for their work focuses on the music itself and attempts to deal with meaning as it is produced in various moments of music history. Their detailed, insightful interpretations of musical compositions have demonstrated over and over again how to write about music with tremendous lucidity and integrity—in a field otherwise noteworthy for its absence and suspicion of intellectual activity.

36. See, for instance, David Epstein's methodological statement in *Beyond Orpheus: Studies in Musical Structure* (Cambridge, Mass.: MIT Press, 1979), 11. While acknowledging that the question of expression is important, he concludes that "it is first of all essential clearly to perceive, to recognize, and to comprehend what it is we hear, *free of external or misconstrued meanings*" (my emphasis). I am dubious that one can ever get from such formalistic explanations to anything having to do with social signification. Moreover, I would argue that hearing Beethoven's *Eroica* through a complex theoretical grid derived from Schenker and Babbitt is a far greater imposition of "external" meanings (available only to a few highly trained professionals) than listening by means of inherited semiotic codes, which informed the composer as well as his various audiences.

37. A great deal of work has been done on how the reader—and not simply the author—produces meaning for literary texts. See, for instance, Stanley Fish, *Is There a Text in This Class: The Authority of Interpretive Communities* (Cambridge, Mass.: Harvard University Press, 1980); Susan R. Suleiman and Inge Crosman, *The Reader in the Text: Essays on Audience and Interpretation* (Princeton: Princeton University Press, 1980); and Judith Fetterly, *The Resisting Reader: A Feminist Approach to American Fiction* (Bloomington: Indiana University Press, 1978). Similarly, feminist film

theory has concentrated heavily on how meaning is construed variously by male and female spectators. See, for instance, Laura Mulvey, "Visual Pleasure and Narrative Cinema," *Screen* 16, no. 3 (Fall 1975): 6-18; Mary Ann Doane, *The Desire to Desire: The Woman's Film of the 1940s* (Bloomington: Indiana University Press, 1987); and Tania Modleski, *The Women Who Knew Too Much: Hitchcock and Feminist Theory* (New York: Methuen, 1988).

The only book dealing with a woman's reception of opera—Clément's *Opera, or the Undoing of Women*—has been heavily criticized since its publication in English precisely because it draws upon Clément's own experiences with opera. What she is doing is in line with much of the intellectual work being done in other areas of the humanities. She is not trying to present an "objective" account of opera (what would that be?), but rather is relating how opera has moved her to tears, how it has helped shape her own identity, and how she has tried to become a resisting listener: how, in other words, opera participates in social formation.

38. Raymond Williams, *The Long Revolution* (London: Cox & Wyman, 1961), 66–69.

39. Johnson, *The Body in the Mind*, all emphases in the original. These passages are excerpted from Johnson's preface, xiii-xvi. See also George Lakoff and Mark Johnson, *Metaphors We Live By* (Chicago: University of Chicago Press, 1980).

40. Schenker—our father of formalist analysis—comes surprisingly close to this position: "As the image of our life-motion, music can approach a state of objectivity, never, of course, to the extent that it need abandon its own specific nature as an art. Thus, it may almost evoke pictures or seem to be endowed with speech; it may pursue its course by means of associations, references, and connectives; it may use repetitions of the same tonal succession to express different meanings; it may simulate expectation, preparation, surprise, disappointment, patience, impatience, and humor. Because these comparisons are of a biological nature, and are generated organically, music is never comparable to mathematics or to architecture, but only to language, a kind of tonal language." *Der freie Satz*, 5. See also the biological metaphors cited in note 16.

41. Jay Clayton likewise has argued for regarding such phenomena as desire as mutable and socially constituted rather than as a biological universal. See his "Narrative and Theories of Desire."

42. For excellent discussions of the political nature of humanities scholarship that pretends to neutrality as well as criticism that announces its agenda, see Said, *The World, the Text, and the Critic*, especially 1-53; Terry Eagleton, *Literary Theory* (Minneapolis: University of Minnesota Press, 1983), especially 194-217; and *The Function of Criticism* (London: Verso, 1984). For music, see Rose Rosengard Subotnik, "The Role of Ideology in the Study of Western Music," *Journal of Musicology* 2 (1983): 1-12.

43. See, for instance, Bruno Nettl, *The Study of Ethnomusicology* (Urbana: University of Illinois Press, 1983); and Koskoff, *Women and Music in Cross-Cultural Perspective*. For a study that reveals especially well the specificity of the cultural metaphors that can inform music, see Stephen Feld, *Sound and Sentiment: Birds, Weeping, Poetics, and Song in Kaluli Expression* (Philadelphia: University of Pennsylvania Press, 1982).

44. A few musicologists are beginning to make use of anthropological methodologies. For instance, Gary Tomlinson, "The Web of Culture: A Context for Musicology," *19th-Century Music* 7 (Spring 1984): 350-62, draws upon the models developed by Clifford Geertz. Henry Kingsbury recently carried out anthropological

fieldwork in an American conservatory. See his *Music, Talent, and Performance: A Conservatory Cultural System* (Philadelphia: Temple University Press, 1988).

For discussions of ethnography that seem especially relevant to musicological work, see Geertz, *The Interpretation of Cultures* (New York: Basic Books, 1973); and, more recently, George E. Marcus and Michael Fischer, *Anthropology as Cultural Critique: An Experimental Moment in the Human Sciences* (Chicago: University of Chicago Press, 1980); James Clifford and George E. Marcus, eds., *Writing Culture: The Poetics and Politics of Ethnography* (Berkeley: University of California Press, 1986); Clifford, *The Predicament of Culture: Twentieth-Century Ethnography, Literature, and Art* (Cambridge, Mass.: Harvard University Press, 1988).

45. "A Musical Dialectic from the Enlightenment: Mozart's *Piano Concerto in G Major, K. 453*, Movement 2," *Cultural Critique* 4 (Fall 1986): 129-70; and "The Blasphemy of Talking Politics during Bach Year," *Music and Society: The Politics of Composition, Performance and Reception*, ed. Richard Leppert and Susan McClary (Cambridge: Cambridge University Press, 1987), 13-62.

46. "Pitches, Expression, Ideology: An Exercise in Mediation," *Enclitic* 7, no. 1 (Spring 1983): 76-86. See Chapter 4 for a discussion of the flat-six excursion in *Lucia di Lammermoor*. This effective rhetorical move is still very much in use in popular music—see Chapter 7.

47. Jacques Attali, *Noise*, trans. Brian Massumi (Minneapolis: University of Minnesota Press, 1985). See my afterword, "The Politics of Silence and Sound," 149-58.

48. See, for instance, Adorno's *Prisms*, trans. Samuel Weber and Shierry Weber (Cambridge, Mass.: MIT Press, 1981); *Philosophy of Modern Music*, trans. Anne G. Mitchell and Wesley V. Blomster (New York: Seabury Press, 1973); and *In Search of Wagner*, trans. Rodney Livingstone (London: New Left Books, 1981).

Rose Rosengard Subotnik has been largely responsible for bringing Adorno's work to the attention of American musicology. See especially her "Adorno's Diagnosis of Beethoven's Late Style: Early Symptom of a Fatal Condition," *Journal of the American Musicological Society* 29 (1976): 242-75; "The Historical Structure: Adorno's 'French' Model for the Criticism of Nineteenth-Century Music," *19th-Century Music* 2 (1978): 36-60. Because Subotnik has been severely chastised for having thus brought Continental criticism into the discipline, I want to go on record expressing my gratitude to her. Hers is the richest critical work to have emerged in musicology in the last fifteen years. See the collection that includes the preceding and other of her essays, *Developing Variations: Style and Ideology in Western Music* (Minneapolis: University of Minnesota Press, forthcoming).

49. See, for instance, Foucault's *The Order of Things: An Archaeology of the Human Sciences* (New York: Random House, 1970); *Madness and Civilization: A History of Insanity in the Age of Reason*, trans. Richard Howard (New York: Random House, 1965); and *The History of Sexuality, Vol. I: An Introduction*, trans. Robert Hurley (New York: Random House, 1978).

50. For perceptive critiques of Foucault, see Irene Diamond and Lee Quinby, eds., *Feminism & Foucault: Reflections on Resistance* (Boston: Northeastern University Press, 1988); and Said, "Criticism between Culture and System," *The World, the Text, and the Critic*, 178-225.

51. Antonio Gramsci, *Selections from the Prison Notebooks*, ed. and trans. Quintin Hoare and Geoffrey Nowell-Smith (New York: International Publishers, 1971); and *Selections from Cultural Writings*, ed. David Forgacs and Geoffrey Nowell-Smith; trans. William Boelhower (Cambridge, Mass.: Harvard University Press, 1985); Mikhail Bakhtin, *The Dialogic Imagination*, ed. Michael Holquist; trans. Caryl Em-

erson and Michael Holquist (Austin: University of Texas Press, 1981); and *Rabelais and His World*, trans. Hélène Iswolsky (Bloomington: Indiana University Press, 1984).

See also Stuart Hall, "Cultural Studies: Two Paradigms," *Media, Culture & Society*, ed. Richard Collins et al. (London: Sage, 1986). For especially fine examples of music criticism utilizing Gramsci, Bakhtin, and Hall, see George Lipsitz, "Cruising Around the Historical Bloc: Postmodernism and Popular Music in East Los Angeles," *Cultural Critique* 5 (Winter 1986-87): 157-78; and "Mardi Gras Indians: Carnival and Counter-Narrative in Black New Orleans," *Cultural Critique* 10 (Fall 1988): 99-122. These essays are included in the collection titled *Time Passages: Collective Memory and American Popular Culture* (Minneapolis: University of Minnesota Press, 1990).

52. See, for instance, Fernand Braudel, *The Structures of Everyday Life: Civilization & Capitalism, 15th-18th Century*, vol. 1, trans. Siân Reynolds (New York: Harper & Row, 1981); Stephen Greenblatt, *Shakespearean Negotiations* (Berkeley: University of California Press, 1988); Joan Kelly, *Women, History, and Theory* (Chicago: University of Chicago Press, 1984); and Nancy Armstrong, *Desire and Domestic Fiction* (Oxford: Oxford University Press, 1987). For an impressive attempt at rereading European literary history in anthropological and sociological terms, see Denis Hollier, ed., *A New History of French Literature* (Cambridge, Mass.: Harvard University Press, 1989).

53. There are no terms for this repertory that are not deeply dissatisfying. It is not accidental that the music produced by the "mainstream" has no convenient adjective: the labels for other repertories (popular, folk, commercial, experimental, and so forth) were invented to hold them apart from this, "the real stuff." In semiotic terms, this repertory is the unmarked member of many loaded binary oppositions, and the inadequacy of labels such as "classical," "concert," "serious," or "art" only emphasizes the problem. I have no solution to offer here—only an indication that I am aware of the dilemma.

54. Roland Barthes, *The Pleasure of the Text*, trans. Richard Miller (New York: Noonday Press, 1989), 53.

CHAPTER 6

Structures of Identity and Difference in Bizet's Carmen

The first act of Georges Bizet's opera *Carmen* opens with a chorus of soldiers who are killing time watching people pass by in the street. The dragoons are ostensibly part of a Spanish army, yet they are of a significantly different class, ethnic, and even—by implication—national constituency from those they observe. They emphasize their difference in their refrain, which they sing repeatedly with accents of mock surprise: *Drôles de gens que ces gens là!* ("What funny people these are!"). This chorus introduces the audience into the terrain upon which the opera will unfold, and it explicitly legitimates distanced, objective, voyeuristic observation. It invites us, the spectators, likewise to gaze unabashedly at these "funny people": a sideshow of women, exotics, and grotesques. Without necessarily noticing how, we enter into the opera's dramatic events from the soldiers' point of view.

For Bizet's original audience, this identification would have been easily made, for the soldiers' music resembles that of light Parisian entertainments of the 1870s: it is French, in other words—unmarked by characteristics used by Bizet in the opera to signal "Spain." The chorus poses no barriers for comprehension: it sounds utterly familiar, yet flatters the ear with its vaguely sophisticated nuances. The soldiers are calculated to sound like "us." In fact, we may not even notice them. (Theirs is not the music we go away humming.) As our stand-ins, they are transparent; we listen past them to the exotic spectacle they offer for our delectation. They both naturalize specta-

torship and situate us as part of the dominant (French) social group that
watches the colorful antics of the local (Spanish) inhabitants from the safety
of the sidelines. But as the opera proceeds, questions of identity and difference become increasingly perplexing. Who precisely are the "funny people"
we are supposed to be observing? And with whom are we to identify, once
the stick soldiers disappear?

Prosper Mérimée's novella *Carmen*, for all its artful ambiguities, is much
more forthright on these matters.[1] He begins his story with a Greek epigraph:
"Woman is bitter as gall, but she has two good moments: in bed and dead."
And he concludes it with a pseudoscientific ethnography of the gypsy people in which the story's narrator attempts to distance himself from and purge
the contagion that fatally infected his acquaintance Don José and that might
well have contaminated him as well. These overemphatic framing devices
leave little doubt that this narrative concerns threatening encounters with the
other: the other primarily understood as woman and as gypsy. However, we
learn in the course of the novella that several other varieties of alterity are at
stake here besides gender and racial or ethnic difference, including class,
nation, religion, culture, legal status, and language. Still, identity is anchored
securely in the voice of the narrator, even though his own sense of self is
severely shaken during the course of the novella.

Our narrator is a French archaeologist who has gone to Spain for field
research. As a scholar, he prides himself on his superior skills in objective
observation and his abilities as a wordsmith. Along the way, he has a fleet-
ing encounter with an outlaw renowned for his violence. He protects himself by befriending this desperate criminal who seems so radically different
but who bears the traces of an upper-class background in his name, Don
José. Like the narrator, José is of a cultivated and privileged class; he is
white, Christian, of northern rather than southern origin; we even learn
that he is a sensitive musician. Yet in behavior, appearance, and reputation
he has taken on the characteristics of the most brutal strata of humanity—
same, yet other. The narrator can only wonder how such a thorough transformation can have occurred.

After parting company with José, the narrator makes his way into
Cordoba, where he learns that the local pastime is watching working-class
women bathe in the river at dusk. Confident in his skills of disinterested
observation, he eagerly joins the assembled group of men to gaze. But his gaz-
ing is interrupted by a charming young woman who engages him in conversation. She is dark in complexion, and he casts about for her proper classification, taking her variously to be Andalusian, Moorish, or Jewish (a word he
cannot bring himself to utter). He finally must be told she is a gypsy. Against
his better judgment, he goes home with her to have his fortune told. But
before they can get down to that or any other kind of business, the door bursts
open and Don José rushes in. He is on the brink of murdering the narrator in
a fit of jealous rage when he recognizes his traveling companion and spares
his life. The narrator flees to the safety of his archaeological pursuits.

On passing back through Cordoba several months later, the narrator learns that Don José has killed Carmen, the gypsy to whose exotic charms he himself had submitted without resistance. He visits José in prison and is told more or less the story we know from the opera: how he was an officer in the military who fell in love with Carmen and consequently (in a kind of Domino Theory of morality) was sucked into the downward spiral of degradation that led eventually to her murder. It is after the narrator has learned of these events that he is compelled to write his hysterical ethnographic essay. For if José had not interrupted his encounter with Carmen and saved him, he might well have found himself in José's predicament.

The narrator therefore attempts to eradicate from himself those inclinations that made him vulnerable to Carmen's charms. He argues in his concluding essay that gypsies are filthy, superstitious, treacherous, and hideous in appearance—especially the women. He seeks by means of a barricade of words to hold at bay the dangerous other and finally focuses on language itself. For Carmen, a colonial subject who has learned of necessity to maneuver within the imposed languages of imperialism, remains fluent in her native tongue. By contrast, the narrator, who eloquently wields the cultural discourses of privilege, has no access to gypsy speech. He is linguistically transparent and vulnerable; she is multilingual, possesses the verbal currency necessary to slip in and out of all social contexts, whether organized by ethnicity, nationality, class, or gender. As he tries to fix her and her people in his analytical writing, his masterful, cultivated words drop impotently into a confused heap. He finishes cryptically with a gypsy adage: "Between closed lips no fly can pass."

Translating a text this convoluted and deliberately conflicted onto the stage was no easy matter, and some critics have complained that Bizet and his librettists betrayed Mérimée's celebrated novella. Indeed, if one locates Mérimée's ingenuity in *Carmen* in its structural and narratological virtuosity rather than in the lurid story, then the linear tracking of the opera may seem unspeakably pedestrian. The most drastic alteration in the adaptation of the novella for purposes of opera involves the elimination of the French narrator—the omniscient voice that guided us through the story, that situated us with respect to subject position, that interpreted what we were permitted to see and hear. Nor is Don José's narrative voice present in the opera: his is simply one of several competing for attention in what appears to be an unmediated presentation of the events themselves. In other words, we move from the monologic conventions of fiction to the polyvocal (and apparently far more democratic) conventions of drama.

This elimination of narrative control was potentially quite perilous. In Mérimée's novella, the figure of Carmen was always multiply mediated: through José's recollections, through the French narrator, through Mérimée's self-consciously literary language. Yet she had been regarded as lethal nonetheless. Not even Don José's knife contains her: the narrator lunges to erect a moralizing scholarly text about gypsy women, hoping thereby to con-

tain the contagion spread through ill-advised contact with the exotic. And in
their turn, French bourgeois critics condemned the unleashing of such a monster onto the literary terrain. Three decades later, the scandal still remained
alive. Thus when Bizet and his collaborators first proposed setting *Carmen* for
the Opéra-Comique, the producers were aghast: how could this infamously
sordid woman be represented in the theater that was a favorite site for family
outings? Halévy, one of the librettists, promised that they would tone the
character of Carmen down and balance her with a proper girl.[2] But they did
intend to present Carmen: not through mere verbal descriptions, but in spec-
tacular enactment and with her treacherous utterances heard directly, rather
than filtered through three layers of male narrators.

In casting aside Mérimée's complex framing devices, Bizet and his collaborators risked creating a simplistic reduction of the novella. But they also
risked unleashing a monster far more dangerous than his, insofar as this
operatic Carmen would appear to speak for herself without the constant
intervention of narrative voices. Given the sensitive, even sensationalistic
nature of this story's subject matter—the humiliation and degradation of
male, white authority at the hands of a woman of color—this was a problem the collaborators could scarcely afford to overlook. But their strategies
of containment had to be radically different from those of Mérimée's
novella, given the nature of their medium.

The most obvious counterweight added by the librettists is the character
promised by Halévy, Micaëla—a girl from José's home who has been sent
to him as a messenger and potential bride by his mother. Mérimée had no
such figure: his is a world in which desperate men circle warily around
Carmen as though she were the only woman on earth and compete to the
death for her favors. However, the dramatic stage—especially the family-
oriented stage of the Opéra-Comique—was regarded as a more influential
site of social formation than the novel. Because the lifelike representations
enacted there were more likely to be perceived by impressionable viewers as
real than the creatures of fiction, the guidelines surrounding theatrical
works were considerably more strict. Micaëla was offered up explicitly as a
foil to Carmen: as the normative good girl who stands as the ideal against
which Carmen is to appear all the more monstrous. With Micaëla aboard
they hoped to receive a PG rating rather than an R or an X.

But the most intricate restructuring of the novella for purposes of this
opera—the delineation of relative subject positions and points of view—is
the work of Bizet alone, and it takes place within the music itself. Although
the opera involves only Spanish characters, Bizet articulates the narrative
tensions of the story in such a way as to reinforce but also to destabilize the
foundations of French national identity. It is he who creates vivid images of
the other—Carmen's frank sexuality, her indicators of racial and class difference—just as he constructs Don José's presumably more cultivated
utterances. And he locates all these within a delicate web of cultural associations, thematic correspondences, and subtle affective commentaries that

match or surpass in complexity the framing devices engineered by Mérimée, even though they operate on the basis of entirely different premises—the formal premises of musical procedure.

We have already seen that the beginning of Act I situates us in the comfortable position of the dragoons, the military presence that sings in the latest Parisian fashion while practicing surveillance over the native Andalusian population. A number of amusing spectacles are presented to them (and us) in untroubled succession: a shy provincial girl, a procession of street urchins pretending to be soldiers, and a group of languorous women who work at the local cigarette factory. The characters who will become prominent in the drama are casually introduced through the "B" sections of the symmetrical ABA formula that governs most of the numbers: Micaëla is interpolated into the soldiers' chorus, Don José into the street urchins' march, and so forth. Musical well-roundedness and plot advancement thus proceed along together, apparently without strain.

Most of Bizet's music during the first several numbers can be justified either as music that is to be heard within the context of the action itself (such as the bugle call that announces the changing of the guard) or as the accompaniment that supports and psychologically amplifies the singers in turn. It seems, in other words, objective. But there is one extremely interesting editorial moment in the first number that subtly situates the listener in a male subject position. The dragoons have just concluded their first full presentation of "Drôles de gens" when Micaëla comes onto the stage. At this point neither they nor (ostensibly) we in the audience know who she is. Bizet might have cued us that this is a sweet girl from home by having the orchestra play one of her guileless motives. Instead, Micaëla is marked by her musical creator as a femme fatale, for her entrance is accompanied by the kind of slinky chromaticism that later will mark Carmen's dangerous sexuality. As Don Giovanni would say, she exudes (at least at this initial moment) an *odor di femina*, and the rising bassline that undergirds Morales's description of her movements leaves little doubt as to the prurient interests of her spectators. Of course, we and the dragoons find out soon that we have misread the signs: she will be sanctioned many times over during this scene and the rest of the opera as a model of modest bourgeois femininity— indeed, precisely the kind of French bourgeois femininity characteristic of the Opéra-Comique. If the plot acknowledges Micaëla as Spanish, she sings in the unmarked discourse that identifies her, like the dragoons, as one of "us" with respect to nation.

Yet for all her modesty, Bizet goes out of his way to slant the piece in the direction of male address through his slight four-bar commentary. Given that this is a piece often taken to be about an innocent young soldier and a temptress, the politics of this first encounter between the sexes are most interesting. In this opera, women are by definition other—even good girls. Micaëla manages to escape the clutches of the aroused soldiers, and they retreat frustrated and bored to their chorus of "Drôles de gens." She provides a diversion—a mere passing dissonance that momentarily enlivens the action before the security of the inevitable return to the beginning. She is the B section that makes the reprise of A meaningful in this ABA structure.

The multivalent dissonance of Carmen herself, of course, proves to be not so easily resolved or contained; when she enters, the confident ABA procedures that had organized the earlier numbers in Act I suddenly lose their certainty. Nevertheless, in a composition in which the listener is so conditioned to expect formulaic returns to opening materials, one might expect that the frame of the quasi-French soldiers will eventually step back in for the sake of structural balance and closure. And we would be correct in anticipating some kind of reprise. But the formal return that ultimately rounds out the opera as a whole involves music we have not yet discussed: the Prelude, which actually occurs prior to the raising of the curtain, prior to the occupying army that would seem to be in control in Act I.

For this opera has two frames competing for the privilege of formal closure. In contrast to the familiar discourse of the dragoons, which invites automatic identification, the Prelude establishes the exotic setting we have presumably come to the theater to sample. I hesitate to call it Spanish, for most of Bizet's writings in this and many of his other works are products of his own synthesized, all-purpose mode of exoticism.[3] If his exotic passages succeed in convincing listeners that they are hearing "the very soul of Spain," it is not because they are ethnographically accurate; he seems not to have been interested in reproducing the traits of any particular ethnic music in his compositions so much as the aura of exoticism itself. Thus when he recycled materials among some of his other works, he occasionally would resituate a piece that was originally supposed to sound Russian in Brazil or in the Orient. Bizet did some small amount of research for *Carmen* and used a couple of snippets of authenticated folk music and some stylistic patterns resembling flamenco. But he also happily incorporated an African-Cuban popular song that became the "Habañera." His success was in large part a result of his uncanny ability to draw upon common assumptions about what the "other" (of whatever stripe) should sound like. Like so many of his contemporaries in French literature and painting, Bizet's imagination only came to life when it engaged with Orientalism: many of his nonexotic compositions were left incomplete or were viewed as quite ordinary by both him and his critics.

Edward Said has written extensively about the appeal of Orientalism for the nineteenth-century artist.[4] On the one hand, the exotic held out the promise of supplementing the increasingly dreary, restrictive world northern Europe had become: it was an imaginary zone where whatever was lacking in the everyday world could be supplied, where behaviors held to be taboo could be indulged in freely, where tedious rationality (the white man's burden) was replaced with its opposite. Nietzsche, for instance, writes:

This music [of *Carmen*] is cheerful, but not in a French or German way. Its cheerfulness is African; fate hangs over it; its happiness is brief, sudden, without pardon. I envy Bizet for having had the courage for this sensibility which had hitherto had no language in the cultivated music of Europe—for this more southern, brown, burnt sensibility. —How the yellow afternoons of its happiness do us good! We look into the distance as we listen: did we ever find the sea smoother? —And how soothingly the Moorish dance speaks to us? How even our insatiability for once gets to know satiety in this lascivious melancholy![5]

On the other hand, these projected characteristics and imaginary constructions were often confused with reality itself and were taken to demonstrate the essential inferiority of the other. This "free zone" became a compensatory space for weary, bored northern Europeans (once again, their/our interest in watching these "funny people") and, at the same time, a site for ideological reproduction of the most lethal variety. Moreover, as imperialist expansion began to reach its limit and people from the colonies started to make their way onto European soil, the insulated, all-white context within which exoticism had served merely as colorful, escapist entertainment became increasingly riddled with the social consequences of French nationalist engagements with the "Orient."[6]

The Prelude opens with bright, festive music. It is flashy, especially when the cornets that have already been heralded by the fanfarelike motive finally enter the ensemble. Such an opening might be regarded as in bad taste if it were not marked as other, but its exotic pretenses justify it. Moreover, its syntax is gaily irrational: each four-bar phrase is stable within itself, but each pivots harmonically at the last moment under a flamboyant trill to the next segment, which sets out a contrasting key area. In sequence the keys established are A major, D major, A major, and C major, with an abrupt return to A major for the conclusion. The Prelude exhibits a high degree of certainty, with the constant reassuring returns to tonic. But the harmonic destabilizations under the flourishes give at least the illusion of risk, and the emergence of the irrationally related key of C major offers the momentary thrill of the unexpected, even if it is pulled back immediately under the control of the tonic. The effect is bold and colorful, though ultimately stable. It also serves as a rapid portrait of the world of the other. It does so not by drawing on exotic materials, but by acting out against the restrictions of "rational" and well-behaved northern European conventions. "Spain" is gaudy, flamboyant, irrational, static (i.e., not progressive), unpredictable, potentially treacherous. So is Carmen.

Even more than the opening scenes of Act I, the Prelude is obsessed formally with nested symmetries: ABA structures that may incorporate contrasting materials but that inevitably loop back for closure. The tiny section we just considered operates that way with respect to its brave excursions away from and back to A major; the section as a whole is the A segment in a small ABA complex that comes back dutifully to round off; and the entire ABA complex in turn becomes the A part of a larger structure that incorporates the F major "Toreador Song" as a B section before returning intact. If the Prelude flirts with a wide assortment of keys, it easily pulls them all back to home base. Formally, the Prelude resembles Freud's game of *fort–da* in which a child experiments with feelings of separation and identity by tossing a spool on a string away (*fort*), then triumphantly retrieving it (*da*). But the Prelude's final toss of the spool destroys this illusion of control.

Following what sounds like the confident final cadence of the Prelude, the orchestra plunges into D minor with a quaking, fortissimo string tremolo. The contrast could not be more dramatic. Time itself (which had been fastidiously meted out in four-bar units until this point) seems to stand still. Under this sustained tremolo, a new, somber motive emerges. It is characterized by the interval of the augmented second: an interval traditionally associated in Western music either with exotic others (Jews, Orientals, gypsies, depending on context) or with anguish. In *Carmen*, both connotations are crucial, and they continually play off of one another as a kind of grim and deadly pun. For the motive will later be linked explicitly both with Carmen and with Don José's fatal, anguished attraction to her.

Another important referent operates here as well: the diminished-seventh tremolos and the foreboding strokes on the timpani that greet each statement of the motive reproduce the signs of horror and suspense first developed in one of Bizet's favorite operas, Weber's *Der Freischütz*. In that earlier context, this cluster of signs had been deployed to stand for pure evil—the evil of the demon Samiel in the Wolf Glen. Now, with the mere addition of the augmented second, the cluster warns us of the Oriental and the femme fatale, which to the late nineteenth century were far more diabolical forces than Samiel ever was.

After writhing its way to two temporary points of rest, the motive rises through increasing intensification to a crisis on a diminished seventh, only to break off onto another diminished seventh followed by silence. After all the cushioned protection of regular phrases and reliably returning opening materials, we find ourselves disgorged into a tonal, rhythmic, and structural void. The *fort–da* game is violently ruptured, and it is within the breach that thereby opens up that the dramatic action of the opera takes place; the unresolved dissonance that concludes the Prelude casts its shadow across the events as they unfold. Given the conventional constraints of formal process (especially as they have been established in this piece), such a gaping wound must eventually be healed or corrected, whatever the cost.

It is here, of course, that the curtain rises on our quasi-Parisian dragoons, confident in their ability to observe these "funny people" as a sideshow, to channel them as the B units of nicely symmetrical ABA forms. But in context, their authority is considerably undermined. It could be argued that the "funny people" have already staked out this terrain, that the soldiers represent but a blip within a far more stringent symmetry. And we don't have the security of Mérimée's narrator to situate us. The Parisian soldiers may manage to erase temporarily the memory of the Prelude, but its claim to being the determining element of the piece becomes increasingly clear as the opera progresses. For unlike any of the materials introduced by the soldiers or their first few tableaux, the various themes of the "Spanish" prelude return to mark significant occurrences in the drama: its final segment (often referred to as "fate") signals critical moments in the relationship between Carmen and Don José; the "Toreador Song" becomes the theme song of Escamillo, José's principal rival; and the festive march of the opening finally reenters in the final act to celebrate the anticipated bullfight and to indicate the beginning of the end—the return of the entire repressed Prelude complex for its postponed closure. In other words, a high tide of exoticism washes up, gradually obliterating the fragile "unmarked" (i.e., French) presence asserted by the dragoons at the beginning of Act I.

Thus far I have said little about the principal characters of this piece, Carmen and Don José, largely because they are part of this much larger set of issues. Most readings of the opera focus exclusively on their personalities and their relationship. But like most love stories we care about, this one has far more baggage attached than the mere matching or mismatching of two individuals. Although in another context I might lavish considerable attention on the details of Bizet's psychological portraits, here I am interested in Carmen and José as discursive types.

Carmen belongs both to the flashy exotic world already introduced in the Prelude and to the succession of women who have been ogled by the dragoons (and presumably by the spectators) since the curtain went up. She is doubly cast as other—as woman and as Oriental, with all the characteristics both entail. Her music is heavily marked both as grounded in the body (unlike Micaëla, Carmen lives up to her slinky introduction) and as treacherously chromatic and exotic.

But there is another kind of alterity projected onto Carmen: that of popular music. With rare exceptions, Carmen sings what are to be construed—even within the terms of the opera itself—as cabaret song-and-dance numbers, not "real" utterances. Thus the "Habañera" was lifted expressly from the Parisian cabaret scene, where exoticism was no less of a box office draw than in high art. And Bizet encountered the flamenco that flavors several of Carmen's other tunes through contact with gypsy night spots of ill repute on the rue Taitbout. In other words, even the most "Spanish" components of the score—those associated with Carmen—resonate with growing cultural tensions within France itself. Institutions such as the Opéra-Comique were designed expressly as wholesome alternatives to these more nefarious forms of entertainment. Thus to have the leading lady in an opera singing the very cabaret songs that opera was supposed to displace was extremely shocking to its bourgeois clientele. Early reviews often refer to Carmen's songs as vulgar and to Célestine Galli-Marié's performance style as obscene.[7] Because Carmen's songs have always been "opera" to us, the transgression is not quite so apparent today. In response to such reviews, musicologist Winton Dean likes to protest that Carmen sings not a vulgar note in the whole opera.

But Carmen's music is *deliberately* vulgar. Bizet draws on practices that were guaranteed to offend his audience, and he knew this in advance. We have often scoffed at listeners who were so narrow-minded that they overlooked the beauty of these tunes. But it was not simply a matter of a prudish bourgeoisie misreading the opera before finally learning that the "Habañera," too, qualifies as great art. The vulgarity of Carmen's tunes (or at least their association with popular urban culture) is crucial to the workings of the opera's dramatic structure.

Andreas Huyssen, in his "Mass Culture as Woman: Modernism's Other," has examined the antagonism between high and low culture from the nineteenth century into the twentieth.[8] To an increasing extent, serious artists took as part of their mission the necessary warding off of the advance of mass culture, which was associated with the working classes, with appeals to sentimentality and sexuality, and thus with the feminine. The move toward abstraction in the modernist painting, poetry, and music of this time was designed expressly as protection against this rising tide of what was regarded as trash.

Carmen was written just as these movements were gaining momentum. Like Orientalism, popular music provided a space where the elite could slum, could satisfy the kinds of pleasures that imperious official culture denied itself. Bizet confessed in a letter in 1867: "I am German by conviction, heart and soul, but I sometimes get lost in artistic houses of ill fame." And it is no accident that the music we remember from *Carmen* is precisely this ill-famed material: the more typical operatic numbers with which it is juxtaposed offer little to compete with its vitality and sensuality. But by the same token, its seductiveness demands that it be regarded (along with Carmen and the gypsies) as a polluting influence, that it be purged.

Purged in favor of the musical discourse of Don José, for it is Don José who bears the Germanic burden of Bizet's split personality. Although some critics recoiled in horror from the pop-culture obscenity of the opera, at least as many despised its moments of confusing Teutonic learnedness, its Wagnerian obscurity: it was heard as aping the difficult symphonic style that was acquiring the status of "universal" music during this period—even (despite the efforts of nationalist critics) in France. The features of complexity singled out by such critics are, in fact, Don José's principal characteristics: his long, impassioned melodies that avoid regular phrasing and cadences for the sake of postponed gratification, his rages in which both his utterances and his psychological amplification in the orchestra threaten to wreck all sense of order. As Winton Dean has pointed out, "The Paris Bourgeoisie liked its music broken up into small watertight compartments set in a framework of ordinary speech."[9] And by those French standards, Don José behaves at least as badly as Carmen.

To those of us who still accept nineteenth-century German style as the universal norm, José's intemperate excesses may not be readily apparent. Indeed, compared with Carmen's insistence on the body, José's visionary spans may seem like a relief. Carl Dahlhaus, for instance, writes approvingly of what he calls José's "lyric urgency," and he sees Bizet's principal challenge in the opera as the problem of how to write for Carmen, a character who is "incapable of lyric urgency."[10] To the extent that we regard both types of utterances—Carmen's and José's—as transparent, we are likely not only to misconstrue contemporary complaints that the piece lacks stylistic unity, but also to underestimate both the essential incompatibility of these two characters and the tensions within French culture they embody.

In an eclectic assemblage that could only have arisen in cosmopolitan (if culturally fragmented) Paris, Don José is a creature of high German style who somehow finds himself on the stage of the petty bourgeois Opéra-Comique playing opposite an exotic cabaret performer. She is contented with the intoxicating grooves of her dance numbers—with the body, sensuality, pleasure. He continually wants to make their encounter into an endless melody of yearning, unquenchable desire—a through-composed drama in which all is sacrificed for the sake of climactic transcendence. And the Opéra-Comique audience and critics found both parties to be distasteful; only Micaëla, Escamillo (whose music Bizet referred to as trash), and the Parisian-style crowd scenes of the opening act were received favorably.

To view José as the discursive norm (as Dahlhaus does) obscures an important point. His high-minded denial of sensuality, his incessant push for something other than the pleasure of the moment cause him to be musically violent. He whips himself up into frenzies that cannot be satisfied except through destruction. Even within the "Flower Song," he cannot attain climax except by establishing musical ceilings and then forcibly penetrating them. For it is not pleasure or sensuality he seeks, but rather control and possession. This is clear to Carmen by the conclusion of the "Flower Song," where she quietly undermines his protestations of love with "Non, tu ne m'aimes pas." And she is right. He loves the narrative trajectory she has induced him to imagine (for this, not her, is what the "Flower Song" is about); but he has no concept of love as it involves other sentient human beings. That is why the tiny exchange between Carmen and Escamillo in the final act—when they sing to each other with the same music and then together in harmony—is so poignant. Such mutuality is impossible for Don José.

In this he follows faithfully his Germanic models, which likewise cannot accommodate pleasure or dialogue and which increasingly find it difficult to believe in the adequacy of the cadence to ground their huge narratives of tonal desire. The more intensively the contradictions between desire and compensation are pursued (say, in Beethoven or Brahms), the more violent the attempts at forcing belief. Compositions such as Mahler's *Resurrection Symphony* reach closure only after apocalyptic explosions and then only through imposition. In each of the last three of four acts of *Carmen*, Don José resorts to charging with his knife. And his final thrust attains closure.

Which brings us back to the question of frame. As was mentioned earlier, two parallel but conflicting framing devices appear at the beginning of the opera: the "Spanish" music of the Prelude and the unmarked soldiers' discourse of the beginning of Act I. Throughout the opera each of these vies for the right to claim ownership over the proper conclusion of the piece. The Prelude's claim rests on two factors: first, its extraordinary symmetries that suddenly are ruptured, thus demanding return and closure; and second, the significant appearances of its various elements to register key moments in the drama. But if the Prelude were to succeed in rounding itself off at the end of the opera, it would mean that the other—the exotic stuff that was supposed to provide the terrain for mere entertainment—had won. A paranoid tale indeed.

The case for the unmarked side is far more complicated, for unlike Mérimée's novella, the opera offers no obvious authorial voice to guide us through the piece. The voyeuristic soldiers provide grounding for a while, but then they fade into the woodwork, leaving us to contend with the polyphony of the various voices on stage. Moreover, Acts II and III take place on terrains established not by our bourgeois stand-ins but by the gypsies themselves, first at Lillas Pastia's tavern and then in the smugglers' hideout. In both these contexts it is José who is positioned as the outsider, the other. The return to Seville for the festival in the final act reintroduces the funny street people we encountered in the opening act, and they now dwarf the dragoons, who had first offered us this scene for purposes of distanced amusement.

Identity in this opera, then, would seem to be pinned on the character of Don José himself. Winton Dean writes, "José is the central figure of *Carmen*. It is his fate rather than Carmen's that interests us."[11] This, of course, might be contested, especially in this age when the classics are being reread from the vantage points of race, class, gender, and nation. For instance, in Catherine Clément's and Nelly Furman's readings of the opera, Carmen herself is the central figure.[12] Social assumptions regarding proper feminine behavior or the entertainment value of ethnic others that used to be taken for granted and that helped to anchor this piece are no longer reliable. To the extent that Bizet could count on French, white, Christian audiences and the "universality" of male address, he did not need to articulate quite so explicitly that side of the argument.

Yet I think Dean is correct in suggesting that the piece as it is written means to be about Don José. But it is the music itself (rather than the libretto) that subtly makes this case. Bizet accomplishes this through a variety of strategies, the most important of which is his use of what I will call "movie music"—the background music that tells the listener how to feel about the action, whether dread, pathos, or anxiety. In its original Opéra-Comique version there were extensive sections of unaccompanied spoken dialogue. Thus the passages that might otherwise seem to be most prone to instrumental inflection and commentary were not generally available within this genre. Bizet does, however, take advantage of a few important moments.

For example. We have to wait for a very long time in the opera to hear Don José actually sing. He enters during the second number—the children's march—and is present throughout the cigarette chorus and the "Habañera," but he only speaks in the course of this entire sequence. His subjectivity is, however, registered in the music itself. After Carmen has insolently thrown the flower at him and the women have repeated their mocking refrain from the "Habañera," the orchestra bursts out in passionate display of lyric urgency. This is unmistakably José's characteristic idiom, and it conveys his powerful feelings long before he has put words to them. Unlike the other characters in this opera, all of whom operate more or less straightforwardly in the social domain, José is presented as having interiority and deep emotions that he can put into words only with great effort. He resists singing and can be compelled to give voice to his private thoughts only in extreme situations. The first of these is when Micaëla tells him that she comes from his home, to which he replies with effusive passion *Parle-moi de ma mère!* The second occasion for his bursting into lyric expression occurs in the "Seguidilla" where Carmen has suggested to him that they might become lovers. (Significantly, he sings back dutifully the phrase Carmen has fed him: her one strategic use of lyric urgency demonstrates that she is fluent enough in this discourse, but like Mérimée's Carmen she deploys it only when necessary.)

From that point on, José is like a loose cannon: his passion, once aroused, can have only one conclusion. And the orchestra supports him in this. The violent rage that bubbles up in the last two acts to overflow the generic boundaries expected in the Opéra-Comique is his: his subjectivity motivates the push for closure at the end and persuades the listener of the necessity, the inevitability, and even the desirability of the murder. If the other characters have more memorable tunes, José possesses the musical techniques of narrative drive that propel the opera toward its bitter end.

But if he can finally demand closure, he apparently has no control over how that closure is articulated. The most brilliant stroke of the opera involves what awaits José at his moment of truth: namely, the thematic materials from the Prelude. The "fate" complex had already returned when Carmen and José met in the first act; the "Toreador" segment returns with Escamillo's entrance in the second. With the return of the very opening of the Prelude for the bullfight procession in the final act, all elements are present, working their way inexorably to their own long-delayed closure. They process by in order as Carmen and José have their final encounter, punctuated with the "fate" materials that failed to reach their conclusion at the outset of the piece. Just before he kills Carmen, José explains that he cannot let her go because she would laugh at him in Escamillo's arms. But it is precisely with Escamillo's signature tune that José's triumph is celebrated. José has no tune—he is identified solely through his goal-oriented techniques, his urgent articulation of subjective passion. And we get one last pathetic glimmer of this before the concluding triad when he sings: "It is I who have killed her, O my beloved Carmen!"

Despite the finality of Carmen's death and the power of the drama that brought us to this moment, it is difficult to unravel with certainty what Bizet's opera (or any given part of it) means. I have deliberately presented a decentered account of the piece—focusing on odd details, tracing its constituent parts back into the social and music worlds that informed them—in part to get away from the kinds of simple love-story synopses that proliferate around *Carmen*. But my decentered account also results from my lack of conviction that a thoroughly coherent, consistent reading of the opera is possible or even desirable.

It could be argued, for instance, that José too is just one of the funny people the soldiers and audience have come to observe—in which case, the spectator (who has perhaps been lured into transferring identification from the distanced soldiers to José) may feel the need to step back at the end and erect an explanation that reestablishes difference. This would, in fact, recreate some of the moves of Mérimée's narrator, who also finds himself implicated in a slippery slope that begins with responding to the charms of a beautiful gypsy and ends in mayhem. And the irony of Bizet's conclusion assists one in achieving distance, for the "movie music" dimension of the piece that had represented José's subjectivity no longer operates in isolation at this point. Its confrontation with Escamillo's fight song can help us disengage ourselves from José's plight.

But like Mérimée's novella, Bizet's *Carmen* raises issues that are insoluble, at least given the premises from which they begin. Both are powerful documents precisely to the extent that they lay bare central faultlines of nineteenth- and twentieth-century French culture: those related to class, race, gender, and cultural hegemony. On some level, both novella and opera present something like the line in one of the more infamous songs by Guns 'n' Roses: "I used to love her but I had to kill her," and this needs to be acknowledged more than it is, whether it is sung by Axl Rose or Plácido Domingo. Yet both Mérimée and Bizet also perform (wittingly or not) a kind of cultural critique. If Don José did not experience his life in terms of lack—lack of sensuality, pleasure, freedom—he would not have been attracted to Carmen in the first place. If we in the audience did not find Carmen and her music irresistible yet somehow not quite kosher, the opera would not work for us. And if we were not still stuck in the dilemmas Mérimée and Bizet point to, we would not be witnessing the endless stream of *Carmen* productions on stage, film, and TV.

But playing the dilemma through over and over again is not sufficient. We have to begin taking apart the very structures of identity and difference that permit such pieces to make sense to us as they drive toward their awful conclusions. Paul Ricoeur has written of the anxieties of our present moment in history: "When we discover that there are several cultures instead of just one . . . when we acknowledge the end of a sort of cultural monopoly, be it illusory or real, we are threatened with destruction by our own discovery. Suddenly it becomes possible that there are *just* others, that we ourselves are an 'other' among others."[13]

If that discovery is threatening, however, it may also be our only hope. Instead of going to *Carmen* to experience the thrill of blurring the distinction between self and contaminating other before violently reimposing boundaries, I suggest that we view it as a mirror. For it is perhaps *we* who are the "funny people": the people who derive pleasure from such stories. We need to find other stories. But first we have to discover how we have organized ourselves to date. And we can learn a great deal about that from our responses to *Carmen*.

NOTES

1. Mérimée's *Carmen* first appeared in *La Revue des Deux Mondes* (October 1, 1845).

2. Ludovic Halévy reported his version of the negotiations between the Opéra-Comique management and the collaborators in "La millième représentation de *Carmen*," *Le Théâtre* 145 (1905). A partial translation of this document appears as "Breaking the Rules," trans. Clarence H. Russell, *Opera News* 51, no. 13 (1987): 36–7, 47.

3. See "The Musical Languages of *Carmen*," in my *Georges Bizet:* Carmen (Cambridge: Cambridge University Press, 1992), 44–61.

4. Edward W. Said, *Orientalism* (New York: Pantheon Books, 1978).

5. Friedrich Nietzsche, *The Case of Wagner*, trans. Walter Kauffman (New York: Vintage Books, 1967).

6. For more on the ways *Carmen* thematizes specifically French issues, see "Images of Race, Class, and Gender in Nineteenth-Century French Culture," in my *Georges Bizet:* Carmen, 29–43.

7. For more on the reception of *Carmen*, see chapter 5 of my *Georges Bizet:* Carmen, 111–29.

8. Andreas Huyssen, "Mass Culture as Woman: Modernism's Other," *After the Great Divide: Modernism, Mass Culture, Postmodernism* (Bloomington: Indiana University Press, 1986), 44–62.

9. Winton Dean, *Georges Bizet: His Life and Work* (London: Dent, 1985), 38.

10. Carl Dahlhaus, *Nineteenth-Century Music*, trans. J. Bradford Robinson (Berkeley and Los Angeles: University of California Press, 1989), 280–82.

11. Dean, *Georges Bizet*, 224.

12. Catherine Clément, *Opera, or the Undoing of Women*, trans. Betsy Wing (Minneapolis: University of Minnesota Press, 1988), and Nelly Furman, "The Languages of *Carmen*," in *Reading Opera*, eds. Arthur Groos and Roger Parker (Princeton: Princeton University Press, 1988). For another feminist critique of *Carmen*, see also "Sexual Politics in Classical Music," in my *Feminine Endings: Music, Gender, and Sexuality* (Minneapolis: University of Minnesota Press, 1991), 53–67.

13. Paul Ricoeur, "Civilization and National Culture," in *History and Truth*, trans. Charles A. Kelbey (Evanston, Ill.: Northwestern University Press, 1965), 278.

CHAPTER 7

CONSTRUCTIONS OF SUBJECTIVITY IN SCHUBERT'S MUSIC

Prelude 1: I Lost It at the Y

*A*LTHOUGH THIS ARTICLE APPEARS here for the first time in printed form, it already has a substantial public history—one that needs, I think, to be addressed. I wrote it initially for a panel on gay issues held at the 1990 meeting of the American Musicological Society: the first such session ever authorized by the AMS. Because I had begun developing methods for analyzing music with matters such as gender in mind, I was invited to discuss how a composer's sexuality might be relevant to the music itself.

I chose Schubert, for two reasons. First, Maynard Solomon's "Franz Schubert and the Peacocks of Benvenuto Cellini" had recently appeared in a prestigious journal.[1] Like many musicologists at the time, I found his arguments persuasive, and I took as more or less established that Schubert had engaged in same-sex erotic activities.[2] The task I set myself for this panel, then, was to explore the question of whether or not his music responded in any way to his sexual orientation.

My second reason was independent of Solomon's work. For some time before his articles concerning Schubert appeared, I had encountered several musicians and listeners (many, but not all of them, gay) who asked *on the basis of the music itself* whether Schubert was gay: there was something about the sensibility projected in his music that led them to intuit some connection. Since I am interested in the ways music engages in constructions of gendered subjectivity—and since I too had long perceived a remarkable difference in

Schubert's musical procedures—I saw this paper as an occasion for examining this issue in a public forum. I must emphasize, however, that without Solomon's publications I would not have framed this project in terms of sexuality per se, for I do not believe that one can discern a composer's sexual orientation (or gender or ethnicity) merely by listening to the music.

While the panelists all felt a bit apprehensive about adverse reactions from those who had already branded our session sensationalistic, we also knew that a considerable number of gay and lesbian scholars would attend and lend support. Accordingly, we prepared our presentations with this latter part of the audience in mind. In retrospect, I must say that I have never participated in a more exciting event. Positive reactions overwhelmed any opposition that surely was lurking in the hall, and it seemed that queer musicology had finally arrived.

About a month later, I received an invitation from Joe Horowitz to present my talk at the annual Schubertiade at the 92nd Street Y in February 1991. I agreed—in part because I had no idea what the 92nd Street Y is. In the Midwest whence I hail, the "Y" in any given town is simply a community center—indeed (as the Village People's anthem "YMCA" proclaims), a place to which men often go for anonymous sex.

Too late I discovered that the Y on 92nd Street is a YMHA (Hebrew) and, moreover, that it is a venerated venue for High Culture events, with the Schubertiade as a yearly event of particular gravity. Who knew? What's more, the 1991 Schubertiade had to be postponed until 1992, by which time the general climate in the country had shifted: backlash—in a word—was in full swing. The AMS meetings in fall of 1991 had witnessed a Schubert session at which audience members seized the mike and made pronouncements in "defense" of Schubert's reputation. Ominous clouds had begun to gather.

In the month before I was scheduled to deliver the talk in New York, I scrambled to devise some version of this project that would not instantly alienate the Schubertiade clientele. The paper adopted a tone of calm reassurance. I pulled my punches; I was practicing Safe Text, and it was boring. Yet I wanted to make the best possible case to an audience predisposed to hostility.

How hostile I had no idea until I arrived at the fateful site and discovered just how hostile hostile can be. Since the Schubertiade lasted an entire day, I had several occasions to stand in a long line in the women's room, where I was privy to unrelieved carping about this woman who was "determined to drag our Schubert through the mud." Solomon's article had been circulated in advance, and some of those who spoke during the course of the day deemed it appropriate to take gratuitous swipes at him ("a pornographer"), with the obvious approval of the crowd.

CONSTRUCTIONS OF SUBJECTIVITY IN SCHUBERT'S MUSIC ∿ 207

By the time my slot rolled around after dinner (dessert, anyone?), the cause was clearly hopeless. But I gave the paper anyway. Nothing much happened, except for some audible squirming during the musical examples (I played excerpts from the "Unfinished" Symphony and presented a voice-over in which I invited them to hear their beloved passages in a somewhat different way). The questions afterward were polite, although one person stood up and announced that *Schubert could not have been homosexual* (applause), while another proposed that Schubert's alleged alienation might have been merely the product of his being a "short, fat man." Many audience members latched onto this latter explanation as though it were a life raft in the middle of the ocean. Although I spotted a few gay people in the crowd, they remained silent—quite understandably—during the hailstorm. I went home, relieved it had not been worse.

In fact, it was only beginning. Two days later the *New York Times* published the first of three reactions to the paper. Working from an early draft the staff at the Y happened to have had on hand, Edward Rothstein reported on the event as a whole, with a somewhat skeptical account of my contribution. He too preferred the "short, fat" explanation. Two weeks later, Rothstein's column in the Sunday edition of the *Times* presented a more antagonistic treatment of my arguments, followed the next day with a smug parody by his colleague Bernard Holland.[3]

Still operating under the illusion that the New York establishment was basically liberal, I wrote a reply, as did Philip Brett and Elizabeth Wood. We waited. Every Sunday I dutifully bought the *Times* to see our letters. Nothing. Finally some phone calls confirmed that the *New York* ("All the News That's Fit to Print") *Times* had not seen fit to print our answers. Nor were they willing simply to admit it: the editor first claimed to have received no letters; next that they had been lost; then that they had been personal letters to Rothstein, who was answering them personally; finally that because they addressed columns in both Sunday and weekday editions they could not be run in either.

By now, this talk was the most notorious queer text in musicology, even though it was not available for anyone to see. The ensuing controversy took place with no trace of my arguments except as the *Times* had reported them. At this point, Paul Attinello suggested that the *Gay/Lesbian Study Group Newsletter* (of which he is an editor) print my speech, so that at least other musicologists concerned with such issues could read my words as I had delivered them. Consequently, that talk—which was tailored specifically for a resistant audience—now exists in the public domain and may be consulted.[4]

Prelude 2: So—Was He or Wasn't He?

Just as *Queering the Pitch* was going to press, Solomon's findings came under severe attack—most pointedly by Andreas Mayer and Rita Steblin, both of whom question matters of translation and issues of historical accuracy in Solomon's article.[5] Whatever the scholarly merit of their research, both are expressly motivated by the need to rescue Schubert from any affiliation with homosexuality.[6] And while their aversion to gay issues does not in itself invalidate the evidence they bring forward, I am saddened to see the debate carried out in terms of such animosity, for it indicates that many scholars still regard same-sex erotic activities as pathological.

I will respond directly to this debate elsewhere,[7] but I want to go on record here as admiring the seriousness, grace, and courage with which Solomon has introduced questions concerning misogyny in Beethoven, homophobia in Ives, or homoeroticism in Schubert into a discipline that has steadfastly refused to address such issues.[8] *Even if* the cases he has presented turn out not to be as airtight as they initially seemed—or, conversely, if they stand up perfectly well under scrutiny—it seems clear to me that Solomon's work has proceeded from the concerns about gender and sexuality that are now studied as a matter of course in the other humanities. His is not some nefarious plot to besmirch the images of our dearest icons, but rather an attempt at factoring in certain crucial dimensions of human life as they intersect with cultural expression.

Until the smoke clears from this controversy, however, we cannot simply assume that we know Schubert was inclined to sexual relations with other males. And—as I mentioned above—my original argument linking Schubert's music and sexuality relied upon what I took to be corroboration from external sources. So why proceed with the publication of this article?

First, my initial positions concerning Schubert's music and sexuality are already a matter of public record, and I cannot retreat from this topic without some kind of public statement. Second, my actual arguments about Schubert's music—for all the sensationalism whipped up in the press in response to them—never have had anything to do with actual sexual behavior; in some sense, I don't really care whom Schubert slept with. My project addresses, rather, his particular constructions of subjectivity, and I still stand by these arguments (thus the change in title), whatever Schubert's preference in bed partners may have been. Finally, some of the idiosyncrasies in Schubert's music—whether criticized or embraced—have long been perceived as having something to do with masculinity. Thus even if we were to declare a moratorium on the subject of Schubert and sexuality, these questions would not go away. The theoretical issues raised by this case are central to research concerning gender, sexuality, and subjectivity in music, and they deserve serious treatment—even in the unlikely event that hard evidence emerges proving that Schubert was involved exclusively with women.

The following article pursues most of the same arguments as its predecessors—indeed, the framing of the article, the readings of the compositions, and the discussions concerning subjectivity have been left virtually unchanged. The alterations principally involve the issue of sexuality itself, which now is articulated more provisionally than in earlier versions.

In 1987 I asked my undergraduates at the University of Minnesota to write short critical analyses of the second movement of Schubert's "Unfinished" Symphony. While I requested that they make a point of some sort in their essays, I was primarily concerned that they demonstrate their ability to deal with keys, themes, and formal structure. A couple of days before the papers were due, a small group of students arrived at my office looking perplexed. They asked shyly if I had been holding back any pertinent information concerning Schubert. When I asked them to elaborate, I was greeted by an embarrassed silence; but finally a young man (whom I knew to be a gay activist) blurted out: "Was Schubert gay?" Since I was not yet familiar with Maynard Solomon's work on Schubert,[9] I had no information to offer them. But I did ask why they had reached such a conclusion. Their answer: Schubert's procedures in this movement diverged so willfully from what they took to be standard practices and in such particular ways that they could find no other explanation.

My students were by no means the first to suggest a link between Schubert's stylistic idiosyncrasies and his sexuality—or at least his masculinity. As David Gramit has shown, critics since Robert Schumann have often characterized Schubert and his music as "feminine," as somehow lacking in the manliness associated with Beethoven.[10] By contrast, my students—some of whom are themselves gay—did not regard the unusual features of Schubert's music as evidence of insufficient manliness. Nor were they trying to sniff out a scandal about Schubert's private life; there was nothing prurient in their question. Rather they perceived in his music a different sensibility, and they wanted to include Schubert as one of a number of homosexual artists who have sought to counter a long history of pernicious cultural stereotypes by producing images of, by, and for themselves.

Their question belonged, in other words, to a branch of research just starting to emerge, as scholars such as Michel Foucault have begun to reveal the
staggering range of explanations for and responses to same-sex erotic practices in many parts of the world and at various times in history.[11] Because
the Christian West has usually branded these activities as illicit, persons
attracted to others of their own sex tend not to appear in historical documents except in trial records or in descriptions that paint them as sordid and
deviant. We are only now investigating the ways in which such people have
understood themselves as individuals and as members of communities or
subcultures—and now only because the relative tolerance of the last two
decades has permitted scholars to venture into this previously unspeakable
terrain, to pursue lines of inquiry earlier generations would have regarded as
professional suicide.

Maynard Solomon's essays argue that Schubert circulated within such a
subculture in early nineteenth-century Vienna. Basing his arguments on
Schubert's journal entries, on accounts of Schubert by his acquaintances,
and on letters among Schubert and his friends, he claims that Schubert probably engaged in sexual activities with other males. More important for my
purposes, he suggests that this aspect of Schubert's life was central to his
understanding both of himself and of his principal affectional and social
relationships.[12]

But although he deems it appropriate to explore these aspects of
Schubert's personal life, Solomon warns readers not to try to relate his findings to Schubert's music itself, and with good reason: many people still
simply assume that gay men—along with whatever they produce—will be
unmanly and, therefore, flawed. Malcolm Brown has demonstrated that
when Tchaikovsky's homosexuality came to light, labels such as "hysterical,"
"effeminate," and "structurally weak" began to proliferate in descriptions of
his music.[13] So long as homosexuality itself is understood as a defect, we
seem to have only two choices: either this inclination is irrelevant to the
music or—to the extent that it exerts any influence—it makes the music
defective as well.

But what of artists who refuse to find their sexualities shameful? An assortment of positions exists, even among gay people today. Many (especially those
of the pre-Stonewall generation) insist that one cannot discern sexual orientation by listening to the music that person produces; they strive to keep that
aspect of their lives separate from their work, in part to resist essentialist projections. And they are right to insist that a gay man may compose however he
pleases—just as a black musician may work within serialism without a hint
of African-based rhythms, a woman may write in an aggressive manner, or a

CONSTRUCTIONS OF SUBJECTIVITY IN SCHUBERT'S MUSIC ∾ 211

white male may attempt to invoke the tone of a lesbian blues singer in his own compositions. Music *need not* reveal anything personal about the composer (although the discursive decisions a composer makes—such as avoiding certain available options, affiliating with others—always signify).

Yet some artists *choose* to make a difference based on sexuality, gender, or ethnicity in what they produce. This has been especially true during the last twenty years, when the consolidation of African-American, Latino, feminist, lesbian, and gay networks has made such self-affirmation both viable and (for some, at least) politically desirable.[14]

When we turn to earlier periods in history, however, we are much less likely to discover evidence of such practices, for the necessary social conditions usually did not obtain. Moreover, the publicly oriented priorities of the arts before 1800 or so tended to preclude personal expression as an artistic goal. Consequently, it would be pointless to seek traces of gay self-identification in the motets of sixteenth-century composer Nicholas Gombert.

But it was around Schubert's time that representations of "the self" began to become prominent in the arts. By the 1830s a few writers who engaged in same-sex eroticism—most notably Théophile Gautier—had started presenting alternative constructions of gender, desire, and pleasure, making their sexual orientations a deliberate (i.e., not inadvert) dimension of their work.[15] Thus the historical conditions by themselves do not preclude the possibility that Schubert too was such an artist, albeit one of the earliest. And whatever his sexual preferences, Schubert's music challenged standard narrative schemata in ways that invite us to reflect on his particular articulations of subjectivity.

Of course, in order to consider Schubert's music as participating in any kind of representation, we have to be able to perceive the genres within which he worked as having something to do with the social world. Unfortunately, instrumental music has been defined for nearly two hundred years as self-contained, available only to the concerns of formal analysis. By maintaining this stance (which may seem quite neutral at first glance), the discipline has prohibited not only questions about sexuality, but *all* studies that would treat music as an active component of culture.

This is not the place to present a full theory of music and social meaning, though I have explained elsewhere my reasons for trying to pry open this music that has been sealed off from criticism.[16] My methods involve paying attention to semiotics, narrativity, genre, reception history, and cultural theory. Rather than protecting music as a sublimely meaningless activity that has managed to escape social signification, I insist on treating it as a medium that participates in social formation by influencing the ways we perceive our feelings, our bodies, our desires, our very subjectivities—even if it does so surreptitiously, without most of us knowing how. It is too important a cultural force to be shrouded by mystified notions of Romantic transcendence. As I proceed through the following discussion, I will sketch my rationales and point to other places where the reader might look for further evidence. But I want to make it clear from the outset that my approach—far from being standard musicological fare—is being developed here partly in tandem with the topic at hand.

Schubert lived at a critical moment in European history, when the ideals of the emerging middle class were replacing the rigid structures of the ancien régime. During this period of radical social transition, many of the concepts we now take for granted as fundamental—such as identity and masculinity—were still very much in flux. The versions of these concepts we now tend to accept as universal were constructed at this time, in part within the context of the arts: as Terry Eagleton has demonstrated, the aesthetic realm served as one of the principal sites where competing models of the individual and subjectivity could be explored.[17]

In literature the privileged genre was the bildungsroman (roughly translated, the novel of character development) in which a protagonist such as Wilhelm Meister or David Copperfield struggles to learn the ways of the world, to nurture inner resources, to reach maturity. Some of these novels involve female subjects (as in Jane Austen), but the genre more typically concerns the shaping of the new masculine subject. Through such novels, we learn how the proper bourgeois male was to acquire the strength of purpose to forge an autonomous identity, but also to cultivate the sensitivity that made middle-class men worthier than the aristocrats they were displacing.[18]

The musical equivalent of the bildungsroman was not opera, which always remains grounded in social interaction, but rather the seemingly abstract sonata procedure that organizes most classic and romantic instrumental music.[19] Sonata movements, which started to appear in the mid-eighteenth century, typically trace the trajectory of an opening thematic complex that passes through episodes of destabilized identity but arrives finally at the reconsolidation of the original key and theme. In its earlier manifestations, sonata was a relatively "objective" process: the dynamic qualities of the tonal schema that fueled it made each movement seem daring in its departures from certainty, yet ultimately reassuring as it displayed its ability to attain—as though by its own efforts—security and closure.

CONSTRUCTIONS OF SUBJECTIVITY IN SCHUBERT'S MUSIC ᕫ *213*

As this standard process became familiar, composers started modifying it in a variety of directions. Mozart, for instance, began to inflect his movements in such a way as to introduce subjective expression into the more objective formal plan of sonata. That is, he worked at striking a balance between the goal-oriented narratives that propel his pieces and the lyrical passages that suggest depth, sensitivity, interiority. In doing so, Mozart not only reflected, but actively participated in, the cultural shaping of the masculine self at this moment in history.[20]

Beethoven and Schubert belonged to successive generations, and while they continued to mine the potentials of sonata procedure, their approaches differed considerably both from Mozart and from each other. Beethoven's solutions were widely accepted as virtual paradigms, especially the one presented in the Third Symphony (the *Eroica*). In the opening movement of this celebrated symphony, the subjective force of the principal theme hammers away, apparently making its own formal pathway as it goes. Any distraction from its agenda—especially the tender motives that keep cropping up during the exposition—must be resisted or annexed for the sake of satisfactory self-development. When the subject finally appears in its definitive form in the coda, the listener can scarcely help cheering the strength and self-denial that made this hard-won, heroic identity feasible. When critics refer to the virility of Beethoven's music, they have in mind this kind of narrative and those types of gestures.

To be sure, Beethoven himself offered many other versions of subjectivity: one thinks immediately of the slow movement of the Ninth Symphony or the cavatina from op. 130 as instances of extraordinary openness, tenderness, and vulnerability. In fact, compositions such as op. 127 seem to try quite deliberately to critique the heroic model later so firmly associated with Beethoven's name.[21] But it is the phantom of the *Eroica* that haunts music criticism throughout the rest of the century and up until the present.[22] This is the standard against which everyone else is measured and—more often than not—found wanting.

Schubert's strategies are quite different from those of the *Eroica*. But they differ not because he was incapable of producing heroic narratives along the lines Beethoven had charted (nothing would have been easier than following that model, which was already available), but rather because he evidently wanted to explore other possibilities.[23] Unfortunately, Schubert's music was little known during his own day, and by the time it came to the attention of the greater public, compositions such as the *Eroica* had already been embraced not merely as *the* standard in music, but also as *the* model of German manhood. Thus began the tradition of casting Schubert as "feminine," in direct comparison with the hypermasculine figure Beethoven had become in the popular imagination. As Sir George Grove wrote:

> Another equally true saying of Schumann is that, compared with Beethoven, Schubert is as a woman to a man. For it must be confessed that one's attitude towards him is almost always that of sympathy, attraction, and love, rarely that of embarrassment or fear. Here and there only, as in the Rosamund B minor Entr'acte, or the Finale of the 10th symphony, does he compel his listeners with an irresistible power; and yet how different is this compulsion from the strong, fierce, merciless coercion, with which Beethoven forces you along, and bows and bends you to his will.[24]

Yet Schubert—no less than Mozart or Beethoven—was constructing models of male subjectivity. His have been read as "feminine," largely because subsequent generations have learned to reserve the term "masculine" for only the most aggressive formulations. And this speaks volumes for our limited notions of gender.

Before we leave the comparison, it is important to emphasize that Beethoven was scarcely a champion of heterosexuality, even if he did succeed in constructing what has been accepted as an ideal of masculinity in music. As Solomon's biography makes clear, this man was highly conflicted with respect to his sexuality: he never managed to sustain an intimate relationship, and his inclinations were decidedly homosocial—often expressly homoerotic.[25] Consequently, we have to be careful not to position him as "straight" in opposition to Schubert, but rather to bear in mind that both men may have been drawn to same-sex activities. The differences between them could be the result of Schubert's acceptance and Beethoven's horror of sexuality. We might hear Beethoven's greater tendency to violence not as strength or confidence, but as overcompensation for fears of inadequacy—fears that not only influenced Beethoven's self-image, but that plague bourgeois masculinity in general.[26] In any case, what is at issue is not Schubert's deviance from a "straight" norm, but rather his particular constructions of subjectivity, especially as they contrast with many of those posed by his peers.

It might be argued that the project of interrogating these aspects of Schubert's music ought to be delayed until the rest of the paradigm is complete. But while we need to know a great deal more about images of gender and narratives of desire within the whole repertory, it makes sense to start with Schubert, whose music has been heard by so many as making some important difference with respect to sensibility. Because we have a history of critics fretting about Schubert's masculinity and his music, his example offers us rare access into what nineteenth-century culture thought was at stake in "absolute music." As Eve Kosofsky Sedgwick has taught us, issues of sexuality are not at the margins of culture during this period, but are centrally what is being contested. Accordingly, studying Schubert can help us unlock the entire repertory.[27]

Let us turn to the second movement of the "Unfinished" Symphony. What is remarkable about this movement is that Schubert conceives of and executes a musical narrative that does not enact the more standard model in which a self strives to define identity through the consolidation of ego boundaries. Instead, each of several moments within the opening theme becomes a pretext for deflection and exploration: the passage drifts through time by means of casual, always pleasurable pivots that entice the E-major theme variously to C# minor, G major, E minor, and then—without warning or fanfare—back to E major (example 1).

This is *not* how one ordinarily establishes one's first key area. In a Beethovenian world, such a passage would sound vulnerable, its tonal identity not safely anchored; and its ambiguity would probably precipitate a crisis, thereby justifying the violence needed to put things right again.[28] Yet Schubert's opening section provokes no anxiety (at least not within the music itself—critics are another matter): it invites us to forgo the security of a centered, stable tonality and, instead, to experience—and even *enjoy*—a flexible sense of self. To be sure, a "proper" subject soon enters, stomping between tonic and dominant to solidify identity as it is more typically construed (example 2). It also soon turns grim, as it stakes out C# minor with the same cadential decisiveness. But the heroic posturing of this passage—clearly not to be heard as protagonist—suddenly yields to the opening materials, quietly proceeding as before. This abrupt intrusion of authority throws the principal theme and its porous ego into even greater relief.

The second key area is perhaps even more remarkable. Its single motive passes through a succession of transformations, from timid quaking (example 3a), to greater confidence (example 3b), to violent Sturm und Drang (example 3c). Yet despite the radical changes in the affective clothing of the theme and its twisting harmonies that appear to seek relief, its tonal position remains stuck on C#/D♭. Stable identity and the security of tonal center are here presented as a kind of prison from which subjectivity cannot escape, regardless of how much it strains. But with the final transformation, the motive splits into two personae that interact and together reach ravishing cadential unions (example 3d). It abandons its rigid key identity and floats easily from D major, to G and C, and back—through a sleight-of-hand modulation—to E for the recapitulation.

This second theme resembles in certain respects the first section of Schubert's Impromptu in C Minor, op. 90, no. 1, in which the theme becomes increasingly violent and yet can find no escape.[29] In the impromptu, a pivot leads to a flexible second subject that—while beautiful—cannot survive within the bleak world already defined by the opening. By contrast, in the second movement of the "Unfinished" it is the flexible opening theme that sets the terms, and the rigid second theme reaches its release by emulating the liberatory ideals of the first.

Significantly, while the recapitulation presents the first three transformations of the second theme more or less as before (albeit transposed), the final version is no longer necessary: it has merged with the opening materials, which reappear to close off the movement. The fusion of the two is most evident near the end, when the riff that previously led into the second theme is met instead by the opening (example 4). As they pass through a mysterious enharmonic pivot between E and A^b major, the two themes become interchangeable.[30]

It is finally the mediant of E major (g#/a^b), rather than its tonic or dominant, that provides the key to transcendence in this movement. This pitch was generated almost as though in a dream at the beginning of the movement: while the previous movement had ended by repeating over and over the futile cycling from b through c# to d, never managing any progress, the second opens with what can be heard as a continuation of that scalar trajectory, e-f#-g#, with this final pitch marking both the escape from the brooding key of B minor and the vulnerable status of the new key. So long as the g# remains, the utopia can continue to prevail; but with the erasure of that g# would come the return (conventionally speaking, the *inevitable* return) of B minor and the loss of the fragile world that has been constituted here. At the close, the melody holds onto the g#; it descends briefly to f# as though toward cadence on e, but then deflects back up to g#. An arpeggiated tonic triad arises from this pitch—harmonic certainty is assured—but the melody itself refuses to be grounded.[31]

Theodor Adorno compared Schubert's musical procedures with the facets of a crystal, noting that Schubert often shuns dynamic narrative and instead assembles compositions from clusters of similar motives.[32] Predictably, Adorno was unnerved by this "deviance" and saw it as evidence that Beethoven's celebrated synthesis between dynamic process and subjective identity was unraveling. Carl Dahlhaus has described Schubert's strategies in

CONSTRUCTIONS OF SUBJECTIVITY IN SCHUBERT'S MUSIC ∽ 217

Example 1

218 ∾ SUSAN McCLARY

Example 1, continued

Example 2

CONSTRUCTIONS OF SUBJECTIVITY IN SCHUBERT'S MUSIC ～ 219

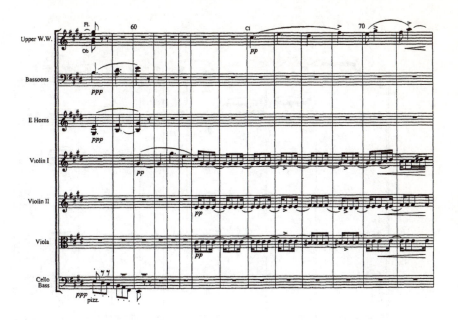

Example 3a

Example 3b

220 ∽ SUSAN McCLARY

Example 3c

CONSTRUCTIONS OF SUBJECTIVITY IN SCHUBERT'S MUSIC ∽ 221

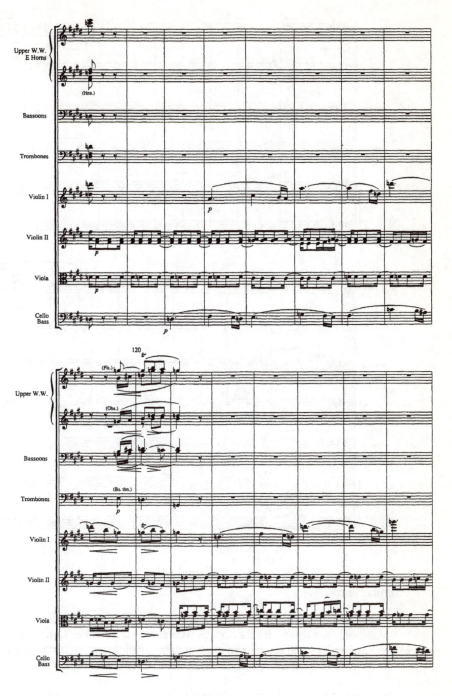

Example 3d

222 ∾ SUSAN McCLARY

Example 4

similar terms:

> The teleological energy characteristic of Beethoven's contrasting derivation
> is surely not absent in Schubert, but it is perceptibly weaker. Conversely,
> Schubert's procedure gains an element of the involuntary: the link between
> the themes is not deliberately brought about; it simply happens.[33]

Dahlhaus goes on to defend Schubert's artistry by arguing that his personae are *purposely* weak and involuntary. Yet despite this qualification, he still uses negative adjectives—"involuntary" and "weaker"—to describe Schubert's difference from Beethoven, his invariable yardstick.

It is important to remember, however, that Schubert's solutions required him to rework virtually every parameter of his musical language: he did not, in other words, slide passively or unwittingly into his imagery. Lawrence Kramer has written in detail about the ingenuity with which Schubert crafted his new harmonic language. Although we often speak of Schubert as if he managed to transmit his own subjective feelings directly into his music, these "feelings" had to be constructed painstakingly from the stuff of standard tonality.[34]

The second movement of the "Unfinished" appears to drift freely through enharmonic and oblique modulations, rather than establishing a clear tonic and pursuing a dynamic sequence of modulations; identities are easily shed, exchanged, fused, and reestablished, as in the magical pivot between E and A^b major near the end. But this illusion of drifting was not easy to accomplish, either conceptually or technically. In this movement, Schubert pushes the formal conventions of tonality to the limits of comprehensibility. Instead of choosing secondary keys that reinforce the boundaries of his tonic triad, Schubert utilizes every pitch of the chromatic scale as the pivot for at least one common-tone deflection. The tonic always rematerializes, but never as the result of a crisis. On some level, centered key identity almost ceases to matter, as Schubert frames chromatic mutation and wandering as sensually gratifying.[35]

To be sure, the exploration of chromaticism is one of the principal projects of nineteenth-century music. But not all chromaticism works the same way.[36] We usually credit the *Tristan* prelude with initiating the dissolution of tonality, but at least Wagner relies on a conventional association between desire and cadence: he imbues his chromaticism with a mixture of pleasure and pain as it continually defers the longed-for and dreaded telos. By contrast, Schubert tends to disdain goal-oriented desire per se for the sake of a sustained image of pleasure and an open, flexible sense of self—both of which are quite alien to the constructions of masculinity then being adopted as natural, and also to the premises of musical form as they were commonly construed at the time.

In this, Schubert's movement resembles uncannily some of the narrative structures that gay writers and critics are exploring today. Literary theorist Earl Jackson has recently identified several traits of what are usually taken as standard modes of narrative organization—traits that (not coincidentally) correspond to commonly held ideals concerning masculinity. These include clear dichotomies between active and passive roles, constant reinforcement of ego boundaries, and avoidance of experiences such as ecstasy or pleasure that threaten to destabilize the autonomous self. By contrast, Jackson describes gay male sexuality in terms of "a dialectic based on an intersubjective narcissism…in which self and other intermesh":

> Subjectivity within male coupling is episodic, cognized and recognized as stroboscopic fluctuations of intense (yet dislocated, asymmetrical, decentered) awareness of self-as-other and self-for-other…[Gay] male sexuality…is a circulatory system of expenditure and absorption, of taking/giving and giving/taking…The gay male body is polycentric and ludic, sexually actualized as a playground.[37]

Of course, even if Schubert's music strongly resembles some contemporary structures by gay artists, we must be wary of assuming that he must therefore have been gay. Gay men are quite capable of producing narratives of a more rigid sort, while heterosexuals might write in ways that resemble Schubert. Yet the association of the standard model with "proper" masculinity has a very long cultural history: Schubert has been labeled "feminine" precisely because he does not conform with the traits Jackson lists as premises of the assumed norm. But the characteristics Jackson admires as typical of narratives by gay men—excess, pleasure, play, porous identities, free exchange between self and other—have little to do with "femininity," nor are they accidental; they actively construct an alternative version of the masculine self. If an earlier period had no way of comprehending Schubert's music other than labeling it "feminine," Jackson presents a model for understanding Schubert's strategies as participating in the cultural construction of masculinity.

Interestingly, while Jackson's work was not yet available at the time, the characteristics he lists are also the elements my students pointed to when I asked why they thought Schubert might have been gay: they understood Schubert to be *refusing* the heroic narrative along with the rigidly defined identity it demands.[38] And I suspect that these associations account for why so many musicologists—myself included—were so willing to accept Solomon's results: Solomon's revelation that Schubert was drawn to same-sex eroticism was but the missing piece of a puzzle that now made all the sense in the world.[39]

We also have to be wary of trusting correspondences between cultures as distant from ours as early nineteenth-century Vienna, about which we know very little concerning sexual practices. Literary historians have traced attempts at depicting a homosexual sense of self only as far back as Gautier's *Mademoiselle de Maupin* (1835), and his solutions differ considerably from

Schubert's. Even Oscar Wilde was circumspect about what would count as homosexual subjectivity: his characters who exhibit signs of perversity tend to be masked and displaced, as in the case of *Salome*.[40]

Only very occasionally (most notably since the emergence of a visible gay movement in 1969) has this community been free to produce alternative constructions of desire and masculinity openly. Jackson developed his theories in conjunction with the fictional works of Robert Glück, who is regarded as a pioneer in what is called the "new narrative"; but Glück does not even pretend to represent all the varieties of gay subjectivities available today, much less some kind of transhistorical "gay sensibility." If Jackson's discussion of Glück has proved useful for this project, it is because Glück's strategies resemble so strongly what I had already perceived in and written about concerning Schubert's music. And it does seem clear that Schubert— for whatever reason—was producing constructions of male subjectivity that differed markedly from most of those that surrounded him.

Movements such as the second movement of the "Unfinished"—as well as sections of many other compositions—celebrate such differences as utopian: in these, the field is established by pleasurable free play, and the forces that threaten to disrupt are successfully defused. But there was another side to Schubert: a side that produced victim narratives, in which a sinister affective realm sets the stage for the vulnerable lyrical subject, which is doomed to be quashed. This is true, for example, of the first movement of the "Unfinished" Symphony.

What distinguishes these from standard movements is that they invite the listener to identify with a subject that stands in the subordinate position, rather than with the opening complex. Critics and listeners have long associated such themes with Schubert himself. Thus in his review of the first performance of the "Unfinished" Symphony (1865), Eduard Hanslick describes the exposition of the opening movement as follows:

> After that yearning song in minor, there now sounds in the cellos a contrasting theme in G major, an enchanting passage of song of almost *Ländler*-like ease. Then every heart rejoices, as if Schubert were standing alive in our midst after a long separation.[41]

When these subordinate themes—the beautiful tunes—are destroyed, there is no triumph of the self, but rather its victimization at the hands of a merciless fate.

226 ~ SUSAN McCLARY

I have written elsewhere about how such movements can be heard as symptomatic of the pessimism that prevailed in European culture in the 1820s: it is possible to back up such an explanation by comparing Schubert's tragic narratives with those that began to appear in literature at the same time.[42] Likewise, Kramer ties Schubert's idiosyncrasies to certain notions of subjectivity that circulated widely in early Romanticism.[43] In other words, we could regard these aspects of Schubert's music as culturally motivated rather than personal.

But at a time when art was concerned with self-expression, personal explanations also might well be considered. Solomon has pointed to the possibility of childhood trauma in explaining Schubert's dark side. Others, such as theorist Edward T. Cone, have linked such narratives to Schubert's reactions to his syphilitic condition, which brought him years of physical anguish and finally death.[44] As Schubert wrote in March 1824:

> Imagine a man whose health will never be right again, and who in sheer despair over this ever makes things worse and worse, instead of better; imagine a man, I say, whose most brilliant hopes have perished, to whom the felicity of love and friendship have nothing to offer but pain at best, whom enthusiasm...for all things beautiful threatens to forsake.[45]

Later the same year he wrote this slightly more accepting account of his situation:

> True, it is no longer that happy time during which each object seems to us to be surrounded by a youthful radiance, but a period of fateful recognition of a miserable reality, which I endeavor to beautify as far as possible by my imagination (thank God). We fancy that happiness lies in places where once we were happier, whereas actually it is only in ourselves.[46]

Both of these testify to Schubert's sense of estrangement from former good times and his immersion in "miserable reality." He still tries to envision beauty; at times he succeeds. But "miserable reality" often gets the upper hand in his musical narratives.

But Schubert might also have been predisposed to producing such narratives because he experienced alienation as a man whose pleasures were deemed illicit by his social context. As I mentioned above, it was suggested at the 92nd Street Y Schubertiade that Schubert's victim narratives might have been inspired by the fact that he was "short and fat," an explanation quickly seized as a preferable explanation to one grounded in sexuality. Yet it is important to notice that what gets punished in these narratives is an extraordinarily open form of pleasure (I must confess to being unsure what would count as the musical representation of "short and fat," but I think I can recognize pleasure when I hear it). Although we may never be able to ascertain why, some of Schubert's constructions—like narratives produced by many homosexual writers, including Marcel Proust, André Gide, Radclyffe Hall, Tennesee Williams, or James Baldwin—often present a tragic vision of the world in which the self and its pleasures are mutilated by an uncomprehending and hostile society.[47]

The hopelessness of the first movement of the "Unfinished," however one reads it, makes the vision of human interaction in the second all the more extraordinary. Because a conventional return to the overarching tonic B minor for subsequent movements would have returned us necessarily to "miserable reality," would have canceled out the g#/a♭ so tentatively established at the end of the movement, Schubert may well have been reluctant to complete this symphony.

Hanslick described the end of the movement as follows:

> As if he could not separate himself from his own sweet song, the composer postpones the conclusion of the [andante], yes, postpones it all too long. One knows this characteristic of Schubert: a trait that weakens the total effect of many of his compositions. At the close of the Andante his flight seems to lose itself beyond the reach of the eye, nevertheless one may still hear the rustling of his wings.[48]

Here once again we find the most loving of insights ruptured by a disclaimer that attempts to distance the anxious critic from the object of desire. I would prefer to say that Schubert concludes with a gentle yet firm refusal to submit to narrative conventions that would have achieved closure only at the expense of his integrity.

Standard accounts from Schumann to Dahlhaus warily label Schubert's music as sentimental, feminine, or weak, even as they mean to praise him. In other words, Solomon and I did not introduce the issue of sexuality into Schubert interpretation: Schubert has long been coded covertly as "effeminate" and downgraded accordingly. But Solomon's research invites us to read this dimension of Schubert's life and music in the affirmative terms made available by gay and feminist theory. For with recent scholarship, we can begin to see how culture has privileged certain models of masculinity and narrative structure, and it becomes easier to recognize and value alternatives. What has been perceived in Schubert's music as defective may at last be heard as purposeful, ingenious, and liberatory—and this is so whether or not he was actually involved in same-sex erotic activities.

Needless to say, Schubert's music need not be heard as having anything to do with sexuality; as we have seen, his idiosyncratic procedures can be interpreted along many other lines as well. I am not interested in dismissing other ways of appreciating this repertory, nor would I want to see his or anyone else's music reduced to nothing but evidence of sexual orientation. Moreover, it is possible to imagine women or heterosexual men devising similar strategies: male or female homosexuality is neither a necessary nor sufficient condition for the production of such narratives.

What does seem clear, however, is that Schubert was constructing images that later were marginalized, but that many of us today prefer to the more aggressive, heroic models that have prevailed. And while his music does not reduce to a simple allegory of sexuality, at the same time, his particular experiences of self, intimacies, and (perhaps) social disapproval might well be understood as factors in the formal procedures he designed. If we hear Schubert's music as offering deliberate counternarratives, we can learn much about how music participated in shaping notions of gender, desire, pleasure, and power in nineteenth-century culture. And we can stop the shameful practice of apologizing for his magnificent vision.[49]

Notes

1. Maynard Solomon, "Franz Schubert and the Peacocks of Benvenuto Cellini," *19th-Century Music* 12, no. 3 (Spring 1989): 193–206.

2. A word on terminology. There are no suitable words for an early nineteenth-century male who had sexual relations with other males. "Homosexual" is anachronistic because it comes from a later historical moment; it also implies an essential and clinically pathological condition. "Gay" comes from an even later time and represents a radically different political environment. Terms from earlier times tend to indicate only that a given individual commits particular kinds of acts (a "sodomite" is merely someone who commits sodomy). Thus while "same-sex erotic activities" is cumbersome, I use it rather than the easier (though misleading) alternatives. The term "queer" has been appropriated recently by many scholars working in this field, both despite and because of its usually pejorative connotations. In addition to its political implications, "queer" also has the advantage of side-stepping the quagmire of clinical terminology to designate identities, activities, or areas of research that resist hegemonic models of sexuality.

3. Edward Rothstein, "Was Schubert Gay? If He Was, So What?" *New York Times* (4 February 1992); "'And If You Play "Boléro" Backward...'" (16 February, 1992); and Bernard Holland, "Dr. Freud, Is It True That Sometimes, Tea Is Only Tea?" (17 February, 1992).

    Holland has continued his crusade of trying to render irrelevant such trivialities as gender, race, and sexuality. In a column "Social Cause As Weapon and Shield" (New York Times, Arts and Entertainment, 9 August, 1992), he advocates critical approaches that deliberately avoid taking such issues into account: "I would also hope that the shape and tone of Robert Mapplethorpe's photography might transcend worry about his sex life." As if part of the point of Mapplethorpe's work were not to insist on his sexuality, as if anyone besides Holland and Jessie Helms were "worrying" about that.

4.   *Gay/Lesbian Study Group Newsletter* 2, no. 1 (April 1991): 8–14. This issue also contains the unprinted responses to the *Times* from Philip Brett, Elizabeth Wood, and myself.

5.   Andreas Mayer, "Der Psychoanalytische Schubert: Eine kleine Geschichte der Deutungskonkurrenzen in der Schubert-Biographik, dargestellt am Beispiel des Textes 'Mein Traum,' " in *Schubert durch die Brille* 9 (1992): 7–31; Rita Steblin, "Franz Schubert und das Ehe-Consens Gesetz von 1815," *Schubert durch die Brille* 9 (1992): 32–42; and "Schubert's Sexuality: The Question Re-Opened," forthcoming in *19th-Century Music*, with a response by Solomon.

6.   For instance, Mayer accuses Solomon of conforming to a "p.c." agenda in his scholarship (20–21) and links him (30, n. 45) with Leonard Jeffries—the professor of African-American Studies at City University of New York who was removed as chair as the result of anti-Semitic statements made in conjunction with his Afrocentric theories.

7.   The editors of *19th-Century Music* have solicited reactions from Edward T. Cone, Robert Winter, and myself, and these will appear in the same issue with Steblin's article and Solomon's rebuttal. To put the matter briefly, some of Steblin's arguments—especially her detection of a couple of questionable translations in Solomon and her discussion of Viennese marriage-consent laws—are well taken. But others reveal a lack of sensitivity to the range of behaviors that might well occur within a subculture organized around shared homoerotic interests—especially at a time when the public affirmation of such interests was not yet possible. For instance, the fact that Schubert and others of his circle had women friends and considered or even entered into marriages does not necessarily mean they were not also involved in male-male sexual activities. While her article raises enough questions to warrant a reexamination of the situation, I do not believe it succeeds in discrediting Solomon's position. Moreover, the overkill quality of her attack makes it clear that she finds utterly intolerable the possibility that Schubert might have been attracted to other men.

8.   See his *Beethoven* (New York: Schirmer Books, 1977) and "Charles Ives: Some Questions of Veracity," *Journal of the American Musicological Society* 40 (1987), especially 466–69.

9.   Solomon first wrote about Schubert's sexuality in "Franz Schubert's 'My Dream,'" *American Imago* 38 (1981): 137–54, and this article received considerable attention from the gay community. Thus it is quite possible that my students had already heard reports of Schubert's homosexuality.

10.   David Gramit, "Constructing a Victorian Schubert: Music Biography and Cultural Values," paper presented for the 1991 meeting of the American Musicological Society, forthcoming in *19th-Century Music*. My thanks to Gramit for providing me with a copy of this paper. This tradition began with Robert Schumann's essay on Schubert's C major Symphony, throughout which Beethoven and Schubert are paired in terms of virility versus "womanliness." And the tradition lives on: Joseph Horowitz's preview article in the *New York Times* for the Schubertiade (19 January, 1992) had "Schubert and the Eternal, Inescapable Feminine" emblazoned across the page as a headline. See below for more on Schubert's image as "feminine." Note that neither Solomon nor I suggest that Schubert was feminine.

See also Eve Kosofsky Sedgwick, *The Epistemology of the Closet* (Berkeley/Los Angeles: University of California Press, 1991). Sedgwick argues that we cannot properly study twentieth-century culture without taking sexual orientation into account, for many of the debates that spawned modernism were reactions to what was perceived as the increasing homosexual presence in the arts. Gramit's article suggests that such tensions—or at least anxieties concerning virility—pervaded much of the nineteenth century as well.

11.   Michel Foucault's *History of Sexuality* is the pioneering work in this area. He died, unfortunately, after completing only the first three volumes of this vast project. See also Martin Bauml Duberman, Martha Vicinus, and George Chauncey, Jr., eds., *Hidden from History: Reclaiming the Gay and Lesbian Past* (New York: New American Library, 1989); and David Greenberg, *The Construction of Homosexuality* (Chicago: University of Chicago Press, 1988).

12.   For a neutral account of Schubert's companions and their ideals, see David Gramit, "The Intellectual and Aesthetic Tenets of Franz Schubert's Circle," Ph.D. dissertation, Duke University, 1987. Gramit presents the following summary of the foreword to one of their yearbooks (1817–1918): "through diligent study of the good, the true, and the beautiful, youths would mature to men who were manly, noble, and beneficial to society as a whole" (38).

While Steblin offers this quotation as evidence of the circle's nonsexual interests, this description fits perfectly within Dorianism: a widespread trend in nineteenth-century Germany and England in which platonic (i.e., homoerotic—as in Plato—rather than strictly nonsexual) relationships between older mentors and younger males were encouraged. The most famous manifestation of such practices is Wilde's Dorian Gray. For a historical and theoretical examination of Dorianism, see Richard Dellamora, *Fin de Siècle/Fin de Siècle: Sexual Politics and the Sense of an Ending in Late 19th- and 20th-Century Writing* (New Brunswick: Rutgers University Press, forthcoming).

13.   Malcolm Brown, paper presented at the 1990 meeting of the American Musicological Society.

14.   This is not to suggest that identity politics are entirely risk-free. A huge bibliography now exists in which theorists affiliated with marginalized groups weigh the benefits and dangers of what has been called "strategic essentialism." See, for instance, Gayatri Chakravorty Spivak, *In Other Worlds: Essays in Cultural Politics* (New York: Routledge, 1988); Judith Butler, *Gender Trouble: Feminism and the Subversion of Identity* (New York: Routledge, 1990); Drucilla Cornell, *Beyond Accommodation: Ethical Feminism, Deconstruction, and the Law* (New York: Routledge, 1991); Jonathan Dollimore, *Sexual Dissidence: Augustine to Wilde, Freud to Foucault* (Oxford: Oxford University Press, 1991); and Kwame Anthony Appiah, *In My Father's House: Africa in the Philosophy of Culture* (Oxford: Oxford University Press, 1992).

15.   I have learned a great deal from discussions with Richard Dellamora on the history of such constructions in literature. See his *Masculine Desire: The Sexual Politics of Victorian Aestheticism* (Chapel Hill: University of North Carolina Press, 1990) and *Fin de Siècle*. For other recent theoretical work on gay and lesbian self-representation in culture, see Dollimore, *Sexual Dissidence*; Diana Fuss, ed., *Inside/Out: Lesbian Theories, Gay Theories* (New York: Routledge, 1991); and the special issue, "Queer Theory: Lesbian and Gay Sexualities," in *differences* 3 (Summer 1991), Teresa de Lauretis, guest editor.

16.   See particularly the first chapter of my *Feminine Endings: Music, Gender, and Sexuality* (Minneapolis: University of Minnesota Press, 1991). For sample case studies, see also "The Blasphemy of Talking Politics during Bach Year," in Richard Leppert and Susan McClary,

eds., *Music and Society: The Politics of Composition, Performance and Reception* (Cambridge: Cambridge University Press, 1987); McClary, "A Musical Dialectic from the Enlightenment: Mozart's Piano Concerto in G major, K. 453, Movement 2," *Cultural Critique* 4 (1986): 129–69; and McClary, "Narrative Agendas in 'Absolute' Music: Identity and Difference in Brahms' Third Symphony," in Ruth Solie, ed., *Music and Difference,* (Berkeley and Los Angeles: University of California Press, 1993).

17. See Terry Eagleton, *The Ideology of the Aesthetic* (Oxford: Basil Blackwell, 1990).

18. For a superb study of the bildungsroman as a terrain where these issues are worked through, see Franco Moretti, *The Way of the World: The Bildungsroman in European Culture* (London: Verso, 1987). For an insightful discussion of how German-speaking intellectuals and artists of this time developed notions such as *Kultur* and *Bildung* in direct counterdistinction to French *civilisation,* see Norbert Elias, *The History of Manners,* trans. Edmund Jephcott (New York: Pantheon, 1978), 1–50.

19. For a similar position, see Leonard B. Meyer, *Style and Music: Theory, History, and Ideology* (Philadelphia: University of Pennsylvania Press, 1989): "In 'pure' instrumental music, the strategies chosen by composers to create unity were responsive to the tenets of Romanticism...Even in the absence of an explicit program, motivic continuity created a kind of narrative coherence. Like the chief character in a novel, the 'fortunes' of the main motive—its development, variation, and encounters with other 'protagonists'—served as a source of constancy throughout the unfolding of the musical process" (201).

20 This conception of sonata and Mozart's specific contributions are developed at length in my "Narratives of Bourgeois Subjectivity in Mozart's 'Prague' Symphony," in Peter Rabinowitz and James Phelan, eds., *Understanding Narrative* (Ohio State University Press, forthcoming).

21. I am now writing an article on Beethoven's implicit critiques of the heroic model.

22. See Sanna Pederson, "The Task of the Music Historian: or, The Myth of the Symphony after Beethoven," unpublished paper. I wish to thank Ms. Pederson for permitting me to see a copy of this paper.

23. For a similar argument concerning the songs, see Lawrence Kramer, "The Schubert Lied: Romantic Form and Romantic Consciousness," in Walter Frisch, ed., *Schubert: Critical and Analytical Studies* (Lincoln: University of Nebraska Press, 1986), 200–36.

24. Sir George Grove, *Beethoven, Schubert, Mendelssohn* (London: Macmillan, 1951), 238. The essays are reprinted from the first edition of the *Grove Dictionary of Music and Musicians* (1882). I doubt that his description of Beethoven is meant to sound negative.

25. Solomon, *Beethoven.* The extraordinary history of scholars fetishizing the letter to the "immortal beloved" dramatizes how desperately we have wanted to prove Beethoven's "normality." That all we have is a single letter to an unidentified person that perhaps was never sent shows the poverty of Beethoven's personal life. Schubert's was incomparably richer.

26. See again Eagleton, *The Ideology of the Aesthetic,* and Moretti, *The Way of the World,* for the contradictions faced by males during this period. For theoretical accounts of masculinity and its discontents, see Victor J. Seidler, *Rediscovering Masculinity: Reason, Language and Sexuality* (London and New York: Routledge, 1989); Jessica Benjamin, *The Bonds of Love: Psychoanalysis, Feminism, and the Problem of Domination* (New York: Pantheon, 1988); and Kaja Silverman, *Male Subjectivity at the Margins* (New York: Routledge, 1992).

27. Given the sexual ambiguity of so many of its foremost practitioners, we might even

consider the nineteenth-century German symphony—the music that dare not speak its meanings—as a genre of the closet.

28.   In a sense, of course, Beethoven resists conventional procedures far more explicitly than Schubert. He marks his departures from usual practices as dramatic events, virtually declaring war on the norms that would constrain him. Yet his transgressions rarely pass without reaction: his narratives both celebrate and punish deviation, in accordance with the contradictory pressures informing masculinity since the early nineteenth century. Even the cavatina in op. 130 and the third movement of the Ninth Symphony (mentioned earlier as open, vulnerable constructions) are met with responses of unparalleled violence: respectively, the Great Fugue and the ripping dissonances that open the finale of the Ninth. Beethoven upholds the Law even as he violates it; by contrast, Schubert simply "changes the subject" (pun intended).

29.   See my discussion of this piece in "Pitches, Expression, Ideology: An Exercise in Mediation," *Enclitic* 7 (Spring 1983): 76–86.

30.   It is interesting to note that Schubert liked to intertwine his name with that of his intimate friend Franz von Schober, creating the fusion "Schobert" (Solomon, "Franz Schubert and the Peacocks," 198). Beethoven occasionally works through similar pivots: see, for instance, the end of the variation movement in op. 127. Here too some kind of union is at issue, but it appears to be linked to the quasi-religious experience in the middle of the movement. By contrast, Schubert's movement bears no semiotic references to anything sacral—except, perhaps, this moment.

31.   See the quotation by Eduard Hanslick below.

32.   Theodor Adorno, "Schubert," *Moments Musicaux* (Frankfurt: Suhrkamp, 1964).

33.   Carl Dahlhaus, "Sonata Form in Schubert: The First Movement of the G-major String Quartet, op. 161 (D. 887)," trans. Thilo Reinhard, in Frisch, *Schubert,* 8–9.

34.   Kramer, "The Schubert Lied."

35.   Literary theorist Ross Chambers has recently been theorizing narrative digressions of this sort as formal expressions of subversive, antipatriarchal desire. I wish to thank Chambers for sharing his insights with me in conversation.

36.   For yet other alternatives, see the discussions of chromaticism in chapters 3 and 4 in my *Feminine Endings,* and in my *Georges Bizet,* Carmen (Cambridge: Cambridge University Press, 1992).

37.   Earl Jackson, Jr., "Scandalous Subjects: Robert Glück's Embodied Narratives," "Queer Theory" issue of *differences,* xv and 118–19. Jackson continues: "Understanding the extensions of these subjects into narratives which at once reflect and constitute them requires a narratology that takes into account the politics of sexual difference and the roles sexualities play in the generation of narrative form" (119).

38.   I have been gratified to hear from a number of gay men who testify to their having long heard Schubert along these lines. My thanks especially to composer Byron Adams and literary theorist/historian Wayne Koestenbaum.

39.   See, for instance, Richard Kramer, review of *Drei grosse Sonaten für das Pianoforte* and *Der Graf von Gleichen, in 19th-Century Music* 14 (1990): 215.

40.   On Wilde, see Dollimore, *Sexual Dissidence,* and Neil Bartlett, *Who Was That Man? A Present for Mr Oscar Wilde* (London: Serpent's Tail, 1988). I wish to thank Mike Steele for introducing me to Bartlett's book.

41.   Hanslick, quoted in Martin Chusid, ed., Norton Critical Score of the "Unfinished"

Symphony (New York: W. W. Norton, 1971), 114.

42. See the account in my "Pitches, Expression, Ideology."

43. Kramer, "The Schubert Lied."

44. Edward T. Cone, "Schubert's Promissory Note," *19th-Century Music* 5 (1982): 233–41. Cone discusses a *moment musical* in which a gentle, happy-go-lucky theme makes contact with another key, only to have the contamination of that key destroy the initial theme. He argues that such a formal plan cannot be explained without recourse to something beyond structural analysis, and he posits Schubert's syphilis as the key to this chilling composition. See also William Kinderman, "Schubert's Tragic Perspective," Frisch, *Schubert*, 65–83.

45. Otto Erich Deutsch, *Schubert: A Documentary Biography*, trans. Eric Blom (London: Dent, 1946), 339.

46. Deutsch, *Schubert*, 484.

47. Note that I am not reading this movement (as Rothstein suggested in his review) as the story of *A Streetcar Named Desire*, with Schubert playing the Blanche Dubois role. I am merely pointing out that something of the abjectness in this narrative runs through a number of prominent literary works as well. Nor is this a Freudian reading: I am claiming that Schubert is quite deliberately channeling his materials to produce such a narrative through a public discourse.

48. Hanslick, as quoted in Chusid, Norton Critical Score, 115.

49. I wish to thank Byron Adams, Paul Attinello, Philip Brett, Peter Burkholder, Ross Chambers, Richard Dellamora, David Gramit, George Haggerty, Joseph Horowitz, Owen Jander, Wayne Koestenbaum, Lawrence Kramer, Richard Kramer, Fred Maus, Tom Plaunt, Eve Sedgwick, Gary Thomas, Robert Walser, and James Westby for reading various versions of this paper and making invaluable suggestions.

Part Three

Popular Music

She was in control of her own sexuality and her life. She was a relatively good role model, compared with what else you saw."

9. Jane Bowers, "Women Composers in Italy, 1566–1700," *Women Making Music: The Western Art Tradition, 1150-1950,* ed. Jane Bowers and Judith Tick (Urbana: University of Illinois Press, 1986): "On 4 May 1686 Pope Innocent XI issued an edict which declared that 'music is completely injurious to the modesty that is proper for the [female] sex, because they become distracted from the matters and occupations most proper for them.' Therefore, 'no unmarried woman, married woman, or widow of any rank, status, condition, even those who for reasons of education or anything else are living in convents or conservatories, under any pretext, even to learn music in order to practice it in those convents, may learn to sing from men, either laymen or clerics or regular clergy, no matter if they are in any way related to them, and to play any sort of musical instrument'" (139–40).

An especially shocking report of the silencing of women performers is presented in Anthony Newcomb, *The Madrigal at Ferrara, 1579-1597* (Princeton: Princeton University Press, 1980). The court at Ferrara had an ensemble with three women virtuoso singers who became internationally famous. Duke Alfonso of Ferrara had the "three ladies" sing for Duke Guglielmo of Mantua and expected the latter to "praise them to the skies." "Instead, speaking loudly enough to be heard both by the ladies and by the Duchesses who were present [Duke Guglielmo] burst forth, 'ladies are very impressive indeed — in fact, I would rather be an ass than a lady.' And with this he rose and made everyone else do so as well, thus putting an end to the singing" (24).

See also the examinations of the restrictions placed on women as musicians and performers in Richard Leppert, *Music and Image: Domesticity, Ideology and Sociocultural Formation in Eighteenth-Century England* (Cambridge: Cambridge University Press, 1988); and Julia Kosa, "Music and References to Music in *Godey's Lady's Book, 1830-77*" (Ph.D. dissertation, University of Minnesota, 1988).

10. David Lee Roth, cited in Marsh, "Girls Can't Do," 165. I might add that this is a far more liberal attitude than that of most academic musicians.

11. This is not always an option socially available to male performers, however. The staged enactment of masculine sensuality is problematic in Western culture in which patriarchal rules of propriety dictate that excess in spectacles be projected onto women. Thus Liszt, Elvis, and Roth can be understood as effective in part because of their transgressive behaviors. This distinction in permissible activities in music theater can be traced back to the beginnings of opera in the seventeenth century. See Chapter 2. See also Robert Walser, "Running with the Devil: Power, Gender, and Madness in Heavy Metal Music" (Ph.D. dissertation, University of Minnesota, forthcoming).

12. Ellen Rosand, "The Voice of Barbara Strozzi," *Women Making Music*, 185. See also Anthony Newcomb, "Courtesans, Muses, or Musicians? Professional Women Musicians in Sixteenth-Century Italy," *Women Making Music*, 90–115; and Linda Phyllis Austern, " 'Sing Againe Syren': The Female Musician and Sexual Enchantment in Elizabethan Life and Literature," *Renaissance Quarterly* 42, no. 3 (Autumn 1989): 420–48. For more on the role of Renaissance courtesans in cultural production, see Ann Rosalind Jones, "City Women and Their Audiences: Louise Labé and Veronica Franco," *Rewriting the Renaissance: The Discourses of Sexual Difference in Early Modern Europe*, ed. Margaret W. Ferguson, Maureen Quilligan, and Nancy J. Vickers (Chicago: University of Chicago Press, 1986), 299–316.

13. See the excerpts from Clara's diary entries and her correspondences with Robert Schumann and Brahms in Carol Neuls-Bates, ed., *Women in Music: An An-*

thology of Source Readings from the Middle Ages to the Present (New York: Harper &
Row, 1982), 92-108; and Nancy B. Reich, *Clara Schumann: The Artist and the Woman*
(Ithaca: Cornell University Press, 1985). *Women in Music* contains many other documents revealing how women have been discouraged from participating in music
and how certain of them persisted to become productive composers nonetheless.

14. For examinations of how the mind/body split intersects with gender in West-
ern culture see Genevieve Lloyd, *The Man of Reason: "Male" and "Female" in Western
Philosophy* (Minneapolis: University of Minnesota Press, 1984); Susan Bordo, "The
Cartesian Masculinization of Thought," *Signs* 11, no. 3 (1986): 439-56; and Evelyn
Fox Keller, *Reflections on Gender and Science* (New Haven: Yale University Press,
1985).

For discussions of how these slipping binary oppositions inform music, see Ger-
aldine Finn, "Music, Masculinity and the Silencing of Women," *New Musicology*, ed.
John Shepherd (New York: Routledge, forthcoming); and my "Agenda for a Feminist Criticism of Music," *Canadian University Music Review*, forthcoming.

15. This binary opposition is not, of course, entirely stable. Imagination, for instance, is an attribute of the mind, though it was defined as "feminine" during the
Enlightenment and consequently becomes a site of contestation in early Romanticism. See Jochen Schulte-Sasse, "Imagination and Modernity: Or the Taming of the
Human Mind," *Cultural Critique* 5 (Winter 1986-87): 23-48. Likewise, the nineteenth-century concept of "genius" itself was understood as having a necessary
"feminine" component, although actual women were explicitly barred from this
category. See Christine Battersby, *Gender and Genius* (London: Women's Press,
1989).

The common association of music with effeminacy is only now being examined
in musicology. See Leppert, *Music and Image*; Linda Austern, " 'Alluring the Auditorie to Effeminacie': Music and the English Renaissance Idea of the Feminine," paper presented to the America Musicological Society, Baltimore (November 1988);
Jeffrey Kallberg, "Genre and Gender: The Nocturne and Women's History," unpublished paper; and Maynard Solomon, "Charles Ives: Some Questions of Veracity,"
Journal of the American Musicological Society 40 (1987): 466-69.

16. See Catherine Clément, *Opera, or the Undoing of Women*, trans. Betsy Wing
(Minneapolis: University of Minnesota Press, 1988); and Chapters 3 and 4 .

17. See Chapter 3.

18. Quoted in Gilmore, "The Madonna Mystique," 87. Nevertheless, Madonna
is often collapsed back into the stereotype of the *femme fatale* of traditional opera and
literature. See the comparison between Madonna and Berg's Lulu in Leo Treitler,
"The Lulu Character and the Character of *Lulu*," *Music and the Historical Imagination*
(Cambridge, Mass.: Harvard University Press, 1989), 272-75.

19. See Richard Dyer, "In Defense of Disco," *On Record: Rock, Pop, and the Written Word*, ed. Simon Frith and Andrew Goodwin (New York: Pantheon Press, 1990),
410-18.

20. See, for instance, Theodor W. Adorno's hysterical denouncements of jazz in
"Perennial Fashion—Jazz," *Prisms*, trans. Samuel Weber and Shierry Weber (Cambridge, Mass.: MIT Press, 1981), 121-32: "They [jazz fans] call themselves 'jitter-
bugs,' bugs which carry out reflex movements, performers of their own ecstasy"
(128). See again the quotation from Adorno on jazz and castration in Chapter 3.

21. However, I have often encountered hostile reactions on the part of white
middle-class listeners to Aretha Franklin's frank sensuality, even when (particularly
when) it is manifested in her sacred recordings such as "Amazing Grace." The argument is that women performers ought not to exhibit signs of sexual pleasure, for

this invariably makes them displays for male consumption. See the discussion in John Shepherd, "Music and Male Hegemony," *Music and Society: The Politics of Composition, Performance and Reception*, ed. Richard Leppert and Susan McClary (Cambridge: Cambridge University Press, 1987), 170–72.

22. Marsh, "Girls Can't Do," 162.

23. See Mary Harron's harsh and cynical critique of rock's commercialism in general and Madonna in particular in "McRock: Pop as a Commodity," *Facing the Music*, ed. Simon Frith (New York: Pantheon Books, 1988), 173–220. At the conclusion of a reading of Madonna's "Open Your Heart" video, Harron writes: "The message is that our girl [Madonna] may sell sexuality, but she is free" (218). See also Leslie Savan, "Desperately Selling Soda," *Village Voice* (March 14, 1989): 47, which critiques Madonna's decision to make a commercial for Pepsi. Ironically, when her video to "Like a Prayer" (discussed later in this essay) was released the day after the first broadcast of the commercial, Pepsi was pressured to withdraw the advertisement, for which it had paid record-high fees. Madonna had thus maintained her artistic control, even in what had appeared to be a monumental sellout.

24. See the discussion of the responses to Madonna of young girls in Fiske, "British Cultural Studies," 269–83. See also the report of responses of young Japanese fans in Gilmore, "The Madonna Mystique," 38. Madonna's response: "But mainly I think they feel that most of my music is really, really positive, and I think they appreciate that, particularly the women. I think I stand for everything that they're really taught to *not* be, so maybe I provide them with a little bit of encouragement." Considine, "That Girl," quotes her as saying: "Children always understand. They have open minds. They have built-in shit detectors" (17).

25. See Chapter 5.

26. When Jackson first signed on with Jam and Lewis, the music for this song was already "in the can" awaiting an appropriate singer. The mix throughout highlights the powerful beats, such that Jackson constantly seems thrown off balance by them. At one point the sound of a car collision punctuates her words, "I never knew what hit me"; and the ironic conclusion depicts the crumbling of her much-vaunted control. Not only was Jackson in a more dependent position with respect to production than Madonna, but the power relations *within the song itself* are very diferent from those Madonna typically enacts.

27. "There is also a sense of pleasure, at least for me and perhaps a large number of other women, in Madonna's defiant look or gaze. In 'Lucky Star' at one point in the dance sequence Madonna dances side on to the camera, looking provocative. For an instant we glimpse her tongue: the expectation is that she is about to lick her lips in a sexual invitation. The expectation is denied and Madonna appears to tuck her tongue back into her cheek. This, it seems, is how most of her dancing and groveling in front of the camera is meant to be taken. She is setting up the sexual idolization of women. For a woman who has experienced this victimization, this setup is most enjoyable and pleasurable, while the male position of voyeur is displaced into uncertainty." Robyn Blair, quoted in Fiske, "British Cultural Studies," 283.

28. For the ways women performers have been seen as inviting tragic lives, see Robyn Archer and Diana Simmonds, *A Star Is Torn* (New York: E.P. Dutton, 1986); Gloria Steinem, *Marilyn* (New York: Henry Holt, 1986). For an analysis of Hitchcock's punishments of sexual women, see Tania Modleski, *The Women Who Knew Too Much: Hitchcock and Feminist Theory* (New York: Methuen, 1988). For treatments of these issues in classical music, see my "The Undoing of Opera: Toward a Feminist Criticism of Music," foreword to Clément, *Opera*, ix–xviii; and Chapter 3 in this volume.

29. In Gilmore, "Madonna Mystique," Madonna states: "I do feel something for Marilyn Monroe. A sympathy. Because in those days, you were really a slave to the whole Hollywood machinery, and unless you had the strength to pull yourself out of it, you were just trapped. I think she didn't know what she was getting herself into and simply made herself vulnerable, and I feel a bond with that. I've certainly felt that at times—I've felt an invasion of privacy and all that—but I'm determined never to let it get me down. Marilyn Monroe was a victim, and I'm not. That's why there's really no comparison"(87). The term "sign crimes" is from Arthur Kroker and David Cook, *The Postmodern Scene: Excremental Culture and Hyper-Aesthetics* (New York: St. Martin's Press, 1986), 21.

30. All previous chapters have dealt extensively with these mechanisms.

31. For an excellent narrative account of the *Eroica*, see Philip Downs, "Beethoven's 'New Way' and the Eroica," *The Creative World of Beethoven*, ed. Paul Henry Lang (New York: W.W. Norton, 1970), 83-102. Downs's interpretation is not inflected, however, by concerns of gender or "extramusical" notions of alterity.

32. See the discussion in Chapter 5.For other readings of the Ninth Symphony, see Leo Treitler, "History, Criticism, and Beethoven's Ninth Symphony" and " 'To Worship That Celestial Sound': Motives for Analysis," *Music and the Historical Imagination*, 19-66; and Maynard Solomon, "Beethoven's Ninth Symphony: A Search for Order," *19th-Century Music* 10 (Summer 1986): 3-23.

33. Fiske, "British Cultural Studies," 262. For more on constructions of masculine subjectivity, see Arthur Brittan, *Masculinity and Power* (London: Basil Blackwell, 1989), and Klaus Theweleit, *Male Fantasies*, Vols. I and II, trans. Stephen Conway, Erica Carter, and Chris Turner (Minneapolis: University of Minnesota Press, 1987 and 1989). I owe my knowledge of and interest in metal to Robert Walser. I wish to thank him for permitting me to see his "Forging Masculinity: Heavy Metal Sounds and Images of Gender," in *Sound and Vision*, ed. Simon Frith, Andrew Goodwin, and Lawrence Grossberg (forthcoming).

34. See again the citations in note 14; Teresa de Lauretis, "Desire in Narrative," *Alice Doesn't* (Bloomington: Indiana University Press, 1984), 103-57, and "The Violence of Rhetoric: Considerations on Representation and Gender," *Technologies of Gender* (Bloomington: Indiana University Press, 1987), 31-50; and Mieke Bal, *Lethal Love: Feminist Literary Readings of Biblical Love Stories* (Bloomington: Indiana University Press, 1987).

35. Compare, for example, the opening movement of Schubert's "Unfinished" Symphony, in which the tune we all know and love is in the second position and is accordingly quashed. George Michael's "Hand to Mouth" (on the *Faith* album) is a good example of the same imperatives at work in popular music. In both the Schubert and Michael, the pretty tune represents illusion up against harsh reality. My thanks to Robert Walser for bringing the Michael song to my attention.

36. This strategy of always staying in motion is advocated in Teresa de Lauretis, "The Technology of Gender," especially 25-26. See also Denise Riley, *"Am I That Name?": Feminism and the Category of "Women" in History* (Minneapolis: University of Minnesota Press, 1988); and Kaja Silverman, "Fragments of a Fashionable Discourse," in *Studies in Entertainment: Critical Approaches to Mass Culture*, ed. Tania Modleski (Bloomington: Indiana University Press, 1986), 150-51. I discuss Laurie Anderson's "O Superman" or "Langue d'amour" in terms of these strategies in Chapter 6.

37. Some of the so-called Minimalist composers such as Philip Glass and Steve Reich also have called the conventions of tonal closure into question, as did Debussy at an earlier moment. See my "Music and Postmodernism," *Contemporary Music Re-*

view, forthcoming. And see the discussions of Schoenberg's (very different) strategies for resisting the narrative schemata of tonality and sonata in Chapters 1 and 4.

38. Andrew Goodwin advances a similar argument in "Music Video in the (Post) Modern World," *Screen* 18 (Summer 1987): 39–42.

39. In the souvenir program book from her 1987 tour, Madonna is quoted as saying: "Madonna is my real name. It means a lot of things. It means virgin, mother, mother of earth. Someone who is very pure and innocent but someone who's very strong." Needless to say, this is not how the name has always been received.

40. For a cynical interpretation, see Steve Anderson, "Forgive Me, Father," *Village Voice*, April 4, 1989: "Madonna snags vanguard attention while pitching critics into fierce Barthesian discussions about her belt buckles. Certainly she's an empire of signs, but the trick behind the crucifixes, opera gloves, tulle, chains, and the recent rosary-bead girdle is that they lead only back to themselves, representing *nothing*" (68).

But see also the complex discussion in Fiske, "British Cultural Studies," 275–76, which quotes Madonna as saying: "I have always carried around a few rosaries with me. One day I decided to wear [one] as a necklace. Everything I do is sort of tongue in cheek. It's a strong blend—a beautiful sort of symbolism, the idea of someone suffering, which is what Jesus Christ on a crucifix stands for, and then not taking it seriously. Seeing it as an icon with no religiousness attached. It isn't sacrilegious for me." Fiske concludes that "her use of religious iconography is neither religious nor sacrilegious. She intends to free it from this ideological opposition and to enjoy it, use it, for the meanings and pleasure that it has for *her* and not for those of the dominant ideology and its simplistic binary thinking."

41. For excellent discussions of the Catholic tradition of female saints and erotic imagery, see Caroline Walker Bynum, "The Female Body and Religious Practice in the Later Middle Ages," *Zone: Fragments for a History of the Human Body*, ed. Michel Feher et al. (New York: Zone, 1989), 160-219; and Julia Kristeva, *Tales of Love*, trans. Leon S. Roudiez (New York: Columbia University Press, 1987), especially 83-100 and 297-317.

This association is in line with many of Madonna's statements concerning Catholicism, such as her claim that "nuns are sexy" (Fiske, "British Cultural Studies," 275). However, she need not be aware of Saint Teresa in order for these kinds of combinations of the sacred and erotic to occur to her. Once again, her experiences as a woman in this culture mesh in certain ways with the traditional symbolism of holy submission in Christianity, and thus her metaphors of spirituality are similar in many ways to Saint Teresa's. She also intends to create this collision in the song and video. In Armond White, "The Wrath of Madonna," *Millimeter*, June 1989, Mary Lambert (director of the "Like a Prayer" video) states: "Madonna and I always work together on a concept. We both felt the song was about sexual and religious ecstasy" (31). The black statue in the church is identified as Saint Martin de Porres. I wish to thank Vaughn Ormseth for bringing this article to my attention.

42. See the many settings of texts from the Song of Songs by composers such as Alessandro Grandi and Heinrich Schütz. The sacred erotic likewise influenced the literary and visual arts. See Bernini's sculpture of, or Richard Crashaw's poem concerning, Saint Teresa. I am at the moment writing a book, *Power and Desire in Seventeenth-Century Music* (Princeton: Princeton University Press, forthcoming), that examines this phenomenon.

43. Quoted in Liz Smith's column, *San Francisco Chronicle*, April 19, 1989, E1. I wish to thank Greil Marcus for bringing this to my attention. Lydia Hamessley first

pointed out to me the significance of inside and outside in the organization of the video.

44. White, "The Wrath of Madonna," 31.

45. For an excellent discussion of the political strength of the music, rhetoric, and community of the black church today, see the interview of Cornel West by Anders Stephanson in *Universal Abandon? The Politics of Postmodernism*, ed. Andrew Ross (Minneapolis: University of Minnesota Press, 1988), 277–86. Madonna speaks briefly about her identification with black culture in Zehme, "Madonna," 58.

46. For another sympathetic discussion of the politics of this video, see Dave Marsh, "Acts of Contrition," *Rock & Roll Confidential* 67 (May 1989): 1-2.

CHAPTER 10

Thinking Blues

One of the anxieties often voiced in accounts of twentieth-century music involves a construct called "the main stream." Donald Tovey's classic essay introduced the term to naturalize what we now refer to as "the canon," and many a composer and critic has attempted to trace the continuation of that main stream in the aftermath of World War I.[1] But as early as 1967, Leonard B. Meyer announced the futility of this venture, arguing instead that our time is characterized most by its stylistic pluralism.[2] Still, in narrative histories of twentieth-century music (by which is meant the continuation of Tovey's classical canon), musicologists continue to grope for the main stream, to grasp hopefully at various trickles, to lament the loss of orientation its disappearance has effected.

But if twentieth-century music has no single main stream, it does at least have something more coherent to bequeath the future than the various trickles we grasp at with a mixture of hope and despair. If I hesitate to label it *the* main stream, I have no qualms comparing it to a mighty river. It follows a channel cut by a force known as the blues.

We can trace something called blues back as far as the beginning of the twentieth century, and it has remained an active generator of new musical movements up until the present moment. When LeRoi Jones

Thinking Blues / 33

published his powerful book *Blues People* in 1963, his title referred to the African American musicians who fashioned the blues out of their particular historical conditions and experiences.[3] Yet a music scholar of a future time might well look back on the musical landscape of the 1900s and label us all "blues people": those who inhabited a period dominated by blues and its countless progeny.

That musical landscape would include such diverse items as the spiritual songs of Blind Willie Johnson, his proto-heavy-metal disciples Led Zeppelin, the stride piano of James P. Johnson, the earthy frankness of Ma Rainey and her heiress Janis Joplin, the electrified Chicago sound of Muddy Waters, the mournful country whine of Hank Williams, the exuberant Cajun stomp of Queen Ida and her Bontemps Zydeco Band, the elegant jazz arrangements of Duke Ellington, the gospel-tinged shouts of Little Richard as he ignited rock and roll, the adolescent surfer songs of the Beach Boys, James Brown's godfathering of soul, echoes from Nigerian and Zulu pop, the modernist irony of Thelonious Monk, the tormented quest for mystical union in albums by P. J. Harvey, the postmodern collages of John Zorn, not to mention contemporary resonances in rap. As much as these musics may differ from each other, they unite in engaging with the conventions of the blues.

Contrary to a popular belief that regards blues as some kind of unmediated expression of woe, the conventions underlying the blues secure it firmly within the realm of culture; a musician must have internalized its procedures in order to participate creatively within its ongoing conversation. Albert Murray writes:

> It is not a matter of having the blues and giving direct personal release to the raw emotion brought on by suffering. It is a matter of mastering the elements of craft required by the idiom. It is a matter of idiomatic orientation and the refinement of auditory sensibility in terms of idiomatic nuance. It is a far greater matter of convention, and hence tradition, than of impulse. . . . It is not so much what blues musicians bring out of themselves on the spur of the moment as what they do with existing conventions.[4]

34 / *Conventional Wisdom*

And yet reliance on convention is rarely held to be incompatible with creativity in blues-based music. How does this musical universe operate, and what can we learn from it?

Before proceeding further, let me say a few words about my purpose in this chapter. I am not presuming to add anything substantial to available knowledge about blues: few genres of twentieth-century music have generated a more extended bibliography.[5] Likewise, I am not attempting to legitimate blues—this music and its practitioners do not need my help or the acknowledgment of academic musicology. Nor—let me hasten to assure you—am I setting up a comparison between African American and European-based musics in order to trash the latter. I promise to be just as affirmative in the next chapter on eighteenth-century tonal procedures.

I have two principal reasons for spending a chapter on this genre. First, I think that blues can help academic music study out of a long-standing methodological impasse: I am drawing on blues as a clear example of a genre that succeeds magnificently in balancing convention and expression, and I will make use of this model as I reexamine the European eighteenth century in chapter 3. Second, I firmly believe that any account of twentieth-century Western music must dwell extensively on the blues in its various manifestations because this is the music that has most shaped our era. Finally, the blues-based repertory deserves our careful attention simply because it contains so much superb music, and I take this to be among the principal reasons we bother to study any repertory.

The blues is largely the product of a diasporic people, though the genre did not originate in Africa. When procedures recognizable as blues first entered the historical record around 1900, they already testified to centuries of fusions with North American genres. I have occasionally heard the claim that no trace of Africa remains in the blues, that African practices were thoroughly eradicated from the music of black people under slavery, and that we must admit this, even while we may mourn the loss involved.[6] And without question, blues harmonies bear witness to European influence—the result of exposure to hymns, dances, popular ballads, fiddle tunes, and marches that circulated widely in the United States during the nineteenth century. Most of the instruments played by blues musicians originated in Europe; lyrics are sung in English; and, as Jones and Lawrence Levine have pointed out, even the emphasis on individual subjectivity in blues poetry and music resembles European practices more than those of Africa.[7]

But most specialists—including not only Jones and Levine but also (among many others) Gunther Schuller, Olly Wilson, Christopher Small, Henry Louis Gates, Peter van der Merwe, Paul Gilroy, and Samuel Floyd—identify in the blues a great many typically African elements.[8] They argue persuasively that African Americans—long after having been uprooted from their homelands and against enormous odds—managed to maintain and transmit a core of collective memory while in exile, especially through their music. For example, blues musicians privilege a vast palette of sounds that European-trained ears tend to hear as distorted or out of tune. As Ernest Borneman explained in a classic essay from the 1940s:

> While the whole European tradition strives for regularity—of pitch, of time, of timbre and of vibrato—the African tradition strives precisely for the negation of these elements. In language, the African tradition aims at circumlocution rather than at exact definition. The direct statement is considered crude and unimaginative; the veiling of all contents in ever-changing paraphrases is considered the criterion of intelligence and personality. In music, the same tendency towards obliquity and ellipsis is noticeable: no note is attacked straight; the voice or instrument always approaches it from above or below, plays around the implied pitch without ever remaining any length of time, and departs from it without ever having committed itself to a single meaning. The timbre is veiled and paraphrased by constantly changing vibrato, tremolo and overtone

36 / *Conventional Wisdom*

effects. The timing and accentuation, finally, are not *stated*, but *implied* or *suggested*. The musician challenges himself to find and hold his orientation while denying or withholding all signposts.[9]

The rhythmic patterns that animate any given realization of blues likewise are related to African attitudes and tied to a vocabulary of physical gestures, kinesthetic motions, and dance steps quite unlike anything European. Music in many African cultures is inseparable from dance on the one hand and spirituality on the other. Historian Sterling Stuckey writes: "For the African, dance was primarily devotional, like a prayer. . . . The whole body moving to complex rhythms . . . was often linked to the continuing cycle of life, to the divine."[10] Thus the groove that sustains the blues serves as a conduit linking the body, words, musicians, listeners, and a realm often experienced as sacred. As we saw in the gospel music of the Swan Silvertones in chapter 1, no transcendence without the body, no individual redemption without the community.

Most important is the way the blues operates according to certain models of social interaction characteristic of African cultures. The practice nineteenth-century blacks called signifying—long before Henry Louis Gates revived the word as "signifyin(g)" for fashionable critical jargon—strives to maintain a socially shared framework within which participants exhibit prowess and virtuosity through highly individualized elaborations. Signifyin(g) thus ensures the continuity of community, at the same time that it celebrates the imagination and skill of each particular practitioner. Gates developed his theory of signifyin(g) in order to account for why African American writers often prefer to reinhabit conventional structures rather than treat formal innovation as the be-all-and-end-all of literary value, as it is for many European-based artists and critics. And he drew heavily on the example of blues in explaining this alternative worldview that pervades so many African American cultural activities.

We cannot trace the precise history of the blues, for those who had the means of preserving music before the twentieth century did not

Thinking Blues / 37

often write down the music produced by African Americans. Occasionally a style ascribed to the black population sparked a response among European or Euro-American musicians, but we cannot tell much about the original music itself from these appropriations—except that its relation to the body and its affective qualities appealed to those with access to notation.[11]

The blues seems to have emerged from many different kinds of musics, including shouts, spirituals, gospel hymns, field hollers, ritual laments, dances, and virtually every musical genre that African Americans had encountered. Whatever its history as a strictly oral practice, we can trace the genre with confidence only after it entered into writing. The first "recording" of blues per se came from the pen of W. C. Handy in 1912, who was promptly granted the title "Father of the Blues."[12] But even as Handy was composing his blues, a far more powerful form of writing—sound recording—was making its first appearances, and it is to this technology that we owe most of what we know about blues history.

It is important to keep in mind that recording and its commercial distributing networks did not merely preserve this music; it also actively shaped the blues as we know it. We cannot, in any case, recover whatever it was that existed before notation and recording crystallized it into something like its standard format. Among the first commercial successes of the new medium were the recordings of the blues queens, Ma Rainey, Bessie Smith, Ida Cox—women who blended modes of performance borrowed from church, rural entertainments, vaudeville, and urban popular idioms when they sang songs such as Handy's "St. Louis Blues" and their own compositions. The Mississippi Delta bluesmen of the late 1920s and the 1930s, many of whom were discovered by recording agents scouring the South for material to supply the burgeoning market of black consumers, had been heavily influenced by early commercial recordings.[13] Even so "authentic" a musician as Robert Johnson learned in part from listening to Bessie Smith on 78s, and he tailored his own songs to accommodate the three-minute limit of sound-recording technology.

In other words, no matter how deeply we excavate the blues in search of a bedrock of pure folk music, we always find the mediating presence of the culture industry.[14] Yet, as George Lipsitz has argued with respect to popular culture and ethnic identity over the course of this century, uncovering commercial interventions in such a genealogy does not discredit it.[15] For it has not been despite but rather *by means of* the power of mass mediation that the explosive energies of the blues managed to spread and develop in as many directions as it did; even so influential an artist as Ma Rainey was unknown outside the South until Paramount Records signed her in 1923.[16] And while the threat of cooptation always accompanies the commercial media, so do the possibilities of worldwide distribution, dialogue across the barriers of class and race, and the unpredictable responses and tangents of development that can proceed from such heightened visibility and audibility.

We often underestimate the impact of the technology of writing on medieval music or of commercial printing on culture since the Renaissance, but it is much more difficult to ignore the cultural explosion made possible by twentieth-century innovations. With sound recording, a previously silenced group, which had been represented to the broader public (when at all) only through European notation, descriptions, and imitations, could begin to explore and literally to broadcast their own various approaches to self-representation. To be sure, these new voices had to negotiate with those who regulated the industry, and the abuses that resulted have sometimes seemed to outweigh the triumphs. Yet this chain of negotiations has had the effect of altering in an African direction the worldwide history of music, the body, sensibilities, and much else.

TWELVE-BAR BLUES

Viewed from a European vantage point and with European criteria, the blues might seem impoverished. Indeed, a more rigid convention is difficult to imagine, as a three-phrase harmonic pattern with a two-line

poetic scheme is repeated in verse after verse, blues number after blues
number. And yet it is the formulaic status of that pattern that has enabled it to give rise to so many rich and varied repertoires, that allowed
it to function so effectively as what literary critic Houston Baker calls a
matrix of African American memory, to sustain personalized improvisation, to maximize communication and the immediate appreciation
by listeners of even the most minute inflections.[17]

I have chosen one of the best-known blues—the opening verse of
W. C. Handy's "St. Louis Blues," as performed by Bessie Smith and
Louis Armstrong—to serve as a schematic model for the blues procedure.[18] For each line of lyrics, I have indicated the underlying harmony
for each successive bar, along with common alternatives. Even when
performed by a single musician (as in the example below by Robert
Johnson), each four-bar section operates on the basis of a call/response
mechanism, with two bars of call followed by two of instrumental "response."

Line 1:	I hate to see	the ev'ning sun go	down	
(1–4 mm.)	I	IV (or I)	I	I^7 (V of IV)

Line 2:	I hate to see	the ev'ning sun go	down	
(5–8)	IV	IV	I	I

Line 3:	It makes me think I'm	on my last go	round.	
(9–12)	V	IV (or V)	I	(V^7)

Unlike the harmonic practices of European classical music (which
is where individualistic expression is most often registered), the
changes in the standard twelve-bar blues serve as a dependable, little-
changing background that articulates the formal divisions within the
lyrics and heightens the rhetorical distinctions among the lines of text.
Typically, the first phrase is harmonically static, beginning and ending
as it does on the tonic, though it may be inflected to IV in bar 2. Following the two-bar "call" (the verbal statement), the "response" stays

40 / *Conventional Wisdom*

grounded on the tonic, though a seventh often enters in preparation for the move to IV.

The second phrase repeats the first line of text, but this time it begins on IV. The "call" takes place in this other harmonic region, then returns to I for a cadence at the beginning of bar 7; the "response" maintains this area of repose. To be sure, the alternation between these two closely related chords—I and IV—creates only a slight degree of tension. Yet it allows for two quite different interpretations of a single line of text: the stable "call" of the first line gets unsettled by its response, leading to a reconsideration of the "call" in the second line, cast now in the new light of a changed harmonic context. A blues singer will usually convey subtle but distinctly different implications of that line when she or he presents it a second time with the harmony tilted slightly askew. Moreover, the second "response" stabilizes by returning to the tonic rather than pushing toward reorientation as in the first line. Thus, even if these fundamental harmonies ensure maximal security, such minimal alterations permit a significant shift in tone. The result is something like the harmonic equivalent of a cross-rhythm, with textual sameness and harmonic sameness held in tension against one another.

The most dramatic contrast comes with the beginning of the third line, which delivers the consequent—the anticipated punchline—to the twice-stated first line of the lyrics. This moment is highlighted by a move to V, which usually relaxes after a bar to IV, and then returns back to I. Note that the harmonic rhythm gradually accelerates through the three segments of the blues: the first line sustains a single area for four bars, and the second spends two bars each on IV and I. Now the harmonies begin to shift every bar, producing greater animation, and placing a strong accent halfway through the "call." In fact, the "call" this time may move through three harmonies, V-IV-I, underscoring the sentiment expressed there; if the first line throws out a proposition, the second mulls over it, and the third draws emphatic conclusions.

Harmonic closure arrives punctually at the beginning of bar 11, yet musicians typically undermine that sense of an ending by stepping away from I to V^7, then building momentum through a "turnaround" that pushes forward into the next cycle. These junctures between verses count as among the most important musical challenges for performers, as they work to arouse a desire for continuation. A good blues band can keep going indefinitely—all night long, as they often boast—by converting what is technically an additive structure into an ever-changing process in which every detail "signifies." Like Scheherazade, blues performers learn how to imply certainty, then suspend it long enough to hook the listener into anticipating another round. And still another. If (unlike Scheherazade) their lives don't depend on the success of their strategies, their livelihoods do.[19]

This simple procedure turns out to be exceptionally resilient, capable of undergirding the most varied of subjects, affects, and styles. If individual blues chords do not operate on the basis of deviation for purposes of expression (as, for instance, an unexpected Neapolitan or a move to $^{\flat}VI$ might in a Schubert song), they do underwrite a powerful rhetorical structure, and the dynamic they chart has been refined by many generations of performers interacting with audiences. While our attention focuses on the imaginative nuances displayed by each new instantiation of the blues, the facilitating pattern itself counts as the most important signifier in the lot: it acknowledges a social history, a lineage descending from a host of tributaries. And with each verse, each performance, it reinscribes a particular model of social interaction.

Within the context of each particular manifestation, however, few people listening to the blues pay much attention to the pattern itself. If the pattern guarantees coherence and the survival of collective memory, it also hovers in the background, accommodating and articulating (as though "naturally") the project at hand. Thus in order to appreciate how the blues operates as a cultural force, we need to examine closely some specific moments and tunes.

It would be absurd to try to treat a genre as pervasive as blues comprehensively in such a short space. My purpose here is to try to demonstrate a critical approach that takes into account the conventions of

42 / *Conventional Wisdom*

blues and historical context, as well as the particularities of the music itself. Accordingly, I will confine myself in this chapter to addressing three tunes only, representing women's Classic Blues, Delta blues, and the blues-based rock of the late 1960s. I will return to the blues in the final chapter when I deal with contemporary compositions by John Zorn, Prince, and Public Enemy that engage once again with blues patterns—no longer as the conventional space they inhabit but as the locus of shared cultural memory, available for citation in the production of new meanings.

BESSIE SMITH: "THINKING BLUES"

Bessie Smith was known during her illustrious career as the Empress of the Blues. Like many of the black women who became stars during the first decade of mass-mediated recording, Smith regarded blues as only one of several marketable genres. For although born and raised in Tennessee, she learned about blues not from oral tradition but from her mentor and rival Ma Rainey; Rainey in turn had learned this mode of expression—at least according to her testimony—from a young girl whom she overheard singing to herself after one of Rainey's tent shows, sometime during the first decade of the century. Rainey incorporated blues into her act (Ma and Pa Rainey, "Assassinators of the Blues," with the Rabbit Foot Minstrels) and found that her audiences responded enthusiastically when she offered them what they perceived as their own music. Smith absorbed both style and format, then, from a context devoted to public entertainment, and when she moved into more urban environments, she continued fusing blues with the popular songs of vaudeville and with a newly emerging idiom known as jazz.

As I have already mentioned, by the time blues started showing up in written or recorded form, it already had merged with commercial enterprises. Yet there exists a cultural mythology (stemming largely from the 1960s and for reasons we will explore later) that wants to trace a pure lineage of blues from a cluster of rural, male blues singers

Thinking Blues / 43

recorded in the 1930s. And that mythology tends either to erase the women who first brought the blues to broad public attention or else to condemn them for having compromised that pure lineage with commercial popular culture.

But Simon Frith and Howard Horne have suggested that the reason for this marginalization might involve even more complex cultural tensions. If the blues came to represent an unassailably virile form of masculinity to British rockers (the musicians largely responsible for the mythologizing of Delta blues), then women could not be acknowledged at all in the canon—let alone as its progenitors. Frith and Horne go on to explain that this association in England of blues/rock with manliness may help account for why so few women art-school students in the 1960s turned to music for self-expression; they became, instead, the vanguard of feminist visual and performance artists.[20] Although these are the concerns of a later and very different group of listeners/ practitioners, they have, in effect, shaped the ways we now usually understand the historical role and contributions of women blues singers.

Purity and authenticity were rarely urgent matters for working black musicians who had to negotiate with real conditions—the securing of gigs, audiences, recording deals—or else face destitution. And prevailing conditions differed considerably according to gender. Male bluesmen often took the option of roaming through the region, playing on the streets, in juke joints, or at festivities as opportunities arose. As a result, many of them remained closely tied to and sustained by the traditional community. Women did not have access to the same kind of mobility, and few became itinerant musicians. Yet with the increasing instability of the southern black population at the turn of the century— the massive migrations to northern cities motivated by poverty, Jim Crow laws, and lynchings—women, too, often were compelled to leave home. By and large, however, they sought the security of steady employment. As Daphne Harrison has shown, many of the performers who came to be celebrated as the blues queens were displaced young women who found they could patch together a living performing in traveling minstrel shows, vaudeville, urban clubs, and (after the industry reluctantly agreed to try black women singers) the new medium of recording.[21]

What resulted was an explosion of female creativity that animated the 1920s—one of the few such moments in Western music history. These women and the market they helped produce exerted significant cultural and economic power for about a decade. As *The Metronome* reported in January 1922 (a scant two years after Mamie Smith recorded the first blues number), "One of the phonograph companies made over four million dollars on the Blues. Now every phonograph company has a colored girl recording. Blues are here to stay."[22]

If the blues produced under these conditions bear traces of its social contexts, that makes it no different from any other kind of music. Rather than hearing women's jazz-and-pop-flavored blues as corrupt, writers such as Hazel Carby, Daphne Harrison, and Toni Morrison have treated it as a genre that registered with keen accuracy the shocks and jolts of early black urban life, including the first direct encounters of the black population with the pressures of capitalist economies.[23] If some of us prefer to turn to the rural bluesmen in an imagined pastoral setting, it is partly because we can thereby pretend to retreat from the harsh realities of industrialized modernity.

One of the extraordinary contributions of so-called Classic Blues is its articulation of desire and pleasure from the woman's point of view. Throughout the span of Western culture, women have been spoken for more than they have been permitted to speak. And given the tendency for women to be reduced to sexuality and the body, many female artists have tried to avoid this terrain altogether.[24] As a result, vocabularies of the body and of erotic feelings have been constructed principally by men, even when they are projected onto women, as in opera and much popular music. Thus the blues queens offer an unparalleled moment in the history of cultural representation. As Carby puts it:

Thinking Blues / 45

> What has been called the "Classic Blues" . . . is a discourse that
> articulates a cultural and political struggle over sexual relations:
> a struggle that is directed against the objectification of female
> sexuality within a patriarchal order but which also tries to reclaim
> women's bodies as the sexual and sensuous subjects of women's
> song. . . . The women blues singers occupied a privileged space;
> they had broken out of the boundaries of the home and taken their
> sensuality and sexuality out of the private into the public sphere. [25]

Accounting for how and why this happened is very complex. On the
one hand, African-based cultures tend to treat the body and eroticism as
crucial elements of human life: the shame or prurience that attends sexuality in so many European cultures is often absent. But on the other hand,
the bodily components of African American culture have repeatedly been
misconstrued within the dominant society.[26] Because black women were
often defined as oversexed by whites,[27] it was risky for them to sing explicitly about desire: entrepreneurs in the culture industry cheerfully exploited the stereotype of the libidinal black female in posters, sheet music,
and staging (recall, for instance, the salacious marketing of so brilliant a
performer as Josephine Baker); and singers who lacked clout sometimes
were pressured into prostitution, which resided just next door to entertainment, as Billie Holiday's painful memoirs make clear. They also encountered severe castigation from the black middle class, which often
adopted the mores and attitudes of white bourgeois culture.

This was yet another set of issues that had to be negotiated with great
care by each female performer, within each song. Despite the personal
dangers and social controversies, however, these women left us an invaluable legacy revealing how female pleasure, sexual independence,
and woman-to-woman address could sound—a legacy Angela Davis
does not hesitate to identify as feminist.[28] Several of them, including
Rainey and Smith, even celebrated their bisexuality in their lyrics.

I want to focus now on "Thinking Blues," one of Bessie Smith's own
blues numbers, which was recorded in New York in 1928.[29] Smith's
lyrics in "Thinking Blues" deal with some of the central themes of

46 / *Conventional Wisdom*

women's blues: broken relationships, remorse, and pleading. Yet in contrast to some of the male-composed lyrics she also performed superbly, "Thinking Blues" articulates a vision of female subjectivity that balances self-possessed dignity with flashes of humor and a powerfully embodied sense of the erotic; simply the stress on the verb "to think" in the opening and final lines presents a different kind of experience from the passive suffering often ascribed to women in general and Smith in particular.[30]

BESSIE SMITH: "THINKING BLUES"
Did you ever sit thinking with a thousand things on your mind?
Did you ever sit thinking with a thousand things on your mind?
Thinkin' about someone who has treated you so nice and kind.

Then you get an old letter and you begin to read,
You get an old letter and you begin to read,
Got the blues so bad, 'til that man of mine I wanna see.

Don't you hear me, baby, knockin' on your door?
Don't you hear me, baby, knockin' on your door?
Have you got the nerve to drive me from your door?

Have you got the nerve to say that you don't want me no more?
Have you got the nerve to say that you don't want me no more?
The Good Book says you got to reap what you sow.

Take me back, baby, try me one more time.
Take me back, baby, try me one more time.
That's the only way I can get these thinking blues off my mind.

Bessie Smith, "Thinking Blues." Used by permission of Hal Leonard Corporation.

As is the case in many blues numbers, "Thinking Blues" suggests a possible narrative framework but moves freely among many forms of implied address from verse to verse. Sometimes she hails the listener as though in conversation ("Did you ever sit thinking?"); at other times, she seems to retreat into soliloquy ("Then you get an old letter"); and finally, she speaks as though directly to the man whom she has evidently left and whom she wants back. As she approaches him, she moves from tentative questioning ("Don't you hear me knocking?"), to audacity ("Do you have the nerve to say?"), to demands ("Take me back, baby").

Thus while there is a clear rhetorical shape to the sequence of five choruses—a move from public address to internalized reflection to simulated encounter, a steady increase in intensity—the blues convention that underlies the piece minimizes the narrative component of the music itself. What we get instead is a series of meditations on a single situation, as Smith returns to the problem nagging her with a new approach in each verse. The repetitions suggest personal obsession, but at the same time, her use of the blues invites the listener to identify with her predicament. What she sings sounds utterly familiar: we can relate. As John Coltrane once said, the audience heard "we" even if the singer said "I."[31] She invokes and brings into being a temporary community that bears witness to and empathizes with her subjective expression, made intersubjective by her use of shared codes.

Yet as transparent as it may seem, her performance refuses to offer a single easily identified affect—even within any particular verse. The structure of the blues, in which the first line of each chorus occurs twice, permits her to shift her implications radically from moment to moment. She couches each statement within an apparently limitless range of ambiguities and ambivalences—she lives a gray area, never truly giving anything away even while suggesting a whole range of possibilities.

At times her moans seem to spell grief, but in the next moment a similar glissando will suddenly turn into a sly, insinuating grind. On "Have you got the nerve to say that you don't want me no more?" is she seducing? Groveling? Taunting? And taunting her lover or herself? This sentence is a central event in the song, and she turns it every which way but loose. Yet what is she saying underneath all those layers of irony? The final line, "Take me back, try me one more time," clarifies a great deal—this is what she wants; no more indirection. But while her words may plead, the power of her delivery and her nuances

48 / *Conventional Wisdom*

destabilize the potential abjection of her appeal. This lady is in charge, even if she "ain't too proud to beg."

In "Thinking Blues," the musicians elect the option of remaining on V for bars 9 and 10 rather than moving down through IV. We may never know who chose to do it this way, but the rhetorical effect is to maintain a single, steady affect through the last line until the moment of cadence in bar 11. Smith's delivery of each verse's final line takes advantage of this detail by driving all the way through rather than releasing the energy in stages, and it becomes especially insistent in verses 3 ("have you got the nerve to drive me from your door?") and 4 ("the Good Book says you got to reap what you sow").

In this recording, Smith is accompanied by some of her favorite sidemen: Demas Dean on cornet, Fred Longshaw on piano, the incomparable Charlie Green on trombone. All three were jazz musicians—Green played regularly with Fletcher Henderson—and the performance presents a fusion between the demands of jazz ensemble-playing and the more intimate qualities of the blues. One of the most obvious jazz elements is standardization: in order to facilitate group improvisation, the blues pattern here (and elsewhere in Classic Blues) has been regularized, so that each chorus follows the twelve-bar progression.

Consistent with the blues, however, is their style of bending pitches, rhythms, timbres, and rhetorical conventions to signify on the standard pattern. The song is structured according to call and response, with Dean and Green answering Smith in turn on alternate lines, thus playing up the asymmetries already inherent in the pattern. Each instrumentalist carefully links his contributions with Smith's words and expressive decisions: in other words, all elements of the song—whether sung or played—are vocal in conception and execution. Green and Dean never tire of intensifying or ironicizing Smith's inflections. Green tends to get down with her growls and innuendoes, while Dean contributes astringent, strutting countermotives that keep Smith and her trombonist from spiraling too deeply into the funky zone. Even

Langshaw—whose principal task it is to maintain the harmonies and the groove at the piano—throws in subtle melodic comments and echoes here and there.

Not only do Smith's three instrumentalists amplify the various shadings of her delivery (they act as extensions of her utterances), but they also serve as an exemplary cluster of listeners who react audibly to her calls, thus granting her the social legitimation of community. If technology had permitted a live performance, we would also hear actual listeners lending their support (as in the Swan Silvertones tune discussed in chapter 1) through sympathetic moans, appreciative hoots for the double entendres, and responses such as "Sing it, Bessie!" or (as we would put it today) "You go, girl!"

ROBERT JOHNSON, "CROSS ROAD BLUES"

When the blues queens proved to be commercially viable, recording companies sent agents out in search of other talent that would appeal to the African American market now being aggressively cultivated. At the same time (the late 1920s and 1930s), folklorists such as Alan Lomax also began traveling through the South in hopes of recording and preserving musics that were in danger of disappearing with the massive migrations north and the onslaught of the mass media. What both commercial scouts and ethnomusicologists found were large numbers of itinerant musicians who performed for various occasions within black rural communities.

Unfortunately, the Great Depression brought to an end the boom that had carried Bessie Smith to fame, and recording companies grew reluctant to gamble on unknown genres or talents. Thus much of what was collected from rural bluesmen circulated only as "race" records designated exclusively for the African American market or as field recordings harvested for purposes of ethnographic study. In the late 1930s, John Hammond—an executive at Columbia Records and a

50   /   *Conventional Wisdom*

blues aficionado—began to mount prestigious concerts of such musicians, along with jazz figures. Around that same time, musicians who had migrated to northern cities were developing urban versions of downhome music that would become extremely influential. Many later blues stars (e.g., Muddy Waters, B. B. King) learned their trade from those earlier musicians—often through recordings. But the bids for commercial success by the Delta bluesmen had occurred at precisely the wrong time.[32]

Robert Johnson figures foremost among this group. Held up as a legend by Waters and made into a virtual god by the British rockers who rediscovered him in the 1960s, he spent his short career playing gigs throughout the South, with side trips to Chicago and New York. In the mid-1930s, Johnson sought out a recording agent, who undertook two sessions with him: three days in November 1936, two in June 1937. In all, he cut eleven 78s, one of which ("Terraplane Blues") sold reasonably well within the southern race-record circuit. But by the time John Hammond tried to recruit him for his 1939 Carnegie Hall concert, Johnson was dead—apparently poisoned by a jealous husband.

Johnson's posthumous reputation rests on an LP released by Columbia in the 1960s. Executives at Columbia speculated that rock'n'roll had generated a market that might be receptive to rock's forerunners, and they turned to their archives for possible materials. Later in this chapter I will discuss some reasons why Johnson became an idol for musicians in England. But for now I want to examine one of his most celebrated cuts, "Cross Road Blues."[33]

ROBERT JOHNSON: "CROSS ROAD BLUES"
I went to the crossroad, fell down on my knees,
I went to the crossroad, fell down on my knees,
Asked the Lord above "Have mercy, save poor Bob if you please."

Standin' at the crossroad, I tried to flag a ride,
Standin' at the crossroad, I tried to flag a ride,
Didn't nobody seem to know me, everybody pass me by.

The sun goin' down, boy, dark gon' catch me here,
Oooo, boy, dark gon' catch me here,
I haven't got no lovin' sweet woman that love and feel my care.

You can run, you can run, tell my friend boy Willie Brown,
You can run, tell my friend boy Willie Brown,
Lord, that I'm standin' at the crossroad, babe, I believe I'm sinkin'
   down.

One of the first things that strikes the ear in "Cross Road" is the peculiar, almost throttled intensity of both guitar and vocal sounds. Although Johnson recorded several very erotic, seductive, slow-hand
blues, his posthumous fame rests with these rather more tortured numbers. An affect of dread and entrapment pervades this tune—partly the
result of his strangulated, falsetto vocals and his uncanny replication of
that timbre on the guitar. Moreover, Johnson's percussive guitar pulse,
which locks in at the eighth-note level, allows almost no sensual movement: even though Johnson's singing constantly strains against that
beat, the listener's body is regulated by those short, aggressively articulated units. The guitar thus seems to represent simultaneously both oppressive outside forces and a desperate subjectivity fighting vainly for
escape.

Another factor contributing to the effectiveness of "Cross Road
Blues" is its elastic sense of phrasing. Because he performs by himself,
Johnson has no need to follow the standardized organization of ensemble blues, whereby each line receives four bars. Instead, phrase-length
becomes one more element he can manipulate rhetorically. Typically,
in "Cross Road" Johnson lingers after the first line, as his call is met
with a varying number of guitar riffs that seem to obstruct his progress.
The presentation of the second line operates similarly, with erratic extensions. But the final phrase often sounds truncated, with some bars of
three rather than four beats. And no sooner does he achieve the conventional closure of the culminating line than he plunges on, as though
dissatisfied, back into the maelstrom. He grants little relief here—as

52 / *Conventional Wisdom*

though hesitation at the cadence would mean that the devil (to whom Johnson's peers believed he had sold his soul in exchange for his guitar technique) would claim him. This phrase irregularity, then, is not a sign of primitivism (he had listened to Classic Blues on the phonograph as much as anyone, and many of his other numbers adhere to the twelve-bar paradigm), but rather a parameter he bends as willfully as pitches, rhythms, and timbres: even the meter expands and contracts to accommodate his rhetorical impulse.

As idiosyncratic as "Cross Road" may be, it relies on the blues format both for its affective quality of obsession and for its public intelligibility. Indeed, Johnson takes for granted that his audience knows the harmonic framework within which he operates: the changes themselves are often only suggested as he concentrates instead on the pungent guitar riff that haunts the song.[34] No longer just a glorified accompaniment pattern or the expected response to fill in the time between vocal lines, the riff comes to dominate "Cross Road," serving double duty both as the amplification of the vocalist's affect and as the object of dread against which he strains. The cross-rhythms set up within the guitar seem to allow no airspaces, no means of escape. Unlike "Hellhound Blues," another of Johnson's songs of metaphysical entrapment, there are no moments of relief—no ribald references to making love while awaiting doom. Instead we are locked into two-and-a-half minutes of concentrated horror—intense social alienation, images handed down from African *vodun* (which holds the cross road to be the terrain of Legba), and the entirely justified fear of what might well befall a black man in Mississippi in the 1930s caught outside after sundown.

Since the 1960s, blues musicians such as Johnson have been elevated as the authentic wellspring from which parasitic, commercially contaminated genres drew their strength. Yet, as George Lipsitz has argued so eloquently, this dichotomy accomplishes little more than ideological mystification.[35] To be sure, Johnson's audience was predominantly composed of southern rural African Americans whose vernacular was blues. He never garnered the prestige to negotiate seriously with a broader, mixed public. Yet it seems quite certain that he happily would have done so, given the opportunity. He was very much a product of his moment in history: his music was influenced by what he had access to by means of recording and radio; he performed Tin Pan Alley songs at his gigs; he drew on the latest technologies (automobile engines, the phonograph) to create some of his most memorable tropes; he sought out recording agents himself. Had he lived, he would probably have moved north and participated in the transformation of traditional blues into R & B. To hold him as the authentic measure against which to condemn both his successors and female predecessors is to cling to a shredded mythology of Romanticism that ought to be laid to rest.

CREAM, "CROSSROADS"

> White folks got money,
> Colored folks got all the signs.
> Signs won't buy nothin'. (1845)[36]

My third example requires that we jump from the rural South to the English art schools of the 1950s and early 1960s. For one of the most unlikely events in recent cultural history involves a group of disaffected art students (including Keith Richards, Pete Townsend, Freddy Mercury, Jimmy Page, Charlie Watts, Cat Stevens, and Eric Clapton; Mick Jagger was from the more upscale London School of Economics)[37] who embraced traditional blues as their own musical language and turned it into what became known in North America as "the British Invasion." Their motivation had at least as much to do with their own context as with the particular music they embraced to form their identities. Yet there are reasons why they chose blues rather than any of the other culturally distant musics available.

54 / *Conventional Wisdom*

The bohemian subculture flourishing around art schools in the 1940s had adopted Dixieland jazz as a sign of proletarian sympathies and resistance to commercialism.[38] When bebop broke on the scene, English jazz aficionados split between those who advocated the "progressive" sounds of modern jazz and those who sought authenticity in "trad" (i.e., Dixieland). In the 1950s, the debate shifted ground somewhat, as John Mayall started to push the blues as an even more authentic source than jazz. Many younger students, who wanted to mark their distinction from the earlier generation, followed Mayall and recreated much the same debate, but now with blues representing authenticity against the commercialism of jazz *tout court*. (This may be difficult for us to grasp now that bebop has come to represent high modernist intellectual rigor in contrast to the simplicity of the now-overexposed blues. But such are the ironies offered up by history.)

It now became fashionable for art students to denounce jazz; John Lennon said of jazz, for instance, "I think it is shit music, even more stupid than rock and roll. . . . Jazz never gets anywhere, never does anything, it's always the same and all they do is drink pints of beer."[39] In place of jazz, they began to exalt the new blues-based rock'n'roll of Chuck Berry, the first model for the Beatles, Rolling Stones, and Clapton. Then they began to look back to acquaint themselves with Berry's musical ancestors. Concerning this conversion, Clapton said:

> At first, I played exactly like Chuck Berry for six or seven months. You couldn't have told the difference when I was with the Yardbirds. Then I got into older bluesmen. Because he was so readily available, I dug Big Bill Broonzy; then I heard a lot of cats I had never heard before: Robert Johnson and Skip James and Blind Boy Fuller. I just finally got completely overwhelmed in this brand-new world. I studied it and listened to it and went right down in it and came back up in it.[40]

Although few of the British art-school students had previous experience with music, many of them acquired guitars and began learning to play—virtually in front of the indulgent coffee-house audiences who shared their enthusiasms and political associations.

In these various debates among English fans, neither side had a particularly clear sense of black culture in America; they used their musical allegiances to meet their own needs.[41] Yet it was significant that it was the music of black males they idolized, for African Americans were thought to have access to real (i.e., preindustrialized) feelings and community—qualities hard to find in a society that had so long stressed individuality and the mind/body split. Moreover, in contrast to what politicized art students regarded as the feminized sentimentality of pop music, blues seemed to offer an experience of sexuality that was unambiguously masculine. This was no mean consideration, for the English had regarded music-making as effeminizing for nearly 500 years.[42] Suddenly it was possible for British males to participate in music without the homophobic stigma of what Philip Brett has theorized as "musicality" attaching to them.[43] But the brand of masculinity that resulted from this identification with black music differed considerably from its model. As Ian Chambers has observed, the rebelliousness of the British bluesmen "tended to take the form of reducing the ironic cast of the blues to a blatant obsession with male sexuality."[44]

Meanwhile Mayall continued to mine the archives for earlier manifestations of blues and to recover obscure race records of the previous thirty years. Some of the old bluesmen were found to be still active as performers, mostly in urban clubs. Overnight Muddy Waters, Howling Wolf, B. B. King, Buddy Guy, and others became celebrities in England—an unanticipated turn of fate they were happy to exploit. For instance, Big Bill Broonzy, who had long played electric blues, converted back to acoustic and developed a "raw" style of delivery in order to satisfy this new audience's demand for ever-greater purity: "authenticity" became his ticket to commercial success.[45]

It was within this highly charged context that Keith Richards and Eric Clapton discovered the newly released Columbia LP of Robert

56 / *Conventional Wisdom*

Johnson. As Richards said later, "To me Robert Johnson's influence—
he was like a comet or a meteor that came along and, BOOM, suddenly
he raised the ante, suddenly you just had to aim that much higher."[46]
Clapton described his experience with Johnson's music this way: "It
was as if I had been prepared to receive Robert Johnson, almost like a
religious experience that started out with hearing Chuck Berry, then at
each stage went further and deeper until I was ready for him."[47] To
both, it was not only Johnson's extraordinary musicianship that drew
them but also what they took to be his freedom from commercialism.
As Clapton says,

> I played it, and it really shook me up because it didn't seem to me that
> he was particularly interested in being at all palatable, he didn't seem
> concerned with appeal at all. All the music I'd heard up till that time
> seemed to be structured in some way for recording. What struck me
> about the Robert Johnson album was that it seemed like he wasn't
> playing for an audience at all; it didn't obey the rules of time or har-
> mony or anything—he was just playing for himself. It was almost as
> though he felt things so acutely he found it almost unbearable.[48]

What a place to encounter the "Who Cares If You Listen?" line![49]
Clapton passed through a number of British blues bands, working
on his guitar skills and listening carefully to Johnson. Eventually he
created the always already legendary band Cream with drummer Gin-
ger Baker and bass player Jack Bruce. Cream was noted for its live performances, in which members of the band would improvise in response to audience feed-back—feed-back heightened for purposes of
the Dionysian fervor cultivated in the late 1960s by hallucinogens. It
was around this time that Clapton began to eclipse his idols, as the
motto "Clapton is God" appeared scrawled on walls throughout Europe and North America. Although they created much of their own
material, they also covered some traditional blues numbers, including
Johnson's "Cross Road Blues."

Cream's version, titled "Crossroads," retains Johnson's lyrics, with a substitute verse (about taking his "rider" or lover to Rosedale) taken from another of Johnson's blues, "Traveling Riverside Blues":

> I'm goin' down to Rosedale, take my rider by my side,
> Goin' down to Rosedale, take my rider by my side,
> We can still barrelhouse, baby, on the river side.[50]

And the model of Johnson's organizing riffs became indispensable to Cream's modus operandi. But the band replaces Johnson's eerie, strangulated riff in "Cross Road" with one that boasts a driving, propulsive beat and an insistent aeolian seventh-degree that announces their refusal of pop-oriented tonality. This riff returns throughout the song, pounding out the tonic whenever it appears.

Several aspects of Cream's performance depart more significantly from Johnson. First, their presentation of the blues pattern is absolutely regular, like the Chicago blues bands rather than Johnson. This is in part because of the presence of an ensemble and also because of the way blues practices had solidified by that time. One can't really imagine a rock band attempting to duplicate Johnson's erratic performance—at least not before the progressive rock bands of the 1970s and thrash metal groups of the 1980s.

Second, the structure of Cream's version articulates a brand of individuality in which self is pitted against society (even as it contributed to and drew from the sensibilities of the counterculture society of the 1960s). In Johnson's version, imagination is manifested in the particularities of his expression; he affirms the convention of proceeding through a series of identically shaped verses, but he signifies constantly throughout the entire number, forcing us to dwell on each moment, each detail as it comes. By contrast, the Cream recording minimizes expression within the verses in order to showcase the virtuosic solos for which Clapton became idolized, thereby reshaping the additive process

58 / *Conventional Wisdom*

of the blues to create an overarching formal trajectory. Clapton's solos operate like those in a concerto or bebop combo, as he strains forward in increasingly more extravagant figuration before yielding to the communal ritornello.[51]

Two solo choruses occur after the verse about Rosedale; then after repeating that verse, Clapton pulls out the stops and plays three choruses that threaten to derail the song with his rebellious individualism. During the solos, Jack Bruce's walking bass contributes to the sense of instability and urgency. The return to the final verse about Willie Brown, which served as the chilling culmination in Johnson, here becomes an aftermath during which listeners can begin to wind down after the ferocious display of improvised pyrotechnics they have just witnessed. Cream pushes the envelope of Johnson's strophic organization, imposing on it the dynamic, climax-oriented shape typical of European-based narratives.[52]

Accordingly, the prominence of the vocal quality of Johnson's performance—even in his guitar playing—and his emphasis on the imagery of the lyrics have been inverted in Cream. Virtually everything in the Cream version revolves around the primacy of the instrumentals, especially in the riff and Clapton's individualistic solos. His singing is fairly perfunctory, even a shade self-conscious ("Crossroads" is the only song in which he contributed lead vocals on *Wheels of Fire*). And the staggering range of timbres employed throughout by Johnson—sonic evidence of his body's intimate engagement with the music—disappears except during the solos. Not too surprisingly, Cream has "hardened" the blues; those elements that signified the body in its vulnerability (whether in vocals, cross-rhythms, or timbral shadings) are exchanged for a driving beat, a narrative trajectory in the music, and the display of alienated Romantic virtuosity.[53]

Thus the priorities of the genre changed when it was adopted by British rockers—as they had, for that matter, when the blues passed from Bessie Smith to Robert Johnson. That the principal interests of the British differed from those of the African American musicians they initially idolized became clear when musicians and critics alike announced that they were ready to leave their black mentors behind and move forward into art rock. As Motown historian Dave Morse complained in 1971: "Black musicians are now implicitly regarded as precursors who, having taught the white men all they know, must gradually recede into the distance, as white progressive music, the simple lessons mastered, advances irresistibly into the future."[54] The mind/ body split—temporarily suspended—returned, motivating the critical dismissal of black dance-oriented music: the British had received access to their bodies by means of their alignment with African American music; but after a point, they felt they had to rescue that music from the body.

When middle-class kids and British art students "universalized" blues by making it the vehicle for their own alienation, many black musicians chose to develop other modes of expression. For some of them, in any case, the blues had come to recall times of rural poverty and victimization—the genealogy sedimented into the blues had moved to the foreground for them, drowning out other registers of meaning. Thus it is no coincidence that rap musicians have worked to construct a different heritage, tracing their roots through sampling and quotation back not to the blues per se but to James Brown and soul—a genre of black music that emerged during the decade when white rockers arrogated the blues unto themselves. For African Americans the blues was always just one particular manifestation of a number of deeper elements that live on in other genres. It was never a fetish, but simply a vehicle for expression. When historical conditions changed, when it became reified, it could be left behind.

To be sure, the blues as a genre still exists intact. Many of the old bluesmen lionized in the 1960s—B. B. King, Buddy Guy—continue to play concerts.[55] Some of the 1920s blues queens, such as Alberta

60 / *Conventional Wisdom*

Hunter, were rediscovered by feminist historians in the 1970s, and women's blues has enjoyed a rebirth with artists such as Etta James and Bonnie Raitt. Moreover, a neo-blues trend may have started with the emergence of younger musicians such as Robert Cray. Even those not identified with the blues continue to find it an invaluable point of reference, a repository from which they may draw gestures, moods, evocations of a variety of times past.

But the way we tell the history of the blues is often shaped by that period of British enthusiasm. Although the enterprise of British rock was certainly not untouched by the desire for commercial success, an ideology of noncommercial authenticity that first led Clapton and others to champion the blues permeated their self-images as rebels against capitalism. It continues to inform many of the rock critics who emerged at that same time as the historians, theorists, and arbiters of popular taste who justified this particular enterprise.

Yet whatever reservations one might harbor concerning that moment in blues history, it is now part of the permanent record. And some of its results were, in retrospect, quite startling. For instance, this fusion between African American models and British aesthetic priorities permitted the first truly international wave of English musical creativity since perhaps Elizabethan times. Moreover, it was in the wake of this fusion that the blues became inescapably a necessary chapter in the history of Western music: one could no longer even explain how white, European males came to compose the music they contributed without a detour through the Mississippi Delta.

This is not to suggest that black music deserves legitimacy only insofar it is found to be of use to Europeans or white Americans. Indeed, I would claim that the musical innovations that have most shaped people in the course of this century have principally come from African Americans, who have given the world a legacy that richly demands (and is finally receiving) attention in its own right. But it is hard to draw the line any longer between various strands of music in North

Thinking Blues / 61

America and Europe, for they have shared the same geographical and temporal spaces, responded to the same historical conditions. And in the second half of the twentieth century, many prominent Western musicians—white as well as black—have come to identify themselves as descendants of African American traditions in addition to or rather than the classical canon. Thus the odd designation of black music as "non-Western," which might have seemed reasonable at one time, was no longer even remotely defensible after the 1960s.

There is no Hegelian reason why this should have happened. This merger occurred as a result of a number of unlikely circumstances—the technology of recording, which made possible (though not necessarily probable) the transmission of African American voices beyond their own times and places; the increasing obscurantism of the European tradition, which created a cultural vacuum; a political faction among British art school students who chose the blues as their symbol of defiance; the explosion of a global counterculture that depended on the demographics of the baby boom and the looming presence of an unpopular war. None of these or their impacts could have been predicted, nor was blues the necessary vehicle, even though the specific qualities of the blues drawn upon—its ability to galvanize community, engage emotions, and animate the body—indicate that the choice was not arbitrary either. Yet music history has always lurched along (I won't say advances) by just such circumstances: we impose the illusion of a smooth narrative unfolding only long after the fact.

In the next chapter, I want to examine one of those sequences in Western music history that seems to flow smoothest—the music of the Enlightenment—in terms that parallel those I have just brought to the blues. For it is not just the procedures of popular music that develop ad hoc according to unforeseen contingencies but also the most "purely musical" elements in the canon. Yet I hope to have established that this process of grabbing established conventions and arranging them according to the needs of the moment can be artistically powerful and

62 / *Conventional Wisdom*

culturally consequential—especially if we pay close attention to the signifying devices engaged in each tune as well as the historical contexts that make them meaningful. If we musicologists often have difficulty grasping how music and social conditions interact, if we still sometimes believe that adhering to conventions means the surrender of individuality and expression, we can learn a great deal by thinking blues.

I don't like it." But, Heilbut reports, the public did, and this particular sound began to be picked up by R & B groups (Heilbut, *Gospel Sound*, 119).

44. See again n. 30, in which Jeter happily acknowledges the group's commercial connections. Tricia Rose deals with a later moment of African American music in which African-based procedures are wed to state-of-the-art technology in her *Black Noise: Rap Music and Black Culture in Contemporary America* (Hanover, N.H.: Wesleyan University Press, 1994). Such practices challenge received notions that equate "authenticity" with acoustical purity.

45. Johannes de Grocheo, *De musica*, trans. Albert Seay (Colorado Springs: Colorado College Music Press, 1974).

46. Lydia Goehr, *The Imaginary Museum of Musical Works* (Oxford: Oxford University Press, 1992), 243.

CHAPTER 2: THINKING BLUES

1. Donald Tovey, "The Main Stream of Music," in *The Main Stream of Music and Other Essays* (Cleveland: Meridian Books, 1959).

2. Leonard B. Meyer, *Music, the Arts, and Ideas* (Chicago: University of Chicago Press, 1967), chapters 6–9.

3. LeRoi Jones (now Amiri Baraka), *Blues People: The Negro Experience in White America and the Music That Developed From It* (New York: Morrow Quill, 1963).

4. Albert Murray, *Stomping the Blues* (New York: Viking, 1976), 126.

5. One of the most enlightening overviews in recent years is Francis Davis, *The History of the Blues: The Roots, the Music, the People from Charley Patton to Robert Cray* (New York: Hyperion, 1995).

6. See Arthur Schlesinger Jr., *The Disuniting of America: Reflections on a Multicultural Society* (New York: Norton, 1991), for arguments denying the African presence in African American practices in general.

7. Jones, *Blues People*, 66, and Lawrence W. Levine, *Black Culture and Black Consciousness: Afro-American Folk Thought from Slavery to Freedom* (Oxford: Oxford University Press, 1977), 221 and 223.

8. Gunther Schuller, *Early Jazz: Its Roots and Musical Development* (Oxford: Oxford University Press, 1968); Olly Wilson, "The Significance of the Relationship between Afro-American Music and West African Music," *Black Perspective in Music* 2 (1974): 3–22; Christopher Small, *Music of the Common*

Tongue: Survival and Celebration in Afro-American Music (London: John Calder, 1987); Henry Louis Gates Jr., *The Signifying Monkey; A Theory of African-American Literary Criticism* (Oxford: Oxford University Press, 1988); Peter van der Merwe, *Origins of the Popular Style* (Oxford: Oxford University Press, 1989); Paul Gilroy, *The Black Atlantic: Modernity and Double Consciousness* (Cambridge, Mass.: Harvard University Press, 1993); Samuel A. Floyd, Jr., *The Power of Black Music: Interpreting Its History from Africa to the United States* (Oxford: Oxford University Press, 1995).

9. Ernest Borneman, "The Roots of Jazz," in *Jazz: New Perspectives on the History of Jazz by Twelve of the World's Foremost Jazz Critics and Scholars*, ed. Nat Hentoff and Albert J. McCarthy (New York: Da Capo, 1959), 17.

10. Sterling Stuckey, *Slave Culture: Nationalist Theory and the Foundations of Black America* (Oxford: Oxford University Press, 1987), 25.

11. For instance, the seventeenth-century *ciaccona* was attributed sometimes to Peruvian Indians, sometimes to displaced Africans; Stephen Foster's songs present themselves as "artful" imitations of slave songs; and the hit tune in Bizet's *Carmen*, the "Habañera," was modeled after an African-based genre from Cuba. For a discussion of the *ciaccona*, see my "Music, the Pythagoreans, and the Body," in *Choreographing History*, ed. Susan Leigh Foster (Bloomington: Indiana University Press, 1995), 82–104; for more on Bizet's borrowings, see my *Georges Bizet:* Carmen (Cambridge: Cambridge University Press, 1993).

12. Murray, *Stomping the Blues*, 70. Although sometimes titled "blues," Handy's tunes were originally classified as rags on the sheet music (70, 81). See 139–40 for Handy's account of how he cobbled "St. Louis Blues" together out of various commercial elements.

13. Daphne Duval Harrison, *Black Pearls: Blues Queens of the 1920s* (New Brunswick: Rutgers University Press, 1988), 57–58.

14. Harrison, *Black Pearls*, 56. See also Murray, *Stomping*, chapter 11, for a discussion of the folk/art debate surrounding blues.

15. George Lipsitz, *Time Passages: Collective Memory and American Popular Music* (Minneapolis: University of Minnesota Press, 1990).

16. Harrison, *Black Pearls*, 35.

17. Houston Baker Jr., *Blues, Ideology, and Afro-American Literature: A Vernacular History* (Chicago: University of Chicago Press, 1984).

18. Recorded on January 14, 1925 (available in the *Smithsonian Collection of Classic Jazz*). The harmonium player, Fred Longshaw, introduces many very

tasty harmonic inflections within the basic blues structure, but I indicate only the basic schema in my diagram.

19. I am greatly indebted to Robert Walser for this discussion of blues conventions. In contrast to him, alas, I cannot pull out a guitar and demonstrate.

20. See Simon Frith and Howard Horne, *Art into Pop* (London: Methuen, 1987), 92.

21. The most thorough account of the material conditions surrounding these women appears in Harrison, *Black Pearls*.

22. Quoted in Harrison, *Black Pearls*, 44.

23. See Hazel Carby, "'It Jus Be's Dat Way Sometime': The Sexual Politics of Women's Blues," in *Unequal Sisters: A Multi-Cultural Reader in U.S. Women's History*, ed. Ellen Carol DuBois and Vicki L. Ruiz (New York: Routledge, 1990), 239; Harrison, *Black Pearls*. For a remarkable fictional exploration of this world, see also Toni Morrison's novel *Jazz* (New York: Alfred A. Knopf, 1992).

24. Carby argues that the black women responsible for literary works tended to minimize sexuality, which is why women's blues become such important documents. Women composers and musicians in the European art tradition too have often tried to minimize references to sexuality: in fact, many feminist musicologists were disconcerted by my discussions in *Feminine Endings*. I owe my serious concern with this repertory to Barbara Christian. When I was first beginning to work on issues involving women and music, I explained to Christian that women had only recently begun to deal explicitly with gender and sexuality in their music. To which she responded: "Ever hear of Bessie Smith?" I have never forgotten that lesson.

25. Carby, "It Jus Be's," 241 and 247. For the importance of joy and pleasure in black culture in general, see Gina Dent, "Black Pleasure, Black Joy: An Introduction," the essay that opens the forum of leading black theorists in *Black Popular Culture*, a project by Michele Wallace, ed. Gina Dent (Seattle: Bay Press, 1992), 1–20.

26. See bell hooks, "Selling Hot Pussy: Representations of Black Female Sexuality in the Cultural Marketplace," *Black Looks: Race and Representation* (Boston: South End Press, 1992), for a critique of several music videos featuring black women. For a discussion of this problem in music studies, see Robert Walser and Susan McClary, "Theorizing the Body in African-American Music," *Black Music Research Journal* 14 (1994): 75–84.

27. See Sander L. Gilman, "The Hottentot and the Prostitute: Toward an Iconography of Female Sexuality," and "Black Sexuality and Modern Consciousness," in his *Difference and Pathology: Stereotypes of Sexuality, Race, and Madness* (Ithaca: Cornell University Press, 1985).

28. Angela Davis, *Blues Legacies and Black Feminism: Gertrude "Ma" Rainey, Bessie Smith, and Billie Holiday* (New York: Pantheon, 1998).

29. Bessie Smith, "Thinking Blues," Demas Dean, cornet; Charlie Green, trombone; Fred Longshaw, piano (February 9, 1928, Columbia 14292-D).

30. See, for instance, Schuller, *Early Jazz:*, 241: "Her tragic early death was perhaps a less painful exit than a long decline into oblivion. For Bessie Smith was one of the great tragic figures, not only of jazz, but of her period." He then adds, "But Bessie Smith was a supreme artist, and as such her art transcends the particulars of life that informed that art." For an important warning against such romanticizing, see again the quotation from Albert Murray near the beginning of this chapter.

31. John Coltrane, quoted in Carby, "It Jus Be's," 242.

32. For an account of the relationship between Delta blues and urban electric blues, see Robert Palmer, *Deep Blues: A Musical and Cultural History of the Mississippi Delta* (New York: Penguin, 1982).

33. Robert Johnson, "Cross Road Blues" (San Antonio, November 27, 1936; Columbia 46222).

34. See the transcription and discussion in Dave Headlam, "Blues Transformations in the Music of Cream," *Understanding Rock: Essays in Musical Analysis*, ed. John Covach and Graeme M. Boone (New York: Oxford University Press, 1997), 62–69.

35. George Lipsitz, "White Desire: Remembering Robert Johnson," in *The Possessive Investment in Whiteness: How White People Profit from Identity Politics* (Philadelphia: Temple University Press, 1998), 118–38. My chapter was completed before I encountered Lipsitz's treatment, but we have talked about these issues over the course of many years. His influence on my work in this area cannot be overestimated.

For a significantly different appropriation of the Johnson legend, however, see Sherman Alexie, *Reservation Blues* (New York: Warner Books, 1995), in which Johnson's ghost bestows his guitar to Thomas Builds-the-Fire and Victor Joseph—both now famous as characters in the 1998 film *Smoke Signals*. Alexie plays ironically with the myth surrounding Johnson as he examines the

poverty and attempts at cultural/spiritual survival in a contemporary Spokane
Indian reservation.

36. Quoted in Simon Frith, *Sound Effects: Youth, Leisure, and the Politics of
Rock'n'Roll* (New York: Pantheon, 1981), 15.

37. See Frith and Horne, *Art into Pop*, 73.

38. Ibid., 72, and Ian Chambers, *Urban Rhythms: Pop Music and Popular
Culture* (New York: St. Martin's Press, 1985), 67.

39. John Lennon, quoted in Frith, *Art into Pop*, 81.

40. Eric Clapton, quoted in Geoffrey Stokes, "The Sixties," in *Rock of Ages:
The Rolling Stone History of Rock 'n' Roll* (New York: Summit Press, 1986),
395.

41. See Stokes, "Sixties," 282–83: "But bitter as it was, the blues-vs.-trad
battle was taking place in an extremely small pond. Recording contracts were
rare, and purism—as that purist Eric Clapton, who quit the Yardbirds to join
John Mayall when they grew too poppish, recalled—was a badge of honor:
'The blues musician is usually a fanatic; that's the common denominator
among blues musicians, they're fanatics. In England, they're a lot more so
'cause they're divorced from the scene and don't really know where it's at.
They don't know what it's like to be a blues musician in America like Mike
Bloomfield does. They're all romantic about it and have a lot of ideals and notions. A lot of ego gets mixed into it and they think they're the only guys playing real music.'"

42. See Richard Leppert, *Music and Image: Domesticity, Ideology, and Socio-
cultural Formation in Eighteenth-Century England* (Cambridge: Cambridge
University Press, 1989), and Linda Austern, "'Alluring the Auditorie to Effeminacie': Music and the English Renaissance Idea of the Feminine," *Music
and Letters* 74 (1993): 343–54.

43. Philip Brett, "Musicality, Essentialism, and the Closet," *Queering the
Pitch: The New Gay and Lesbian Musicology*, ed. Philip Brett, Elizabeth Wood,
and Gary C. Thomas (New York: Routledge, 1994), 9–26.

44. Chambers, *Urban Rhythms*, 67.

45. See ibid., 20.

46. Keith Richards, "Well, This Is It," in liner notes for *Robert Johnson:
The Complete Recordings* (Columbia/CBS Records, 1990), 22.

47. Eric Clapton, "Discovering Robert Johnson," in liner notes for *Robert
Johnson*, 22.

48. Ibid., 22.

49. See Milton Babbitt, "Who Cares If You Listen?," *High Fidelity Magazine* 8, no. 2 (February 1958): 126. See my "Terminal Prestige: The Case of Avant-Garde Music Composition," *Cultural Critique* 12 (1989): 57–81.

50. Cream, "Crossroads," reissued on *Wheels of Fire* (Polygram, 1976). This performance was recorded live at the Fillmore. Clapton's much-publicized identification with Johnson in general and this song in particular inspired the title of one of his biographies: Michael Schumacher, *Crossroads: The Life and Music of Eric Clapton* (New York: Hyperion, 1995).

51. Robert Walser has shown that this particular fusion prepared the way for the literal incorporation of Vivaldian passagework into heavy metal. See *Running with the Devil: Power, Gender, and Madness in Heavy Metal Music* (Hanover, N.H.: Wesleyan University Press, 1993).

52. Gregory Bateson has written on the convention of climax in Western cultural artifacts. See *Steps to an Ecology of Mind* (New York: Ballantine Books, 1972), 113. I once attended a performance by Joe Turner's blues band in which Turner delivered his famous shouts, the piano player boogie-woogie, the sax player a series of alienated postbop squawks, and the white guitarist a narrative excursion into greater and greater frustration with a final spray-down release, followed by Turner shouting out a verse in conclusion. This sequence occurred without fail on every number in the concert.

53. See also Lipsitz, "White Desire." For a formal analysis of Cream's performance of "Crossroads," see Headlam, "Blues Transformations in the Music of Cream," 69–72. Once again, Headlam's transcriptions prove very useful.

54. Dave Morse, quoted in Chambers, *Urban Rhythms*, 117. Chambers comments: "Employing the accusation of 'commercialism', black performers were compared unfavourably to what were referred to as the 'blue-eyed white soul singers' . . . The soul and R & B strains of Janis Joplin, Rod Stewart, Joe Cocker and Van Morrison were praised, while Ray Charles and Aretha Franklin, not to mention the unredeemable Tamla Motown stable . . . were accused of decaying in the swamps of a commercial jungle" (118).

55. Mick Jagger said of the appropriation of black music: "These legendary characters wouldn't mean a light commercially today if groups were not going round Britain doing their numbers" (quoted in Stokes, "Sixties," 283). From the other side, Muddy Waters said of Jagger: "He took my music. But he gave me my name" (quoted in Chambers, *Urban Rhythms*, 69).

Part Four

Early Music

CHAPTER 11

The Cultural Work of the Madrigal

Ah, dolente partita!
Ah, fin de la mia vita!
Da te parto e non moro? E pur i' provo
la pena de la morte
e sento nel partire
un vivace morire,
che dà vita al dolore
per far che moia immortalmente il core.

> (Giovanni Battista Guarini,
> *Il pastor fido*)

Ah, sorrowful parting!
Ah, end of my life!
I part from you and do not die? And yet I suffer
the pain of death
and feel in this parting
a vivacious dying,
which gives life to sorrow
causing my heart to die immortally.

In this highly concentrated verse, the pastoral lover Mirtillo attempts to put into words the contradictory impulses he experiences in but a single moment.

Multiple passions—longing, abjection, disbelief, anguish, resignation—assail him from within, finally to condense into the oxymoron of "un vivace morire." Banished from Amarilli's presence, Mirtillo hangs suspended between an agony so violent that it ought to bring about his immediate demise but that, because of its very intensity, prevents the release from suffering promised by death. In this brief speech, Giovanni Battista Guarini displays his celebrated epigrammatic style: an economy of means that sketches in a mere eight lines an emotional state comprising opposites that cannot even hope for reconciliation. He manifests his virtuosity particularly well in his successive redefinitions of "vita" and "morte," binary opposites that shift positions back and forth until they become hopelessly (and deliciously) fused.

Imagine, however, having the ability to convey all these sentiments at once, as though one could read the lines of Mirtillo's speech together vertically as a score. The resulting performance, alas, would amount to little more than noise, each string of words canceling out the others; instead of a realistic representation of Mirtillo's conflicting affects we would get something akin to John Cage tuning in randomly to twelve different radio stations. For despite all its potential for precision and sophistication, language relies for its intelligibility on the consecutive presentation of ideas in linear grammatical order. We may marvel at the extent to which Guarini appears to overcome the limitations of additive speech. Indeed, literary figures of the twentieth-century literary avant-garde—James Joyce and Virginia Woolf, for example—labored to push language in these directions through stream-of-consciousness technique, leading some literary theorists to latch onto the concept of counterpoint to explain such experiments; Julia Kristeva even offers double-column prose to simulate the experience of jostling two contrasting thought processes at the same time (a simulation that often leaves the reader feeling little more than wall-eyed).[1]

The very term *counterpoint*, however, alludes to the cultural medium in which such feats occur as a matter of course: namely, music. And in his madrigal setting of Mirtillo's lament, Claudio Monteverdi manages to achieve the simultaneity toward which Guarini gestures. Given the performing force of five independent voices, the composer can actually superimpose the sentiments of the first four lines of text, allowing them to circulate within the same space and time. Thus, in the first motive two voices divide from a

1. Julia Kristeva, "Stabat Mater," in *Tales of Love*, trans. Leon S. Roudiez (New York: Columbia University Press, 1987).

FIGURE I. Monteverdi, "Ah, dolente partita": First four motives

unison to a sequence of close dissonances to enact the searing anguish of separation expressed in the first line; a too-rapid collapse toward premature closure on "Ah, fin de la mia vita!" parallels Mirtillo's futile death wish in the second; a slowly ascending melodic motive that cancels out the would-be closure of the death wish registers the incredulity of the third; and an insistent repetition of a high pitch on "E pur i' provo / La pena de la morte" shrieks out the stabbing pain of the fourth (Fig. 1). The dynamic vectors of Monteverdi's motives, in other words, offer analogues to these divergent affects, giving us a visceral enactment of the suffering, resignation, doubt, and protest that surge through Mirtillo's mind and body during this single moment. Moreover, in keeping with Guarini's sense that Mirtillo cannot escape his internally conflicted state, the madrigal moves on in time to yet other combinations that recycle these mutually antagonistic elements but come no closer to resolution.

What Monteverdi offers here is a sound-image of subjective interiority on the verge of psychological meltdown, and he thereby gives us what music can do that language cannot, even at its most ingenious. Of course, not everyone has celebrated this particular strategy. Some of Monteverdi's own contemporaries, including most prominently Vincenzo Galilei (the father of the astronomer), complained that the contrapuntal excesses of late sixteenth-century madrigals prevented the intelligible projection of the words; such critics advocated instead a solo-voice model whereby the music serves primarily to inflect the lyrics, declaimed in an unimpeded fashion approximating public oratory.[2]

To be sure, it takes a leap of faith to accept a five-voice ensemble as reproducing the swooning of a single individual. Musicologists trip all over themselves to explain away this embarrassing convention, so far removed from the realistic expressivity of seventeenth-century solo singing. They gain support from sixteenth-century critics such as Galilei, who likewise detested the contrapuntal artifice of polyphonic text-settings. But this convention should seem quite familiar to fans of gospel, doo-wop, or any of the boy-group collectives that rise to the top of today's pop charts with great regularity. Like madrigal ensembles, these feature simulations of complex interiorities: rational grounding in the bass, melodic address in the middle, ecstatic melismas on the top. No contemporary teenager needs to be told how the various vocal roles in, say, *NSYNC function together to produce a viable representation of the Self.[3]

Even as Monteverdi was delivering "Ah, dolente partita" to the publisher, he and his colleagues were embarking on a style that brought music into the arena of dramatic spectacle we now call opera. The realistic performance of individual subjects afforded by the *stile recitativo* made opera the dominant genre of musical representation for the next three hundred years. But we often forget that recitative accomplished its coup at the cost of harnessing music to the linear imperatives of language: as music attaches itself to the exigencies of rhetorical declamation, it finds itself restricted to speech's limitations. We could thus count "Ah, dolente partita" (to which we will return later in this chapter) as not only Mirtillo's wistful adieu to Amarilli but also as a reluctant farewell to the multivoiced medium honed to perfection in the sixteenth century as a means for depicting the phenomenological interior Self.

Music historians like to start the clock for the early modern period in 1600. Several factors lend support to that date: the first opera, the first oratorio,

---

2. Vincenzo Galilei, *Dialogo della musica antica, et della moderna* (1581); an excerpted translated appears in Oliver Strunk, *Source Readings in Music History*, rev. ed. (New York: Norton, 1998), 463–67. See my Chapter 6 for a more extended discussion of Galilei.

3. I have not included girl groups in my discussion here because their voice parts interact differently. These too find their equivalent, however, in the *concerti delle donne* in late sixteenth-century Ferrara and elsewhere. See Chapter 6.

the first solo sonata—in other words, the first "realistic" musical representations of the individual persona—all appear in that year. Moreover, these emergent genres all rely on the new technology of *basso continuo* responsible for securing the tonal era that still persists to this day, if not in expressions of the avant-garde then at least as the lingua franca that underwrites film, advertisement, and popular music. But the coincidence of all these elements makes it perhaps too easy to draw a line of demarcation whereby all cultural agendas before that point count as radically Other. Nor does this problem arise solely within musicology: witness Michel Foucault's similar partitioning of epistemologies in *The Order of Things* at around 1600 or philosophy's designation of point zero at Descartes's "Cogito."[4] If we take these interdisciplinary resonances as further confirmation, then the early seventeenth century seems irrefutably the dawn of modern subjectivity.

Of course, something momentous *does* occur in European culture around 1600. Yet that break is not so radical that it can justify the flattening out of what happened prior to that time—an inevitable effect of Othering. As Eric Wolf explains in his classic *Europe and the People without History*, our historiographies tend to ascribe Selfhood and complex sequences of significant events to those we choose to regard as "us," and they project everyone else into a kind of timeless, unconscious arcadia.[5] Thus, the decades preceding our countdown year often count as interesting insofar as their cultural practices point toward the advent of the new; but to the extent that they align themselves with soon-to-be-obsolete genres and techniques, they still seem to belong to the old world, the backdrop up against which the innovations under consideration can stand in bold relief.

Truth to tell, some distinctions of this sort will appear in this book: I too wish to trace a history of Western subjectivity and will even refer occasionally to the Cogito as a crucial verbal manifestation of the phenomenon I examine. I also plead guilty to drawing a line for the sake of de-

---

4. Michel Foucault, *The Order of Things: An Archaeology of the Human Sciences* (New York: Vintage Books, 1973). For Foucault-oriented epistemology within musicology, see Gary Tomlinson, *Music in Renaissance Magic: Toward a Historiography of Others* (Chicago: University of Chicago Press, 1993) and *Metaphysical Song: An Essay on Opera* (Princeton: Princeton University Press, 1999).

5. Eric R. Wolf, *Europe and the People without History* (Berkeley and Los Angeles: University of California Press, 1997). See also Johannes Fabian, *Time and the Other: How Anthropology Makes Its Object* (New York: Columbia University Press, 1983).

limiting my study, such that what lies before my designated time and outside of northern Italy will have to remain suspended (at least for now) in a vague atemporality.[6]

My argument *in nuce* is that from around 1525 the Italian madrigal serves as a site—indeed, the first in European history—for the explicit, self-conscious construction *in music* of subjectivities. Over the course of a good century, madrigal composers anticipate Descartes in performing the crucial break with traditional epistemologies, plunging musical style and thought into an extraordinary crisis of authority, knowledge, power, and identity. They do so, however, not by repudiating the modal edifice they had inherited from centuries of scholastic theorizing but rather by systematizing, allegorizing, and finally blowing it up from the inside. During the process, they move not closer to but instead further and further away from what might qualify as "tonal" (at least in the standard eighteenth-century sense of the word). And they do so in the service of an agenda that interrogates what it means and feels like to be a Self—to be more specific, a morbidly introspective and irreconcilably conflicted Self.

If similar issues also show up in various other cultural media, they need not advance together in lock-step. Indeed, my other work suggests that music often yields a somewhat different chronology of issues such as subjective formations or conceptions of the body than would a study based solely on written documents. On the one hand, the madrigal resuscitates a tradition of vernacular love song—together with its infinitely fascinating ruminations on the affects of passion on identity—stretching from the Moorish courts of medieval Spain, through the troubadours, and climaxing in the works of Petrarch, whose fourteenth-century sonnets prove a major source of texts for the sixteenth-century genre we are tracing.[7] From that point of view, the madrigal might count as a throwback, and indeed, one of the important strands we will follow involves the association of madrigals with individu-

6. See, however, Bruce W. Holsinger, *Music, Body, and Desire in Medieval Culture* (Stanford: Stanford University Press, 2001). Kate Bartel is writing a dissertation at UCLA on Josquin and his contemporaries that takes many of these issues back into the fifteenth century. See her *Portal of the Skies: Topologies of the Divine in the Latin Motet* (in progress). Moreover, Elizabeth Randell Upton is developing methods for the critical interpretation of Dufay's love songs.

7. See María Rosa Menocal, *The Shards of Love: Exile and the Origins of the Lyric* (Durham and London: Duke University Press, 1994), and Robert M. Durling, Introduction to *Petrarch's Lyric Poems*, trans. and ed. Durling (Cambridge: Harvard University Press, 1976).

als and/or communities in exile who yearn nostalgically for their homeland in the guise of the Lady. But on the other hand, the musical settings that comprise madrigal composition often articulate astonishingly modern insights into subjectivity, for in the process of converting lyrics into the more corporeal and time-oriented medium of music, they necessarily bring to bear aspects of human experience and cultural assumptions not available to poetry. The historiographer Hayden White has pleaded with musicologists to start paying back for what they have gleaned from historians and literary scholars by offering information not available except through music.[8] This book serves as an installment of that payback.

It is, of course, notoriously difficult (I won't accept the word *dangerous*—dangerous to what? to whom?) to rely on nonverbal media for historical data. Pitches and rhythms reside a long distance away from the apparently solid semiosis of language. Yet if music is to figure as anything other than a mere epiphenomenon (and those of us who lived through the music-driven 1960s fervently believe as much), then we must find approaches that will allow us to examine its meanings.[9] Otherwise, we will continue simply to graft music onto an already-formulated narrative of historical developments; more important, we will fail to learn what music might have to teach us or to question seriously what may be incomplete accounts of the past. At the very least I want in this book to shake loose a version of early modern subjectivity too neatly packaged in recent studies and to encourage a process of historical revision that takes music as a point of departure. I also wish to treat in depth a repertory too long neglected as a site of crucial cultural work: the sixteenth-century Italian madrigal.

The madrigal scarcely qualifies as an obscure genre. Within its own time, it occupied the center of musical production: the aesthetic debates concerning sixteenth-century Italian music revolved around the experiments

8. Hayden White, "Form, Reference, and Ideology in Musical Discourse," afterword to *Music and Text: Critical Inquiries,* ed. Steven Paul Scher (Cambridge: Cambridge University Press, 1992). My book *Conventional Wisdom: The Content of Musical Form* (Berkeley and Los Angeles: University of California Press, 2000) explicitly paid homage to White's *The Content of the Form* (Baltimore: Johns Hopkins University Press, 1987) in its title and project.

9. This slight difference in generation explains, I think, the differences in orientation between those "new musicologists" who search to discern meanings (e.g., Lawrence Kramer, Rose Subotnik, and myself) and those who adopt a more postmodernist approach in their work (e.g., Carolyn Abbate and Mary Ann Smart).

performed by its principal composers,[10] and its success contributed greatly to the viability of the new commercial enterprise of music printing.[11] Moreover, a large number of prominent musicologists have long concentrated their efforts to uncovering its history and making this music available to modern musicians and audiences.

Why, then, this book? In point of fact, I have no new archival sources to offer nor hitherto-unknown composers to tout. Indeed, *Modal Subjectivities* deals only with the most familiar artists and madrigals of the tradition— the ones most celebrated in their own day for their impact on cultural life, the ones most readily available in textbooks, anthologies, and recordings. And it concentrates far more on these musical texts than on the contexts that surrounded their origins. I hope, however, to accomplish three major goals, all of them similar to those pursued in my work on later periods.

First, I want to begin interpreting critically a major repertory that has received mostly stylistic descriptions. By "interpreting critically" I mean interrogating the formal details through which the selected compositions produce their effects—structural, expressive, ideological, and cultural. A few musicologists have previously undertaken projects that link sixteenth-century musical procedures with the social: for instance, Joseph Kerman has written extensively on English madrigals, especially those of William Byrd;[12] Anthony Newcomb's work on the court of Ferrara strongly influenced my own training and much of my subsequent work;[13] Gary Tomlinson and Eric Chafe have examined in detail the music of Claudio Monteverdi;[14] Martha

---

10. See the account of the tensions between Willaert and Rore in Martha Feldman, "Rore's 'selva selvaggia': The *Primo libro* of 1542," *JAMS* 42 (1989): 547–603; the flap surrounding Nicola Vicentino's enharmonic experiments in Henry Kaufmann, *The Life and Works of Nicola Vicentino*, Musicological Studies and Documents, vol. 11 (Rome, 1966); Galilei's critique of the polyphonic madrigal in his *Dialogo della musica antica et della moderna* (1581); and the Artusi/ Monteverdi controversy, discussed at length in my Chapter 8.

11. See Mary Lewis, *Antonio Gardane, Venetian Music Printer, 1538–1569: A Descriptive Biography and Historical Study*, 1:1538–49 (New York, 1988); Suzanne Cusick, *Valerio Dorico: Music Printer in Sixteenth-Century Rome* (Ann Arbor: UMI, 1981); and Stanley Boorman, "What Bibliography Can Do: Music Printing and the Early Madrigal," *Music & Letters* 72.2 (May 1991): 236–58.

12. Joseph Kerman, *The Elizabethan Madrigal* (New York: American Musicological Society, 1962).

13. Anthony Newcomb, *The Madrigal at Ferrara, 1579–97* (Princeton: Princeton University Press, 1980).

14. Gary Tomlinson, *Monteverdi and the End of the Renaissance* (Berkeley and Los Angeles: University of California Press, 1987); Eric Chafe, *Monteverdi's Tonal Language* (New York: Schirmer, 1992).

Feldman in her book on the Venetian contexts of Adrian Willaert and Cipri-
ano de Rore brings into focus the kinds of questions I wish to pursue;[15] and,
of course, we all stand on the shoulders of Alfred Einstein, whose monumental *The Italian Madrigal,* while no longer definitive in its details, is not
likely ever to find an equal in terms of sheer prodigious learning.[16] These
scholars and others will emerge as important figures in the chapters that follow. But although it draws on the work of predecessors, this book will push
the enterprise of sixteenth-century music criticism to delineate rather different approaches to theory, analysis, and interpretation.

Second, I want to strengthen the intellectual connection between musicology and scholars in the other humanities. Many of the issues raised over
the course of *Modal Subjectivities* bear traces of my engagement with writers such as Michel Foucault, Stephen Greenblatt, Jonathan Dollimore,
María Rosa Menocal, Charles Taylor, and Peter Burke, all of whom proceed from the premise that human subjectivity has a history—a history for
which modern scholars may receive invaluable insights from the arts.[17] Most
New Historicists depend principally on literature, theater, and painting for
their evidence; they rarely refer to music as a resource (except in the work
of Theodor Adorno or Carl Schorske),[18] in large part because of the specialized training demanded by the task. They sometimes look to musicologists for assistance, but music scholars have concerned themselves only
very recently with the questions typically asked by cultural historians. I
maintain that the madrigal can tell us all a great deal about constructions
of subjectivity—notions of the body, emotions, temporality, gender, reason, interiority—during a crucial stage of Western cultural history. And if
some of these notions find direct corroboration in contemporaneous cul-

15. Martha Feldman, *City Culture and the Madrigal at Venice* (Berkeley and Los Angeles:
University of California Press, 1995).

16. Alfred Einstein, *The Italian Madrigal,* trans. Knappe, Sessions, Strunk (Princeton:
Princeton University Press, 1949; repr., 1971).

17. Foucault, *The Order of the Things;* Stephen Greenblatt, *Renaissance Self-Fashioning from
More to Shakespeare* (Chicago: University of Chicago Press, 1980); Jonathan Dollimore, *Death,
Desire and Loss in Western Culture* (New York: Routledge, 1998); Menocal, *The Shards of Love;*
Charles Taylor, *Sources of the Self: The Making of the Modern Identity* (Cambridge: Harvard
University Press, 1989); Peter Burke, *Eyewitnessing: The Uses of Images as Historical Evidence*
(Ithaca: Cornell University Press, 2001).

18. See, for example, Carl E. Schorske, *Fin-de-Siècle Vienna: Politics and Culture* (New York:
Vintage Books, 1981) and *Thinking with History: Explorations in the Passage to Modernism*
(Princeton: Princeton University Press, 1998). For Adorno see *Essays on Music,* ed. Richard
Leppert (Berkeley and Los Angeles: University of California Press, 2002).

tural discourses, others do not. Thus, although my work is indebted to Foucault and others, I cannot subscribe in advance to any master narrative against which to map my history of subjectivity, for doing so would foreclose anything I might find in this radically different medium.

Before proceeding further, I should explain why I treat musical texts—here and elsewhere in my other work—as potential sources of historical evidence, why I rely at least as heavily on what I discern in musical procedures as on verbal documents. I do not claim that we can read straight through music to history: without question, many levels of cultural tropes, artistic conventions, and social contingencies mediate between the dots on the page and the complexities of a world now more than four centuries removed. But the same holds true for verbal documents, which likewise require careful contexualization and which never can deliver anything approaching Truth. If we wait for the discovery of a treatise that will tell us everything we want to know about this repertory, we will be able to ice-skate in Hades while we read it. For the questions I ask of this repertory often differ from those posed by its composers and first audiences, all of whom found themselves enmeshed in other cultural debates.

Yet I would not thereby concede that my enterprise qualifies as anachronistic. Take for example the question of sexuality. Renaissance music theorists generally did not discuss strategies for simulating desire, arousal, or climax in their writings; they had (as it were) other fish to fry. Nevertheless, the madrigal repertory deals consistently, obsessively, even graphically with experiences of erotic engagement. I know in advance that those critics who find problematic my ascription of sexual dimensions to Richard Strauss's *Salome* will also balk at this project. And I can also anticipate some who will continue to worry about my hermeneutic incursion into the cultures of historic Others. But if we are ever to move beyond the mere hoarding of old music and enter into cultural interpretation, then we have to take such chances. We must, of course, also take into account whatever documents do happen to survive. But for musicologists (and, if we can make the case, for other cultural historians as well), these documents should also include the music itself. The verbal does not trump the musical.

At issue here is a methodological problem concerning the relative weight of texts and contexts. Music historians have tended to privilege what they know (or think they know) about the historical terrain, then situate their interpretations of music accordingly. But what if—as Jacques Attali quirkily but astutely posits—music frequently registers epistemological changes before they are manifested in words?[19] What if John Cage (as Jean-François Lyotard, among others, claims) sparked postmodernism as it appeared in the other arts, decades before other musicians thought to write what they themselves labeled as postmodernist music?[20] What if Mozart was (as E.T.A. Hoffmann insisted) the first great Romantic—the model for the poets and novelists who followed?[21] And what if the madrigalists anticipated Foucault's seventeenth-century episteme a good seventy years earlier, performed the Cogito when Descartes wasn't even a twinkle in his father's eye? I firmly believe that to demand verbal confirmation for anything we want to say about music assumes that music can add nothing to our understanding of a society that we cannot glean perfectly well from other kinds of sources. And it can lead to grave underestimations of music's impact on structures of feeling in a culture.[22]

I have a third purpose in writing this book. In recent years, most of my efforts have centered on music of the seventeenth century: a period that witnessed the emergence of tonality, the musical system we still too often regard as natural. As I began writing a chapter devoted to musical practices *before* that change, I discovered that I could not do justice to its complexity and vast range of possibilities in the course of a mere introduction, not even in an introduction that threatened to stretch to inordinate length. That chapter clearly needed to become a book in itself—a book necessary if my account of style in the 1600s, *Power and Desire in Seventeenth-Century Music*, were not to seem like yet one more celebration of tonality's inevitable emergence. I hope to demonstrate in *Modal Subjectivities* that there existed no prima facie reason why musical grammar needed to have changed in the 1600s, that the syntactical and expressive sophistication manifested in the sixteenth-century madrigal equals that of any subsequent musical repertory. And, having done that, I can in relatively good conscience proceed to an examination of the transformation, to ask why—given the extraordi-

19. Jacques Attali, *Noise: The Political Economy of Music* (Minneapolis: University of Minnesota Press, 1985); afterword by Susan McClary.

20. Jean-François Lyotard, "Several Silences," in his *Driftworks*, trans. Joseph Maier (New York, 1984), 91–110.

21. E.T.A. Hoffmann, "Beethoven's Instrumental Music" (1813), trans. Oliver Strunk, *Source Readings in Music History* (New York: Norton, 1950; rev. ed., 1998).

22. I owe the expression "structures of feeling" to Raymond Williams. See his *Marxism and Literature* (Oxford: Oxford University Press, 1977), 128–35.

nary capabilities of this modus operandi —composers opted to alter drastically not only their musical procedures but (more important) their fundamental conceptions of temporality and Selfhood.[23]

Now an apology: I would like to be able to assure the interdisciplinary reader that technical music-theoretical jargon will not enter into this text. But my argument proceeds from my conviction that musical procedures themselves constitute an indispensable aspect of the cultural content of any repertory. Formal properties, in other words, operate neither as "purely musical" elements relevant only to music theorists nor as neutral devices on top of which the content gets deposited, inasmuch as the stuff of music is sound and time. And given the extensive grammatical mediation that regulates the relationships between sounds and their temporal arrangements, we cannot hear straight through to the content.

Moreover, our contemporary ears—all long since oriented toward the tonal strategies of the eighteenth and nineteenth centuries—have to be reoriented to hear in significantly different ways if they are to discern the madrigal's expressive and allegorical strategies. This process of rewiring will doubtless prove difficult even for those who have learned to accept as universals the structural and harmonic norms of later musics. But as it turns out (or does so according to the historical narrative I will weave over the course of this book), the cultural agenda of the madrigal's successive stages cannot be disentangled from the successive developments of the highly intricate musical system with which it was allied, which sustained and often inspired its various moments, and which eventually served as the conventional base that needed somehow to be repudiated and sacrificed to the cause of radical individualism.

I will always attempt to translate the principal points I make into language comprehensible to those without specialized musical training. Yet I cannot avoid the formal frameworks within which these pieces unfold without falling back on the assumption that their meanings all proceed directly from the lyrics: an assumption that underlies most accounts of the madrigal, so prevalent that text/music relationships of virtually all varieties are pejoratively termed "madrigalisms" or text-painting. It is as though composers stumbled blindly from line to line, relying for coherence on their chosen verses like children requiring training wheels on their bikes. At best,

---

23. My *Power and Desire in Seventeenth-Century Music* is now in preparation for Princeton University Press.

then, a composition would reflect its text, and its meanings would reduce to those of the poem. Without question, madrigalists (like later composers of opera or Lieder, for that matter) saw their task as enhancing and interpreting their chosen texts, and we can come to understand their signifying practices in part by following correspondences with words. But if the *music* of the madrigal matters (and I submit that it does), then we must examine how it produces its powerful imagery over and above—and sometimes in contradiction to—the lyrics.

HOW TO DO THINGS WITH MODES

Music theorists of the sixteenth century discussed the formal organization of their music in terms of what they called mode. Yet musicologists have long regarded that penchant as a mere holdover from earlier theoretical traditions designed to classify Roman Catholic plainsong, and they have tended to dismiss sixteenth-century theories as woefully inadequate or fundamentally misguided for purposes of explaining contemporaneous polyphonic practices. Part of the reason for that dismissal is a model of historiography that envisions a teleological trajectory from modal monophony through a gradual breakdown of modality to the consolidation of standardized tonality in the later seventeenth century. Given this intellectual predisposition, music historians often want to hear the music of the sixteenth century as the penultimate step in that evolutionary process: after all those centuries of wandering in the wilderness, we arrive finally within spitting distance of the promised land![24]

Without question, a humanist such as Gioseffo Zarlino—the music theorist upon whom I rely most heavily—blurred the boundaries between his displays of classical erudition, his continued respect for ecclesiastical tradition, and the systems he himself formulated to account for the music of his own contemporaries.[25] The section of Zarlino's *Istitutioni harmoniche* that deals with modes (Book IV) actively works to keep all these very differ-

24. See, for example, Edward Lowinsky, *Tonality and Atonality in Sixteenth-Century Music* (Berkeley and Los Angeles: University of California Press), 1962, and Carl Dahlhaus, *Studies on the Origin of Harmonic Tonality*, trans. Robert Gjerdingen (Princeton: Princeton University Press, 1990). Rather than cluttering my exposition with disciplinary debates, I will return to the relevant literature in Chapter 9.

25. Gioseffo Zarlino, *Istitutioni harmoniche* (Venice: 1573; facsimile ed., Gregg Press, 1966).

ent agendas braided together: thus, he appeals to Ancients such as Ptolemy
for support of his statements, even as he seeks to explain the music of his
own Venetian mentor, Adrian Willaert. Modern scholars rightly despair of
Zarlino's universalizing obfuscation of the vast differences between theories borrowed from Greek sources (some of them ostentatiously quoted in
Greek) and those appropriate for musical repertories of the High Renaissance. Furthermore, no one would deny that the music of sixteenth-century
Italy resembles that of the tonal era far more than it does that of mythol-
ogized Dorians and Phrygians. Hence, the sixteenth-century pretense that
its composers were reconstituting the musical practices of Hellenic civilization deserves much of the scorn it receives.

But we have too often read Zarlino as a committed antiquarian rather
than as the reigning authority on music of his own time who brings in the
trappings of classical learning for show and cultural prestige. The fact that
he leads off with so much dirty bathwater does not justify throwing out
the baby itself, for what Zarlino has to say about mode as a structuring
principle provides greater insight into sixteenth-century Italian repertories
than does any other source available—not because this music works the
same way as does Greek song or liturgical chant (obviously it does not),
but because Zarlino constructs his theories with the express purpose of dealing with the most up-to-date practices. In point of fact, his model does
not necessarily even help us with much music of the fifteenth century, composed largely without this reworking of mode as part of the precomposi-
tional conceptual framework.[26] But beginning with Johannes Tinctoris,
who states quite off-handedly and without much further explanation that
mode also applies to polyphony, a series of intellectuals—including most
prominently Pietro Aron and Heinrich Glareanus, in addition to Zarlino—
grappled with formulating theories of modal polyphonic practice.[27] Sub-

---

26. See, however, Leeman L. Perkins, "Modal Species and Mixtures in a Fifteenth-
Century Chanson Repertory," in *Modality in the Music of the Fourteenth and Fifteenth Centuries,* ed. Ursula Günther, Ludwig Finscher, and Jeffrey Dean, Musicological Studies and Documents 49 (Neuhausen-Stuttgart: Hänssler-Verlag, 1996), and "Modal Strategies in Okeghem's
Missa Cuiusvis Toni," *Music Theory and the Exploration of the Past,* ed. Christopher Hatch
and David W. Bernstein (Chicago: University of Chicago Press, 1993).

27. Johannes Tinctoris, *Liber de natura et proprietate tonorum* (1476); Pietro Aron, *Trattato
della natura e cognitione di tutti gli tuoni di canto figurato* (Venice: 1525; partial translation in
Strunk, *Source Readings*); Heinrich Glareanus, *Dodecachordon* (Basle: 1547; trans. Clement A.
Miller, Musicological Studies and Documents 6, 1965). See my Chapter 9 for a more extensive discussion of modal theory in history and practice.

sequent musicians learned their craft in part by studying such texts, which predisposed them to conceive of their compositional strategies in precisely these terms.

In other words, the sixteenth-century repertory manifests a kind of self-conscious *neo*modality—not the modality of plainsong (let alone that of Greek antiquity!), yet nevertheless a practice that reinhabits and reanimates some of those old and still-prestigious structures of the past for its own purposes. More recent episodes of neomodality—for instance, those of avant-garde jazz or thrash metal—attest to the ways in which those old bottles can serve to ferment entirely new (if quite unlikely) wines,[28] and High Renaissance polyphony counts as another such moment. But just as George Russell and Metallica turned to modes for reasons having little to do with antiquarian authenticity (though the prior existence of ready-made categories such as Lydian and Phrygian helped legitimate and propel their experiments), so too the musicians of the sixteenth century found in these old structures something that appealed to and deeply influenced their own cultural practices. Recall that much of the music of the earlier part of the sixteenth century—the frottolas and dances that enjoyed considerable popularity in northern Italian courts of that time—actually comes much closer to behaving in ways we now call "tonal" than does the more complex music of several subsequent generations. Thus, instead of regarding the music of the sixteenth century as a series of successive attempts to evolve out of modality toward something else, it makes greater sense to see it as a period that deliberately revived, refashioned, and reveled in mode.

J. L. Austin transformed permanently the philosophy of language with his *How to Do Things with Words,* which directed inquiry away from the ontological and toward the performative.[29] So long as we imagine a static entity called "mode" and ask whether or not the Greeks, the early church, Palestrina, John Coltrane, and Megadeth all abide by it in the same ways, the clear answer is: of course not! But although modes do not remain static throughout their various manifestations in Western culture, the very fact

28. For jazz, see George Russell, *Lydian Chromatic Concept of Tonal Organization* (New York: Concept Publishing,1953). I once had the opportunity to hear Russell explain his brilliant ideas of how the Lydian fourth degree freed bop from the imperatives of the tritone that drive tonality. For metal, see Robert Walser, *Running with the Devil: Power, Gender, and Madness in Heavy Metal Music* (Hanover, NH: Wesleyan University Press, 1992).

29. J. L. Austin, *How to Do Things with Words,* 2nd ed. (Cambridge: Harvard University Press, 1975).

that this set of time-honored categories exists has inspired and sustained an unending stream of new possibilities. Thus, we should alter our question and ask instead: What did musicians in the 1500s actually *do* with modes? Why did modes appeal to composers of this particular moment? How did modes (albeit in a very new manifestation) underwrite and facilitate the musical strategies of the time?

Over the course of this book, I will demonstrate how sixteenth-century composers deployed modes in the service of a new cultural agenda that sought to perform dynamic representations of complex subjective states. For the first time in European history, musicians strove deliberately and explicitly to simulate in their work such features of human experience as emotions, bodies, sexual desire, and pleasure. This is not to suggest that earlier music never engaged with such matters: the music of Machaut or Josquin provoke powerful affective reactions in listeners, and the stimulation of such reactions had to have been part of their artistic purpose. Yet most earlier musicians did not appear to have had representations of interiority as their primary goal. Beginning with the madrigal, however, the performance of subjectivity moved to the fore as the dominant and self-consciously acknowledged project.

Stephen Greenblatt, in his important book *Renaissance Self-Fashioning,* demonstrates the ways in which this agenda operated in English literature of the time.[30] It so happens that the moment at which music entered into the representation of what Greenblatt calls "inwardness" was also a moment that regarded inwardness not as a simple phenomenon innocent of the contradictions of modern life but as always already ambivalent and self-divided. The systematization of modality in the sixteenth century became the technology that allowed for the simulations of such conflicted conceptions of Selfhood in sound.

Moreover, inasmuch as these pieces highlight the fundamentally unstable status of the Self, they produce images of "modal"—that is, always provisional—subjectivities, which is why they do not translate easily into the imperative sense of centered subjectivity that grounds eighteenth-century tonality ideologically. Indeed, we might even fail to recognize their configurations as relating to subjectivity. In his *Aesthetic Theory,* for instance, Theodor Adorno grants subjective consciousness to the Hellenic Greeks

---

30. Greenblatt, *Renaissance Self-Fashioning* (see again n. 17).

and to Renaissance sculptors, but he ascribes this attribute to music starting only with Bach.[31]

After a recent talk, in which I had discussed the considerable expressive range in the music of Hildegard von Bingen, I was asked by a nonspecialist whether I would characterize her music as "happy" or "sad." The question took me aback for a moment, but like all good questions, this one stimulated far more than the simple information requested. Of course, the "happy/sad" dichotomy does not even adequately serve the needs of the tonal music within which it developed: the idea of reducing any given movement to one or the other of these alternatives has driven many critics to advocate the banning of adjectival description altogether. Yet the major/minor polarity of standardized tonality does often operate to reinforce something of this pair of options—especially in pieces by composers such as Schubert that depend heavily on fluctuating mediants for their meanings.

But the binary opposition between major and minor fails to engage effectively at all with earlier repertories, not because these musics lack expressive dimensions, but because their expressivity is conceived up against a grid offering at least eight and sometimes twelve possible categories—or subjective modalities. In other words, we cannot interpret this music through the dualisms that orient the emotional landscape of so much later music, for the technologies underlying modal composition presuppose a much broader range of possible expressive grammars. Just as (according to linguistic mythology) the Arctic languages that possess dozens of words for *snow* cannot find equivalents in English, so the affective qualities of the various modes correspond to no readily identifiable types in later music. The implications of this untranslatability not only involve musical procedure but also bear witness to significantly different structures of feeling. By pointing to alternative ways of experiencing affect than the ones we often assume, they also may lead us to interrogate the reasons behind the radical reduction of this more multifaceted emotional syntax to one with two principal options: major (positive) and minor (negative).

I will not set out here an elaborate theory of modal practice; instead, I will present only the minimal amount of information necessary for understanding

31. Theodor Adorno, *Aesthetic Theory* (1970), trans. and ed. Robert Hullot-Kentor (Minneapolis: University of Minnesota Press, 1997).

the compositions that I examine over the course of this book, providing more detail for specific pieces as needed. The brief expositions offered by most theorists of the sixteenth century prove ample, for they aim only to delineate the basic framework within which to comprehend the enormous variety of strategies available within this practice; they opt for a deliberately baggy concept that lends itself to an infinite number of possible arrangements. I will concentrate for most of *Modal Subjectivities* on the strategies exemplified by a series of madrigals, though those seeking a more detailed discussion of sixteenth-century sources and present-day debates may consult the final chapter. For purposes of the book, I will assume the following general guidelines:

1. Modes are *not* the same as scales. Modern misunderstandings concerning this practice in sixteenth-century music stem in part from our misconceived notion that modal identity requires scalar purity, that accidentals testify to the inadequacy of the system and thus point toward the dissolution of mode and the inevitability of tonality. But most sixteenth-century accidentals no more weaken modal identities than they do in their corresponding places in tonality; it's just that we have internalized a wide range of extensions, loopholes, and techniques for explaining departures from scalar purity in tonal pieces. We must extend the same courtesy to the Renaissance repertory, instead of defining mode by means of the narrowest possible criteria (criteria not ratified, incidentally, by theorists of the time) and then seizing onto accidentals as evidence of the modal system's increasing incoherence and impending demise. Indeed, as we will see, accidentals in the madrigal more often than not operate to distinguish one mode from another and thus to consolidate identity.

2. Modes involve the melodic and structural projection of a particular species of octave (diapason), fifth (diapente), and fourth (diatessaron) throughout a composition. (I make use of Aeolian for these examples because it is the mode within which Monteverdi's "Ah, dolente partita"— the example for this chapter—operates.) The boundaries of the species usually emerge as the most frequent sites for cadences. Moreover, they define the grammatical implications—that is, the relative degree of tension and repose, the sense of direction—of each pitch in the principal melodies and imitative motives (Fig. 2).

3. The syntax of sixteenth-century modal music is primarily horizontal, presented through the melodic patterns of the surface. The clearest pro-

FIGURE 2. Aeolian species

diapason   diapente   diatessaron

FIGURE 3. Diapente descent

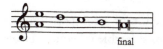

final

FIGURE 4. Harmonizations of diapente

Passamezzo antico   Romanesca

gression available involves the stepwise descent from the fifth degree to the final (designated in my schematic examples with a double whole note) (Fig. 3). Harmonization matters: for instance, a melodic cadence may be confirmed or frustrated by the extent to which the other voices concur with its primary implication. But it functions as a secondary, inflectionary parameter; the example in Figure 4, for instance, presents two standardized harmonizations—known respectively as the Passamezzo antico and the Romanesca—of this fundamental progression. This principle proves true even in relatively diatonic passages with the most obvious harmonies, which frequently end up sounding very much "tonal" to our modern ears but for which linear explanations provide more reliable accounts. Otherwise, we end up with patchwork analyses that posit tonal islands surrounded by seas of incoherence, instead of consistent interpretations of strategic choices within a single practice.

4. The diapente (or fifth) underwrites the most stable sections of a composition, and its pitches usually remain unchanged. Especially crucial to identity are the boundary pitches and the third degree (the mediant)— the pitch that determines major or minor quality. Chromatic inflections may occur for the sake of leading tones to secondary-area cadences (for instance, in Aeolian, a cadence on the fourth degree, D, will de-

mand a temporary C♯), but such inflections are regarded literally as "accidental"; they may even remain unnotated, though assumed by *musica ficta*—a performance practice that allowed for and sometimes even required such pitches but that did not clutter up the score with theoretically "irrational" pitches. Otherwise, the pitches of the diapente cannot be bent chromatically without disrupting modal certainty. (Note, however, that such disruptions often operate as the expressive crux of particular compositions.)

5. Within a stable section of a composition, the diatessaron (or fourth) often submits to considerable inflection *for the sake of enhancing modal identity*. Thus, both the sixth and seventh degrees in Aeolian will be raised to F♯ and G♯ at cadences to provide a heightened sense of direction (Fig. 5). Yet the actual diatonic pitches of the fourth become hardwired in at the structural level, where they may be altered only for the sake of temporary leading tones or for purposes of signaling irrationality. Consequently, the Aeolian modes differ from Dorian on the higher level of available secondary areas: while the inherently high sixth degree of the Dorian diatessaron facilitates authentic cadences onto the fifth degree (for which it serves as scale-degree $\hat{2}$), the low sixth degree of Aeolian does not for allow such cadences. In those cases in which an Aeolian sixth degree is inflected upward to F♯ to provide the second degree for an authentic cadence on E, the alteration counts as a significant violation and should be regarded as such (Fig. 6).[32]

6. The modal species may be arranged with either diapente or diatessaron on top, producing two possible systems. When the diapente and the modal final occur at the bottom of the range, theorists classify the mode as authentic; when the diapente occurs on top with the final in the middle of the range, they label it plagal (Fig. 7). Clearly, when the composition involves genuinely equal-voiced polyphony, some of the voices will occupy the plagal range and others the authentic. Theorists such as Zarlino recommend that composers and analysts privilege tenor and soprano above the other voices, and they assign mode accordingly. The

32. See, for instance, John Dowland's song "In darknesse," especially on the words "The walls of marble black." In his *L'Orfeo*, Monteverdi uses the F♯ in Aeolian contexts to manifest extreme grief.

FIGURE 5. Diatessaron

descending   ascending

FIGURE 6. $\hat{5}$ in Dorian vs. Aeolian

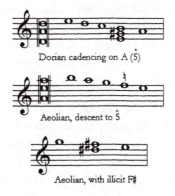

Dorian cadencing on A ($\hat{5}$)

Aeolian, descent to $\hat{5}$

Aeolian, with illicit F♯

FIGURE 7. Authentic and plagal

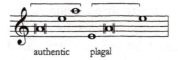

authentic   plagal

very fact of the mixture complicates easy classification, of course. But music does not exist for the sake of mere pigeonholing, and we do better to ask why and how such strategies proved useful in the production of musical meaning at this time. As we will see in the analyses that follow, mixtures of this sort facilitate the articulation of internal conflict, making such complexities not a sign of theoretical weakness but rather a factor contributing to the richness of modal practice.

7. On the structural level, a composition may visit the same three or four pitches repeatedly for cadences, in contrast with tonal pieces, which typically follow a linear and nonredundant trajectory on the background. The recurrences of cadences on a few pitches do not, however, imply an arbitrary or primitive approach to structure. Quite the con-

trary: the tensions among cadence points operate to define the text-re-
lated allegories central to the strategies of individual pieces. In other
words, the structure of each piece corresponds to a particular reading
of its text and is tailor-made to dramatize its meanings. The extraordinary variety of modal designs could even be counted as evidence of
greater formal sophistication within the sixteenth-century repertories
than those of the eighteenth, in which most pieces delineate more or
less the same background trajectory in their unfoldings. In contrast with
what is often relegated to the status of the "purely formal" in standard
tonality, the structural features of a modal piece function among the
dimensions of the piece concerned most expressly with articulating idiosyncratic meanings.[33]

8. Sixteenth-century modal theorists differ greatly from one another
    mostly with regard to their respective numbering systems. The scholas-
    tics had maintained eight modal types: two each (authentic and plagal—
    the latter with the prefix *hypo-* to designate its arrangement) for D, E,
    F, and G, numbered one through eight. But as Pietro Aron discovered
    when he attempted to analyze contemporary practice, some composi-
    tions of the time also shape themselves around C and A as apparent
    finals. Glareanus and Zarlino solved that inconsistency by positing two
    extra modal pairs, respectively on C and A, that operated just like the
    others of the system except for their newly recognized finals. Alas, the
    two dodecachordans chose to locate their added categories in different
    arrangements: Glareanus started with A, then runs the gamut stepwise
    from C to G, while Zarlino decided to offer a more symmetrical, aes-
    thetically pleasing series from C to A. Consequently, what a tradition-
    alist would label as Mode 1 (authentic, with D as the final), Glareanus
    would label as Mode 5, and Zarlino would count as Mode 3. Although
    composers continue to title their pieces with respect to mode numbers
    (e.g., *Missa sexti toni*), these numbers become very confusing, given the
    competing systems—even though the theorists concur on most other
    matters concerning modal practice. Accordingly, I prefer to refer to
    modes by their traditional Greek names, which sidesteps the confusion
    over numbers: in other words, an authentic mode with D as the final

---

33. For an extended discussion of eighteenth-century tonality along these lines, see my
Conventional Wisdom: The Content of Musical Form (Berkeley and Los Angeles: University of
California Press, 2000), chap. 3.

FIGURE 8. Twelve modes

(Hypo)Dorian   (Hypo)Phrygian   (Hypo)Lydian   (Hypo)Mixolydian   (Hypo)Aeolian   (Hypo)Ionian

will count for me as Dorian (a label, incidentally, endorsed by Zarlino and others) (Fig. 8).

I do not wish to belabor the theoretical aspect of this study; indeed, it must seem strange that someone so associated with the critique of formalism would spend so much time discussing abstract syntactical matters. But in my studies of the tonal repertory, I have found it necessary to counter the exclusively structuralist accounts that characterize scholarship in those areas so as to introduce some consideration of content. The opposite situation obtains, however, in early and popular musics: most writers have been all too happy to deal only with what they term the "extramusical"—that is, lyrics, biographies, social contexts, and even encrypted references—with virtually no serious engagement with critical analysis. Thus, in order to pursue the same kinds of interpretations of these theoretically neglected repertories that I regularly offer of tonal pieces, I have to shore up the formal side this time. For my concerns have always centered on the interrelationship between form and content—on how structural procedures themselves contribute to the production of expressive and cultural meanings. The discussions of the madrigals that make up the larger part of this book require some amount of knowledge concerning the conventional practices within which they operate. As we shall see, the too-common habit of labeling chords in this music frequently obscures some of the most significant moments in a piece; it may even so misconstrue the basic framework of a piece as to prevent recognition of the fundamental tensions upon which its governing allegory relies. I am not, in other words, insisting on this theoretical sidetrack for the sake of historical pedantry, nor am I casting sixteenth-century pieces as mere examples in the service of an analytical project. Yet we do need a sufficient grasp of the theoretical principles underlying this music if we are to have access into the cultural work performed by each piece.

And I can best demonstrate the efficacy of the guidelines just presented by turning to the music itself. The remainder of this chapter deals, consequently, with the madrigal that opened this chapter: Monteverdi's "Ah, dolente partita."

AH, DOLENTE PARTITA

For his musical setting of Mirtillo's lament (Book IV, 1603), Monteverdi chose the Aeolian mode: a mode that offers even in the abstract certain formal predispositions that the composer perceived as parallel to Mirtillo's condition. We often assume that Aeolian operates much as tonal minor does, in that its scale—including even the location of its sixth degree a half step above the fifth—is exactly the same. But scale does not equal mode; as we saw above, mode also entails a whole package of melodic tendencies, structural demands, and probable ambiguities that convert mere scalar properties into dynamic potentialities.

Like all modes, Aeolian features an octave (A to A) divided into a species of fifth (the diapente, A to E) and of fourth (the diatessaron, E to A). The boundary pitches of these species should appear in prominent positions— at cadences, as principal melodic points—if the mode is to maintain its identity. A glance at the motives in the first half of "Ah, dolente partita" (see again Fig. 1) confirms that the composer complies with this basic criterion of modal propriety.[34]

But Aeolian also brings with its pitch arrangement certain idiosyncrasies, the most critical of which involves the relative weakness of its fifth degree. Whereas the fifth degree in Dorian often threatens to usurp the authority of the final, that same boundary pitch in Aeolian cannot establish itself through temporary finalization: the F♯ needed for a cadential confirmation of E does not occur within the system. By contrast, Dorian has access to both versions of its sixth degree, in that the higher one (the one responsible for tonicizing the fifth degree) exists within its species, while the lower one may be annexed through principles of *musica ficta*. We learn to wink at these "fictional" pitches, to regard them as not *truly* there, even as they perform undeniably important functions; leading tones both count and don't count because of this "just kidding" status. But although *musica ficta* freely grants Aeolian any number of chromatic leading tones, it cannot legitimately supply the F♯ needed as second degree to E.

---

34. Monteverdi alludes in some of his motives to Giaches de Wert's setting of the same text, though their concepts—including choice of mode and all that implies—differ radically from one another.

FIGURE 9. Emphasis of $\hat{5}$

with A   with C   with E

FIGURE 10. Alternative divisions of A octave

final on A   final on D

This difference—which only emerges as significant at the structural level—accounts largely for the affective distinctions between Dorian and Aeolian. For lacking the gravitational pull in Dorian toward the fifth degree, Aeolian can assert that boundary pitch only with considerable difficulty: as part of a stable Aeolian configuration; as part of the area on the third degree, C; or as an unstable half cadence, arrived at by equivocal Phrygian movement. It can never shore itself up as a temporary region in and of itself (Fig. 9).

What Aeolian offers instead is a tendency (also available, incidentally, in Dorian) to divide its octave at the fourth degree (Fig. 10). Depending on context and harmonization, the Aeolian fifth degree, E, may sound as though it is poised to confirm D as the stronger pitch. And because D lies to the flat (i.e., less dynamic) side of the Aeolian center, this propensity to collapse over onto the fourth degree lends a quality of passivity to many Aeolian pieces—passivity answered with an uphill struggle to reassert E as the proper boundary pitch, however limited its systemic resources to do so.

Here we may begin to appreciate the relevance of Aeolian to poor Mirtillo's inner turmoil. He never musters the energy to take action (as an aggressive move to the fifth degree might register, making Dorian the preferred mode for recriminations) but rather draws the conflict down within himself. He wills himself dead (often on D) yet ends up somehow always in the same position: that is, with his whiny, ambivalent E, confirming his ineffectual identity even as it always seems ready to collapse in keeping with his death wish. In other words, Aeolian already maps out in its formal predispositions an analogue to Mirtillo's psychological state (as we shall see in Chapter 8, Amarilli's psychology turns out to be far more complex than Mirtillo's—or at least it is so in Monteverdi's hands).

When introducing the various components of Mirtillo's simultaneous yet contradictory feelings, Monteverdi follows Guarini's sequence. One could even envision a monodic setting of the text for solo voice, in which the reactions succeed each other in linear, speechlike fashion: Monteverdi does as much in his celebrated *Lamento d'Arianna*. But, as we saw at the beginning of this chapter, the five-voice idiom characteristic of the madrigal allows for the gradual layering of these sentiments. They can do so, however, only if the materials that initially make sense in horizontal arrangement can also accommodate themselves to vertical stacking.

As it happens, all the motives associated with the first lines of text feature some configuration of Aeolian's sore pitches, E and D, with F always ready to follow the lead of the others. As the new layers enter, the entire complex begins to waver back and forth between A and D orientations: a mere fictive C♯ can cause the even the most stable of Aeolian configurations to tilt dangerously toward octave division on D, whereas E (the rightful divisor) has nothing more in its arsenal for purposes of stabilizing itself than an equivocal half cadence (Fig. 11). Thus, the ambiguities of this section are not limited to just the incompatible vectors of the various motives; in addition, the superimposition of motives alters the syntactical implications of each, injecting self-doubt and slippage into even those ideas that seem completely clear at first glance. They come to affect—indeed, to *in*fect—each other to an extent only hinted at in Guarini's generating text.

The madrigal opens with two high voices singing a unison E, a pitch initially undefined with respect to mode—though stylistic probability would argue for a beginning on either final or fifth degree (see Ex. 1). Only on the last syllable of "dolente" do the voices start to distinguish themselves, as the canto moves to produce a painful half-step dissonance above the quinto—the sorrowful parting mentioned in the text. But Monteverdi's sorrowful parting extends itself through a suspension chain: if the quinto moves reluctantly down to relieve the tension, the canto (as if already regretting the separation) returns, only to find itself now dissonant with respect to its partner. At this point, the quinto leaps to the F previously occupied by the canto, but it finds there a lonely void. It writhes slowly around E (F-E-D-E) in belated imitation of the now-absent canto, striving in vain to restore the unity of the opening sonority. The music thus tracks the parting of the two would-be lovers, with their clinging hesitations, misunderstandings, failures to synchronize, and futile attempts at reconciliation. But it also de-

FIGURE II. Combinations of E, D, and F

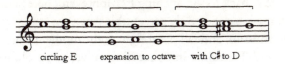

circling E   expansion to octave   with C♯ to D

picts Mirtillo's internal anguish, his feeling of being torn apart on the inside. The quality of being identical with himself, suggested by the unison E of the first measures, has disappeared, never again to be restored. Yet his condition of equanimity always was (at best) extremely tenuous, hovering as it did on that high, unsupported, undefined pitch.

While the quinto is twisting around E to complete its verbal phrase, the canto launches into the next line of text, "Ah, fin de la mia vita," with a gesture that plunges downward suddenly into the abyss—toward cadence or (given the words) toward death. Whereas the canto lands in a position of relative powerlessness (the opening E now reproduced at the octave below), the alto (a new voice) succeeds in tracing a linear descent to A: the final that would spell closure in Aeolian. But in contrast to the excruciatingly slow motion of the opening, this motive moves too quickly—more quickly, in fact, than the half-note pulse (or *tactus*) that marks the rate of actual progression. Because its pitches occur at the level of diminution or ornament, it counts technically as a throwaway, an exasperated and fruitless wish to escape the entire situation. Despite its impetuousness, it cannot break free from that tortured web of motives that continues on, quite oblivious to these attempts at bailing out. Mirtillo might as well will himself out of his own skin.

Still, "Ah, fin de la mia vita" does register as a motivic unit, and as the madrigal progresses, this gesture will repeatedly rip—even if impotently—against the exquisite languor of the other voices. Indeed, following its initial appearances in canto and alto, the canto and quinto take up the motive, elevate it to various pitch levels until they find one that guarantees at least the linear cadence on A in m. 15, bringing to a conclusion the first section of the piece.

Meantime, however, another idea has slipped in, disguised at first as a mere supporting bass. The motive on "Da te parto e non moro?" not only casts verbal doubt on the self-deluded attempts at cadence in the upper voices but also unravels their apparent progress: while the canto is plummeting down confidently to A, the bass reverses the action as it climbs inexorably from C back to the opening E. Monteverdi here masks skepticism as affirmation—a paradox only perceptible when the lower voices complete their motivic mission and fall silent right at the moment when they should, if they were *only* harmonic in conception, advance to solidify A. (Performance decisions make all the difference here: the bass and tenor must crescendo through their lines to the moment when they break off if they are to convey successfully their double-edged functions.) The sighing upper voices consequently arrive on their A without external corroboration; the cadence presents itself as a classic case of false consciousness.

But Monteverdi *does*, of course, supply an A to greet and support (at least provisionally) the canto's conclusion: the tenor enters with the missing pitch—if only to begin a concentrated passage on "Da te parto e non moro?" involving the three lower voices. Up to this point, the madrigal's ambiguities have centered on the fact of simultaneous yet contradictory impulses, but these impulses at least all point to A as final. And although none of the voices presents anything other than full-fledged motivic materials, certain of them have appeared more prominent with respect to modal definition, while the others seemingly acquiesce to the role of harmonic support.[35]

This slight comfort now evaporates as the three lower parts all trace exactly the same motive—that statement of incredulity, "Da te parto e non moro?"—at different pitch levels. At first, the alto might seem to qualify as the one with the "real" modal information; like the bass in the phrase just completed, it ascends from C to E: $\hat{3}$-$\hat{4}$-$\hat{5}$ in Aeolian. Moreover, it gets to present this material in the uppermost voice instead of getting buried in the mix. But then there's that worrisome bass, trailing behind and offering the same tune a fifth below—an odd harmonization of the alto's line, to say the least. If all three voices concur in their verbal sentiment, which now mounts in a veritable chorus of skepticism, together they instill syntactical unease. The first presentation of that skepticism in the bass brought us circling back to the opening position, but this rising tide of doubt in mm. 15–18 threatens to destabilize any clear sense of pitch orientation: it's not just that we return to the disappointment of the beginning, as did the bass

---

35. Note that mm. 9–10 have what appear to be clanging parallel fifths: one of the great taboos of sixteenth-century contrapuntal practice. The fact that the bottom pitches belong to different voices mollifies the situation only slightly. I would argue that Monteverdi deliberately plants this stark parallel progression in order to emphasize the descent to $\hat{4}$ in the reigning modal line.

in the previous phrase, but now the reliability of that anchor point is itself in question.

The dark-horse voice, the tenor that was threading its way along apparently as harmonic filler, suddenly takes control with its C♯ and follows through to D in m. 21, causing the entire complex suddenly to pivot disastrously. Even though the two upper voices have recommenced their opening gambit of "Ah, dolente partita," their once-secure boundary pitch, E, now registers as a second degree prepared to cadence on D. Indeed, all motives here find themselves twisted on their axes: the alto's E likewise reads as second degree, the bass's A sounds like a harmonic dominant that stops short of the implied resolution onto D. It is as if that growing realization of doubt fed on itself and led beyond mere rejection of the false closure of "Ah, fin de la mia vita" to an even greater horror—one that severely undermines Mirtillo's subjective center. Note that Guarini's lyrics convey none of this directly; we owe the psychologizing of this moment (which draws for its effect on the innate dynamics of the Aeolian mode) to Monteverdi. Thus, the apparent repetition of materials that begins in m. 18 is colored with a quality of panic: whereas the soprano voices originally luxuriated in their sweet torment, now they hang on to a quickly unraveling rationality, their D or F escape notes now spelling capitulation to the tenor's paranoiac *musica ficta*. Who could have guessed that the situation could become worse than that of the beginning? Mere unadulterated separation now sounds in retrospect like a picnic.

No sooner does the crisis break, however, than another motive enters with the words "E pur i' provo / La pena de la morte"—which lends verbal confirmation to precisely the sentiment already rendered so vividly by the swerve onto D that has just occurred. This motive jumps to the octave above the final and literally shrieks out in anguish on repeated, stabbing tones; if the alto part is sung by a man, it anticipates the quality of vocal strain heard when the tenor enters on the same pitch two measures later.[36] But the motive loses heart and ultimately droops back to the neutral E of the beginning. Indeed, its protest submerges itself into the mix that now includes all four other motives, as one reaction among many (yearning, resignation, incredulity) to the calamity at hand. The alto soldiers onward, stating the en-

---

36. In his long-definitive edition of Book IV (1927), Gian Francesco Malipiero marks this motive pianissimo, no doubt to pull this shriek back into the unbroken serenity expected of madrigals during his own day. It should, however, register as a shriek.

tire motive twice, but the tenor—following its first outburst—swallows its indignation, abjectly drops in register, and ends an octave below the actual bass voice. The alto maintains some sense of protest, but the tenor converts Guarini's line into a resentful whine.

Yet this motive has served some productive purpose syntactically, for its insistent A, coupled with the disappearance of C♯, gradually allows Aeolian to fade back in as the probable mode, confirmed with the cadence in m. 31. Although this cadence sounds stronger than the one in m. 15, it too has liabilities, most obviously the tenor's E that prepares the arrival in the three lower voices—the pitch that ought by right to lead to A but that emerges as a defeated termination, unable even to make the causal leap from dominant to tonic. The A in the bass that greets the sopranos' moment of closure merely initiates the next futile cycle.

This time the sorrowful parting occurs in the lower voices, while the sopranos take up the affects of incredulity and protest. The bass voice at first seems only to be supplying the final, A, to lend harmonic support the rest of the voices. But even this most reliable of functions—a sustained tonic in the bass—proves deceptive as its move to B♭ in m. 37 suddenly reveals our anchor pitch to be a double agent: all along, that A was actually serving as the fifth degree of D, and in collusion with the tenor's C♯, it leads to another arrival on D in m. 39. As before, the traumatic swerve to D triggers howls of protest, death wishes, and incredulity. And once again, the Aeolian mode gradually coalesces and manages a third halfhearted cadence in m. 47, this time with the soprano changing the usual conclusion (E) of the protest motive to the bitter confirmation of A. The lower voices refuse to participate in this arrival. Instead they embark on a series of short ruminations on the third and fourth motives, and in each case, the energy drains away in Phrygian approaches to E: the starting position Mirtillo can neither escape nor confirm as a viable alternative. The last of these approaches, which edges its way along through equivocal *fauxbourdon* voicing (parallel chords in first inversion), culminates in m. 56 with a sonority that even lacks a mediant, so empty is its arrival, so devoid of fervor its complaint.

A few words about the madrigal up to this point. Although it may seem that I have twisted and turned every pitch in these fifty-six measures, I have in fact omitted many that might well serve as the beginning of yet other readings. For Monteverdi presents here a process nearly as organic as any by a latter-day serialist, except that he has a commitment not only to the saturated integrity of his piece but also to the conventions that make it publicly intelligible. No voice in this first half sings a throwaway pitch or presents a line written for the mere sake of harmonic support or filler. At the same time, the simultaneous appearances in the five voices of mutually antagonistic affects, coupled with the ways in which they change their modal implications in context, produce a web of unwilling (though invariably consonant) fellow travelers.

Once these motives begin to interact, they generate whole chains of meanings that go far beyond Guarini's verbal blueprint to chart an interiority pulled not just between the pain of living and the impossibility of death, but also in directions not specified by the words. For instance, if the madrigal starts by suggesting allegorical links between E as unresolved agony and A as wished-for death, then what do all those swerves toward D signify? I have based my reading of these moments (which do not align themselves with any particular line of text but rather surge through the entire complex, capsizing the orientation of every single motive) on the modal dynamics themselves. The binarisms of Guarini's lyrics map fairly easily onto the A/E axis of basic Aeolian identity, to which Monteverdi then adds a third dimension. It is as if the cumulative pressure of these competing emotions pushes Mirtillo to the point where reason itself becomes unhinged, and he struggles not just between the poles of life and death, but also with an increasingly frayed sanity and a tendency to tip over into madness. In each case, the symptoms (C♯ or B♭ chromatic alterations) trigger a frantic pull back toward the proper boundaries of Aeolian. But the ease with which a single voice can veer over the edge and hence pollute the whole ensemble makes rationality particularly precarious. Although Guarini may hint at such ramifications, Monteverdi makes them fundamental elements of his structural logic.

Later music has conditioned us to situate ourselves according to sequences of verticalities or chords. Indeed, the great technological breakthrough of the early seventeenth century involved new notational conventions—figured bass—based on this conception. One may easily listen to "Ah, dolente partita" as a succession of chords, for the individual lines have been contrived in such a way as to yield perfectly consonant sonorities during their superimpositions. But this reduction eliminates much of the madrigal's effectiveness. Moreover, although these pieces were presented before select audiences, they were designed not only for spectators but also for the performers themselves. Each singer would have had a part book inscribing only a single vocal line, and each would have seen at a glance that her/his score made modal sense independent of the others; in fact, each singer might well have anticipated leading the ensemble as *the* mode-bearing voice. Only in performance would that part's susceptibility to the contrary impulses of the other voices have become manifest, as each singer experienced something of that unbidden and unanticipated log jam of emotions about which Mirtillo complains.

This multifaceted representation of conflicted interiority requires, in other words, the contributions of five separate performers; utterly private feelings come to voice only by virtue of this communal effort. Seventeenth-century musicians (though not our more recent *a cappella* pop groups) would soon balk at the artificiality of this construct and exchange this representational convention for the greater realism of the solo singer. But in doing so, they would sacrifice the capacity for paradox and troubled inwardness cultivated in the polyphonic madrigal. In effect, a culture focused on the hidden secrets of the inside will give way to one oriented toward the outward, theatrical display of the public figure. And while I would not want to decry the arrival of tonality (the conventions that emerged to sustain the semblance of rhetorical speech), I do insist that we acknowledge the heavy price paid for that change.

Meanwhile, back to Mirtillo, whom we left lying depleted on his open-E sonority. In Guarini's text, the next line—"E sento nel partire / Un vivace morire"—offers the flip side of the previous line ("E pur i' provo / La pena de la morte"). Monteverdi might well have superimposed these two lines, causing them literally to cancel each other out, but he has already played that card throughout the first section of the madrigal. Instead, he opts for a new strategy: a controlled, homophonic recitation that proceeds to a strong cadence on A in m. 61. Mirtillo seems to marshal his powers of reason and to pull himself from the morass of contradictory impulses in which he has wallowed thus far, as though he thinks that stating his dilemma calmly and succinctly will solve the problem. He puts his faith in logical discourse—or so Monteverdi suggests in this most speechlike passage of the madrigal.

But despite all the homophonic clarity of this passage, it harbors some very odd internal convolutions. In Monteverdi's setting, Mirtillo strives to hold the elements of effect and cause apart from each other; he calmly acknowledges his phenomenological state (OK, so I feel . . . a vivacious dying) while trying to bracket the memory of the separation that has thrown his world into havoc. Monteverdi achieves this double-level effect by tracing a linear descent from E to A, but embedding along the way a paren-

FIGURE 12. Expansion process

Romanesca

E   sen - to nel par - ti - re   Un vi - va - ce mo - ri - re.

"Ah, dolente partita," mm. 56–61

thetical expansion of D, thus recalling the unforeseen difficulty of the first half. He isolates and even tonicizes briefly this treacherous pitch,[37] then steps gingerly around it and secures the cadence on A, almost as though Mirtillo is inoculating himself against the threat of further contagion.

What makes this detour possible is Monteverdi's use of most familiar improvisatory progression in sixteenth-century music, the Romanesca,[38] which allows the listener to keep track of the implied goal despite the balloon embedded along the way (Fig. 12). Of course, that balloon never sounds entirely innocuous. With the broken-off leading tone in m. 58, the floor

37. Monteverdi's intricate part writing marks this parenthetical effect. He leaves the C♯ by leaping down, thereby compromising its force as a leading tone to D. Within the parenthesis, the collection on D sports an edgy F♯, which suggests that it might return to the G of m. 57. Both these potential areas—D and G—are redefined as provisional, however, with the reappearance in m. 59 of the canto's D, which resumes the diapente descent and the principal thrust of the sentence.

38. Standardized harmonizations of the diapente descent, such as the Romanesca and the Passamezzo antico, count as the blues progressions of the Renaissance. Working musicians improvised thousands of dances and songs by means of these patterns, and they eventually became the background framework for common-practice tonality. I will take this topic up at much greater length in my *Power and Desire in Seventeenth-Century Music*. See also my discussions of tonality in *Conventional Wisdom* and "Constructions of Gender in Monteverdi's Dramatic Music," *Feminine Endings: Music, Gender, and Sexuality*, 2nd ed. (Minneapolis: University of Minnesota Press, 2002), chap. 2.

seems to drop out from under us, and we hover along with Mirtillo in that space of alienated suspense. But when in m. 61 the passage arrives (as promised) on A, the danger seems to have been successfully quarantined.

Alas, Mirtillo is simply in denial: he cannot arrest so easily the logic already set in motion over the course of the first section, and this crystalline presentation of Aeolian merely gives way to an identical presentation of the same materials transposed to D, all the more chilling for its apparent lucidity. At this point in the madrigal—the moment that presents its dilemma in its most condensed form, its *mise-en-abîme*—A has no greater claim over the meaning of events than its Other; both have acquired equal status, as sanity and insanity become indistinguishable, unreason speaks with the voice of reason itself.

As before, the swerve toward D precipitates a shriek of protest, this time in the highest soprano range and with the very words with which the lower parts are cadencing: "Un vivace morire." The motive purposely recalls the repeated stabbing A of "E pur i' provo," the motive that entered to counteract earlier moves to D. But whereas the earlier motive usually ended slumped on E (an Aeolian boundary pitch, even if not the strong conclusion desired), the soprano now dithers and finally confirms through linear descent in m. 68 the very D that had provoked the outburst. The problems the middle section purported to have untangled—simultaneous but incompatible utterances, modal identity—snarl up again, now more virulently than ever because of the false hopes raised by mm. 57–61. Thus, although the quinto and alto coax the soprano back to a reiteration of that descent, now to the "correct" pitch of A (m. 70), the damage is done: from here to the end, the madrigal will list back and forth between A and D orientations, granting both equal weight and authority. The pitch A, because it is common to both areas, cannot decide the matter, and without the possibility of shoring up E as a powerful counterbalance, the piece has difficulty asserting A as final instead of fifth degree. The foreign element introduced by Monteverdi in m. 19 is now so entangled with its host that it constitutes half of a permanently hybrid identity.

It remains only for the final phrase of Guarini's verse ("Per far che moia immortalmente il core") to specify what we already know from the musical process: Mirtillo is locked in a condition whereby he dies yet doesn't die—in perpetuity. This final motive returns to the intertwining yet irreconcilable serpentine lines of the opening measures. Whereas initially they performed the painful separation of the title, here they just flicker among those sore pitches (D-E-F), now favoring one interpretation, now the other;

they duplicate each other (as do Mirtillo and Amarilli) yet remain forever out of phase. Cadences punctuate the last section of the madrigal, but they mechanically alternate between confirmations of A and D. At last, as if to set the matter straight once and for all, the two top voices undertake an octave scalar descent from A to A, and a prolonged dominant preparation in the bass allows for an unequivocal arrival on A in m. 89. If only the floodtide could be stopped here! But the twisted logic of Mirtillo's subjectivity cannot halt; it continues on inexorably, as the tonic A in the bass now comes to function as a dominant preparation, prepared to cadence on D. The diapason descent from A to A recurs in the alto and tenor, but against voices that make the octave seem to divide at D rather than E.

How does one conclude such a piece? Can the composer satisfy both the integrity of the materials and the powerful rule that one must cadence within the mode? As we shall see in subsequent chapters, Monteverdi did not invent the solution he deploys here, but he uses it to great effect. He breaks the piece off on the stipulated A sonority, thus confirming the mode. But that sonority contains a C♯, which can be—indeed, given the context of this piece, *must* be—heard doubly: as the conventionally raised mediant in a final chord (the *tierce de Picardie*) or as the dominant of D, poised to resolve all the weight of the madrigal onto the rival final. By halting there, he produces a musical equivalent of Mirtillo's immortal undeath: a freeze-frame that stops while implying like an ellipsis that the flip-flop between A and D will go on forever.[39]

What Monteverdi accomplishes in this final gesture is very difficult to do within standard tonality, which creates its long-term structural effects at the expense of forgoing these sorts of ambiguities. Yet we do on occasion find this strategy resuscitated—most obviously in Bach's C♯-Minor Fugue from *WTC* I and in Beethoven's C♯-Minor String Quartet, Op. 131, and his "Moonlight" Sonata of the same key. Why did this Aeolian problematic come to be identified with C♯ minor?[40] That would be a different

---

39. Of course, performance matters enormously here. If the ensemble chooses to mark the arrival on A in m. 89 as a moment of genuine closure, followed by a plagal extension, we will hear the madrigal as having reached conventional resolution. But if the singers render the section starting in m. 89 as I have described it, they can produce an electrifying effect: one that both matches the burden of Guarini's text and counts as the payoff for Monteverdi's strategy over the course of the entire madrigal. In other words, we *can* hear this culminating ambiguity—but only if it has been made audible by the performers.

40. I have traced this key association back to a ricercar in C♯ minor by Johann Jacob Froberger, the final composition in his *Libro di capricci e ricercati* (c. 1658). This ricercar's theme

project. But it would require that we take mode rather more seriously than we have in the recent past.

Within the context of Guarini's play, Mirtillo would deliver his soliloquy passionately but within the codes of decorum appropriate to theatre. If he went through the spasms and conniptions of Monteverdi's score, he would look like an epileptic speaking in tongues. In retrospect, it is as though the Guarini's character can only put bland verbal labels on the warring affects Monteverdi causes to be heard and viscerally experienced.

Monteverdi has long received more than the lion's share of attention in madrigal studies. Many factors contribute to his prominence, including his fame among his contemporaries, his pivotal role in the change from sixteenth- to seventeenth-century cultural enterprises, and the ways in which his compositional priorities happen to coincide with those of later periods—especially, as we have just seen, his penchant for organic economy. We also often think of him as having progressive or radical qualities, in contrast with his lesser known predecessors. But as impressive as "Ah, dolente partita" unquestionably is, it does not really break new ground. Quite the contrary, it hearkens back in its contrapuntal density, allegories of inwardness, and willingness to operate strictly within the exigencies of his chosen mode to the music of, say, Adrian Willaert. He thereby brings to an aesthetically satisfying close the era of the madrigal.

But the radical edges reside elsewhere in the repertory. It was Monteverdi's forebears who opened up this arena of conflicted Selfhood for cultural elaboration and scrutiny, who defied the long-standing authority of Pythagoras, who developed musical analogues to the entire range of affects, who experimented with the graphic simulation of sexual experience. Monteverdi reaped the benefits of this heritage, but he did not invent its principles. And his relatively conservative reinhabiting of the madrigal even makes the genre appear tamer, more classically bounded in retrospect, than it actually was.

In this introduction, I hope to have whetted the reader's appetite for the kinds of things that can be done with mode: the conceptions of subjectivity that shaped its procedures, the ways its procedures informed represen-

---

bears a striking resemblance not only to Bach's C♯-Minor Fugue but also to the theme of his *Musical Offering*. Of course, tracing the problem back to Froberger only defers the question of why C♯ minor. I include a chapter on Froberger and his C♯ ricercar in *Power and Desire in Seventeenth-Century Music*.

tations of Selfhood. As the book proceeds, I also hope to encourage a sense
of aesthetic connection between the contemporary listener/reader and the
madrigal, for the tunes I discuss in *Modal Subjectivities* count among the
great artworks of all time. Without question, an enormous gulf lies between
us and the individuals who composed, sang, and first heard this music; no
one survives to testify for them as we try to interpret their cultural artifacts.
But to the extent that we still study, perform, and record these works, their
meanings should matter to us, no less than do those of their contemporary
Shakespeare. With the next chapter I will move back in history to the works
of earlier practitioners, to those who first began exploring the possibility of
revealing how emotions feel in music.

CHAPTER 12

Cycles of Repetition: Chacona, Ciaccona, Chaconne, and *the* Chaconne

Over the course of the nineteenth and twentieth centuries, repetitive procedures in music acquired a singularly bad reputation. Frankfurt School critic Theodor W. Adorno – who based his aesthetic principles on the resistance to reiteration in the music of Beethoven and Schoenberg – fulminated against the moral dangers of such procedures, especially as they lured unwary listeners into mindless dances such as the jitterbug, into Stravinsky's primitivism, or into the herd mentality encouraged by bourgeois affirmative culture and later exploited by the rise of European fascism.[1] The ethical imperative of Schoenberg's serialism grounded itself in this horror of repetition and of the kinds of subjectivities it breeds; decades after everyone had forgotten the original rationale behind prohibitions of musical redundancy, the commandment 'Thou shalt not repeat patterns in thy compositions' still held sway over university-trained musicians.

Of course, any rule that strident and seemingly arbitrary only invites reaction, and the minimalist musics of the last thirty years have revelled in repetition, in deliberate violation of High Modernism's most cherished taboo.[2] The musicians who have participated in this return to repetition have paid for their sins by getting excluding from official histories of Western music, which still want to trace an upward trajectory away from ritualistic reiterations and towards increasingly autonomous, non-redundant formal processes. As a result, most textbooks make it as far as Pierre Boulez and Milton Babbitt, then lose their narrative thread. Surely Philip Glass, Laurie Anderson, and John Adams (to say nothing of James Brown, Parliament, or Missy Elliott) cannot be the next step along this carefully plotted path! There must be some mistake.

This collection of essays concerns not the crises of contemporary culture, but rather the institutional functions of repetition in a much earlier era – the seventeenth and eighteenth centuries. Yet I have begun with this discussion of repetition's fate in more recent years because that allergy to repetition has also coloured the analytical methods and standards of judgment developed in musicology in the wake of Beethoven. To the extent that Beethoven teaches us implicitly in his music to abhor repetition, he instills in us a principle we apply to all musics.

My work, along with that of a growing number of musicologists and ethnomusicologists, has attempted to interrogate those 'purely musical' standards – to understand how they developed as ideological constraints and to construct other ways of approaching the musics that do not yield to Beethovenian (or Schoenbergian) standards.[3] It seems clear to many of us that the linear, narratively conceived art music of the last two hundred years has set itself up as a false universal; in fact, most musics of the planet – and even of western Europe – have happily embraced repetition for purposes of ritual, dance, religious trance, community consolidation, and much else. Historian William McNeill's *Keeping Together in Time* even argues that a society's survival depends on its ability to implement such repetitious practices successfully.[4] Up against that larger picture, the imperative to eschew repetition appears as a mere blip on the screen – and a fairly perverse blip at that. The question that now arises is why European art musics since the eighteenth century have pursued this very different course.

In view of this set of issues, I want to revisit a moment in European art music that engaged in musical procedures of repetition, to ascertain how those procedures operated within their own social frameworks, how they performed cultural work. As it turns out, the seventeenth and eighteenth centuries nurtured one peculiar pattern that was within itself highly redundant and that spawned hundreds of reiterations from the late sixteenth to the mid-eighteenth century. It qualifies, in other words, as a *mis-en-abîme* of the concept of repetition.

Yet if this procedure inspired copycat imitations everywhere it went, each new site embued it with very particularized sets of meanings, often very different from and even antagonistic to those developed within other institutional contexts. The procedure continued to signify strongly wherever it went, but its implications changed radically, depending on the ideological priorities of each place and time. It thus affords us a glimpse into several very distinct cultural worlds, united in their interest in inhabiting this simple pattern, even if diametrically opposed in their deployments of it.

Chacona, Ciaccona, Chaconne, and *the* Chaconne   23

The Chacona: Origins and Disseminations

Our story begins somewhere in the New World, where sixteenth-century conquistadors encountered a kind of music they liked well enough that they included it (or some version of it) in the booty they brought back to Spain. Musicologist Richard Hudson has speculated as to the chacona's origins: possibly Mexico, a site sometimes mentioned in early sources; perhaps South America, where Andean musicians still play rhythmic and harmonic patterns uncannily like those of the chacona; perhaps even African settlements, for the slave trade had already flourished for some decades by the time the chacona made it back across the Atlantic, and the cross-rhythms characteristic of the chacona also mark many of the impulses of African-Latin musics.[5] Like so many musics born of the cultural collisions brought about by colonization and diaspora, the chacona bears tantalizing (if imprecise) witness to events buried in a past incompletely recorded. Moreover, its transporters inevitably translated whatever it was they heard in its original contexts into patterns familiar to their European ears and conceptual schemata.

Nonetheless, transferal of something from the New World back to the Old took place, and many Spanish sources – including mentions by Cervantes and Lope de Vega – testify to its rapid spread in its new environment.[6] It sparked a dance craze that inspired a familiar set of reactions: on the one hand, it was celebrated for liberating bodies that had been stifled by the constraints of European civilization; on the other, it was condemned as obscene, as a threat to Christian mores. But all sources concurred that its rhythms – once experienced – were irresistible: its practioners had only to shout 'Vida bona!' (the good life) to signal the beginning of the music that would pull everyone within earshot into its compelling groove. For instance, the lyrics for one extended chacona describe a funeral at which the officiating priest by mistake mutters 'vida bona,' the signal for the dance to begin; the clergy, the nuns, the family of the deceased, and even the corpse itself respond by wiggling and leaping with uninhibited glee. When they go afterwards to beg forgiveness, the bishop asks (strictly as a point of legal information) to hear one refrain and spends the next hour gyrating with his skirts raised; his congregation shakes the house for another six. At the conclusion of this carnivalesque fantasy, the bishop forgives his flock.[7]

In a sequence of events paralleled still today whenever a dance-type bubbles up from the wrong social group, a backlash against the chacona soon ensued. Like rhythm and blues at a later historical moment, the chacona crossed over cautiously guarded class and racial boundaries.

Whatever the chacona signified in its original contexts, it quickly came to be associated in Europe (by friends and foes alike) with forbidden bodily pleasures and potential social havoc. Like syphilis, which also followed the conquistadors back home, the chacona qualified as a venereal contagion, and the sensual pleasure associated with both ensured their unchecked spread throughout Europe. Attempts were made to insulate upper-class ladies from the chacona's influence, and the church banned it in 1615 on grounds of its 'irredeemably infectious lasciviousness.'

But the horse had already left the stable, thanks in large part to new technologies of music printing, which made its dissemination quick, cheap, and unstoppable. For the introduction of the chacona coincided with a market dedicated to self-help manuals – in this case, books that promised to teach you how to play guitar in the comfort of your own home. Aimed exclusively at amateurs, these publications offered only the bare essentials of tuning and frets, along with a few easily executed patterns. The older virtuosic mode of performance, which required complex plucked finger work (*punteado*), was replaced by *rasgueado*, the technique of strumming simple chords. The chacona fit perfectly into this new demand for music playable by three-chord wonders, who employed their quickly acquired *rasgueado* for rhythmic vitality and could happily play the chacona – like the blues – all night long. Very much like the folk, art-school, or garage musicians of a later era who sometimes learned how to play their requisite three chords the same day as their public premieres in bands, people could, with these manuals, take musicking into their own hands, to provide the soundtrack for la vida bona.[8]

These self-help manuals are our principal source of written documentation for the musical details of the early chacona. A few slightly different patterns appeared in print under this name; they all share, however, a very restricted number of chord changes (conforming to the most basic of contemporaneous cadential formulas), a strong rhythmic accent on the offbeats, and the instruction that one simply play the tiny pattern (four to eight seconds in duration) over and over again (fig. 1.1). The harmonic pattern itself did not arouse consternation, but that offbeat accent seemed to provoke explicitly sexualized motions in the bodies of dancers,[9] while the infinite iterations of the pattern became addictive, putting its listeners into the ecstatic trance-state sought after by many rituals, from those of whirling dervishes to Cuban *Santeria* to raves.[10] The fact of the chacona's 'barbaric' pedigree enhanced simultaneously its appeal for its devotees and the hysterical denunciations of its opponents.

Chacona, Ciaccona, Chaconne, and *the* Chaconne   25

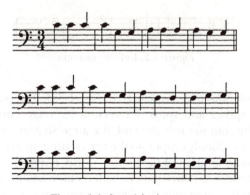

Figure 1.1. Spanish chaconas

Had the chacona stayed within the realm of amateur guitar manuals and community music-making, musicologists probably would have paid no more attention to it than to dozens of other practices that similarly left only the barest of outlines for purposes of improvisation. Imagine having to reconstitute the richness of the blues tradition or trying to make sense of all the verbal testimonies to its power if, instead of recordings, we had only the twelve-bar schema that underwrites it. Fortunately for our story, the chacona soon trickled upward from its humble origins to infiltrate the highest levels of cultural production, to enter contexts within which court composers wrote out and thus preserved their inventions in lavish detail for posterity. Some memory of the chacona's titillating past came with it to each new environment, but its mythology and the effects of its repetitions meant very different things as it jumped from host to host.

The Italian Ciaccona

The chacona first travelled from Spain to Italy along with fashionable guitarists and the international marketing of improvisatory manuals. In its new home, the ciaccona (as Italians called it) soon became the musical background for dancing and a common item in instrumental variations. The renowned organist at Saint Peter's in Rome, Girolamo Frescobaldi, included ciaccona sections within his keyboard partitas, for instance, and references – labelled as such or not – show up frequently in Italian vocal and instrumental musics of the early 1600s (fig. 1.2).

By far the most famous of Italian ciaccona settings is Claudio Monteverdi's accompanied duet for two tenors 'Zefiro torna,' published

26   Susan McClary

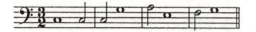

Figure 1.2. Italian ciaccona

in the collection *Scherzi musicali* in 1632 (fig. 1.3a). The poetic text hails
the return of spring and spins out verse after verse enumerating the
season's delights; but towards the end, the anguish and alienation of the
poet's inner self suddenly erupt into the text, setting up a stark Petrarchan
contrast with the splendour of the natural world. For most of the duet, the
ciaccona proliferates its dance pattern with reckless abandon, each temporary conclusion breeding only the desire for yet another repetition.

As the lines concerning the poet's emotional condition appear, however, the music swerves into a concentrated passage featuring some of
the most chromatic, dissonant writing available to the mannerist avant-
garde. The duet ends by pivoting between the overwrought agony that
guarantees the 'authenticity' of the subject's interiority and the carefree,
seductive ciaccona rhythms of 'nature,' of the body[11] (fig. 1.3b).

Note that this 'body' is no longer the body of colour or of the lower
classes from which the ciaccona was taken; it now stands for the 'universal' (i.e., white) body – albeit a body yoked explicitly in binary opposition
with the tortured, deeply feeling soul. It thus traces a Cartesian mind/
body split, whereby the unbridled pleasures of the flesh compete with
the White Man's Burden: the alienation nurtured by thought and zeal-
ous self-fashioning.[12] Monteverdi allows us to have it both ways, as he
indulges us in course after course of the ciaccona's contagious impulse,
though periodically dunking us into the chilly waters of tormented
interiority.

Nor did the ciaccona remain strictly within the realm of secular composition in Italy. In his capacity as *maestro di cappella* at San Marco (a church
frequently resistant to Roman authority), Monteverdi happily brought to
his sacred music his entire toolkit of devices, which included the ciaccona.
For instance, in a solo setting of Psalm 150 (the psalm that recites the inventory of King David's instruments), the ciaccona suddenly enters with
the verse: 'Praise God upon the loud cymbals, praise him upon the high
sounding cymbals.' The mere mention of 'primitive' percussion instruments diverts the music from its rather more gracious impulse and, as
though someone had shouted 'vida bona,' immerses us in the party
rhythms of the New World. Whereas each of the previous verses of the
psalm had received a brief setting, the cymbals and their attendant

Chacona, Ciaccona, Chaconne, and *the* Chaconne   27

Figure 1.3a. Monteverdi, 'Zefiro torna'

28   Susan McClary

Figure 1.3b. 'Zefiro,' mm. 122–37

ciaccona run on for nearly a quarter the length of the whole piece. Only the need to proceed to the final verse, 'Let everything that hath breath praise the Lord,' brings a reluctant halt to the festivities; even here, the high spirits of the ciaccona seem to have compromised the decorum established earlier in the psalm setting, requiring that the voice go out in a blaze of glory – in a delirium of coloratura ornamentation.[13]

Although the ciaccona enjoyed a period of considerable popularity in early seventeenth-century Italy, it nearly always functioned as though within quotation marks, as in the two Monteverdi examples just dis-

Chacona, Ciaccona, Chaconne, and *the* Chaconne   29

Figure 1.3b. (*concluded*)

cussed. To be sure, Italian courtiers included dance among their entertainments, and dance-oriented rhythms appear in both vocal and instrumental genres of the time. But elite Italian composition during the
sixteenth and seventeenth centuries focused on the arousal of the
passions, on representations of interiority – especially interiority under
duress. The Renaissance madrigal developed an extensive arsenal of
devices for simulating conflicted inner states, and opera, which emerged
around 1600, likewise pursued this highly subjective agenda.[14] Dance
occupied a decidedly backseat position with respect to cultural prestige.

Thus even when the ciaccona intrudes into pieces such as the ones
mentioned above, it is marked as pleasurable yet somehow as a distraction; variously aligned with nature, with the dancing body, or with percussion, it resides on a lower level within the aesthetic hierarchy than
those components that lend insight into interiority. The tenors in 'Zefiro
torna' sing exuberantly about how nice it would be to feel at one with the
unproblematic springtime landscape, but the entire ciaccona section –
regardless of its length and energy – converts to a subjunctive 'as if' as
soon as the 'reality' of tortured emotions pushes to the surface.[15] Psalm

150 includes no anguished imagery to juxtapose to the ciaccona, but Monteverdi still situates his reference to New World rhythms in the position of the primitive.

In short, the ciaccona constitutes a guilty pleasure within the Italian cultural lexicon. This is not to suggest that the Italians hesitated to indulge in such delights, for hedonism ranked high among their values. But we would be missing something important if we failed to notice how Italian composers framed the ciaccona as cheap thrill.

The French Chaconne

Some time around 1650, Cardinal Mazarin brought the Italian virtuoso Francesco Corbetta to the French court to teach Spanish guitar to Louis XIV himself. No three-chord wonder, Corbetta had brought to this lowly instrument the kinds of *punteado* techniques associated with the high-class lute, making him the first in a line of Guitar Gods (as my generation called Eric Clapton and his heavy-metal descendants). Corbetta published some of his compositions based on the ciaccona, and we can follow in his scores some of the strategies a skilled performer of the time could bring to this dance: they begin with the simple *rasgueado* strumming featured in instruction manuals, then build with ever more difficult figuration to encompass finally the whole range of devices available to fretted instruments.[16] In Corbetta's hands, the ciaccona became a pretext for intellectual exploration. If he retains something of the old second-beat accent, Corbetta's successive variations pull the ear further and further away from the mere physical impulse and exact repetition it had offered in previous incarnations. As the changes unfold, the infectious dance rhythms get sacrificed to ornamental filigree and to contrapuntal display, slowing the tempo and making the ciaccona increasingly an abstract platonic form.

When French harpsichordists such as Jean-Henry D'Anglebert started writing chaconnes for solo keyboard, they established an essentially new genre. First, they revised the repetitious quality of the old ciaccona. Instead of proceeding through consecutive iterations of the basic unit, the keyboard chaconne fused with the rondeau format. Although the rondeau refrain still clings to the harmonic patterning of the ciaccona (again a very simple cadential formula; Fig. 1.4), it alternatives with episodes that introduce other keys, that explore other musical options. Without question the refrain serves as the focal point of the resulting composition: the listener waits through the imaginative episodes with

Chacona, Ciaccona, Chaconne, and *the* Chaconne   31

Figure 1.4. D'Anglebert, Chaconne

the sure expectation that the refrain will return intact. But the structural priorities of the keyboard chaconne differ from those of the much simpler ciaccona.[17]

More important, the French brought the chaconne back into the realm of actual dance. In contrast to the Italians, who preferred the passionate medium of vocal music, the French shaped their court rituals around dance, which served both to provide recreational distraction and to inscribe courtiers physically into the neoplatonic ideology prescribed by the Sun King.[18] Far from referring to the unbridled exuberance of the primitive body, the French chaconne delineates the most stately of rhythmic impulses – parallel, in fact, with the upwardly mobile ascent of the sarabande, a dance likewise reputed to have originated in orgiastic rituals of the New World but gradually refined at court to represent the height of elegance. Both chaconne and sarabande maintain an accent on the second beat; but in their much slower tempos, they no longer inspire (nor would they condone) the ill-behaved gestures of the body that had so scandalized the chacona's early foes.

In its new French manifestation, the chaconne climbed even further up the ladder of cultural prestige until it reached the summit. Jean-Baptiste Lully, Louis's dance-and-music czar, often positioned a chaconne as the concluding element in his ballets and operas.[19] At this point following the plot's *dénouement,* spectators joined professional performers in dancing around the body of the King, thereby simulating the orbit of planets around the sun. The repetitious – and thus timeless – quality of the chaconne provided the musical stimulus for this ritual in which the court participated in affirming immutable verities of power and pleasure.

For instance, in Lully's tragédie-lyrique *Amadis* (1684), the legendary hero Amadis of Gaul (intended as a thinly disguised allegorical stand-in for Louis himself) finally triumphs, leading to a chaconne-finale, in which nature and humanity join in celebration.[20] The chaconne lasts for quite a long time: long enough certainly to induce the state of bliss that

32   Susan McClary

Figure 1.5. Lully, Chaconne from *Amadis*

comes of 'keeping together in time' and through a process identical to that practiced by religions that seek the erasure of self-awareness through musical drones and recitation of mantras (fig. 1.5).

The ideological shift in the meanings of the ciaccona/chaconne that occurred at Versailles relates to fundamental differences in cultural priorities. Spanish, Italian, and French observers recognized the extraordinary effect of this dance-type, but in Spain and Italy its mesmerizing quality encouraged motions of the body defined as illicit or somehow dissonant with the proper focus on individualistic feelings and reason. In France, where dance served as one of the principal tools for instilling conformity, the chaconne represented a means of eliciting the highest degree of pleasure and, simultaneously, the greatest sense of neoplatonic order and group identification. Not surprisingly, the French authorities viewed the Italian obsession with interiority with suspicion, to the extent that Lully had Italian music banned in France. The ability of the chaconne to erase the boundaries of the self and to produce in dancers the sense of unity with the cosmos made it an invaluable resource.

Recent neurobiologists have found that radical changes in brain function occur in people involved in such rituals, especially those involving music and dance. The parts of the brain responsible for orienting us as individuated selves as we move through space actually shut down their

Chacona, Ciaccona, Chaconne, and *the* Chaconne   33

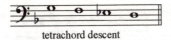

tetrachord descent

chromatic passacaglia

Figure 1.6. Passacaglias

activity, causing subjects to experience *as reality* that merger with time-lessness.[21] Mystics interpret this phenomenon as evidence of divine union. But long before scientific evidence confirmed this set of connections, Louis XIV deployed the chaconne pragmatically to turn 'the God trick': to seduce his courtiers into that neurological condition in which they dissolved into a state of jouissance – not coincidentally with the king himself as centre.

The chaconne had a *Doppelgänger*, however – one that sometimes alternated unproblematically with the chaconne itself but that could also carry rather different affective charges. In the *Amadis* finale, for instance, the major-key chaconne gives way to a minor-mode version of the same cadential figure. Nothing ruffles the serenity of the apotheosis; the shift into the minor only produces a welcome contrast for a short while before the major reappears. But the minor-key version of the chaconne, often known as the passacaglia, had a somewhat different chain of cultural referents. Even if both procedures appeared in early guitar manuals as pretexts for improvisation, the passacaglia more frequently fused with the signs not of 'la vida bona' but rather of lament[22] (fig. 1.6).

The most famous ostinato of this sort is Monteverdi's famous *Lamento della ninfa*, in which a solo female singer bewails her entrapment and abandonment, all over an unchanging tetrachord descent in the bass. The association of this figure with ritualized mourning became so strong that it could signal grief all by itself in instrumental as well as vocal pieces. Purcell's celebrated farewell aria for Dido, 'When I Am Laid in Earth,' draws brilliantly on the sedimented history of this formula, elaborated chromatically, and Marin Marais's *Tombeau pour Mr de Saint-Colombe* for viol starts off with an allusion to the descending-tetrachord lament as a means of establishing the elegiac tone of his funeral commemoration.[23]

Musicologists used to love to write articles that attempted to draw a decisive line between 'chaconne' and 'passacaglia': graduate exams back

34   Susan McClary

Figure 1.7. Lully, Passacaille d'Armide

in the early 1970s still typically demanded that students produce a rule of
thumb for distinguishing the two. The fact is, however, that seventeenth-
century musicians cared much less about generic boundaries than do
historians, and they sometimes used the two terms interchangeably. Yet
the music of the time often treats the two in very different ways; if there
exists a gray area of overlap in which one can substitute for the other,
there are also contexts in which the carefree ciaccona/chaconne has
nothing to do with its melancholy twin, the lamenting passacaglia. And
even the gray area of overlap can present difficulties: not of the sort
pursued by musicologists who want each to have its own separate box,
but for anyone concerned with musical meanings.

Consider, for instance, the Passacaille in the final act of Lully's tragédie-
lyrique *Armide* (1686). Armide, a Saracen sorceress, has seduced the
great crusader Roland from his task of 'liberating' Jerusalem. She holds
him captive in bonds of pleasure so powerful that he lies helpless in her
lair. At the beginning of this last act, Armide finds she must leave Roland
for a short while, and she entrusts him to a gaggle of demons, who
maintain his paralytic condition by performing a passacaille.[24] To gentle
dance rhythms identical to those of the *Amadis* chaconne, they serenade
him for nearly seventeen minutes with soft strings and woodwinds, with
occasional choral entries in praise of 'plaisir' and 'amour' (fig. 1.7). The
spell shatters only when Roland's companions-in-arms awaken him from
his stupor and persuade him to go back to battle with them. (Armide
returns, finds that Roland is gone, delivers a brief tirade, and thus ends
the opera; the Passacaille qualifies as the show-stopper for the act.)

To some extent, this passacaille functions identically to the chaconne
from *Amadis*: both serve to induce that state that eradicates inside and
outside, that pulls theatrical characters and spectators alike into that
timeless zone of infinite pleasure. Yet the minor key of the passacaille, its
rather more yearning melodic shapes, and its dramatic context make it
available for a somewhat different reading: one that resonates with

entrapment by a surfeit of sensual pleasure, one that may even connect back to the non-European origins of such musical procedures. Roland's French *raîson* is held hostage by this repetitious soundscape, requiring that his comrades forcibly rescue him from the blandishments of his Saracen captor, who knows that her music itself suffices to keep him blissfully enslaved.[25] This passacaille, I would argue, brings us much closer to warnings against repetitious music implicit in 'Zefiro torna' and ecclesiastical bans. Too much depends on who controls such a powerful resource – the king or diabolical forces of Oriental witches – to make the *Armide* Passacaille an unambiguously innocuous procedure, even in the heavily regulated French court.

J.S. Bach and *the* Chaconne

By far the most famous chaconne in the repertory is the final movement of Johann Sebastian Bach's Partita II in D Minor for Unaccompanied Violin. It still stands at the pinnacle of violin virtuosity: to say 'chaconne' to a developing violinist is tantamount to saying 'Everest' to an aspiring mountain climber. Many of us have encountered the chaconne and other baroque genres (French dances, chorale elaborations, Italian concertos, fugal techniques) solely through Bach's compositions, and we treat Bach as a kind of ground zero of music history, the earliest canonic source we think we need. As a result, we miss much of the cultural work Bach achieved in his music. If we honour him as self-contained and beyond history or criticism, we also fail to engage with his compositions as socially meaningful texts.[26]

I have argued elsewhere that Bach worked throughout his career to translate everything he had inherited – the dances of the Absolutist court, the relatively static fugues of earlier North German organists, even the Lutheran chorale – into the dynamic, narrative-oriented style elevated to the status of an international lingua franca by Antonio Vivaldi.[27] A virtual sponge, Bach acquired and processed all new ideas as soon as they became available, whether through printing or trips to sites of musical innovation. He remained, however, in what were then regarded as the backwaters of European culture, always resentful of his lack of worldly recognition, yet enabled by that very isolation to conduct musical experiments and to produce any hybrid he could imagine.

Bach's re-readings of French dance-types have gone unnoticed, in large part because we have taken his 'French' dances (including the chaconne) as the standard and have judged those by, say, D'Anglebert as

36   Susan McClary

Figure 1.8. Bach. 'Jesu, der du meine Seele'

insipid. But if we take D'Anglebert's compositional aesthetic seriously,
then we can also begin to see how Bach more or less assaulted the
foundations of French cultural values.[28] Given a choice between the
timeless physicality of Versailles and the dramatic impulse of the concerto, Bach opted every time for the latter. In his simulations, the
elegant hovering of a courante became intolerable stagnation, to be
converted forcibly into the progressive, modulatory dynamism of Vivaldi.
The tension between the French and Italian models involves far more
than mere taste or personal preference; to Bach, faced with mutually
exclusive structures of temporality and subjectivity, the differences war-
ranted a lifetime of creative struggle. If he bequeathed to us a predisposition towards the Italianate mode of being (adopted by his German/
Austrian successors tout court as 'the way music is supposed to go'), he
also managed to hide his tracks to the extent that few even realize the
stakes of his fundamental choices.

The French chaconne, with all its Absolutist trappings and extreme
suspension of time, posed a particular challenge to Bach, and in his
composition for solo violin we have something of a microcosm of his
modus operandi – his obsession with saturating his pieces with far-flung,
often contradictory references, which must then work their way towards
some kind of formal and semiotic détente. We cannot doubt that Bach
knew the codes already discussed above. The tetrachord-descent with its
roots in Monteverdi and Purcell underwrites the Crucifixus in the B
Minor Mass. Moreover, he seems to have had access to Lully's frequently-
anthologized *Armide* passacaille, which he interpreted in his own reworking as unambiguously sinister. In the astonishing opening movement of
his Cantata 78, *Jesu, der du meine Seele*, he appropriates Lully's passacaille
as a simulation of entrapment in sin (fig. 1.8). The repetitious pattern
relents only once: on the line of text expressing the hope that Christ will
pull us forcibly from the jaws of the Devil. But this statement remains
provisional, and the movement ends back in the passacaille with the plea

Chacona, Ciaccona, Chaconne, and *the* Chaconne   37

132

Figure 1.9a. Bach, Chaconne, mm. 132–140

that God will stand by us. The lyrics to Armide's plaisir-drenched lullaby
have no place in this musical landscape that resembles those circles in
Dante in which sinners – stuck in slime up to their ears – cry out with
remorse. Subsequent movements of the cantata, based on the acknowledgment of guilt and the confession of faith, pull us gradually out of the
mire and into the teleological temporality that Bach uses to simulate a
trajectory towards redemption.

The movement for unaccompanied violin, of course, has no lyrics to
render specific its meanings. In modern editions it usually sports the title
'Chaconne,' although Bach's manuscript labels it 'Ciaccona.' (The same
'correcting' of Bach's labels also occurs when pieces he properly calls
'Corrente' get published as 'Courante,' as though all dances must come
from France, as though differences between the types must be negligible.) Moreover, as the piece begins, it quite clearly aligns itself more
closely with the minor-mode, lament-oriented passacaglia. I will follow
convention and call it 'Chaconne,' for any single title to Bach's hybrid
composition proves inadequate. Indeed, the history of the alternate
titles and the first four measures of the movement, which announce the
passacaglia, suffice to set the conflicted terms for this remarkable movement – the condensation and ultimate transformation of all the traditions we have been tracing, and deservedly the most renowned instance
of the genre.[29]

We first hear something genuinely resembling a dignified French
chaconne about two-thirds of the way through the movement when Bach
suddenly alters the minor mode to its parallel major (fig. 1.9a).[30] In
other words, he presents formally a reverse image of the *Amadis* chaconne,
which begins and ends in major but includes a minor-key episode in the
middle. Here, in this extended passage at least, Bach gives us a taste of
timeless bliss, of repetition welcomed and celebrated. The rich harmonies and apparently effortless arpeggios of this extended passage immerse us in a haven of warmth and freedom of physical motion – so long
as we remain content with endless refrains in D major.

But this island of D-major reminiscent of *Amadis* serves only as a delusion, a refuge of false consciousness, as Bach's larger compositional strategy indicates. For he frames this placid section within a movement that works desperately to extricate itself from the repetitive coils of the chaconne (or passacaglia). And the fact that the lone violinist must both furnish the redundant ostinato and also fight tooth and nail against it locates the antagonism inside a single subject. Like Monteverdi's nymph, the violin fights to escape the obsession that holds it down; it is as though we witness Roland awakening from his drugged state but finding himself incapable – even with the most heroic exertion – of liberating himself from Armide's spell. A song by Purcell states: 'I attempt from Love's sickness to fly in vain, since I am myself my own fever and pain.' Bach's piece presents with far greater affective intensity that same struggle to pull oneself out of one's own skin, to transcend the material conditions of being, to resist the jouissance afforded by repetitious structures so as to follow a progressive trajectory of *Bildung* – a German idealist model of subjectivity just beginning to appear on the cultural map. Yet as in the first movement of *Jesu, der du meine Seele*, the Chaconne's formal commitments will not allow us into the promised land. We witness instead Laocoön or Samson wrestling valiantly despite all odds, concluding not with triumph but with unbowed determination not to concede defeat or to accept the terms offered by the ciaccona/chaconne/passacaglia.

Bach's Chaconne begins with a tonic triad – simple harmonically but requiring that the performer sweep the bow across three strings of the violin in order to execute what the mere drop of a hand could accomplish on a keyboard; even in this starting position, a sense of unresolvable tension already arises, as this melody instrument has to take upon itself the tasks of the harmonic bass in addition to its own singing voice (fig. 1.9b). The tension increases exponentially at the downbeat, as the melodic line leaps up a fifth, producing a harsh dissonance against the bass – now articulated as the lowest of four pitches, demanding the sweep over all four strings. For a few beats the melodic (read: subjective) line of the violin seems to prevail, and the passacaglia bass seeems to conform to its dictates. The top line gives the appearance of escaping the downward pull of the ostinato. But the escape turns out to be provisional; the energies expended in launching the top line up through its leap and its subsequent ascent to F deplete its resources, and the line then falls parallel to the generating bass until it even closes up the initial triad: in m. 4, the melody collapses to meet the bass on D. A flurry of activity pushes towards a renewed effort, and this time the top line jumps all the way to a high B^b, from which vantage point it almost seems to bring about the cadence by itself.

Chacona, Ciaccona, Chaconne, and *the* Chaconne   39

Figure 1.9b. Chaconne

But, of course, the cadence only initiates another statement of the ostinato, this time with an inner voice leading while the top line makes itself heard solely through intermittent gasps. As the variations unfold, the distinctions between voices sometimes dissolve into running ornamental notes and hair-raising passages of arpeggiation for which the performer must saw raucously through chord progressions, concentrating the attention on the almost unbearable strife between the inevitable

40   Susan McClary

Figure 1.9c. Chaconne, 118–41

bass and the resistant melodic line. When the smoke clears, we find
ourselves right back at the beginning, for Bach casts his opening strain
also as a refrain – a refrain that both first establishes the stakes of the
composition and also reappears periodically to consolidate identity, even
as it concedes the inability of the persona, despite its superhuman
efforts, to progress beyond the conundrum first posed at the very outset
(fig. 1.9c).

It is after this concession that Bach suddenly drops us into the far
more serene realm of D-major and the tight, consonant harmonies of
the courtly chaconne. As the violin's persona becomes accustomed to
this new world of plaisir, it expands virtuosically to nearly equal the
technical feats of the opening segment. Alas, this whole D-major passage
functions in the subjunctive mode.[31] Following the confident final arrival on octave Ds, the piece suddenly awakens to find itself back in the
context of the minor. With nothing more than a sleight of hand, the
illusory vision collapses like a house of cards: 'if this, then ...' But no.

Chacona, Ciaccona, Chaconne, and *the* Chaconne   41

The concluding D-minor segment allows another series of variations, each of which expands both the pyrotechnic scope of the violin and the attempts at pushing beyond the dilemma to some kind of narrative development and closure. Yet at the very end, the violin simply reiterates the refrain that opened the composition, and the two antagonistic lines – the top one of which repeatedly defied gravity in its determination to escape the inexorable pull of the bass – fall to a unison, a single pitch.

The title of this volume emphasizes the intersections between institutions and rituals of repetition, and my discussions of Italy and France located the meanings of the ciaccona/chaconne squarely within the cultural centres of courts and churches. Bach's Chaconne is more difficult to situate institutionally, however. He probably wrote it during his tenure at Cöthen around 1720, but it would not have contributed to social dance, especially given its tormented gestures and extreme discontinuities. Like much of Bach's music, it served as a showpiece for any virtuoso equal to the task, but even more as the exhaustive, comprehensive pedagogical exploration of a specific compositional technique. In short, he intended this as the chaconne to end all chaconnes.

If Bach did not write his piece for a particular institution, however, he himself became the cornerstone of the German canon that still dominates our conceptions of music history. We inherit from Bach many of the musical values we take as self-evident, values that themselves have defined the institutions of concert music and pedagogy for the last two hundred years. Adorno never refers in his Bach essay to the Chaconne,[32] but his philosophy of music might have proceeded from this composition alone. For here we have the dramatic enactment of repetition as narcotic, as that which prevents the Self from developing autonomously. Try as it might, the violin in the Chaconne cannot throw off its chains – the connections back to the autocratic oppressions of French court life (still alive and flourishing in the Potsdam of Frederick the Great at the end of Bach's life), the siren song to regress to the warm certainties of social dance and domesticity; it cannot make the leap from these ideologically saturated procedures to the dynamic drive of Vivaldi, for even when it annexes Vivaldi's virtuosic figuration, its will to proceed through progressive modulation is blocked by the generically imposed imperative to repeat.

The pleasurable dance rhythms evoked by Monteverdi, the simulations of cosmological order choreographed by Lully have turned into nightmares, from which only the ability to self-invent can extricate us. Mozart will similarly pit *Bildung* against pleasurable regression in his mature works,[33] and Beethoven will nearly blow up the tonal ground on which he stands in his anxiety to eschew conventional formula – or else he will, like Bach does in his Chaconne, so overdo repetition that it calls attention to itself as imprisonment.[34] We need Freud only to explain in words the drives and contradictions associated with this particular brand of subjectivity, already firmly in place in Bach. Adorno will then build his rise-and-fall narrative of Western art music by moving from Bach to Beethoven to Schoenberg.

The Bach Chaconne stands, then, as the final chapter in the history of the repetitive procedure imported from the New World in the late 1500s. It sums up both the sensual delights and the autocratic tendencies already aligned with various branches of the tradition, and points in the direction of other musical structures and devices – ones that will rule classical music for a couple of hundred years. But those exalted structures and devices have proved no match against the next wave of repetitive procedures that have now emerged from the New World in the form of blues, jazz, rock, rap, and electronic dance music. This time around, it seems, the descendants of the chacona get to win.[35]

Notes

1 See Theodor W. Adorno, *Philosophy of Modern Music*, trans. Anne G. Mitchell and Wesley V. Blomster (New York: Seabury Press, 1973), especially the sections on Stravinsky; and 'Perennial Fashion: Jazz,' in *Prisms*, trans. Samuel Weber and Shierry Weber (Cambridge, MA.: MIT Press, 1980).

2 See my 'Rap, Minimalism, and Structures of Time in Late Twentieth-Century Culture,' in *Audio Culture: Readings in Modern Music*, ed. Christoph Cox and Daniel Warner (New York: Continuum/The Wire, 2004), 289–98; and 'Terminal Prestige: The Case of Avant-Garde Composition,' *Cultural Critique* 12 (Spring 1989): 57–81.

3 See my *Conventional Wisdom: The Content of Musical Form* (Berkeley and Los Angeles: University of California Press, 2000).

4 William H. McNeill, *Keeping Together in Time: Dance and Drill in Human History* (Cambridge, MA.: Harvard University Press, 1995).

5 Richard Hudson, *Passacaglia and Ciaccona: From Guitar Music to Italian Keyboard Variations in the 17th Century* (Ann Arbor: UMI Research Press, 1981).

6 See Alex Silbiger's entry for 'Chaconne,' in *The New Grove Dictionary of Music and Musicians*, ed. Stanley Sadie (London: Macmillan, 2000).

7 The poem appears in translation in Hudson, *Passacaglia and Ciaccona*, 4.

8 I owe the concept of 'musicking' to Christopher Small, whose insistence on

shifting from the noun 'music' to the verb emphasizing action and partici- pation has had a radical effect on musicology. See his *Musicking* (Hanover, NH: Wesleyan University Press, 1998).

9 We know very little about the actual choreography of the chacona. Gordon Haramaki, who specializes in the dance music of this era, has reminded me that the elaborate garb of noblewomen would have severely restricted movements of the torso. Yet the dance did reach the courts by way of the lower classes, who would not have had to contend with such corseting. My thanks to Gordon for his insights.

10 See Gilbert Rouget, *Music and Trance: A Theory of the Relations between Music and Possession,* trans. Brunhilde Biebuyck (Chicago: University of Chicago Press, 1985); and Simon Reynolds, *Generation Ecstasy: Into the World of Techno and Rave Culture* (New York: Routledge, 1999).

11 Many recordings of 'Zefiro torna' exist. My favorite is Nigel Rogers and Ian Partridge, tenors; Jürgen Jürgens, director, *Madrigals and Sacred Concertos* (Archiv 415 295-2, 1972/73).

12 For more on this phenomenon, see Stephen Greenblatt, *Renaissance Self-Fashioning from More to Shakespeare* (Chicago: University of Chicago Press, 1980). See also my *Model Subjectivities: Self-Fashioning in the Italian Madrigal* (Berkeley and Los Angeles: University of California Press, 2004).

13 Monteverdi, *Laudate dominum* (1640), Judith Nelson, soprano; Concerto Vocale, René Jacobs, director, *Un concert spirituel* (Harmonia Mundi 1901032, 1980). The ciaccona section begins at 2'.

14 See my *Modal Subjectivities.*

15 I owe the concept of the 'subjunctive' in musical structure to my graduate student Stuart De Ocampo, who has found it operating in repertories as distant from each other as Chopin ballades and Alessandro Grandi's early-seventeenth-century setting of the Song of Songs.

16 Francesco Corbetta, *Chiacona*, Paul O'Dette, guitar, with The King's Noyse; David Douglass, director, *Pavaniglia: Dances and Madrigals from 17th-c. Italy* (Harmonia Mundi 907246, 1997).

17 Jean-Henry D'Anglebert, Pieces in D Major, Chaconne Rondeau, Christophe Rousset, harpsichord (Decca 458 588-2, 2000).

18 For an extended discussion of the political uses of music and dance under Louis XIV, see my 'Unruly Passions and Courtly Dances: Technologies of the Body in Baroque Music,' in *From the Royal to the Republican Body: Incorporating the Political in Seventeenth and Eighteenth Century France,* ed. Sara Melzer and Kathryn Norberg (Berkeley and Los Angeles: University of California Press, 1998), 85–112.

19 See Geoffrey Burgess, 'The Chaconne and the Representation of Sovereign

44   Susan McClary

Power in Lully's *Amadis* (1684) and Charpentier's *Médée* (1693),' in *Dance and Music in French Baroque Theatre: Sources and Interpretations*, ed. Sarah McCleave (London: Institute of Advanced Musical Studies, King's College London, 1998), 81-104.

20 Jean-Baptiste Lully, *Amadis* (1684); act 5, finale: 'Chaconne,' Chatham Baroque, *Danse Royale: Music of the French Baroque Court & Theatre* (Dorian Recordings 90272, 1999).

21 See Andrew Newberg, Eugene D'Aquili, and Vince Rause, *Why God Won't Go Away: Brain Science and the Biology of Belief* (New York: Ballantine Books, 2001).

22 For a useful overview of this figure, see Ellen Rosand, 'The Descending Tetrachord: An Emblem of Lament,' *Musical Quarterly* 55 (1979): 346–59.

23 For recordings, try Monteverdi, *Lamento della Ninfa*, book VIII (1638), Montserrat Figueras, soprano; La Capella Reial de Catalunya, Jordi Savall, director, *Madrigali guerrieri et amorosi, Book VIII* (Auvidis/Naïve ES 9944, 2000); Marin Marais, *Tombeau pour M' de Sainte-Colombe*, Jordi Savall, soundtrack to *Tous les matins du monde* (Auvidis/Valois V4640, 1991). Many recordings of the Purcell exist.

24 Lully, *Armide*, act 5, scene 2: 'Passacaille,' Collegium Vocale/La Chapelle Royale, Philippe Herreweghe, director (Harmonia Mundi 901456.57, 1992). The keyboard arrangement in fig. 1.7 is D'Anglebert's.

25 Strong evidence points to Lully's affiliation with sodomitical activities at Versailles. His association of entrapment with feminine evil and of rescue with renewed homosocial bonding may have had other resonances for original audiences. See Davitt Moroney's entry on Lully in *Encyclopedia of Lesbian and Gay Histories and Cultures*, ed. Bonnie Zimmerman and George Haggerty (New York: Garland, 2000).

26 See my 'The Blasphemy of Talking Politics during Bach Year,' in *Music and Society: The Politics of Composition, Performance and Reception*, ed. Richard Leppert and Susan McClary (Cambridge: Cambridge University Press, 1987), 13–62; and Adorno, 'Bach Defended against His Devotees,' *Prisms*, 133–46.

27 See my *Conventional Wisdom*, chap. 3.

28 See my 'Temporality and Ideology: Qualities of Motion in Seventeenth-Century French Music,' *ECHO* 3 (November 2000), http://www.humnet.ucla.edu/ECHO.

29 Bach also composed the piece most often thought of as *the* Passacaglia: a virtuoso piece in C minor for organ. Bach's 'Passacaglia' unfolds over a mostly unbending ostinato pattern of eight bars, and he follows it with a fugal treatment of the ground. The organ composition parallels the violin chaconne in its sense of profound disquiet, articulated by syncopated figures

Chacona, Ciaccona, Chaconne, and *the* Chaconne 45

that attempt in vain to escape the law of the repeating pattern. It does not, however, share the Chaconne's accented second beat, which recalls – however faintly – the dance patterns of its predecessors.

30 I recommend the recording by Rachel Podger, *Bach: Sonatas and Partitas*, vol. 1 (Channel Classic 12198, 1999).

31 See n.13 above.

32 Adorno, 'Bach Defended.'

33 See my 'Narratives of Bourgeois Subjectivity in Mozart's "Prague" Symphony', in *Understanding Narrative*, ed. Peter Rabinowitz and James Phelan (Columbus: Ohio State University Press, 1994), 65–98.

34 See the discussion in Rose Rosengard Subotnik, 'Adorno's Diagnosis of Beethoven's Late Style: Early Symptom of a Fatal Condition,' in *Developing Variations: Style and Ideology in Western Music* (Minneapolis: University of Minnesota Press, 1991).

35 I wish to thank Gordon Haramaki, Robert Walser, and the late Philip Brett for reading and commenting on an earlier draft of this essay. Special thanks go to Maiko Kawabata, who performed the Bach Chaconne with exemplary bravado at the Clark conference where I presented these ideas as a talk.

Index